S0-EIH-131

A BIBLIOGRAPHY OF PROSTITUTION

GARLAND REFERENCE LIBRARY
OF SOCIAL SCIENCE
(VOL. 30)

A BIBLIOGRAPHY OF PROSTITUTION

edited by

Vern Bullough
Barrett Elcano
Margaret Deacon
Bonnie Bullough

assisted by

Robbie Tyrell
Gordon Kent
Margaret Moe
Pat Kleinhammer
James Bullough

GARLAND PUBLISHING, INC. • NEW YORK & LONDON
1977

Library of Congress Cataloging in Publication Data

Main entry under title:

A Bibliography of prostitution.

(Garland reference library of social science)
Includes index.
1. Prostitution--Bibliography. I. Bullough, Vern L.
Z7164.P95B52 [HQ111] 016.30141'54 75-42891
ISBN 0-8240-9947-8

PRINTED IN THE UNITED STATES OF AMERICA

CONTENTS

INTRODUCTION

This is a bibliography of works dealing with prostitution. But what constitutes prostitution? The investigator who pursues the subject will find that thcrc is not always agreement on the definition. In law, prostitution has been defined as the hiring out of one's body for purposes of sexual intercourse. Many state statutes, however, fail to stipulate that a monetary exchange need take place. Thus prostitution can also be defined as the giving or receiving of one's body for indiscriminate sexual intercourse without hire. Both definitions, however, tend to neglect important psychological criteria, including the prostitute's own attitude. Roman law was perhaps more encompassing when it emphasized the woman's lack of individual preference, although it also considered the pecuniary aspect. St. Jerome thought that a prostitute was a woman who served the sexual urges of many, but he never bothered to define what he meant by "many." Other churchmen, concerned with the ambiguity of St. Jerome's statement, attempted to be more specific, but in the process often added to the confusion. One writer claimed that a woman could be called a "whore" only if she had known intimately some 23,000 men, a number that would eliminate any but the hardiest lifetime professional.

The confusion over definition exists throughout this bibliography. We have tried to be all encompassing, gathering together books and articles by people who *said* they were writing about prostitution, and this can and does include almost any aspect of extramarital sexual activity. Listed are works dealing with mistresses, concubines, streetwalkers, call girls, brothels, and both amateur and professional women and even occasionally men. We have attempted to organize these works under various subheadings, but sometimes the decision as to how to classify a work was difficult to make. Many of the works listed here can logically be classified under several subjects. Usually, however, we list a work under only one subject heading, although in a few instances a work is so significant that it is listed under more than one in order that it not be overlooked. As we approach the present, the number of categories increases. For example, many titles from the late nineteenth and early twentieth centuries that would earlier have been classed under history are listed under "area studies."

A brief perusal of the categories reveals changing attitudes toward prostitution as well as the changing nature of studies of prostitution. The category most consistent over time and cultural setting has been literature—fiction, drama, poetry, essays—and we include such references as far back as the ancient Greeks. Since in the past, history was often regarded as a branch of literature, there were frequent references to prostitution in historical works even though historians as a group have been reluctant to deal with other aspects of sexual behavior.

For a time, religious writings about prostitution seem to have been the most plentiful, and these writings emphasized the prostitute as sinner and prostitution as evil. Western culture in general has been what I have elsewhere defined as a sex-negative culture, emphasizing celibacy as the most desirable form of sexual—or rather non-sexual—activity but permitting sex within marriage for purposes of procreation. Still, religious writers had to deal with the realities of sexual activity, and much of their writing on sex dealt with prostitution. In general, they regarded prostitution as similar to a sewer, noxious and evil but essential to public well being. Although the prostitute might be tolerated, she was also condemned, and much effort was spent in trying to get her to repent and achieve salvation.

In the sixteenth century there was renewed interest in prostitution on the part of medical writers, primarily because of the syphilis epidemic that swept Europe and the Americas. In the nineteenth century there was again concern over venereal disease when the third stage of syphilis was recognized, and since that time, much of the medical writing about prostitution has concentrated on its association with venereal disease. Also in the nineteenth century, a medical model of sexual behavior generally replaced the old religious model that emphasized the sinful nature of the prostitute and her customers. The medical model tended to see the prostitute as an ill person and prostitution itself as pathological. Not surprisingly, in view of the male-dominated medical profession, much of the medical interest in the pathology of prostitution concentrated on the prostitute and not on her customer. This aspect of prostitution appears most often in this bibliography under the heading of psychiatry, but some of it also spills over into the general medical and psychology sections.

The emerging social sciences of the twentieth century also turned to the study of prostitution, and some of the earlier quantitative studies, many of them medically inspired, had had strong social science implications. Sociologists, psychologists, and the more social science-oriented historians began to study prostitution; anthropologists usually included references to it in their studies, although few studied it in any detail. This century also witnessed a growing movement to abolish tolerated and regulated prostitution, a movement closely allied with the growing political power of women. Joining forces with the women were religious groups, physicians who felt that medical inspection was not the answer to venereal disease, and police officials who worried about the connection between prostitution and organized crime. The abolition movement reached its peak in the period immediately following the end of World War II, after which there was a reassessment and reorientation, in large part encouraged by the greater freedom of women to express themselves sexually.

Women themselves have become increasingly concerned with prostitution, as the bibliography indicates. In the past, male writers, even when condemning the prostitute and prostitution, recognized the need for a double standard of sexual behavior. Inevitably, when women entered the field as reformers or researchers, they were concerned with exposing and investigating this aspect of prostitution. Ultimately, the prostitute was seen somewhat differently than she earlier had been, and increased support for initiating programs designed to arrest and prosecute the customer of the prostitute replaced the past concentration on the prostitute.

These changing concerns are amplified by the works included in this bibliography, the first of its kind. The nucleus of the collection was gathered through the researches of myself and Bonnie Bullough, who traveled throughout much of the world collecting, photocopying, and purchasing materials, many of which are now in the library at California State University, Northridge. A more professional touch was lent to the project by Barrett Elcano and Margaret Deacon, who supplemented the original bibliographical collections with a concentrated search through the published literature, a somewhat easier task for prostitution than for some other forms of sexual behavior since card catalogues have usually included references to prostitution. Nevertheless, there are hundreds of titles dealing with prostitution that can be discovered only through personal investigation. Often discovery has been accidental. We have included the hundreds of titles we have discovered, but we have probably missed many hundreds more. Although we have attempted to be comprehensive, there are bound to be omissions, some serious. We hope to be able to add them through periodical supplements, a task made simple because this bibliography is stored on computer tapes at the Center for Sex Research, California State University, Northridge. We hope our readers will send us additions and at the same time notify us of the errors and mistakes they find in the bibliography.

Three students have been particularly helpful in putting the information into final form, including coding, collating, and proofreading: Robbie Tyrell, Gordon Kent, and Margaret Moe. Special thanks should also be given to the Computer Center at CSUN and to its director, W. J. Bowles. The program design was directed by Joyce Hayes. The man who did most of the day-to-day work, however, was Pat Kleinhammer, and his work was so crucial to this enterprise that he is also credited as a contributing editor. Also listed is James Bullough, who copied notes for us and helped code. Final corrections were made by Doris Williams and Elfrida Stone. The index was prepared by Gertrude Dinman.

Vern Bullough
January 1977

A BIBLIOGRAPHY OF PROSTITUTION

1000 Abraham, Karl. Selected Papers. Translated by Douglas Bryan and Alix Strachey. London: The Hogarth Press and the Institute of Psychoanalysis, 1942.

1001 Abraham, Karl. Selected Papers on Psychoanalysis. New York: Basic Books, Inc., 1953, 36 pp.

1002 Acton, William. The Functions and Disorders of the Reproductive Organs in Childhood, Youth, Adult Age, and Advanced Life Considered in Their Physiological, Social, and Moral Relations. 5th ed. London: J. A. Churchill, 1871.

1003 Acton, William. Prostitution Considered in Its Moral, Social, and Sanitary Aspects. London: J. A. Churchill, 1857; reprinted ed., London: MacGiffon and Kee Limited, 1968, 175 pp.

1004 Amador-Guevara, J."The Problem of Prostitution." Rev Med Costa Rica 20:93-103, March 1963. In Spanish.

1005 "Anthology of Prostitution." Time 81:34, April 12, 1963

1006 Armand, E."La Prostitution et ses multiples aspects." Orleans 1933, 24 pp.

1007 "L'Art et la maniere d'obtenir a son gre des garcons ou des filles." Paris 1900

1008 "Bashing Away." Economist 247:11-12, June 2, 1973.

1009 Balena, L. M."Solutions for Reducing the Supply and Demand for Prostitution." Sem Med (B.Aires) 121:1789-94, November 12, 1962.

1010 Basserman, Lujo. The Oldest Profession. Translated by James Cleugh. New York: Stein and Day, 1967, 244 pp.

1011 Bataille, Georges. L'eroticisme. Paris: Les editions de Minuit, 1957.

1012 Benjamin, Harry, and Ellis, Albert. "An Objective Examination of Prostitution." International Journal of Sexology 8:100-105, 1954. Prostitution relative to the Kinsey Reports. Finds prostitution a "virtual necessity" in a monogamous nation.

1013 Bergh, Henri L. Irrwege der Liebe. Gottingen: Delphn, 1951.

1014 Blacker, C. P. Birth Control and the State. New York: E. P. Dutton, 1926.

1015 Bloch, Iwan. Die Prostitution 2v. Berlin: L. Marcus, 1912.

1016 Briffault, Robert. The Mothers: a study of the origins of Sentiments and Institutions. 3v. New York: Macmillian, 1927.

1017 Bullough, Vern L. Sexual Variance in Society and History. New York: Wiley Interscience, 1976.

1018 Bullough, Vern L. Sex, Society, and History. New York: Neale Watson, 1976.

1019 Burnett, Stan and Seeger, Alan. Prostitution Around The World. Derby, Connecticut: Monarch Books, Inc., 1963, 220 pp.

1020 Calderone, Mary Steichen, ed. Abortion in the United States. New York: Hoeber-Harper, 1958.

1021 "Call me madam; COYOTE conference." Newsweek 84:65, June 8, 1974.

1022 Calvino, P. La prostituzione. Il male e il remedio. Geneva: Federation Abolitionniste Internationale, n.d. before 1942. 48 pp.

1023 Caprio, Frank, and Brenner, Donald. Sexual Behavior, Psycho Legal Aspects. New York: Citadel Press, 1961.

1024 Carpenter, Edward. Love's Coming of Age. New York: Boni and Liveright, 1911.

1025 Casan, V.S. La Prostitucion. 7th ed. Barcelona: M. Maucci, 1948.

1026 Caufeynon, Docteur [Jean Fauconney]. La Prostitution. Paris: Charles Offenstadt, 1902.

1027 Cavaillon, (Dr.). The Prevention of Prostitution: The Reduction of Demand. Geneva: Federation Abolitionniste, 1942. 2 pp.

1028 Cocks, Orrin Giddings. The Social Evil and Methods of Treatment. Sex Education Series, Study No. 5. New York: Association Press, 1912, 68 pp.

1029 "Code Message." Newsweek 22:39, July 12, 1943. Prostitution.

1030 Collisson, M. Chave. Prostitution to-day, the international scene. London: Alison Neilans Memorial, 1966, 9 pp.

1031 Cooper, C. R. Design in scarlet. New York: Little, 1939.

1032 Deutsch, Helene. The Psychology of Women. New York: Grune and Stralton, 1944.

1033 Diehl, B., and D'Amico, T. "From Caves to Cafes." American Mercury 77:85-90, September, 1953.

1034 Elliott, Albert Wells. The Cause of the Social Evil. 3rd ed. Macon, Ga.: Elliott, 1919. 122 pp.

1035 Ellis, Albert, and Abarbanel, Albert. The Encyclopedia of Sexual Behavior. 2 vols. New York: Hawthorn Books, 1961.

1036 Ellis, Albert. Sex Without Guilt. New York: Lyle Stuart, 1958.

1037 Ellis, Havelock. "Sex in Relation to Society." In Studies in the Psychology of Sex, pp.225-226. Vol. 2, pt. 3. New York: Random House, 1936.

1038 Ernst, Morris L., and Loth, David. American Sexual Behavior and the Kinsey Report. New York: Greystone Press, 1948.

1039 Eulenburg's Real-Enzyklopadie der gesammten Heilkunde. Berlin, Vienna: 1898. "Prostitution," by Gustav Behrend.

1040 Fels, Florent. L'art et Amour. Paris: Editions Arc en Ciel, 1952-53. Also New York: 1953.

1041 Felice, Th. de. "Situation Abolitionniste mondiale," Horitsu Jiho 3 (1958):219-225.

1042 Fere, Charles Samson. Sexual Degeneration in Mankind and in Animals. Translated by Ulrich Van der Horst. Reprinted New York: Anthropological Press, 1932. pp. 284-85.

1043 Fischer, Wilhelm. Die Prostitution. Leipzig: Verlag von Hans Hedwig's Nachfolger Curt Ronninger, 1920.

1044 Flexner, Abraham. Prostitution in Europe. New York: Century Co., 1914.

1045 Frappa, J. J. Enquete sur la prostitution. 1937, 212 pp.

1046 French Institute of Public Opinion. Patterns of Sex and Love: A Study of the French Woman and Her Morals. Translated by Lowell Blair. New York: Crown Publishers, Inc., 1961. Not directly on prostitution--just sex education and ideas.

1047 Freud, Sigmund. Collected Papers. Translated under the direction of Joan Riviere, et al. 5 vols. New York: Basic Books, 1959.

1048 Freud, Sigmund. The Standard Editions of the Complete Psychological Works of Sigmund Freud. London: Hogarth Press, 1971. I:180; III:150.

1049 Gebhard, Paul, et al. _Pregnancy, Birth and Abortion_. New York: Harper-Hoeber, 1958.

1050 Guyot, Yves. _La Prostitution_. Paris: G. Charpentier, 1882, 577 pp.

1051 Hall, G. M. _Prostitution: a survey and a challenge_. London: William and Norgate, 1933, 196 pp. Reprinted New York: Emerson Books, 1936.

1052 Harris, H. Wilson. _Human Merchandise: A Study of the International Traffic in Women_. London: Ernest Benn, 1928.

1053 "How to Create Good Will." _Time_ 61:91, March 4, 1957.

1054 Kemp, T. _Prostitution_. Stechert, 1936.

1055 Kinsey, Alfred, et al. _Sexual Behavior in the Human Female_. Philadelphia: W. B. Saunders, 1953.

1056 Kinsey, Alfred C. et al. _Sexual Behavior in the Human Male_. Philadelphia: W. B. Saunders, 1948.

1057 Krafft-Ebing, Richard von. _Psychopathia Sexualis_. Translated by Charles Gilbert Chaddock. Philadelphia: F.A. Davis Company, 1894. There are other translations and numerous German editions.

1058 Kuhn, Franz. _Femes Derriere un Voile_. Paris: Calman-Levy, 1972.

1059 Leonhard, Stephan. _Die Prostitution_. Munich: E. Reinhardt, 1912.

1060 Lyttelton, E. "League's Big Little Jobs." _Outlook_ 138:448-50, November 19, 1924. Prostitution.

1061 Mancini, G. _Prostitution et Proxenetisme_. Paris: 1962, 125 pp.

1062 Mantegazza, Paola. _The Sexual Relations of Mankind_. Translated by Samuel Putnam. 11th ed. Reprinted New York: Eugenics Publishing Co., 1957.

1063 Masters, William H. and Johnson, Virginia E. _Human Sexual Response_. Boston: Little, Brown, and Co., 1966.

1064 Mathur, A. S. and Gupta, B. L. _Prostitutes and Prostitution_. Agra: Ramprasad and Sons, 1965, 255 pp.

1065 May, G. "Prostitution," in, _Encyclopedia of Social Science_. 1934 ed. 12:553-559.

1066 May, Geoffrey. "Prostitution," _Encyclopedia of Social Sciences_. 1935 ed. New York.

1067 Mencken, H. L. _In Defense of Women_. New York: Alfred A. Knopf, 1922.

1068 Miner, M. E. _Slavery of Prostitution: A Plea For Emancipation_. Macmillan, 1916. This book is readable and reasonably complete. It touches on causes, legislative remedies, and individual treatment, but emphasizes in every chapter the ultimate reliance on education, economic reform, and the whole network of social measures which affect prostitution.

1069 "Mrs. Warren's Profession." _Nation_ 143:6, July 4, 1936.

1070 Murray, James A. H., et al. "Prostitution,: in, _Oxford English Dictionary_ Oxford: Clarendon Press, 1933.

1071 Philippon, Odette. _L'esclavage de la femme dans le monde contemporain ou la prostitution sans masque_. Paris: 1954, 232 pp.

1072 Pierce, C. C. "Prostitution." _American City_.

1073 Pierson, H. _Die Prostitutionsfrage_. Mulheim, 1885, 31 pp.

1074 Pillay, A. P. and Ellis, Albert. _Sex, Society and the Individual_. Bombay, India: The International Journal of Sexology, 1953.

1075 Pomeroy, Wardell B. "Some Aspects of Prostitution." _The Journal of Sex Research_ 1:177-187, November, 1965. Previously unpublished material on prostitution in the Kinsey study.

1076 "Private and Public Vice." _New Statesman_ 54:261, September 7, 1957. Discussed in 54:317, 349, September 14-21, 1957.

1077 Profeta, G. _Sulla prostituzione_. Palermo, 1898.

1078 "Prostitution." _Melcora_ 1:70.

1079 "Prostitution." _Melcora_ 3:145.

1080 "Prostitution." _Problems_ No. XX, March-April, 120 pp.

1081 "Prostitution." _Tait_ new series, 25:110.

1082 "Prostitution." _Tait_ new series, 27:251.

1083 "Prostitution." _Survey_ 47:571-2, January 7, 1922.

1084 "Prostitution." _Westm_ 53:448.

1085 "Prostitution and its causes." _Melcora_ 6:308.

1086 Putnam, Samuel. "Prostitution," in Encyclopedia Sexualis, edited by Victor Robinson. New York: Dingwall-Rock, 1936, pp.640-670.

1087 Reuss, L. La Prostitution. Paris, 1889, 636 pp.

1088 Robinson, Victor, ed. Encyclopedia Sexualis. New York: Dingwall-Rock, 1936.

1089 Rohden, G. von. Die Prostitutionsfrage. Kirchlich-soziales Heft., no 8. Leipzig: 1917.

1090 Ross, Colin. Loose Women Throughout the World. New York: Lyle Stuart, 1959. Paper crummy.

1091 Rougemont, Denis de. Love in the Western World. Translated by Montgomery Belgion. New York: Pantheon, 1956. Revised and augmented.

1092 Sacotte, Marcel. La Prostitution. Paris: Buchet/Chastel, 1965, 180 pp. A second edition of this work because of ratification by France of the International Convention. 1924.

1093 Scharlieb, Mary, editor. Sexual Problems of to-day, 1924. See "Prostitution" by Father Andrew, pp.212-239.

1094 Scheinfeld, Amram. Women and Men. New York: Harcourt, Brace, 1943.

1095 Servir. Prostitution et proxenetisme. Sociale, Number 25. Paris: c1960, 4 pp.

1096 Sicot, Marcel. La Prostitution dans le monde. Paris: 1964, 239 pp.

1097 Simons, G. L. Sex and Superstition. London: Abelard and Schuman, 1973. A popular survey.

1098 "Social evil." Outlook 70:606-608, March 8, 1902.

1099 Strohmberg, C. Die Prostitution. Stuttgart: 1899.

1100 Tammeo, G. La Prostituzione. Torino: 1890.

1101 United Nations. International Survey of Programmes of Social Development. New York: 1959. Sales No. 59, 1 v. 2. E/CN.5/324/Rev.1.

1102 United Nations. Report on the World Social Situation. United Nations, 1957. Sales No: 1957 IV 3. E/CN.5/324/Rev.1.

1103 United Nations. _Study on Traffic in Persons and Prostitution_ New York, 1959. Document ST/SOA/SD/(8).

1104 Walton, J. W. "A Study of Prostitution." _Am J Pol_ 3:605.

1105 Wilson, H. _Is Prostitution Inevitable? A Discussion of Causes and Remedies._ International Abolitionist Federation, 1914. 39 pp.

1106 Worthington, G. E. "Prostitution: What a City Should Know About Itself." _American City_ 30:63-6, January, 1924.

1107 Young, W. H. "Sitting on a Fortune." In _Encounter_, pp. 106-27. New York: Basic Books, 1963.

Studies which include discussions of prostitution.

1108 Abraham, Roy Clive. The Tiv People. Lagos: The Government Printer, 1933.

1109 Ames, David Wason. Plural Marriage Among the Wolof in the Gambia: With a Consideration of Problems of Marital Adjustment and Patterned Ways of Resolving Tensions. Unpublished dissertation. Evanston, Illinois: Northwestern Univ., 1953.

1110 Baillant, George Clapp. Aztecs of Mexico: Origin, Rise and Fall of the Aztec Nation. Garden City, New York: Doubleday, Doran and Co., Inc., 1941.

1111 Balandier, Georges. Sociologie Actuelle de l'Afrique Noire: Changements Sociaux au Gabon et au Congo. (Contemporary Sociology of Black Africa: Social Changes in Gabon and the Congo). Paris: Presses Universitaires de France, 1955.

1112 Bandelier, Adolph F. On the Social Organization and Mode of Government of the Ancient Mexicans. Reports of the Peabody Museum of American Archaeology and Ethnology in Connection with Harvard Univ., Vol.II, pp.557-699. Cambridge: 1880.

1113 Barton, Roy F. The Half-Way Sun: Life Among the Headhunters of the Philippines. New York: Brewer and Warren, Inc., 1930.

1114 Beals, Ralph Leon. Cheran: A Sierra Tarascan Village. Smithsonian Institution. Institute of Social Anthropology. Pub. no.2. Washington, D.C.: 1946.

1115 Bennett, Wendell C. and Robert M. Zingg. The Tarahumara: An Indian Tribe ot North Mexico. University of Chicago Publications in Anthropology: Ethnological Series. Chicago: University of Chicago Press, 1935.

1116 Blackwood, Beatrice. Both Sides of Buka Passage: An Ethnographic Study of Social, Sexual, and Economic Questions in the North-Western Solomon Islands. Oxford: Clarendon Press, 1935.

1117 Blunt, E. A. H. The Caste System of Northern India. London: Oxford Univ. Press, 1931.

1118 Boelaert, Edmond. "Terminologie Classificatoire Des Nkundo." (Classificatory Terminology of the Nkundo). Africa 21:218-222. London: International African Institute, 1951.

1119 Bogoraz-Tan, Vladimir Germanovich (Bogoras, Waldemar). The Chukchee: Material Culture (Part 1), Religion (Part 2), and Social Organization (Part 3). Memoirs of the American Museum of Natural History, vol. XI. Leiden: E. J. Brill, Ltd., and New York: G. E. Stechert and Co. 1904 (Part 1), 1907

(Part 2), 1909 (Part 3).

1120 Bohannam, Paul and Laura Bohannam. "Three Source Notebooks in Tiv Ethnography". New Haven: Human Relations Area Files, 1958. Unpublished manuscript.

1121 Brand, Donald D. "A Brief History of Araucanian Studies." New Mexico Anthropologist 5(2):19-35. Albuquerque: Dept. of Anthropology, University of New Mexico, 1941.

1122 Breton, Raymond and Armand de la Paix. "Relation de l'Isle de la Guadeloupe." (An account of the Island of Guadeloupe), in Les Caraibes, La Guadeloupe, 1635-1656, Joseph Rennard, ed. Vol. I: Histoire Coloniale, pp.45-74. Paris: Librairie Generale et Internationale, 1929.

1123 Briffault, Robert. The Mothers. New York: Macmillan Co., 1927. Vol. III, p.209.

1124 Brodrick, Allan Houghton. Little China: The Annamese Lands. London: Oxford University Press, 1942.

1125 Burgesse, J. Allan. "The Woman and the Child Among the Lac-St-Jean Montagnais," in Primitive Man, Vol. 17, nos. 1-18. Washington, D.C.: Catholic Anthropological Conference, 1944.

1126 Burrows, Edwin Grant. The People of Ifalik: A Little-Disturbed Atoll Culture. Coordinated Investigation of Micronesian Anthropology. Washington: Pacific Science Board, National Research Council, 1949. Unpublished manuscript submitted as a final report.

1127 Butt, Audrey. The Nilotes of the Anglo-Egyptian Sudan and Uganda. Ethnographic Survey of Africa, East Central Africa, pt.4, pp.45-67. London: Interational African Institute, 1952.

1128 Christian, John Leroy. Modern Burma: A Survey of Political and Economic Developments. Berkeley and Los Angeles: Univ. of California Press, 1942.

1129 Cline, Walter, et al. The Sinkaietk or Southern Okanagon of Washington. Ed. by Leslie Spier. Contributions from the Laboratory of Anthropology, 2. General Series in Anthropology, no.6. Menasha, Wis.: George Banta Publishing Co., 1938.

1130 Cline, Walter. Notes on the People of Siwah and El Garah in the Libyan Desert. General Series in Anthropology, no.4. Menasha, Wis.: George Banta Publishing Co., 1936.

1131 Colson, Elizabeth. The Makah Indians; A Study of an Indian Tribe in Modern American Society. Minneapolis: University of Minnesota Press, 1953.

1132 Conzemius, Eduard. Ethnographical Survey of the Miskito and Sumu Indians of Honduras and Nicaragua. Bureau of American Ethnology Bulletin, no.106. Washington: Smithsonian Institution, 1932.

1133 Cooper, John M. The Araucanians. Bureau of American Ethnology Bulletin no.143, Vol.2, pp.687-760. Washington, D. C.: Smithsonian Institution, 1946.

1134 Cornell University. India: Sociological Background. Subcontrctor's Monograph, HRAF-44, Cornell-8. New Haven, Conn.: Human Relations Area Files, 1956.

1135 Crawley, Ernest. The Mystic Rose. Revised and enlarged by Theodore Besterman. 2v in 1. Reprinted New York: Meridian Books, 1960, pp.1, 25-58.

1136 Czekanowski, Jan. Forschungen im-Kongo-Zwischengebiet. Erster Band: Ethnographie; Zwischenseengebiet Mpororo: Ruanda. (Investigations in the Area Between the Nile and the Congo. First volume: Ethnography, the Interlacustrine Region of Mporo and Ruanda). Wissenschaftliche Ergebnisse der Deutschen Zentral-Afrika-Expedition 1907-8 unter Fuhrung Adolf Friedrichs, Herzogs zu Mechlenburg. (Scientific Results of the German Central African expedition 1907-08 under the Leadership of Adolf Friedrich, Duke of Mechlenburg). Vol.6, pt.1: Ethnography-Anthropology I, ed. by Dr. Jan Czekanowski. Leipzig: Klinkhardt and Biermann, 1917.

1137 Dall, William H. "On the So-Called Chukchi and Namollo People of Eastern Siberia." American Naturalist 15:857-68. Philadelphia: Press of McCalla and Stavely, 1881.

1138 Damm, Hans, et al. Zentralkarolinen, Part II: Ifaluk, Aurepik, Faraulip, Sorol, Mogemog (The Central Carolines, Part II: Ifaluk, Aurepik, Faraulip, Sorol, Mog-Mog). Ergebnisse der Sudsee-Expedition, 1908-1910, sec. B, vol.10, pt.2. Hamburg: Friederichsen, De Gruyter and Co., 1938.

1139 Delgado, M. J. "Sexual Morals of Indians of Southern Peru in Relation to Penal Code (especially in relation to prostitution and venereal diseases)." Cron Med Lima 53:379-83, Oct. '36.

1140 Delobsom, A. A. Dim. L'Empire du Mogho-Naba, Coutumes des Mossi de la Haute-Volta. (The Empire of the Mogho-Haba, Customs of the Mossi of Upper Volta). Institut de Droit Compare, etudes de Sociolologie et d'Ethnologie Juridiques, Vol. II. Paris: Les Editions Domat-Montchrestien, 1932.

1141 Deyoung, John E. Village Life in Modern Thailand. Berkeley: Univ. of Calif., 1955. p.62.

1142 Dickson, H. R. P. The Arab of the Desert; a glimpse of Badawin Life in Kuwait and Sau'di Arabia. London: George Allen and Unwin, Ltd., 1951.

1143 Diguet, Col. E. Les Montagnards du Tonkin. (The Mountaineers of Tonkin). Paris: Augustin Challamel, 1908.

1144 Dorgeles, Roland. On the Mandarin Road. New York: The Century Co., 1926.

1145 Dorsey, Rev. J. Owen. Omaha Sociology. Smithsonian Instituion, Bureau of Ethnology, Third Annual Report, 1881-82, pp.205-370. Washington D. C.: Govt. Printing Office, 1884.

1146 Douglas, William O. Beyond the High Himalayas. Garden City, N. Y.: Doubleday and Co., Inc., 1953.

1147 Drucker, Philip. The Northern and Central Nootkan Tribes. Smithsonian Institution, Bureau of American Ethnology, Bulletin no.144. Washington, D. C.: 1953.

1148 Dubois, J. A. Hindu Manners, Customs and Ceremonies. Oxford: The Clarendon Press, 1906.

1149 Dundas, Charles. "The Organization and Laws of Some Bantu Tribes in East Africa." J Royal Anth Instit Gt Brit and Ire (London) 45:234-305, '15.

1150 East, Rupert, ed. Akiga's Story; The Tiv tribe as seen by one of its members. London: International Institute of African Languages and Cultures, Oxford Univ. Press, 1939.

1151 Elwin, Verrier. "Maria Murder and Suicide." Bombay: Published for Man in India by Oxford Univ. Press (Humphrey Milford), 1943.

1152 Emsheimer, Ernst. "Preliminary Remarks on Mongolian Musical Instruments," in The Music of the Mongols, pt.1: Eastern Mongolia. The Sino-Swedish Expedition, Pub. no.21, VIII: Ethnography, 4, pp.69-100. Stockholm(?): Tryckeri Aktiebolaget Thule, 1943.

1153 Evans-Pritchard, Edward Evans. The Divine Kingship of the Shilluk of Nilotic Sudan. The Grazer Lecture, 1948. Cambridge: University Press, 1948.

1154 Ferrars, Max and Bertha. Burma. London: Sampson Low, Marston and Co., 1901.

1155 Ffoulkes, Arthur. "Fanti Marriage Customs." J African Society, 8:31-48. London and New York: Macmillan Co., 1909.

1156 Firth, Rosemary. *Housekeeping Among Malay Peasants.* Monographs on Social Anthropology no.7. London: London School of Economic and Political Science, 1943.

1157 Fletcher, Alice C. and Francis La Flesche. *The Omaha Tribe.* Twenty-seventh Annual Report of the Bureau of American Ethnology, 1905-6. Washington D. C.: Govt. Printing Office, 1911.

1158 Forde, Daryll. "The Nupe," in Forde, ed., *Peoples of the Niger-Benue Confluence.* Ethnographic Survey of Africa. Western Africa, pt.10, pp.17-52. London: Int. African Institute, 1955.

1159 Franck, Harry A. *East of Siam: Ramblings in the Five Divisions of French Indochina.* New York: The Century Co., 1926.

1160 Frazer, James George. *The Golden Bough.* 3d ed New York: Macmillan: 1935.

1161 Gamble, David P. *The Wolof of Senegambia.* Ethnographic Survey of Africa, Western Africa, pt.14. London: Int. African Institute, 1957.

1162 Ghurye, G. S. *Caste and Class in India.* Bombay: published for the Popular Book Dept., 1950.

1163 Glubb, J. B. *The Sulubba and Other Ignoble Tribes of Southwestern Asia.* General series in Anthropology, no.10, pp.14-17. Menasha, Wis: George Banta Pub. Co., 1943.

1164 Gorer, Geoffrey. *African Dances; a book about West African Negroes.* London: Faber and Faber, 1935.

1165 Gorer, Geoffrey. *Himalayan Village; an account of the Lepchas of Sikkim.* London: Michael Joseph, Ltd., 1938.

1166 Grajdanzev, Andrew J. *Formosa Today; an analysis of the ecomomic development and strategic importance of Japan's tropical colony.* New York: Institute of Pacific Relations, 1942.

1167 Greenfield, S. M. "Bruce Effect and Malinowski's Hypothesis on Mating and Fertility." *Am Anthro* 70:761, Aug. '68. Replies by M. Nag and A. Chrowning, 71:1119-1125, Dec. '69.

1168 Guerin and Bernard. *Les Aborigenes de l'Ile de Formose. Bulletin de la Societe de Geographie,* series 5, vol.15, pp.542-568. Paris: 1888.

1169 Harrison, Paul W. *The Arab at Home.* New York: Thomas Y. Crowell Co., 1924.

1170 Hammond, Peter B. "Economic Change and Mossi Acculturation," in Bascom, William R. and Melville J. Herskovits, eds., Continuity and Change in African Cultures, pp.238-256. Chicago: Univ. of Chicago Press, 1959.

1171 Hartland, Edwin Sidney. "Concerning the Rite at the Temple of Mylitta," in Anthropological Essays Presented to Edward Burnett Taylor, pp.189-202. London: 1905.

1172 Hawes, Charles H. In the Uttermost East. London and New York: Harper and Bros., 1903.

1173 Honigmann, John J. Culture and Ethos of Kaska Society. Yale Univ. Publications in Anthropology, no.40. New Haven: Yale Univ. Press, 1949.

1174 Howell, P. P. "Observations on the Shilluk of the Upper Nile, Customary Law: marriage and the violation of the rights of women." Africa 23:94-109. London: Int. African Institute, 1953.

1175 Hulbert, Homer B. The Passing of Korea. New York: Doubleday, Page and Co., 1906.

1176 Hulstaert, Gustave. Le Marriage des Nkundo. Institut Royal Colonial Belge, Section des Sciences Morales et Politiques, vol.1. Brussels: Librairie Falk Fils, Georges Van Campenhout, Successeur, 1938.

1177 Indiana University. Finland. Subcontractor's monogragh, HRAF-2, Indiana-4, prepared for HRAF in 1955.

1178 James, Jennifer. Ethnographic Semantic Approaches to the Study of an Urban Subculture: Streetwalkers. Dissertation for the Univ. of Washington. Available from Univ. Microfilms, 1972. 192 pp.

1179 Jones, Livingston F. A Study of the Thlingets of Alaska. New York: Fleming H. Revell Co., 1914.

1180 Joseph, Alice, et al. The Desert People; a study of the Papago Indians. Chicago: Univ. of Chicago Press, 1949.

1181 Junod, Henri A. The Life of a South African Tribe, vol.1. London: Macmillan and Co., 1927.

1182 Karve, Irawati. Kinship Organization in India. Deccan College Monograph Series. Poona: 1953.

1183 Kelly, Howard A. The Influuence of Segregation Upon Prostitution and Upon the Public. Issued by the Executive Committee of the Pennsylvania, 1912. 15 pp.

1184 Kenyatta, Jomo. Facing Mount Kenya; the tribal life of the Kikuyu. London: Secker and Warburg, 1953.

1185 Knapp, Frances, and Rheta Louise Childe. The Thlinkets and Southeastern Alaska. Chicago: Stone and Kimball, 1896.

1186 Krause, Aurel. The Tlingit Indians; results of a trip to the Northwest Coast of America and the Bering Straits. Published for the American Ethnographical Society. Seattle: Univ. of Washington Press, 1956.

1187 Kuttner, R. E. and A. B. Loring, "Promiscuity and Prostitution in Urbanized Indian Communities." Mental Hygiene 54:79-91, Jan. '70. Bibliography.

1188 Lebarre, Weston. The Aymara Indians of Lake Titicaca Plateau, Bolivia. American Anthropologist, Memoir no.68, vol.50, no.1, pt.2. Menasha, Wis.: American Anthropological Assn., 1948.

1189 Lambrecht, Francis. The Mayawyaw Ritual. Publications of the Catholic Anthropological Conference, v.4, nos.1-5. Washington, D. C.: 1932, 1935, 1938, 1939, 1941.

1190 Latcham, Richard E. "Ethnology of the Aracanos." J Royal Anthro Instit Gt Brit and Ire (London) 39:334-370, '09.

1191 Lattimore, Owen. Mongol Journeys. New York: Doubleday, Doran and Co., 1941.

1192 Leakey, Louis S. B. Mau Mau and the Kikuyu. London: Methuen and Co., 1952.

1193 Lewis, I. M. Peoples of the Horn of Africa. Ethnographic Survey of Africa, North Eastern Africa, pt.1. London: Int. African Institute, 1955.

1194 Lips, Julius E. "Naskapi Law and Order in a Hunting Society." American Philosophical Society. Transactions ns 37(4):379-492, '47.

1195 Little, Kenneth L. The Menda of Sierra Leone. London: Routledge and Kegan Paul, 1951.

1196 Logan, J. R. "Plan for a Volunteer Police in the Muda Districts, Province Wellesley, submitted to the government by the late J. R. Logan in 1867." J of Straits Branch of Royal Asiatic Soc (Singapore) 16:173-202, 1886.

1197 Longmore, Laura. The Disposessed; a study of the sex-life of Bantu women in urban areas in and around Johannesburg. London: 1959, 334 pp. Considerable prostitution.

1198 Lorimer, Emily Overend. Language Hunting in the Karakoram. London: George Allen and Unwin, Ltd., 1939.

1199 McLennon, John. The Patriarchal Theory. London: Macmillan, 1885.

1200 Mair, Lucy P. Native Marriages in Buganda. Memorandum 19 of the Int. Institute of African Languages and Cultures. London: 1940.

1201 Mair, Lucy P. An African People in the Twentieth Century. London: George Routledge and Sons, 1934.

1202 Malinowski, Bronislaw. The Sexual Life of Savages in Northwestern Melanesia. New York: Horace Liveright, 1929.

1203 Manoukian, Madeline. Akan and Ga-Adangme Peoples of the Gold Coast. London: Oxford Univ. Press for the Int. African Institute, 1950.

1204 Mayne, John D. Treatise on Hindu Law and Usage. 11th ed Madras: Higgensbothams Ltd., 1953.

1205 Menen, Aubrey. The Ramayana. New York: Charles Scribner's Sons, 1954.

1206 Messing, Simon David. The Highland-Plateau Amhara of Ethiopia. Dissertation for the University of Pennsylvania. Philadelphia: 1957.

1207 Meyer, Hans. Die Barundi: Eine Volkerkundliche Studie aus Deutsch-Ostafrika. Leipzig: Ott Spamer, 1916.

1208 Middleton, John. The Central Tribes of the North-Eastern Bantu; the Kikuyu, including Emby, Meru, Mbere, Chuka, Mwinbi, Tharaka, and the Kamba of Kenya. Ethnographic Survey of Africas, East Central Africa, pt.5. London: Int. African Institute, 1953.

1209 Modi, Mivanji Jamshedji. "The Pundits of Kashmir." J Anthro Society Bombay 10('13, '14, '15, '16):461-485, '17.

1210 Morgan, L. H. Ancient Society. Reprinted New York: World, 1963. Originally published 1871.

1211 Morgan, L. H. The League of the Iroquois. Rochester: 1851.

1212 Morse, Edward S. Korean Interviews. New York: D. Appleton and Co., 1897.

1213 Nadel, Siegfried Frederick. A Black Byzantium: the Kingdom of Nupe in Nigeria. London: Published for the Int. Institute of African Languages and Cultures by Oxford Univ. Press, 1942.

1214 Nemeck, Ottokar. Virginity: Prenuptial Rites and Rituals. New York: Philos Lib., 1958.

1215 Neumann, Erich. The Great Mother; an analysis of the archetype. Bollinger Series, no.47. New York: Pantheon Books, 1955. p.43, 96n.

1216 Oberg, Kalervo. "Crime and Punishment in Tlingit Society." Am Anthropologist 36(2):145-156, '34.

1217 Orleans, Prince Henri d'. Around Tonkin and Siam. London: Chapman and Hall, Ltd., 1894.

1218 Osgood, Cornelius. The Koreans and Their Culture. New York: The Ronald Press Co., 1951.

1219 Pasquier, Pierre. L'Annam d'Autrefois. Paris: Augustin Challamel, 1907.

1220 Paul-Boncour, Georges. "La Prostitution Devant la Science Anthropologique (sa definition, sa nature)." Rev Anthropologique (Paris) 43:110-124, '33.

1221 Paulitschke, Philipp. Beitrage zur Ethnographie und Anthropologie der Somal, Galla, und Harari. Leipzig: Eduard Baldamus, 1888.

1222 Peter, Prince of Greece. Tibet, Toda, and Tiya Polyandry; a report on field investigations. New York Academy of Sciences. Transactions Ser.2, vol.10, pp.21?-225, '48.

1223 Petrullo, Vincenzo, The Yaruros of the Capanaparo River, Venezuela. Anthropological Papers, no.11. Bureau of American Ethnology, Bulletin no.123, pp.161-290. Smithsonian Institution, 1939.

1224 Phillips, Arthur, ed. Survey of African Marriage and Family Life. London: Oxford Univ. Press for Int. African Institute, 1953.

1225 Pospisil, Leopold. Kapauku Papuans and Their Law. Yale Univ. Publications in Anthropology, no.54. New Haven: Yale Univ. Press, 1958.

1226 Pumphrey, M. E. C. The Shilluk Tribe. Sudan Notes and Records, vol.24, pp.1-45. Khartoum: 1941.

1227 Purcell, Victor. The Chinese in Southeast Asia. London: Oxford Univ. Press, 1951.

1228 Reichard, Gladys A. Navaho Religion; a study of symbolism. New York: Bollingen Foundation, vol.1, 1950.

1229 Reinach, Lucien de. Le Laos. Paris: A. Charles, Librairie-Editeur, 1901.

1230 Sarytschew (Sarychev), Gawrila. Account of a Voyage of Discovery to the Northeast of Siberia, the Frozen Ocean, and the North-East Sea, vol.2. London: Richard Phillips, 1806.

1231 Schmacher, Robert. Formosa und Seine Gebirgsbewohner. Petermanns Mitteilungen aus Justus Perthes' Geographischer Anstalt, vol. XVIV, pp.22-226. Gotha: 1898.

1232 Scott, George Ryley. Curious Customs of Sex and Marriage. Reprinted New York: Key Pub. Co., 1960.

1233 Singh, Mohinder. The Depressed Classes; their economic and social condition. Bombay: Hind Kitabs, Ltd., 1947.

1234 Sources of Chinese Tradition. Compiled by W. T. de Bary, Wing-tsit Chan and Burton Watson, et al. New York: Columbia Univ. Press, 1960.

1235 Spiro, Melford E. Ifaluk; a South Sea Culture. Unpublished manuscript submitted as a final report. Coordinated investigation of Micronesian Anthropology. Washington: Pacific Science Board, Nat. Research Council, 1949.

1236 Srinivas, M. N. Marriage and Family in Mysore. Bombay: New Book Co., 1942.

1237 Stanford Univ. Taiwan (Formosa) Handbook. New Haven: Human Relations Area Files, 1956. HRAF-31, Stanford-5.

1238 Staub, ____. Beitrage zur Kenntnis der Materiellen Kultur der Mendi in der Sierra Leone. Solothurn: Buchdruckerei Vogt-Schild, 1936.

1239 Sumner, William. Folkways. Reprint of 1909 ed. New York: Dover, 1959, 692 pp. A cross-cultural survey.

1240 Swanton, John R. Social Organization and Social Usages of Indians of the Creek Confederacy. Forty-second Annual report of the Bureau of American Ethnology, 1924-25, pp.23-472, 859-900. Washington, D. C.: Govt. Printing Office, 1928.

1241 Tarnowsky, P. Etude Anthrometrique sur les Prostituees. Paris: 1889, 226 pp.

1242 Tauxier, Louis. Le Noir du Sudan, Pays Mossi et Gourounsi Documents et Analyses. Paris: Emile Larose, Librairie-Editrur, 1912.

1243 Tauxier, L. Le Noir du Yatenga: Mossis, Nioniosses, Samos, Yarses, Silmi, Mossis, Peuls. Paris: Emile Larose, 1917.

1244 Tessman, Gunter. Die Pangwe, Volkerundliche Monographie Eines West Afrikanischen Negerstammes, vol.1. Berlin: Ernst Wasmuth A. -G., 1913.

1245 Thevet, Andre. Les Singularitez de la France Anarctique, Autrement Nommee Ameriaue: et isles decouvertes de nostre temps. Paris: Maisonneuve et Cie., 1878.

1246 Thompson, Virginia. French Indo-china. New York: Macmillan, 1937.

1247 Titiev, Mischa. Araucanian Culture in Transition. Occasional Contributions from the Museum of Anthropology of the Univ. of Michigan, no.15. Ann Arbor: Univ. of Michigan Press, 1951.

1248 Trezenem, Edouard. "Notes Ethnographiques sur les Tribus Fan du Moyen Ogooue (Gabon)." J Soc Africanistes (Paris) 6:65-93.

1249 Underhill, Ruth Murray. Papago Indian Religion. New York: Columbia University Press, 1946. p.64.

1250 Unwin, J. D. Sex and Culture. London: Oxford Univ. Press, 1934.

1251 Valkenburgh, Richard van. "Navaho Common Law: Etiquette, Hospitality, Justice." Museum of Northern Arizona, Note, 10(1938):39-45. Flagstaff: N. Arizona Society of Science and Art, Inc.

1252 Vanoverbergh, Morice. The Isneg Life Cycle. Publications of the Catholic Anthropological Conference, vol.3, no.2, pp.18-186 (Birth, Education, and Daily Routine); no.3, pp.187-280 (Marriage, Death, and Burial). Washington D. C.: The Catholic Anthropological Conference, 1936-1938.

1253 Vassal, Gabrielle M. On and Off Duty in Annam. London: Wm. Heinemann, 1910.

1254 Vidal, F. S. "Date Culture in the Oasis of Al-hase." Middle East J (Washington, D. C.) 8:417-428, '54.

1255 Westermann, Diedrich. The Shilluk People; their language and folklore. Philadelphia: The Board of Foreign Missions of the United Presbyterian Church of North America, 1912.

1256 Whitehead, Right Rev. Henry. The Village Gods of South India. 2d ed Calcutta: Oxford Univ. Press, 1921.

1257 Williams-Hunt, P. D. R. An Introduction to the Malayan Aborigines. Kauala Lumpur: Government Press, 1952.

1258 Windsor, Edward. Cultural and Anthropological Studies in the Hindu Art of Love. New York: Falstaff, 1937.

1259 Zimmerman, Carle C. and Phra Vaidyakara. "A Demographic Study of Eight Oriental Villages Yet Largely Untouched by Western Culture." Metron (Rome) 2(3):179-198, '34.

1260 De Leeuw, H. _Cities of Sin_. N. Douglas, 1934, 297 pp. Also revised New York: Willey Book Co., 1947; and Casement Publications, 1953.

1261 De Leeuw, Hendrik. _Sinful Cities of the Western World_. New York: Citadel, 1949, 285 pp.

1262 "Existing conditions with respect to the traffic in persons and prostitution in selected British trust and non-self-governing territories." _Internat R Criminal Policy_ June 1956, pp.58-67.

1263 Mortimer, Lee. _Around the World Confidential_. New York: G. P. Putman's Sons, 1956.

1264 "Mrs. Harrell's harem." _Newsweek_ 82:39, October 1, 1973.

1265 "Prey of the blind tigers." _Lit Digest_ 103:22-3, November 2, 1927.

1266 Ross, Colin. _Loose Women Throughout the World--The story of what the world's oldest profession is doing today_. New York: Lyle Stuart, 1959, 64 pp.

1267 Spencer, A. G. "World crusade." _Forum_ 50:182-95, August, 1913.

1268 Tammeo, G. _La Prostituzione_. Torino: 1890, 324 pp.

1269 "Twelve O'Clock Sharp." _Commonweal_ 10:660-1, October 30, 1929.

1270 Bosman, W. 'Slaves and public women,' excerpts from "A New and accurate description of the coast of Guinea," in *The Great Travelers*, ed. by M. A. Rujoff, v.1, pp.257-62. Simon and Schuster, 1960.

1271 Du Bois, Victor D. *Prostitution in the Ivory Coast: a social problem and it's treatment*. (Repts service: West Africa ser. v.10, no.2). American University field staff, Nov. 1967, 11 pp.

1272 Freed, Louis Franklin. *The Problem of European Prostitution in Johannesburg: a Sociological Survey*. Cape Town, South Africa: Juta, 1949, 430 pp. Thesis: University of Praetoria.

1273 Freedman, R. S. "Aspects of Bantu domestic life in relation to some gynaecological conditions." *S Afr Med J* 46(38):1383-6, September 23, 1972.

1274 Manafub, Maurice (Champeua). *Plaidoyer pour les prostituees*. Yaounde, 1957, 27 pp. An expose of prostitution in the Cameroons.

1275 Pumphrey, M. E. C. "The Shilluk Tribe." *Sudan Notes and Records* 24(1941): 34, 44.

1276 South Africa. Laws, statutes, etc. *Commentary on the Immorality Act (act no. 23 of 1957)* by Garth M. Hardie and Gordon F. Hartford. Cape Town: Juta, 1960. 113 pp. This act consolidated and amended the laws relating to brothels.

1277 Turnbull, Colin M. "The taught," in *The Lonely African*, pp. 121-39. Simon and Schuster, 1962.

1278 Bey, Diza. _Darkest Orient_. London: Arco Publications, 1953. Describes prostitution in the Near East. Partly fiction.

1279 Carver, J. L. "Slavery's Last Stronghold." _United Nations World_ 2:24-7, June 1948.

1280 Champley, H. _The Road to Shanghai. White Slave Traffic in Asia_. Translated from the French by W. B. Wells. Long, 1934, 288 pp. and McBride, 1935.

1281 Guthrie, A. "Traffic in Women." _Journal of the American Asiatic Association_ 37:522-3, July 1937. Delegates of many nations, meeting in Java, plan to check prostitution and child slavery in the Orient.

1282 Pommerenke, Millicent. _Asian Women and Eros_. New York: Vantage Press, 1958.

1283 Scott, George Ryley. _Far Eastern Sex Life_. London: Gerald G. Swan, 1943 and 1949.

1284 Snyder, Paul. "Prostitution in Asia." _Journal of Sex Research_ 10(2):119-127, May 1974. Various non-communist countries.

1285 "Traffic in women and children in the Far East." _Journal of Social Hygiene_ 19:169-70, March 1933.

1286 Balmann, A. de. "Prostitution in Society Islands." Marseille-med 1:185-191, Feb. 15, 1937.

1287 Barry, J. Vincent. "Prostitution: A Report from Australia." Brit J Delin 9(3):182-191, Jan. '59.

1288 Wilson, P. R. and Chappell, D. "Australian attitudes towards abortion, prostitution and homosexuality." Australian Q 40:7-17, Jun. '68. Based on sample of 1045 informants.

1289 Adams, C. "Special house in Hamburg." New Statesman 85:521-2, April 13, 1973. Male prostitution.

1290 Alexander, Rolf B. Die Prostitution in Deutschland. Munich: Lichtenberg: 1969, 187 pp.

1291 Anthony, Katherine. Feminism in Germany and Scandinavia. London: Canstable, 1916.

1292 Bartsch, Georg. Prostitution, Kuppelei und Zuhalterei. Hamburg: Verlag Deutsche Polizei, 1956, 93 pp.

1293 Bauer, M. Die Dirne und ihr Anhang. Dresden: 1924, 228 pp.

1294 Burchard, E. Erpresser-Prostitution. Berlin: Kampf-Verlag, 1905, 14 pp.

1295 Dieckhoff, Albr. "Die Helenstrasse in Bremen." Kriminalistik November 1958, p.463. Helenstrasse is a street reserved for prostitution.

1296 Doutine, H. "Eros centre." Encounter 30:65-8, March 1960.

1297 Federation Abolition Internation. Enquete Sur la prostitution en Suisse. Federation Abolition Internation, 1949, 27 pp.

1298 Fiaux, L. "La Prostitution en Suisse et particulierement en Geneva." Progres Med (Paris) 9:65, 132, 183, 209, 329, 364, 394, 1899, 3. s.

1299 Fichte, Hubert. Interviews aus dem Palais d'Amour. Hamburg: Rowohlt Taschenbuch-Ver., 1973, 203 pp. Also includes Lesbianism.

1300 Guillot, A. La lutte contre l'exploitation et la reglementation due vice a Geneve. Geneva: Federation abolitionniste internationale, n.d. (before 1902).

1301 Hessen, Robert. Die Prostitution in Deutschland. Munich: Albert Laugln, 1910, 240 pp.

1302 Hoppe, Ludwig. Sexueller Bolschewismus und seine Abwehr Berlin: Vaterlandische verlag-und Kunstanstalt, 1921, 55 pp.

1303 "Hostel is not a house; West Germany's quarters for prostitutes." Time 86:26+, June 23, 1965.

1304 Joerissen, Luise. Die Lage der Prostitution in Deutschland. Koln: 1957, 24 pp.

1305 Kessler, Rainer. Die rechtliche Regelung der Prostitutionsfrage seit dem RSTGB 1871 und deren soziologische Bedeutung in diesem Zeitraum. Munchen: 1952, 151 pp.

1306 Knack, U. B. Groz-Hamburg im kampfe gegen geschlechtstrantheiten und bordelle. Hamburg: Verlagsanstalt Auer and Co., 1921, 32 pp.

1307 Kocmata, C. F. Die Prostitution in Wien. Vienna: 1925, 71 pp.

1308 Kun, Gerhard. Das phenomen der strichjugend in Hamburg. Wiesbaden: Schriftenreihe des Bundeskriminalamtes, 1957, 120 pp. A study of 352 professional prostitutes between 1948 and 1954.

1309 Laurent, Dr. Emile. Prostitution et degenerescence (Prostitution und Entartung. Ein Beitrag zur Lehre von der geborenen Prostituierten). Translated and edited by G. Montanus. Freiburg i. Br. and Leipzig, 1903, 51 pp.

1310 Loeffler, F. "Die Zuhalterbewegung und ihre Bekampfung." Krim Mh 8:277-278, 1934.

1311 Meyer, T. Massnahmen von offentlichen, Kirchlichen und privaten Stellen der Stadt Zurich zur Verminderung und Eindammung der Prostitution. Geneva: 1956, 61 pp. Work presented to the School of Social Studies.

1312 Montane, H. Die Prostitution in Wien. Vienna: 1925, 182 pp.

1313 Niss, Alexander. Das Strich-Buch. Frankfurt: Zero Press, 1971, 178 pp.

1314 Pappritz, Anna. Die gesundheitlichen Gefahren der Prostitution. Dresden: 1902. A brochure issue by Anna Pappritz of the Berlin affiliate of the Federation.

1315 Pongratz, Lieselotte. Prostituiertenkinder, Umwelt und Entwicklung in denersten acht Lebensjahren. Stuttgart: G. Fisher, 1964.

1316 Rogan, Carl. Berlin's beruhmte und beruchtigte hauser. Zweiter Band, Heft I. Berlin: Debit von Leopold Lassar, Bruderstrasse, n.d., 288 pp.

1317 Rohr, Dorothea. Prostitution: eine empir. Frankfurt am Main: Suhrkamp, 1972, 201 pp.

1318 Sarason, D. Vorschlag einer neuen Organisation des Prostitutionswesens. (Blaschko, A. Welche Aufgaben erwachsen dem Kampf gegen die Geschlechtskrankheiten aus dem Kriege?) 1915.

1319 Schmidt, H. "Therapy of prostitutes and history of prostitution in Hamburg." Dermat Wchnschr 114:257-260, Mar. 28, 1942.

1320 Schultze, E. Die Prostitution bei den gelben Volkern. Abhandlungen aus dem Gebiete der Sexualforschung. Bd. 1. Heft 2. Bonn: 1918, 46 pp.

1321 Searle, Ronald. Secret Sketchbook The Back Streets of Hamburg. London: Weidenfeld and Nicolson, 1969.

1322 Seekel, Friedrich. Frankreich, Zentrale des internationalen Madchenhandels, etc. Schriften des Deutschen Instituts fur Aussenpolitische Forschung. Heft 71. Berlin: 1940, 46 pp.

1323 "Sex mit Herz; K. Kofl's chain of brothels in West Germany." Time 101:104, April 23, 1973.

1324 "Sexporter; West German brothel chain." Newsweek 81:40, Apr. 23, '73.

1325 Sexikon, Heluetikuss. Ein Fuhrer Z. Nutzen d. "Fremden-Verkehrs." Berlin: Dulk, 1971, 176 pp.

1326 Simmat, William E. Prostitution und Offentlichkeit; Soziologische Betrachtungen zur Affare Nitribitt. Stuttgart: F. Decker Verlag Nachf, 1958, 169 pp.

1327 "Suppression of Prostitution in Germany; German Emperor as Supreme Conscience." Spec 67:585.

1328 Touraine, A. and Fouassier. "Results of 10 years of abolition of official recognition of prostitution in Strasbourg." Bull Soc franc de dermat et syph 44:1940-1954, November 1937.

1329 Wintsch-Maleeff. "Struggle against the venereal diseases and prostitution in Switzerland." Soc Hygiene 6:255-62, April 20.

1330 "Women Withour Husbands." The Bulletin. Press Office, German Embassy, February 21, 1961.

1331 Canada's War on the White Slave Trade. Canada, 1911.

1332 "Canadian Slavers; in London." Time 27:15, February 17, 1936.

1333 Cavers, C. W. "Vice and venereal disease in Montreal: preliminary report of the committee of sixteen." Public Health J 9:529-33, November 1918.

1334 "Jadeo Jarvis Street, Toronto." Newsweek 46:60, November 14, 1955.

1335 Limoges, Therese. La prostitution a Montreal. Montreal: Editions de l'Homme L'Agence, 1967, pp.123-125.

1336 Montreal Committee of Sixteen. Some facts regarding toleration, regulation, segregation and repression of commercialized vice. (Pub. no.2). 80 pp.

1337 Toronto, Ontario. Social survey comm. Report presented to the city council October 4, 1915. 72 pp. 1915. Carswell Co. Contains: Introductory; Conditions in Toronto in relation to the social evil; The social evil and the law; Contributory factors in the problem of social morality; Medical aspect of prostitution.

1338 Champley, Henry. Doroga v. Shanghai. Translation of Le Chemin de Changhai. Warsaw: 1935.

1339 Chang, Ching-chi. Prostitution. lv. Toronto: n.p., 1892. Romanized title Ch 'in-huai pa yen t'u yung. Nanking.

1340 Chang, P. Chuang lou chi. 1796. Ts'ui, Ling-ch'in, 1939.

1341 Hsieh, K'ang. Mai yin chih tu yu T'ai-wan ch'ang chi went'i. Formosa: 1972, 470 pp.

1342 Ichok, G. "Combat against induced sexual crimes with special reference to prostitution in China. Rev d'hyg 56:133-14, February, 1934.

1343 Nakagawa, K. and Watanabe, F. "Wasserman reaction in prostitutes of prefecture of Taihoku (Formosa)." Taiwan Igakkai Zasshi 35:1275, June 1936.

1344 Penlington, J. N. "Licensed women of Japan." Current History 34:887-91, S 1931.

1345 Peter, Prince of Greece. "Tibetan, Toda, and Tiya Polyandry: a report on field investigations," in New York Academy of Sciences, Transactions, Ser.2, 10(1948):217.

1346 "Russian women and League's report on prostitution." China W R 72:375-6, May 18, 1935.

1347 Ste-Croiz, Avril de. "Reform of 'regime des moeurs' in France," translated as "Venereal diseases in relation to prostitution in China," by F.J. Heath. Social Pathology 1:270-3, 278-84, 1925. Tables.

1348 "Shanghai moral conditions and the British troops." China W R 43:300, February 18, 1928.

1349 "Shanghai's open air houses of prostitution." China W R 69:169, June 30, 1934.

1350 Tasaki, K. and Kamimura, T. "Frei and Ito reactions in licensed prostitutes in Mukden." J Orient Med (Abstr. Sect.) 27:117, November, 1937. Comment on contagious origin of lymphogranuloma inguinale.

1351 "Traffic in women problem for China." Trans-Pac 23:15+, March 28, 1935.

1352 Tseng, P. S. "The Chinese Woman Past and Present," in Symposium on Chinese Culture, edited by Sophia H. Chen Zen. Shanghai, China: Institute of Pacific Relations, 1931.

1353 Ts'ui, Ling-ch'in. Chiao fang chi. Chung-kuo wen hsueh ts'an tzu kiao hsaio ts'ung shu. Ti.1 chi.8 (Series). 1959, 66 pp.

1354 Ts'ui, Ling-ch'in. _Chiao fang chi chien ting_. 1962, 288 pp. Tables.

1355 Van der Valk, M. H. _Conservatism in Modern Chinese Family Law_. Luden: E. J. Brill, 1956.

1356 Wei, Yu and Wong, Amos. "A study of 500 prostitutes in Shanghai." _Int J Sexol_ 2:234-8, 1949.

1357 Weiger, L. _Moral Tenets and Customs in China_. In Chinese and in English translations by L. Daurout, Hokien-fu: Catholic Mission Press, 1913.

1358 Yao, Ling-hsi. _Wei k'o chen p'in ts'ung_. Toronto: 1936, 112 pp.

1359 Baloff, A. "Derevenskaya Prostitutsiya v Yaroslavskoi Gubernii." (Village Prostitution in Yaroslav Government) Feldscher St. Petersb. 1901, 11:427-429.

1360 Czappert, L. "Ein Beitrag zur Prostitutionsfrage, mit Besonderer Beruksichtigung des Prostitutionswesens zu Prag." Wien Med Wchnschr (Vienna) 1851, 1:278-293.

1361 "Hard currency girls; hotel prostitutes in Europe." Time 101:39, May 7, 1973.

1362 Jincinska, B. "Czechoslovakia's oldest profession." East Europe 16:23-4, June 1967.

1363 Kasinska, Magdalena. Proces spolecenego wykolejenia mlodocianych dziewczat. Warsaw: Wydawnictwo prawnicze, 1967, 196 pp. The second of two studies.

1364 Minkevicius, P. Metodai ir priemones kovai su prostitucija. Teises ir economijos studijos. tom.2. kn.3. Kaunas, 1938, 52 pp. Lithuanian.

1365 Posner, S. Nad Otchiania. Czese. Warsaw: 1903, 95 pp.

1366 Turzanski, G. "Kilka uwag w Sprawie Popraway Obecnych Stsunkow Prostytucyi." Przegl Chorob Skor I Wen Wars. 1907. 2:376-403.

1367 Zahovova-Nemcova, J. "The organization of anti-prostitutional work in the Czechoslovak republic." J Social Hygiene 11:407-16, October 1925.

1368 Berg, Alex. *Sex in Sozialismus: Report.* Munich: Heyne, 1972, 158 pp. Communist countries.

1369 "Cherchez la fraulein; million dollar Dunengetto scheme." *Newsweek* 61:25 January 7, 1963.

1370 Flexner, Abraham. *Prostitution in Europe.* (Bureau of Social Hygiene pubs). Century, 1913 and 1914. Reprinted by Grant Richards, 1919 and by Patterson Smith in 1969. 455 pp. Dr. Flexner spent a year investigating eleven European countries under a commission from the Bureau of social hygiene, of which J. D. Rockefeller, Jr., was chairman.

1371 Flexner, A. "Regulation of prostitution in Europe." Am Social Hygiene Assn. Also printed in *Social Hygiene* 1:15-28, December 1914.

1372 "Hopeful book on the social evil: prostitution in Europe." *Outlook* 106:293-4, February 7, 1914.

1373 Kissmeyer, A. "Voyage made in 1938 to port cities of Western Europe to study organization of antivenereal campaign," *Prophylax antiven* 11:623-624, November 1939.

1374 Lux, H. *Die Prostitution.* Berlin: 1892, 38 pp.

1375 Nance, W.O. and Geiger, E. *Control of vice conditions in European cities.* Chicago:1914. Municipal reference library.

1376 "Prostitution in Europe: a study of supply, demand, regulation." *Survey* 31:471-3, January 17, 1914.

1377 "Real social evil treatise: prostitution in Europe." *Nation* 98:75-6, January 22, 1914.

1378 Wicksell, K. *Om Prostitutionen.* Stockholm: 1887, 56 pp.

1379 Bair, L. "Lost Women of Paris." Reader's Digest 66:57-61, April 1955.

1380 Berenger, M. Rapport sur la prostitution et les outrages aux bonnes moeurs. Senat francais, 1895. 68 pp.

1381 Bizard, L. "Errors in regulation in Paris." Prophylax antiven 11:452-476, July 1939.

1382 Bizard, L. "Number of prostitutes in Paris." Paris med (annexe) 1:ii-iv, March 10, 1934.

1383 Bourret, M. and Jarret. "Experiences with voluntary registration for health in Marseille." Prophylax antiven 20:564-67, July-August 1948.

1384 "Bring back the brothels? France considering municipal bordellos." Time 96:30, November 9, 1970.

1385 "Call Them Social Workers: Paris House of Prostitution." Time 59:31, January 14, 1951.

1386 Carlier, F. Les deux Prostitutions. Paris: 1887, 514 pp.

1387 Carroll, L. "Paris in a Clean-up Era; The City of No Red Lights." Newsweek 31:32-3, January 5, 1948.

1388 Cere, E. "Femmes du monde." Mercure Fr 189:604-20, August 1, 1926.

1389 Clouzet, Maryse. Parizhsakiia nochi. (Paris Nights). Riga: Lukoporniy, 1933, 138 pp. In Russian.

1390 Commenge, Oscar. Hygienc Sociale: La prostitution clandestines a Paris. Paris: Schleicher Freres, 1897. Also Paris: Schleicher Freres, 1904.

1391 Deux "filles" sur trois sont des mamans. Numero special de Moissons nouvelles, Clichy: 1959, 88 pp. Another brochure from Nid analyzing prostitution.

1392 Durban,___, and Durban,____. "La Prostitution feminine a Toulouse." Toulouse Med 52:524-47, 1951.

1393 Filhol, P. Le monde des particulieres. Paris: Gallimard, 1959, 262 pp.

1394 Gemahling, Paul and Parker, Daniel. Les maisons publiques, danger public. Paris: Ligue francaise pour le relivement de la moralite publique, 1945, 77 pp.

1395 "How the French deal with prostitutes." Soc Hygiene 5:601-6, October 1919.

1396 Isou, Isidore. Histoire philosophique illustree de la volupte a Paris. Paris: Publications et editions Alger, 1960, 128 pp.

1397 Kunstle, Marc. Notre-Dame des Esclandres. Paris: Presses de la Cite, 1973, 212 pp.

1398 Lasserre, Jean. Les bagnes de la prostitution reglementee. Comment les "maisons" furent fermees. Geneva: Federation abolitionniste internationale, 1955, 144 pp.

1399 Leitch, D. "The brothels of Lyons." New Statesman 84: 309-10, September 8, 1972.

1400 Lennon, Peter. "The falling stars (Suburban part-timers)." Guardian November 18, 1966, pp.9.

1401 "Les Telefilles in Paris." Time 75:27, March 14, 1960.

1402 Limouzi, M. "Arguments for and against reglementation in France." J de Med de Paris 68:45-48, Mar.; and 65-70, Apr., 1918.

1403 "Lost Women of Paris." Readers Digest 66:57-61, 1955.

1404 Mace, Gustave. Gibier de Saint-Lazare. Paris: G. Carpentier, 1888, 320 pp. Prostitution in Paris.

1405 Mancini, Jean Gabriel. Prostitution et proxenetisme. Paris: Presses universitaires de France, 1972, 127 pp.

1406 Merlin, Jean de. La Debauche a Paris. Paris: 1900, 246 pp.

1407 Metra, Louis. Les dessous de Paris; souvenirs vecus par l'ex-inspecteur principal de la brigade mondaine. Paris: Editions du Scorpion, 1955, 255 pp.

1408 Mireur, H. La prostitution a Marseille. Paris-Marseille, 1882.

1409 Morin, Edgar. La Rumeur d'Orleans. Paris: Editions du Sevil, 1969, 237 pp. Orleans, France. Also, translated by Peter Green. New York: Pantheon Books, 1971, 276 pp. Public opinion and prostitution.

1410 "New French law for repression of prostitution goes into effect." J Soc Hygiene 32:383-5, November 1946.

1411 Orvingo, C. "Morals bureau of Paris." J Soc Hygiene 10:139-63, March 1924.

1412 "Paris: After Dark Where?" Newsweek 28:53, October 21, 1946.

1413 "Paris: La Skylark." _Newsweek_ 27:52, March 18, 1946.

1414 Perrin, M. "Prevention in Grenoble." _Rev med de Nancy_ 66:879-90, November 1, 1938. Also _Prophylax antiven_ 11: 8-23, January 1939.

1415 Philippon, Odette. _L'esclavage du siecle_. Paris: Tequi, 1969, 251 pp. Another one of her studies.

1416 Pignier, Francois. _La prostitution feminine--Ses formes--Sa prevention_. Paris, n.d. (1960?), 28 pp. A survey of prostitution in Paris.

1417 "Prostitution in Paris." _Westm_ 119:494.

1418 Richard-Mollard, G. "La prostitution en France. adjourd'hie." _Etudes_ 340:713-26, May 1974.

1419 "Ring out Wild Belles; Prostitution in France." _Newsweek_ 26:39-41, December 31, 1945.

1420 Roheim, G. "Ceremonial prostitution in Duau (Normandy Island)." _J Clin Psychopath Psychother_ 7:753-764, 1964. Information on Trobriand Islander Anthropology.

1421 Sacotte, Marcel. _La Prostitucion_. Translated by Rafael Andreu and Caroline Audenia. Barcelona: Fontanella-Pulcra, 1964. 2nd edition, 1966 and 3rd edition, 1969.

1422 Sacotte, Marcel. _La Prostitution, que peut-on faire?_. Paris: Buchet-Chaslel, 1971, 315 pp.

1423 "Street Cleaning in France." _Newsweek_ 53:58, April 6, 1959.

1424 Suriant, ___. "La 'Dame aux yeux gris'." _Mercure Fr_ 278:18-38, August 15, 1937.

1425 Vigne, P. and Bourret, M. "Effects of application of law of April 13, 1946 on sanitary control at Marseille." _Ann de dermat et syph_ (Bull. Soc. franc. de dermat. et syph 2) 7:109-110, April 1947.

1426 Vigne, P. "Organization of control in Boughard Rhone province." _Prophylax antiven_ 13:349-54, October 1941.

1427 Vivien, Robert Andre. _Solution au probleme de la prostitution_. Lille: L. Daniel, 1960, 152 pp.

1428 "Voice of Conscience of New France." _Time_ 46:32, Dec. 31, 1945.

1438A Touraine, A. and Fouassier. "Results of 10 years of abolition of official recognition of prostitution in Strasbourg." _Bull Soc Franc de dermat et Syph_ 44:1940-1954, November 1937.

1429 "Angry M.P. and Vice; London's West End." Newsweek 47:55, March 19, 1956.

1430 "Austerity Hits the Mile in London." Newsweek 29:41, May 19, 1947.

1431 Chesterton, A. E. In Darkest London. Stanley Paul, 1930, 188 pp.

1432 "Cities of the plain; Wolfenden report." Economist 189:769-70, November 29, 1958.

1433 "Cleaning the streets." Economist 189:1142, December 27, 1958.

1434 "Colchester and the Contagious Diseases act." Brit Med J Lond. 2:886, 1884.

1435 Edwards, Quentin. What is unlawful? Does innocence begin where crime ends? Afterthoughts on the Wolfenden report. Westminister: Published for the Church of England Moral Welfare Council by the Church Information Office, 1959, 13 pp.

1436 "Eire puts out the red lights." Survey 50:97, April 15, 1923.

1437 "Experiment with sex." New Statesman 58:209, August 22, 1959.

1438 "Farsical proceedings of the committee on street offenses." New Statesman 30:457-8, January 21, 1928.

1439 "First cases; street offenses act." Economist 192:575, August 22, 1959.

1440 Gilmour, I. "Echoes of a report; Wolfenden and the 'scandal'." Spec 213:106, June 24, 1964.

1441 Gosling, John and Warner, D. The Shame of a City: An Inquiry into the Vice of London. London: W. H. Allen, 1960, 208 pp.

1442 Great Britain. Committee on Homosexual Offences and Prostitution. Report. London: H. M. Stationery Office, 1957, 155 pp.

1443 Great Britain. Committee on Homosexual Offences and Prostitution. The Wolfenden report. Authorized American edition. Introduction by Karl Menninger. New York: Stein and Day, 1963, 243 pp. Tables.

1444 Great Britain. Home office. Report of the street offenses committee. London: H. M. stationery office, 1928, 49 pp.

1445 Hall-Williams, J. E. "Wolfenden report--an appraisal." Pol 2 29:132-43, April 1958.

1446 Harrison, M. Fanfare of strumpets. London: W. H. Allen, 197 pp.

1447 Higson, Jessie E. The story of a beginning; an account of pioneer work for moral welfare. London: S. P. C. K., 1955, 168 pp.

1448 "Jack the stripper; hunt for murderer of London prostitutes." Time 83:32+, May 8, 1964.

1449 "London's campaign against vice." Literary Digest 53:1177-8, November 4, 1916.

1450 Lowndes, F. W. Prostitution and Venereal Diseases in Liverpool London: 1886.

1451 Lowndes, F. W. "Prostitution and Syphilis in Liverpool." Med Times and Gaz 2:569-571, 1875

1452 MacInnes, C. "Other man." 20th Cent 167:152-7, February 1960.

1453 Mayhew, H. London's underworld. Spring Bks., 1958.

1454 "Messina girls in London." Newsweek 30:32+, June 14, 1947.

1455 Morrison, Majbritt. Jungle West. Great Britain: Tandem Books Limited, 1964, 288 pp.

1456 Neilans, A. "Abolition anniversary." Spec 156:709, April 17, 1936.

1457 "New style tart." New Statesman 58:616+, November 7, 1959.

1458 Norman, Frank and Bernard, Jeffrey. Soho Night and Day. London: Secker and Warburg, 1966, 96 pp.

1459 "Off the streets of London." Time 74:22+, August 31, 1959.

1460 Panter-Downes, M. "Letter from London; report of the Committee on homosexual offenses and prostitution." New Yorker 33:101-3, September 28, 1957.

1461 Pearl, C. The Girl with the Swans Down Seat. Horwitz, 1969.

1462 (Physican) The greatest of our Social Evils: Prostitution as it now exists in London, Manchester, Glasgow, Edinburgh, and Dublin. London: 1857.

1463 Postgate, R. "London: Goodbye to Hullo, Darling." Holiday 28:50+, November 1960.

1464 "Prostitution statistics of London." *Tait* n.s. 24:747.

1465 "Pushed off the sidewalk; London." *Time* 73:21, February 9, 1959.

1466 Richelot, G. "Hygiene Publique. De la Prostitution en Angleterre et en Ecosse." *Union Med* Paris, 11:181;195; 207;221;245;257;269;281;293;305;317;329;341;355;367;379;391, 1857.

1467 Scarlet, I. *The professionals: prostitutes and their clients*. Sidjuich, 1972.

1468 Scott, B. *A state of iniquity*. Kelley, 1968.

1469 Shepherd, F. H. W., ed. *Survey of London*. Vol. 23: "The Parish of St. Anne, Soho." London: Athlone Press, 1966.

1470 Tait, W. *Magdalenism*; an enquiry into the extent, causes, and consequences of prostitution in Edinburgh. Edinburgh, 1840, 80pp.

1471 Terrot, Charles. *Traffic in innocents, the shocking story of white slavery in England*. Dutton, 1960, 230 pp.

1472 Thomas, Mrs. Howell. "Prostitution in Great Britain today." *Social Defence* 8(30):14-26, October 1972.

1473 "Traffic in women and children." *Spec* 139:47, June 9, 1927.

1474 "View from Curzon street." *Newsweek* 53:43, February 9, 1959.

1475 "Westminster commentary (House of Commons debate on the Wolfenden Report)." *Spec* 201:742, November 28, 1958.

1476 Wilkinson, G. S. "Soliciting and offences by prostitutes [Great Britain]: Vagrancy act, 1824, Section 3." *Police J* 22:50-7, January 1949.

1477 Willis, W. N. *White slaves in a Piccadilly flat*. Anglo-Eastern Pub. Co., 1932(?) Reprinted London: Camden Publishing Co., 1949.

1478 Willis, W. N. *White slaves of London*. R. G. Badger, 1913. Reprinted London: Camden Publishing Co., 1949.

1479 Stamatiades, M. *O Etaipiemoe*. Athens: 1954, 168 pp. A study of prostitution in Greece, written to obtain the grade of doctor in the faculty of law and economics at the University of Salonique.

1480 Craps, M. "Reglements, legislation et contributions medico-sociales belges dans le domain de la lutte antivenerienne depuis la fin du hygiene, medecine du travail et medicine legale." July 1959, 29 pp.

1481 Fremery Kalff, J. Met gesloten duren. Den Haag: Daamen, 1956, 276 pp.

1482 "Girls from De Walletjes, Amsterdam." Time 75:23, January 11, 1960.

1483 Groothuyse, Johan Wilhelm. Het menselijk tekort van de pooler. Amsterdam: Wetenschappelijke Uitge-verij, 1973, 213 pp. Alcoholism, crime, and prostitution.

1484 Haeften, W. L. van. Prostitute vroeger en nu. Amsterdam: Nederlandsche Keur Boekeri, 1969, 252 pp.

1485 Hoogenkamp, W. F. "The Mr. de Graaf-Institution in Amsterdam." Tijdschr Ziekenverpl 19(19):643-4, October 1, 1966.

1486 Prostitutie onder de oude en rieume volken. Amsterdam: 1885, 185 pp.

1487 Slobbe, J. F. van. Bijdrage tot de geschiedenis en de bestrijding der prostitutie te Amsterdam. Amsterdam: 1917(?), 172 pp.

1488 "The war and prostitution in Holland:" Social Hygiene 2:617-21, October 1916.

1489 Agnihotri, Vidyadhar. Fallen Women: A Study with Special Reference to Kanpur. Kanpur, India: Maharaja Printers, 1954(?), 99 pp.

1490 Anderson, H. Calcutta Vice. Calcutta: 1921, 40 pp.

1491 Anderson, H. "Changes in the Outlook on Prostitution in India." J Social Hyg 20:361-2, October 1934.

1492 Association for Moral and Social Hygiene in India. The First All-India Conference on Moral and Social Hygiene. New Delhi: 1950, 121 pp. Report on Conference held on October 19-21, 1950 at Red Cross Building, New Delhi.

1493 Banerjee, G. R. "Crusade against social vice [India]." Indian J Soc Work 10:1-8, June 1949.

1494 Banerjee, G. R. "Prostitution requires prohibition." Indian J Soc Work 19:11-17, June 1958.

1495 Bedekar, Malati Vishram. Gharala mukalelya strlya va kajael eahula. 1962, 238 pp.

1496 Bengal. Legislative Department. The Bengal Suppression of Immoral Traffic Act 1933. Alipore: Government Printing, 1940, 15 pp.

1497 Bombay, Presidency of. Prostitution Committee. Report. 1923, 16 pp.

1498 Carter, Herbert Dyson. Sin and Science. Bombay: Current Book House, 1950 [c. 1946], 223 pp.

1499 "Changes in Prostitution act in Bombay." J Soc Hyg 15:429-30, October 1929. Abstract.

1500 Correia, A.C. G. da Silva "Bayaderes and Other Courtesans of Portuguese India; anthropometry, sexology, ethnography, sociology, venereology and prophylaxis." Arq Esc Med.-cir de Nova Goa Ser. A, pp.61-384, '39.

1501 Correia, A. C. G. da Silva "History, demography, ethnography, hygiene and prophylaxis." Arq Esc med cir de Nova Goa Ser B, mem. 1, pp. 1-404, 1938.

1502 Correia, A. C. G. da Silva India). J de sif e ura 11:208, August; 230, September; 268, October; 287, November; 361, December; 1940.

1503 Correia, Alberto C. Germano S. Prostituicao e Profilaxia Anti-venerea. Bastora: Portuquese India, 1938.

1504 Dixon, K. An Appeal to the Women of the Empire concerning present moral conditions in our cantonments in India. Association for Moral and Social Hygiene, 1916, 11 pp.

1505 Gask, R. C. and Isaacs, H. "Twain do meet; oldest profession thrives in India." Newsweek 24:62-4, September 11, 1944.

1506 Gokhale, B. B. "Study of Prostitution in Poona." Samaj-Seva (Poona) January 1, 1955.

1507 Hausurrth, Frieda. Purdah: The Status of Indian Women. London: Kegan Paul, Trench, Trubner and Co., 1932. Some historical material.

1508 India. Laws, statutes, etc. Commentaries on suppression of immoral traffic in women and girls act (Act no. 104 of 1956); with states' rules and forms, by Shrinath Prasad Srivastava. Patna: Pahuja Bros., 1960.

1509 India. Laws. The Suppression of Immoral Traffic in Women and Girls Act, 1956. (No. 104 of 1956.) With critical commentary and case law. By Mazhar Husain. Lucknow, Delhi: Eastern Book Co., 1958, 103 pp.

1510 India. Laws, statutes, etc. The suppression of immoral traffic in women and girls act, 1956; (with states rules), by B. R. Beotra. Allahabad: Law Book Co., 1962 and 1970, 388 pp.

1511 "India Signs Convention on Traffic in Persons." United Nations Bulletin 8:494, June 1, 1950.

1512 Jahore. Enactment to make provision for the protection of women and girls, the suppression of brothels, and other purposes. (No. 7, Enactments 1926).

1513 Krishnan, O. U. The Night Side of Bombay. Cannanore, 1938, 83 pp.

1514 Kuttner, R. E. and Loring, A. B. "Promiscuity and prostitution in urbanized Indian communities." Ment Hy 54:79-91, January 1970.

1515 Lapping, Brain. "The wickedest street of them all." Guardian December 28, 1968. Pakistan.

1516 Laurent, Emile. Die Prostitution in Indien. Eine Kulturhistorische Studie. Translated by G. Montanus. Freiburg i. Br. and Leipzig: 1901.

1517 "Les Girls in Calcutta." Time 71:25, May 19, 1958.

1518 Madras, Presidency of. Administration Report on the Working of the Madras Suppression of Immoral Traffic Act for the year 1956. Madras: 1958. From the Office of the Chief Inspector of Certified Schools and Vigilance Service.

1519 Mathur, A. S. and Gupta, B. L. _Prostitutes and Prostitution_. Ram Prasad, 1965.

1520 Misra, N. "A Survey of Prostitutes in Kanpur." _Sociologist_ 1(1):59-65, 1956-57.

1521 Mukherji, S. K. "Sexual promiscuity (in India)." _Indian M Rec_ 53:305, October; 342, November; 369, December, 1933.

1522 Nadu, Tamil. _Administration report on the working of the suppression of immoral traffic in women and girls act, 1956_. Madras: 1968.

1523 Nadu, Tamil. _Office of the Chief Inspector of Approved School and Vigilance Service_. Madras: 1968.

1524 Noronha, M. "Commercialized prostitution in Bombay and its effects; measures of combat." _Indian J Ven Dis_ 2:60-65, March 1936.

1525 North-West Frontier Province Government. _The North-West Frontier Province Anti-prostitution and Suppression of Brothels Act 1936_. Peshawar: 1937, 4 pp.

1526 Punekar, S. D. and Roa, Kamala. _A study of prostitutes in Bombay, with reference to family background_. Bombay: Allied Publishers, 1962, 242 pp. Family background emphasized.

1527 Ranga, Rao M. and J. V. R. Rao. _The Prostitutes of Hyderabad: A Study of the Socio-Cultural Conditions of the Prostitutes of Hyderabad_. Hyderabad, India: Association for Moral and Social Hygiene in India, Andhra Pradesh Branch, 1970, 79 pp.

1528 Ross, Allen V. _Vice in Bombay_. London: Tallis, 1969, 192 pp. Plates.

1529 Rothfield, Otto. _Women of India_. Bombay: D. B. Taraporevala Sons and Co., 1920.

1530 Santosha-Kumara Mukhopadhyaya. _Prostitution in India_. Calcutta, 1934, 528 pp.

1531 _Social health_. v. 1-. New Delhi: July 1962. Quarterly.

1532 Uamaria, C. B. "Prostitution in India." _Ind J Soc Work_ 17:106-12, S 1956.

1533 Accettella, "Terza Statistica Civile Amministrative e Clinica della Prostituzione di Terra di Lavoro per l'anno 1871." Campania Med Castera, 2:1;21, 1872-3.

1534 "Addio casino!" New Statesmen and Nation 39:482, April 29, 1950.

1535 "Battle of the Brothels; Merlin Anti-Brothel Bill in Italy." Time 54:18, December 26, 1949.

1536 Bacon, G. M., "Brief Account of the Government Regulations on Prostitution in Italy, and of the Sifilicomio at Naples." Lancet Lond., 1:357, 1864.

1537 Bacon, G. M., "The Statistics of Public Prostitution in Italy." Lancet Lond., 1:157, 1867.

1538 Bernocchi, Franco. Prostituzione e rieducazione. Padua: Cedam, 1966, 253 pp.

1539 Bucalo, Salvatore. Prostituzione e salute pubblica. Terni: Poligrafico Alterocca, 1958, 204 pp. Legge 20 febbraio 1958 n. 75 sulla abolizione della regolamentazione della prostituzione e lotta contro lo sfruttamento della prostituzione altrui. Legge 25 luglio 1956 n.837 sulla profilassi della malattie veneree. Storia, legislazione, giurisprudenza.

1540 Cazzani, C., "Osservazioni Intorno al Vigente Regolamento sulla Prostituzione." Ann Univ di Med Milano, 180:607, 1862.

1541 "Coffee for every taste; Rome." Time 96:35, December 14, 1970.

1542 Cutrera, Antonino. La mala vita di Palermo. 2nd ed. Palermo: A Reber, 1900, 89 pp. Prostitution.

1543 d'Alo, Giuseppe. Abolizione delle case di meretricio. Pisa: 1950, 28 pp.

1544 Gamberini, P., "Rapporto Politico-Aministrativoclinico della Prostituzione di Bologna, 1861-1886." Bull d Sc Med Bologna 1864, 4 s., 21:1869, 5 s. 7. Cont. in Gior Ital d Mal Ven Milano, 1870, 1:1887,22.

1545 Garbelli, Giambattista. La prostituzione in Italia oggi. Francavilla al Mare: Edizioni paoline, 1973, 57 pp.

1546 Granata, Luigi. "Aspetti sociali e giuridici delle Legge Merlin. Lo sfruttamento di prostitute e l'applicazione delle misure di dicuerzza." Giustizia penale (September 1960), 337-340.

1547 Grazzini, G. "Sin on the doorstep." Atlas 9:18-21, January 1965.

1548 Gustapane, Giuseppe. Casa di prostituzione e lenocinio (disposizioni penali della Legge Merlin). Galatina. Edtr. Salentina di Pajano, 1959, 307. Esposizione critica rassegna di dottrina e giurispudenza. Presentazione di Michele de Pietro.

1549 "Italy: house and home; move to amend Merlin law." Newsweek 66:53, November 8, 1965.

1550 "Italy; Lost Distinction." Time 72:25, September 29, 1958.

1551 "Klaxton Girls of Italy." Time 76:37, October 10, 1960.

1552 La Prostituzione continua... Firenze: Vallecchi, 1960, 163 pp.

1553 Lettere dalle case chiuse. Milano and Roman, 1955, 204 pp. A cura di Lina Merlin e Carla Barberis. Letters written to Senator Merlin dealing with closing tolerated houses.

1554 Manocchia, Benito. Indagine su dieci squillo di losso. Torino: MEB, 1971, 154 pp.

1555 Neves, Azevedo. "Campaign against Prostitution and Exploitation of Women in Italy." Arch de Med leg 6:1-15, 1933.

1556 Penco, Giovanni. Donna caduta e donn redeota. 2nd ed. Milan: 1954, 185 pp. Prostitution in Milan.

1557 "Die Prostitution in Mailano." Wien Med Halle 3:389, 1862.

1558 Saffiro, Luciano. "Prostituzione femminile contemporanea." Rivista di Psicologica Sociale (October-December 1960), pp.271-302, published at Turin. Prostitution considered from a nuber of points of view, moral, sexual, psychoanalytic, psychological, sociological, et al.

1559 Sapolini, "Statistica della Prostituzione e dei Sifilicomi nel Regno d'Italia." Atti Cong Gen d Ass Med Ital 1871 Rome, 5:281-322, 1872.

1560 Schmit, F. E., "Regulativ Uber Offentliche Preisgebung im Konigreiche Italien." Deutsche Ztsch f d Staatsarznk Erlang n.F.28:3-35, 1870.

1561 "Statistik der Prostitution in Italien und in Paris." Bl f Reform d San Wes Vien., 81-83, 1869.

1562 United Nations. Malta. Department of Information, 1968, 5 pp.

1563 Adachi, Naoro. Asobkne fuzoku sugata. 269 pp. Available at Harvard University, Chinese-Japanese Library.

1564 "After 1000 years prostitution becomes illegal in Japan." Newsweek 49:60, April 1, 1957.

1565 Anstice, E. H. "Licensed prostitution in Japan: complete abolition versus regulation." Chinese Nation 2:287-8+, Aug 12, '31.

1566 Bacon, Alice. Japanese girls and women. Boston: Houghton-Mifflin, 1891; reprinted edition, 1919.

1567 "Brothels must go in Japan." Time 67:40, June 4, 1956.

1568 "By Public Demand: Tokyo's Red-Light District." Time 70:40+, November 25, 1957.

1569 Camerer, C. B. and Huth, P. E. "Social evil in Japan," U S Nav M Bull 41:1189-1198, July 1943.

1570 Cohen, Yehudi A. "The Sociology of Commercialized Prostitution in Okinawa." Soc Forces 37(2):160-168, December 1958.

1571 DeBecker, J. E. The Nightless City: or the "History of Yoshiwara Yukwau". 5th edition revised. London: Probsthain and Co., 1905. Reprinted 1971.

1572 De Becker, Joseph Ernest. The Sexual Life of Japan: Being an Exhaustive Study of the Nightless City or the "History of Yoshiwara Yukwaku". New York: American Anthropological Society, 1934, 386 pp.

1573 De Becker, J. E. Yoshiwara. Reprinted third edition, 1905. New York: Frederick Publications, 1960.

1574 De Mente, Boye. The Pleasure Girls and Fleshpots of Japan. London, England: Ortolan, 1966, 159 pp.

1575 De Mente, Boye. Some Prefer Geisha: The Lively Art of Mistress-Keeping in Japan. Rutland, Vt.: Tuttle, 1966, 167 pp. Wayward Press; Ryudo-cho, Azaba, Minato-Ku, Toyko.

1576 Goryachkovshaya, Mariya. Japanese Orgies. Berlin: 1909, 39 pp.

1577 "Green Light for Red Lights in Japan." Time 66:25, August 1, 1955.

1578 Harris, Sara. House of the 10,000 Pleasures: A Modern Study of the Geisha and of the Streetwalker of Japan. London: W. H. Allen, 1962, 222 pp. Also New York: Dutton, 1962, 273 pp.

1579 Hashimoto, Yoshio. Hyakuokuen no baishun shijo. 1958, 238 pp. Available Hoover Institution.

1580 Hassel, J. W. "Blot on Japan's Escutcheon." Miss R of the World. 46:27-8, January 1923.

1581 Hennigar, E. C. "Battle for Purity in Japan." Miss R of the World 50:664-8, September 1927.

1582 Hennigar, E. C. "Fight against Licensed prostitution in Japan." J Soc Hyg 12:530-8, December 1926.

1583 Hintze, K. "Yoshiwara; die Regelung der Prostitution in Japan." Ztschr f Bekampf d Geschlech Leip. 7:189-228, 1907.

1584 Japan. Baishun Taisaku Shingikai. Baishun tsisaku no genkyo. 1959, 529 pp. Includes legislation. Available from Princeton University, Oriental Library.

1585 "Japans dangerous flowers." Economist 185: 599-600, November 16, 1957.

1586 Japan. Ministry of Justice. Material Concerning Prostitution and Its Control in Japan. Toyko, 1957, 55 pp. Gives materials from Japan from 1872 to 1957.

1587 "Japanese and the Social Evil." Missionary Review of the World 47:672-4, September 1924.

1588 Kagawa, T. "Licensed vice must go; the harm Japan is doing herself by the maintenance of prostitution." Trans-Pac 13:5, Sep. 11, '26.

1589 Kanzaki, Kiyoshi. Balshun. 1955, 208 pp.

1590 Kanzaki, Kiyoshi. Musunne(?) o uru machi. 1952, 231 pp. Avaialble at Hoover Institution.

1591 Kanzaki, Kiyoshi. Sengo Nihon no baishun mondai. 1954, 326 pp., maps, diagrs., tables.

1592 Kanzaki, Kiyoshi. Yoru no kichi. 1953, 305 pp.

1593 Kimura, Bumpei. Nihon schichinenkan no nazo. 1959, 198 pp.

1594 Krauss, Friedrich Salamo. Dasgueschlechtleben inglauben sitte brauch und gewohnheitrecht der Japaner. Leipzig: Ethnologisches verlag, 1911.

1595 Kuck, L. E. "Procession of taiyu is a colorful event." Trans- Pac 21:6+, May 18, 1933.

1596 "Licensed quarters may be ended soon." Trans-Pac 22:14+, January 11, 1934.

1597 Longstreet, Stephen and Longstreet, E. _Yoshiwara: City of the Senses_. New York: McKay, 1970, 225 pp. Deals with prostitution in Toyko.

1598 MacMurtrie, D. C. _Prostitution in Japan_. New York, 1913, 11 pp.

1599 Martin, S. C. "Prostitution in Japan in early years of this century." _Urol and Cutan Rev_ 51:574-585, October 1947.

1600 Matignon, J. J. "La Prostitution au Japon; le Quatier du Yoshiwara de Tokio." _Arch d'anth Crim_ Lyon and Par. 21:697-715, 1906

1601 Matsumoto, Y. "Statistics of prostitutes, in Kioto, Japan." _Mitt a d med Akad zu Kioto_ 9:483, 1933.

1602 "Memo from Toyko. Pup Costs $50, a Child, $22." _U.S. News and World Report_ 53:70-3, November 27, 1953. Slave Trade.

1603 "Messina Girls in London." _Newsweek_ 30:32+, July 14, 1947.

1604 "Ministry to fight selling of women." _Trans-Pac_ 22:9, November 22, 1934.

1605 "Modernism's Stride in Japan." _Literary Digest_ 114:11, September 3, 1932.

1606 Murphy, U. G. _The Social Evil in Japan_. Tokyo: 1904, 113 pp. 4th edition revised, with plates, 1908.

1607 Nagato, Hiromi. _Prevention of Prostitution and Rehabilitation of Prostitutes in Japan_. Tokyo: 1956, 30 pp.

1608 Nakamura, Saburo. _Hakusen no onna_. 1958, 209 pp.

1609 Nakayama, Taro. _Baisho sanzennen shi_. 1956, 698 pp. Available Harvard University, Chinese-Japanese Library.

1610 Nakayama, T. "3000 years of prostitution." _Trans-Pac_ 73:5 November 13, 1926.

1611 "Nazi trinity in Japan." _China W R_ 94:153, October 5, 1940.

1612 Nishiyam, Matsunosuke. _Kuruwa_. 1963, 310 pp.

1613 Omura, B. "Passing Yoshiwara." _(Asia) Journal of the American Asiatic Association_ 36:86-93, February 1936.

1614 Penlington, J. N. "Licensed Women of Japan." _Current History_ 34:887-91, September 1931.

1615 Prostitution legally outlawed in Japan." _Christ Cent_ 75:486, April 23, 1958.

1616 "Red Lights in Japanese Lantern." Survey 36:405, July 15, 1916.

1617 Richie, D. "Letter from Toyko: Anti-Prostitution Law," Nation 187:217-19, October 11, 1958.

1618 Rossiter, A. P. "Two Faces to Japan." New Statesm and Nation 2:367-8, September 26, 1931.

1619 Russell, O. D. "Prostitution in Japan." American Mercury 36:328-33, November 1935.

1620 Saburo, Mashimo. Yurigo no Kenkyu. 1966, 396 pp. Primarily glossary, vocabulary, and bibliography.

1621 Sakurai, Kodo. Sei rippo no riron. (Shakai seisaku, bunka seiaku ni okera sei rippo no riron). 1956, 101 pp. Available Hoover Institution.

1622 "Sayonara; Japan's new anti-prostitution law." Newsweek 51:30, Jan. 6, '58.

1623 Scott, A. C. The flower and willow world; the story of the Geisha. Tokyo, Hong Kong: 1958. New York: Orion Press, 1960. 208 pp.

1624 "Sin and Politics." Newsweek 47:36, June 4, 1956.

1625 "Slave trade in Japan." China W R 79:119, December 26, 1936.

1626 Takeyasu, M. "Prostitution in Japan." Internat R Crim Policy pp.50-61, Jan. '54.

1627 Tresmin-Tremolieres, Dr. La Cite d'amour au Japan. Courtisanes du Yoshiwara. Paris: 1905, 301 pp.

1628 Tsujikawa, Kinosuke. Ori no naka no onnatachi. 1957, 245 pp. Available Hoover Institution.

1629 Uenoda, S. "System of licensed vice aimed to abolish secret prostitutes." Trans-Pac 19:4, July 23:4+, July 30, 1931.

1630 Uenoda, S. "Yoshiwara doomed to disappear; was once center of night life." Trans-Pac 22:4+, November 29, 1934.

1631 Watanabe, Eizaburo. Nihon baishun shi. 1960, 204 pp.

1632 Watanabe, Yoji. Gaisho no shakaigakuteki kenkyu. 1950, 252 pp, maps, diagr., form, tables. Bibliographical footnotes.

1633 Yamaguchi, Nana. Onna to MP. 1957, 253 pp. Available Hoover Institution.

1633A Yamamuro, G. "Social evil in Japan." Miss Rev 46:801-4, October 1923.

1634 Yamazaki, Roki. Sharebon. 1932, 36 pp. Japanese Literature 1600-1868.

1635 "Yoshiwara Democratized." Time 47:36, February 4, 1946.

1636 Abreu, Joao Theodoro de Salles. *A prostituicao no Distrito Federal*. Brasilia: Fundacao do Servivo Social, 1965, 120 pp.

1637 Abreu, Waldyr de. *O submundo da prostitucao, viadiagem e jogo do bicho; aspectos socias, juridicos e psicologos*. Rio de Janeiro: Freitas Bastos, 1968, 145 pp. Prostitution, vagrancy and lotteries.

1638 Ardiles Gray, Julio. *Memorial de los infiernos; Ruth Mary, prostituta*. Buenos Aires: Ediciones La Bastilla, 1972, 165 pp.

1639 Ariza, Barrios Ramon H. *Prostitucion y delito (estudio sociologico juridico y de la posible incorporacion de esta doctrina en la legislacion Colombiana)*. Cartagena, Columbia: Impr. Departamental, Servio Commercial, 1968, 431 pp.

1640 "Back to the bordello in Argentina." *Time* 65:29-30, January 10, 1955.

1641 Bejarano, J. "Can a town progress normally while living in prostitution and vice." *Rev Columbia Pediat* 21:53-5, February 1963. In Spanish.

1642 "Body politic: Chile." *Time* 88:28, August 12, 1966.

1643 "Brothels, Ltd., in Buenos Aries." *Time* 65:39, May 2, 1955.

1644 Casazza, Pedro. *El patoteroy la Ley de profilaxis social*. Buenos Aires: 1952.

1645 Cea Quiroz, Waldo. *La prostitucion y el delito de contagio venereo*. Santiago: 1950, 62 pp.

1646 *Comite Abolicionista Peruano Segunda Jornado Peruana Antivenerea Lima, 1945*. The results of a Congress held at Peru in 1953 dealing with abolitionism and venereal disease.

1647 Cranston, C. "Wings; Glass Cages of Rio." *Good Housekeeping* 101:156-8, October 1935.

1648 Davalos y Lisson, Pedro. *La prostitucion en la ciudad de Lima*. Lima: . Imprenta la Industria, 1909, 97 pp.

1648A Fernandez, J. M.M. "Results of abolition laws in Rosario," *Rev med del Rosario* 24:750-9, August, 1934

1649 Franco y Guzman, Ricardo. *La prostitucion*. Mexico: Editorial Diana, 1973, 309 pp.

1650 Fuccio, Francisco de. *Prostitucao Aborta criminoso*. Sao Paulo: Editora Cultura Popular, 1949 (?), 107 pp.

1651 Gonzalez Perez, Beatriz. *Problema de la prostitucion en Mexico*. Mexico: 1949, 57 pp.

1652 Goodman, H. "Porto Rican experiment." Soc Hygiene 5:185-91, April 1919.

1653 Hildreth, E. L. W. "Awakening in Porto Rico." Union Signal 44:4 October 3, 1918.

1654 Ielpi, Rafael Oscar. Prostitucion y rufianismo. Buenos Aires: Editorial Encuadre, 1974, 203 pp.

1655 Fernandez, J. M. M. "Results of abolition of laws in Rosario." Rev med del Rosario 24:750-9, August 1934.

1656 Jenkinson, C. "Social evil in Vera Cruz." Survey 33:136-8, November 7, 1914.

1657 Lagenest, H. D. Barruel de. Lenocinio e prostituicao no Brasil; estudo sociologico. Capa de Milton Ribeiro. Rio de Janeiro: AGIR, 1960, 195 pp.

1658 ______________. Mulheres em leiao; um estudo da prostituicao no Brazil. Petropolis: Editora Vozes, 1973, 86 pp.

1659 Landaburu, Jr., L. and Aftalion, E. R. "Basis for reform of legal regulation in Argentina." Rev argent dermatosif 28: 180-185, June 1944.

1660 Londres, Albert. Le chenun de Buenos Aires. Paris: A Michel, 1927. Translated by Eric Sutton as The Road to Buenos Aires. London: Constable, 1928 and 1935. Also New York: Boni and Liveright, 1928, and also Blue Ribbon Books, 1930.

1661 Luisi, Paulina. Otra voz clamando en la desierto (proxenetismo y reglamentacion). 2 volumes. Montevideo: 1948.

1662 Marroquin, J. "Prostitution and syphilis in native Peruvian population." Cron med Lima 60:339-45, December 1943.

1663 Mendine Martinez, Cirino. El problema de la prostitucion en Mexico. Mexico: 1948, 84 pp.

1664 Minot, P. "Sex in Puerto Rico." American Mercury 73:55-60, September 1951.

1665 "Murdering madams; sisters Gonzalez Valenzuela." Newsweek 64:60, November 2, 1964.

1666 O'Callaghan, S. Damaged baggage. R. Hale, 1969.

1667 Odorico de Morais, M. "Present status in Rio de Janeiro." Folha med 23:148, July 5, 1942; 160, July 25, 1942.

1668 Payne, G. L. "Vice problem in Puerto Rico." Soc Hygiene 5:233-42, April 1919.

1669 Pereira, Armando. Mulheres deitadas. Rio de Janeiro: Grafica Record Editora; distribuidores: Irmaos Pongetti, 1961, 256 pp.

1670 Porto Rico. Laws, statutes, etc. Laws of Porto Rico in regard to prostitution, adultery, sale of intoxicating liquors, etc. San Juan: Department of Justice, 1918.

1671 Porto Rico. Office of the attorney-general. Special report concerning the suppression of vice and prostitution in connection with the mobilization of the national army at Camp Las Casas. San Juan: Bureau of supplies, 1919.

1672 Prostibulario. Buenos Aires: Editorial Merlin, 1969, 143 pp. Stories of prostitution.

1673 "Qualified cleanup in Havana." Time 57:34, January 22, 1951.

1674 Raban, S. "Trip to paradise." Contemp R 210:298-301, June 1967. Mexico.

1675 Ramos Lugo, Luis Antonio and Cartagena, Salomon Equihua. "La prostitucion en Mexico." Criminalia (Mexico) July 1956, pp. 400-27.

1676 Revilla, G. F. "Problem of pandering in Mexico: critique of reforms of penal code." Arch mex ven y dermat 5:86-111, March-April 1946.

1677 Rodman, Hyman. "Illegitimacy in the Caribbean Social Structure: A reconsideration." American Sociological Review 31(1966):673-83.

1678 Rodriguez-Solis, E. Historia de la Prostitucion en Espagna y America. Madrid, 1921, 335 pp.

1679 Roebuck, Julian and McNamara, Patrick. "Ficheras and free lancers: Prostitution in a Mexican border city." Archives of Sexual Behavior 2(3):231-44, June 1973.

1680 Rojal, J. F. Mujeres tras la red. Pamphlona et d "Villa Tesitu". Ona: Facultad de Teologia, 1962. 52 page pamphlet on the horrors of prostitution.

1681 Rovira, Alejandro. Prostitucion y proxenetismo. Montevideo: 1951, 318 pp.

1682 Saavedra, A. M. "Prostitution in Mexico (The problem as observed over a century ago)." Medicina (Mexico) 41:(Suppl) 145-50, September 25, '61.

1683 Santos, E. M.; Juca, L.; and Arruda, H. P. "Prostitution, venereal diseases and recreation; situation in Rio de Janerio, D. F." Folha med 25:89, June 25, 1944; 97, July 5, 1944.

1684 Sa Pereira Coutinho, Jose de. Madalenas. Palestra...Marta. Palestra...em beneficio do Instituto Feminino de Educacao e Regeneracao Corpus Cristi. Porto: 1935, 38 pp.

1685 Sepulveda Nino, Saturnino. La prostitucion en Colombia. Bogota: Editorial Andes, 1970, 204 pp.

1686 __________. La Prostitucion en Columbia: una quiebra de las estructuras sociales. Bogota: Tercer Mundo, 1974, 205 pp.

1687 Servic o social do Estado--Divisao tecnia Seccao de amparo a mulher. O baxio meretricio na regiao de Ribeirao Preto. Sao Paulo: 1967, 70 pp.

1688 __________________. Relatorio de estaudo sobre o problema do meretricio na capital de Sao Paolo. Sao Paulo: (May) 1966, 50 pp.

1689 "Sisters of shame; Mexican white slaves." Time 84:50, October 30, 1964.

1690 Solano, Susano. El problem de la prostitucion y las Naciones Unidas. Accinelli, Mario. La education sexual de la mujer. And Gonzalez, Margarita de. Que es el abolicionismo. Lima, 1952, 14 pp. pamphlet. Written for the delegate of Comite Abolicionista Peruano a la Ve Conference regionale Latino-americane des organisaion non-gouvernmentales (La Paz, 1952).

1691 Solano, S. "White slavery in Peru." Cron med Lima 62:13-6, January 1945.

1692 "Vice and evil in republic of Panama." Cong Rec 57:4432-3, February 25, 1919. Tables.

1693 Villavicencio, V. "Otros aspectos de le prostitucion Peruana. (Other aspects of Peruvian prostitution.)" Bol de Crimin 7:565-78, 1928.

1694 Villela, E. "Cooperative antivenereal campaign in Mexico." Arch mex ven sif y dermat 3:106-16, May-June 1944. Also Bd Ofic san panam 23:984-90, November 1944.

1695 "White slavery in the Argintine." Lit Digest 106:22, June 19, 1930.

1696 Blanchard, R. "La Prostitution en Palestine." Bull Soc Franc Hist Med 11:123-7, 1912.

1697 Broadhurst, J. F. "Underworld of Egypt." Gt Brit and East 48:354, March 11, 1937.

1698 Cairo. al-Markaz al-Qawmi lil-Buhuth al-Ijtimaiyah wa-al-Jinalyah. 1961, and 1971, 270 pp. tables. Available from Princeton University Library.

1699 Duchesne, E. A. De la Prostitution dans la Ville d'Alger Depuis la Conquete. Paris: 1853.

1700 Duchesne, E. A. "Lettre Medicale sur la Prostitution dans la Regence de Tunis." Monit d Hop Paris 4:537-540, 1856.

1701 Gibb, Hamilton and Bowen, Harold. Islamic Society and the West. Oxford University Press, 1951-57. One volume in two parts have been published so far.

1702 Gripon, B. Sidi-Moulay-Moussa--Arssimoussa. Recit documentaire. 1936, 105 pp.

1703 Hitata, Mohammed Niazi. Delits de la prostitution. A doctoral thesis in the faculty of law, University of Cairo, July 1961, 629 pp. An excellent study of prostitution in Egypt.

1704 Horowitz, Menachem. "A survey of procurers in Israel, 1961-63." Israel Annals of Psychiatry and Related Disciplines 4(2):219-227, Autumn 1966. Relationship between prostitute and pimp emphasized.

1705 Khalaf, Samir. Prostitution in a Changing Society: A Sociological Survey of Legal Prostitution in Beirut. Beirut: Khayats, 1965. 163 pp.

1706 La Fontaine, Jean S. "The free women of Kinshasa: prostitution in a city in Zaire," in Choice and change, pp. 89-113. Edited by J. Davis, 1974.

1707 Lepinay, E. "Campaign against prostitution and venereal disease in Morocco." Prophylax antiven 21:248-53, June 1949.

1708 Lepinay, E. "Moroccan Courtesans: life in the reserved quarter." Paris Med (annexe) 1:iii-vii, Mar. 7, '36.

1709 Lorenzo, Jack M. Sexual vice with special reference to Egypt. Cairo: 1945, 52 pp.

1710 Marchand, H. "Curious custom of Arabian prostitutes." Practien du Nord de l'Afrique 7:537-40, November 15, 1934.

1711 Parent-Duchatelet and Urbain, Ricard. _La prostitution contemporaine a Pris en Province et en Algerie_. Paris: 1902.

1712 Sabry, Amin. "Syphilis and gonorrhea at hospital of Hod El Marsoud reserved for prostitutes." _Prophylax antiven_ 6:235-42, February 1934.

1713 Salerno, Luigi. _La polizia dei costumi a Tripoli_. Lugo: Edit Trisi, 1922, 99 pp. Libya.

1714 United Arab Republic National Center for Social and Criminological Research. _Prostitution in Cairo: A Social Survey and Clinical Study_. Cairo: 1964, 14 pp.

1715 Upson, A. T. "Purity movement in Cairo." _Miss R_ 43:29-33, January 1920.

1716 Viola, S. "Historic flight from Algiers." _Atlas_ 13:20-3, February 1967.

1717 Vychodil, Z. "Control of prostitution in new Algeria." _Cesk Dermatol_ 41(3):142-4, June 1972.

1718 Anthony, Katherine. Feminism in Germany and Scandinavia. London: Constable, 1916.

1719 Denmark. Kriminalforsorgsudvalget. Betaenkning om prostitution. Copenhagen: Staten trykningskontor; Eksp: Dek, 1973, 93 pp.

1720 Denmark. Udvalget til overvejlse af foranstaltninger overfor prostituerede kvinder og andring af de galdende bestemmelser til modarbejdelse af prostitutionen. Copenhagen: Betaenkning om foranstaltninger til bekaempelse af prostitutionen, 1955, 145 pp.

1721 Ehlers, Edvard. "Prostitution et maladies veneriennes en Danemark." Conference internationale pour la prophylaxie de la syphilis et des maladies veneriennes. Vol.1, fasc.2. Brussels: 1899.

1722 Kemp, T. Prostitution. Copenhagen: Levin and Munksgaard, 1936, 253 pp.

1723 Playfair, Giles. "How Denmark reforms prostitutes." New Society November 12, 1964, pp.18-19.

1724 Rasmussen, Agnete. Dansk kvindesamfund og saedelighedsfejden 1887. Copenhagen: Forlaget GMT, 1972, 89 pp.

1725 Welander, E. Blad ur Prostitutionsfragans Historia i Sverige. Stockholm: 1904.

1726 Winquist, Tore. Bordeller i Suerige? Framsteg eller Nederlag. Stockholm: Natur och kultur, 1972, 177 pp. Sweden.

1727 "Apologia Pro Verbis Suis: Expression of Regret over Recent Remarks About Moral Conditions in Saigon." Time 87:70, May 27, 1966.

1728 "Back to the Brothel; Discussion in Senate Foreign·Relations Committee Hearings of Conditions in Saigon." Time 87:29, May 20, 1966.

1729 Balfour of Burleigh, D. "Licensed Vice at Singapore." Spec 134:927, June 6, 1925. Discussion 134:972, 1006; 135:144, June 13-20, 25, 1925.

1730 "Campaign Against Prostitution in Rangoon." Missionary Review of the World 38:46-7, January 1915.

1731 "Goodbye Suzie Wong; Hong Kong." Newsweek 81:44, Feb. 19, '73.

1732 Joseph, R. "Travel notes: Hong Kong and Peitore." Esquire 80:59-60, June 1973.

1733 Parise, G. "Strange sad story: sex and Saigon." Atlas 14: 26-31, S 1967.

1734 Vigilance society of Rangoon, Burma, is issuing a series of pamphlets to aid in carrying on its campaign against the segregation of prostitution. Pamphlets exist but titles are unknown to us.

1735 Virgitti, M. H. and Joyeux, B. "Houses of Prostitution in Hanoi." Rev du Palud 5:81-86, March 15, 1947.

1736 Wimmers, F. "Social medical notes from Bangkok. A visit to the Pierra Maternity and Child Welfare Foundation." Munch Med Wochenschr 114(9):406-8, March 3, 1972.

1737 Amdel, Doctor. (pseud). La Prostitucion en Espana. Madrid: 1934, 63 pp.

1738 Brazao, Arnaldo. Um inquerito da Uniao internacional para proteccao da moralidade publica. Lisboa: 1952, 21 pp.

1739 Carboneres, Manuel. Picaronas y Alcahuetes o la mancebra de Valencia. Valencia: 1876, 140 pp.

1740 Cardia, M. and Fonseca, A. da. "Prostitution in the City of Porto (Portugal); its present status." Acta Gynaec Obstet Hisp Lusit 9:416-19, 1960. In French.

1741 Cela, Camilo Jose. Izas, rabizas y colipoterras. Barcelona: Lumen, 1971, 109 pp.

1742 Cossio y Gomez Acebo, M. de. La Trata de Blancas en Espana. Madrid: 1911, 64 pp.

1743 De Castro, S. V. "Evolucion de la Prostitucion en Espana." Gac Med de Espana Gran. 25:491-498, 1907.

1744 Fonseca, Aureliano de, et al. Alguns aspectos da prostituicao na cidade do Porto. Porto: 1963, 24 pp.

1745 Gernaldo de Quiros, C. and Aguilandiedo, J. M. L. "Verbrechterum und Prostitution in Madrid." In Sexualpsychologischen Bibliothek, Volume 3. Edited by Iwan Bloch. Berlin: Louis Marcus, 1910.

1746 Lapa, Albino. A prostituicao, subsidios para o seu combate e para a sua historia. Lisbon: 1949, 39 pp.

1747 Lima de Sousa Pinto, Maria Jose Vahia. O problema da prostitucao. Porto: 1962, 65 pp.

1748 Navarro Fernandez, A. La Prostitucion en la villa de Madrid. Madrid: 1909, 296 pp.

1749 Navarro, Maria Jose. En busca de un porque. Barcelona: Casiopea, 1972, 199 pp. Spain.

1750 Riesco, L. "A medico-sanitary investigation of a section of the city of Cordova. Prostitution as a social disease." Rev Med Cordoba 48:30-40, January-March 1960. In Spanish.

1751 Rojal, J. F. Mujeres tras le red. Pamplona, Valencia, Granada: 1958, 52 pp.

1752 Santalo, J. La Trata de Blancas ante los principios fundementales del derecho. Madrid: 1913, 50 pp.

1753 Santo Cruz, Francisco Ignacio dos. De prostituicao na cidade de Lisboa. Lisbon: 1841, 457 pp.

1754 Tovar de Lemos, A. Dispensario central de higiene social de Lisboa. Lisbon: 1954, 65 pp. Statistics of prostitution in Lisbon for 1953.

1755 Tovar de Lemos, A. Relatorio dos Servicos referentes a Prostitutuicao, no anno de 1951. Lisbon: 1952, 15 pp. A similar pamphlet for 1952: Lisboa, 1953, 18 pp.

1756 "Wall of Flesh in Spain." Time 66:29, October 24, 1955.

1757 Acuna, Chile Mapocha. *Women for Sale*. New York: Godwin, 1931, 201 pp. Deals with prostitution in New York City.

1758 Adams, G. and Hutter, E. "Sex in old New York; story of the birth and death of the Magdalen Society." *American Mercury* 52:550-7, May 1941.

1759 Addams, Jane. *A new conscience and an ancient evil*. Arno Press, 1972. Chicago.

1760 Additon, Henrietta Silvis. *City Planning for Girls*. Chicago: University of Chicago Press, 1928. Prostitution in Philadelphia.

1761 Allison, S. D. "Honolulu myth." *J Social Hyg* 32:77-81, February 1946.

1762 American social hygiene association. *Some early stages of the Chicago fight against prostitution*. American Social Hygiene Association, 1920.

1763 Arizona. Governor Hunt recommends statute imposing no additional penalties upon the fallen women, but penalizing the property owner.

1764 Astor, G. "Legal prostitution spreads in Nevada." *Look* 35:34-6, June 29, 1971.

1765 Asbury, H. "Loose ladies of New Orleans; excerpt from 'The French Quarter'." *American Mercury* 39:235-43, October 1936.

1766 Asbury, H. "Pennsylvannia's greastest rogue." *American Mercury* 53:738-46, December 1941.

1767 "Back at the Ranch; integration at bordello in Nevada." *Newsweek* 75:78+, March 9, 1970.

1768 Baltimore, Maryland. Board of police commissioners. *Report, 1915*. 1916, pp.12-13 (Social evil). Describes the good effects attained by the board's order to close all assignation houses and to gradually eliminate all houses of prostitution.

1769 Baltimore, Maryland. *Double shame of Baltimore: her unpublished vice report and her utter indifference*. Baltimore: Howard A. Kelly. Two articles reprinted from the *Survey*.

1770 Baltimore, Maryland. Grand jury made a report, May 7, 1915, favoring segregation of disorderly houses. The opinion was reached after an investigation made by a special board of inquiry. The report has not been printed.

1771 Baltimore. Society for the Supression of Vice of Baltimore City. Abolition of the red-light districts in Baltimore. 1916, 23 pp. Discusses the history of the movement, recommendations of the Maryland vice commission, past and present conditions in Baltimore, care of the women leaving the red-light districts, and regulation in Europe and its failure.

1772 Baltimore. Society for the Suppression of vice. Annual report for the year ending December 31, 1914. 6 pp.

1773 Bare, C. C. "Clean slate for Cleveland where big-city prostitution is held to a minimum." J Social Hyg 39:92-3, February 1953.

1774 Barnes, C. W. "Story of the Committee of fifteen of Chicago." Social Hygiene 4:145-56, April 1918.

1775 "Bawdy business; New York vice investigation." Time 27:15, May 25, 1936.

1776 Benet, J. "New York's Vice Ring." New Republic 87:124-6, June 10, 1936.

1777 Betts, F. W. "History of the moral survey committee of Syracuse." Social Hygiene 1:183-93, March 1915.

1778 Bliss, N. A glimpse of shadowed lives in a great city. Chicago: 1913, 63 pp.

1779 Boston. Police department. Record of the enforcement of the laws against sexual immorality since December 1, 1907. Boston: Police department, 1913.

1780 "Bother over Brothels in Reno." Newsweek 32:19, August 30, 1948.

1781 Bowen, L. H. Road to destruction made easy in Chicago. Chicago: Juvenile protection association of Chicago, 1916.

1782 Braden, Forrest. "Steady pressure on the prostitution racket: a police chief needs support." J Soc Hygiene 38:193-203, May 1952. Report of the successful program of suppression in Terre Haute, Indiana, since 1943.

1783 Bredemeier, Harry C. and Jackson, Toby. Sexual Problems in America. New York: John Wiley, 1960.

1784 Bridgeport, Conn. Vice commission. Report and recommendations. Bridgeport: City club, 1916, 94 pp. Recommends strict supervision of saloons, reporting of venereal infection, establishment of a venereal disease and a psychopathic clinic, welfare work, better recreational and housing facilities, teaching of sex hygiene, continued abolition of segregated district, passage of an abatement and injunction law, a farm and reformatory for prostitutes, and creation of a morals commission.

1785 Bruno, Mike and Weiss, David B. Prostitution, U.S.A. Los Angeles: Halloway House Publishing Company, 196?, 223 pp.

1786 "California dux." Ind 74:1064-5, May 15, 1913.

1787 "California women and the vice situation." Survey 30:162-4, May 3, 1913.

1788 "Call wives, Long Island Housewives." Newsweek 63:18, February 17, 1964.

1789 Carroll, L. "Paris in a clean up era: the city of no red lights." Newsweek 31:32-3, January 5, 1948.

1790 Boston, Mass. (Address on prostitution in relation to the liquor traffic.) J. F. Chase. In Chicago, Ill. City council. Com. on license. Report to the mayor and aldermen on the public licensing, regulation and control of the liquor traffic in Boston and New York city, p.52-6, December 1917. Address before the committee on license of the Chicago city council in the court of the Boston licensing board, August 8, 1917.

1791 Chicago. Committee of fifteen. Annual report for the year ending April 30, 1915. Chicago, S. P. Thrasher. The purpose of the organization is to aid the public authorities in the enforcement of laws against pandering and to take measures calculated to prevent traffic in women.

1792 Chicago. Illinois Commission of fifteen. Annual report for the year ending April 30, 1917. 1917, 16 pp.

1793 Chicago. Committee of fifteen. Annual report. Chicago: 1917.

1794 Chicago. Committee of fifteen. Annual report for the year ended April 30, 1918. 1918, 18 pp.

1795 Chicago. Committee of fifteen. Supplemental report of the work since May 1, 1917.Chicago: 4 pp.

1796 Chicago. Mayor's commission to study municipal problem in Europe. "Report on prostitution in certain European cities." In Chicago city manual, 1914, pp. 125-9. The commission visited a number of cities and gathered authentic data respecting many important matters in municipal policy and administration.

1797 Chicago. Ordinance creating a morals commission. Chicago: City clerk, November 12, 1914, 2 pp.

1798 Chicago. Vice commission. _Social evil in Chicago_. Chicago municipal reference library, 1911. Reprinted by the American Vigilance Association, 1911; Gunthrop-Warren Printing Co., 1911. Distributed in 1912 by the American Social Hygiene Association. Reprinted New York: Arno Press, 1970, 399 pp. Illus.

1799 "Chicago vice commission; symposium." _Survey_ 26:215-8, May 6, 1911.

1800 "Chicago's morals court." _Lit Digest_ 46:1228-9, May 31, 1913.

1801 Chicago. Municipal court. _Report for 1913_, pp.93-9. The work of the Morals branch of the court is described.

1802 Clarke, C. W. "Cheechako; a tenderfoot's report on Alaska and the line." _J Soc Hyg_ 37:392-404, December 1951. General social conditions in the towns and the incidence of prostitution.

1803 Clark, M. "Oldest profession; reply to 'Prostitution in New York City'." _New Republic_ 69:245, January 13, 1932.

1804 Cleveland welfare department conducted a survey of vice and crime in the city. Civic bodies, church leaders, and women's organizations were asked to cooperate with the proposed commission, which included citizens identified with various activities of the city, as well as social workers. A printed report was made but edition is now exhausted. (August 1916).

1805 Coffee, R. I. "Pittsburgh under world at bay." _Survey_ 29:173-4, November 9, 1912.

1806 Columbus, Ohio. Vice Commission, A. B. Riker, chairman. "Report." _City Bulletin_ (Columbus) Sup v.4 no.7, February 15, 1919, 12 pp.

1807 Columbus, Ohio. Mayor Karb has approved the vice commission ordinance passed the previous week by council. This ordinance authorizes the president of the council to name a commission of five to investigate couses and conditions of vice and report to council recommendations for the improvement of the local situation. April 14, 1917.

1808 _Commercialized prostitution in New York city November 1,1915, a comparrison between 1912 and 1915_. New York: Bureau of social hygiene, 15 pp.

1809 "Commercialized vice in Pittsburg." _Survey_ 36:215-6, May 27, 1916.

1810 "Conclusions from a field of investigation of the workings of the injunction and abatement law in Iowa and Nebraska made by the American social hygiene association, May, 1914." _American Social Hygiene Association Bulletin_ 1:1-3, September 1914.

1811 Connecticut. State defense council. Manual on vice control. Hartford: January 1943, 41 pp.

1812 "Control of venereal diseases and the problem of prostitution in the city of New York." J Soc Hyg 22:425-6, December, 1936.

1813 Coolidge, R. M. "California women and the abatement law." Survey 31:739-40, March 14, 1914

1814 "Difficulty in prostitution control, Dayton, Ohio." American City 57:11, October 1942.

1815 "Discussing the social evil; decision of some Chicago post-office censors." Nation 93:308-9, October 5, 1911.

1816 "Disneyland east; brothels built exclusively for American soldiers." Time 87:29-30, May 6, 1966.

1817 Dosch, A. "Extinguishing the Red-light Operation of Abatement Laws on the Pacific Coast." Sunset 37:38-40, August 1916.

1818 Edgcumb, Pinchon. Life Among Hollywood's "Extra" Girls. Girard, Kansas: Haldeman-Julius Publishing, 64 pp.

1819 Engle, R. Brothels of Nevada. Los Angeles: Melrose Square Publishing Company, 1973.

1820 Eselstyn, T. C. "Prostitution in the United States." Annals of the American Academy of Political Science 376:123-35, March 1968.

1821 "Everthing's Up to Date in Lida Junction: Brothels in Nevada." Time 93:54, June 27, 1969.

1822 Fertig, J. G. Commercialized prostitution in St. Louis. Com. of 100 for the suppression of commercialized vice in St. Louis, 1916.

1823 "Fighting Prostitution in Michigan." Survey 41:70-1, October 19, 1918.

1824 "Fighting Vice in Chicago." Lit Digest 45:848, November 9, 1912.

1825 "Flatfoot Floozies; Policewomen Arrest Customers in Washington, D. C." Newsweek 75:99, May 18, 1970.

1826 Forbes, James. "Prostitution." In Wage-earning Pittsburg, pp.348-65. Edited by P. U. Kellogg. 1914.

1827 "Fun City: Prostitution Increases in New York." Newsweek 70:74, July 3, 1967.

1828 "Gaining Control Over Vice in New York." Survey 33:572, February 27, 1915.

1829 Gentry, C. The Madams of San Francisco. Toronto: Doubleday, 1964.

1830 Geiger, J. G. "Prostitution and venereal disease in San Francisco." J Soc Hyg 255:243, May 1939.

1831 Goodchild, F. M. "Social Evil in Philadelphia." Arena 15:574-86, March 1896.

1832 "Graft Report Hits Golden Gate; San Francisco's Debate Licensing Vice Following Quiz." Literary Digest 123:3-4, April 3, 1937.

1833 Grand Rapids, Michigan. Public Welfare Commission. Report. Grand Rapids: City clerk, 1913, 39 pp. Report of a special commission appointed by the common council to investigate the relation of wages to the social evil. It is a comprehensive survey of vice conditions, wages, housing, etc., and contains legislative recommendations for the betterment thereof.

1834 Grant, Edwin. Redlight Padlocking. San Francisco: 1952, 18 pp. Brochure for book The Passing of Barbary Coast.

1835 Grant, E. E. "Vice Repression in San Francisco." National Municipal Review 13:264-9, May 1924.

1836 Harding, T. S. "Prostitution in a Nice Way; reply to 'Prostitution in New York city'." Nation 142:531, April 22, 1936.

1837 Harland, Robert O. The Vice Bondage of a Great City. Chicago: The Young People's Civic League, 1912, 200 pp.

1838 Harris, Sara. House of Ten Thousand Pleasures. New York: E. P. Dutton, 1962. Standard Sara Harris.

1839 Hartford Vice Commission. Report. Hartford, Conn. Woman suffrage association, 1913.

1840 "Heir and Dolls." Newsweek 40:27, August 25, 1952.

1841 Hichborn, F. Anti-vice movement in California. American social hygiene association, 1920.

1842 Hichborn, Franklin. California campaign commission for the redlight abatement law has issued a series of leaflets on the general problem of the social evil. Santa Clara, California.

1843 Hichborn, Franklin. "Organization that backed the California red light abatement bill." Social Hygiene 1:194-206, March 1915.

1844 Hichborn, Franklin. _Social evil in California as a political problem._ Santa Clara: Franklin Hichborn, 8 pp.

1845 Himelhoch, Jerome and Fava, Sylvia Fleis, editors. _Sexual Behavior in American Society._ New York: Norton, 1955.

1846 Holcomb, E. "Social Work and Social Hygiene in the United States." _Pakistan J Health_ 12:37-41, April 1962.

1847 "Honolulu's complicated vice problem." _Survey_ 32:627, September 26, 1914.

1848 "Hooker's Market: Prostitutes in Manhattan." _Time_ 90:23, August 18, 1967.

1849 "House on the range; state closing of La Grange, Tex., bordello." _Time_ 102:69, August 27, 1973.

1850 "How Atlanta cleaned up." _Literary Digest_ 46:1012-3, May 3, 1913.

1851 Illinois. Senate vice commission, headed by Lieutenant-Governor Barratt O'Hara. _Report._ Springfield, Illinois: 1916, 979 pp. Contains: History of the inquiry; Findings and recommendations; Present laws, their perfections and imperfections; Public meetings and testimony; Inquiry in cities under 100,000 population; Public opinion reflected in correspondence; Recommendations of other vice committees; Prevalence of social diseases; Social evil in foreign countries; Colleges participate in inquiry; Woman's legislative congress; Importance of inquiry to the nation.

1852 Iowa district court has upheld the validity of the "redlight" law by issuing instructions to tenants in four of the five cases brought before the court. Two orders of abatement were issued against property, and tenants were taxed $300 in each instance. All those enjoined have given notice of appeal. (Press rept. January 23, 1916)

1853 Jackson, M. M. "Atlanta campaign against commercialized vice." _Soc Hygiene_ 3:177-84, April 1917.

1854 Janney, O. E. _White slave traffic in America._ New York: National vigilance committee, 1911.

1855 Johnson, Bascon "Are we holding our own against prostitution? Post-war review of progress in United States." _J Social Hyg_ 33:57-64, February 1947.

1856 Johnson, Bascon. "Moral conditions at the Panama Pacific exposition in San Fransico in 1915." _J Social Hyg_ 19:172-4, March 1933.

1857 Johnson, Bascom. "Prostitution in the United States." J Soc Hygiene 19:467-91, Dec. '33; Erratum, 20:52, Jan. '34.

1858 Johnston, C. "Chicago's social morality commission." World To-Day 18:554-6, May 1910.

1859 Kansas City society for suppression of commercialized vice, incorporated. By the Society, 11 pp.

1860 Kemp, T. Prostitution. Copenhagen: Levin and Munksgaard, 1936, 253 pp.

1861 Kilman, E. "Galveston's Street of Shame." American Mercury 54:567-74, May 1942.

1862 Kneeland, G. J. Commercialized prostitution in New York city. (Bur of social hygiene pubs.). Century Co, 1913, 334 pp. Reissued by Century Co., 1917. Reprinted Patterson Smith, 1969. Reviewed in Hearst's Magazine 24:147-9, July 1913.

1863 Kneeland, George J. A Report on Vice Conditions in Elmira, New York. 1913 For the Department of Investigation of the American Vigilance Association.

1864 Lang, F. M. "Lebanon County looks after its girl. Pennsylvania community combats delinquency and venereal disease." J Social Hygiene 31:284-289, May 1945.

1865 Laune, F. F. "Fighting 'sin in paradise'." Soc Hygiene 32:67-81, Feb. '46.

1866 "Las Vegas Goose Egg." Newsweek 38:26, September 10, 1951.

1867 Lathrop, C. N. "California abatement law." Am soc. hygiene assn. First annual report. 1914, pp.146-9.

1868 Lehman, Frederick Martin. The White Slave Hell; or With Christ at Midnight in Slums of Chicago. Chicago: The Christian Witness Company, 1910, 418 pp.

1869 Lexington, Kentucky. Vice commission. Report 1915 By George Hunt, Chairman. Lexington: 1915. Discusses its findings under the following headings: Child protection and education, The question of dealing with the situation, Medical inspection of prostitutes as a sanitary policy, Experience of other cities, Existing laws and the recommendations of the vice commission; and recommends a state abatement and injunction law, immediate closing of all houses of prostitution outside the segregated district, and the closing of all such houses as soon as a house of shelter shall be provided for the inmates. The commission believed this could be accomplished by January 1, 1916. This committee was succeeded by the Committee on Social Hygiene, December 28, 1915.

1870 Lexington, Kentucky. Vice commission. Report. 2nd edition. R. K. Massie, Chairman. Lexington, Kentucky: Vice commission, 1919.

1871 Lewis, L. L. "Man who saved Chicago." American Mercury 20:178-84, 1930.

1872 Lewis, L. L. "Survey of a nice district in tne Middle West." J Soc Hygiene 13:93-6, Fall 1927.

1873 Libman, Joan. "Prostitution law in Oregon may end a double standard: clients are prosecuted too but sporadically, urge legalization instead." Wall Street Journal 184:1+, October 18, 1974.

1874 Little Rock, Ark. Vice commission. Report May 20, 1913 and the order of Mayor C. E. Taylor to close all resorts in Little Rock by Aug. 25, 1913. Little Rock, Ark.: City clerk, 1913, 29 pp.

1875 Locke, C. E. White slavery in Los Angeles. Los Angeles: By author, 1913.

1876 Longstreet, Stephen. Sportin' House: A History of the New Orleans Sinners and the Birth of Jazz. Los Angeles: Sherbourne Press, Inc, 1965, 293 pp.

1877 Los Angeles. Municipal confidential bureau for girls has been established under the supervision of "City Mother" Aletha Gilbert, former police-woman. The bureau is housed in quarters far removed from any connection with the police department and the usual detention homes and is given the aid of a board composed of society women, social rescue workers and women inclined to philanthropic work. The bureau is an innovation, and police officials predict the rapid spread of the idea.

1878 Louisville, Kentucky. Mayor Buschemeyer, February 27, 1915, appointed a vice commission with authority to investigate anything in Louisville which might be physically or morally debasing. Reverand E. L. Powell, chairman.

1879 Louisville, Kentucky. Vice commission. Report: survey of existing conditions with recommendations to the Honorable John H. Buschemeyer, mayor. A. Y. Aronson, secretary. 1915, 94 pp. Describes conditions in Louisville and other cities and recommends abolition of the red-light district within two years, with as little sensation as possible, prohibition of sale of liquor and the use of musical instruments in houses of prostitution, and of new recruits, strict supervision over all places of public amusement, creation of a recreation commission, closing parks at eleven, more adequate supervision of delinquent girls, including a reformatory, teaching of sex hygiene and a campaign of education in regard to sexual diseases.

1880 Louisville, Kentucky. Segregated district has been abolished by order of the chief of police, effective September 1, 1917. This order was issued in deference to the requirements of the Secretary of war and is intended to effect the repression of prostitution in all its forms throughout the city.

1881 "Man's commerce in women." McLure's 41:185+, August 1913.

1882 Markun, Leo. Prostitution in the United States. Girard, Kansas: Little Blue Books, 61 pp.

1883 Marsh, Marguerite. Prostitutes in New York City: Their Apprehension, Trial, and Treatment, July 1939-June 1940. New York: Welfare Council, 1941, 178 pp.

1884 Marsh, N. J. "Treatment of cases of prostitution in New York city." Social Hygiene 2:515-26, October 1916.

1885 McQuaid, E. B. "Frontiersman with a mission: a social hygiene worker in Alaska." J Soc Hyg 38:179-85, April 1952.

1886 McQuaid, E. "Polls open... Brothels close; San Antonio breaks with tradition." J Soc Hyg 38:250-60, June 1952.

1887 Marshall, Constance. "Racketeering in vice: scandals in vice repression in New York have started a civic housecleaning that offers pointers to other cities." Woman's J 18-19+, May 1931.

1888 Massachusetts Commission for investigation of white slave traffic. Report (House no 2281). Massachusetts superintendent of documents, February 1914, 86 pp.

1889 Mills, J. "Murphy man misses, then scores at last." Life 59:94-5, December 3, 1965.

1890 Miner, C. E. "Repression versus segregation in Chicago." J Soc Hyg 17:283-7, May 1931.

1891 Minneapolis. Vice commission. Report to his honor, James C. Haynes, mayor. Minneapolis: Byron and Willard, 1911.

1892 Morris, L. R. "High, Wide and Handsome." In Empire City, pp.203-06. Edited by A. Klein. New York: Rinehart, 1955. About New York City.

1893 Murtagh, John. M and Harris, Sara. Cast the first stone. New York: McGraw-Hill, 1957, 307 pp.

1894 "National merger to fight white slavery." Survey 27:1991-2, March 30,1912.

1895 Newark, New Jersey. Citizens committee of 100 made a report October 17th on conditions. The report is summarized in the _Newark News_ for October 17, 1914.

1896 Newman, A. "Freedom? Brothels Girls Thank Mac for Nothing." _Newsweek_ 27:41, February 11, 1946.

1897 Newman, Barry. "Losing battle? New York's campaign to stop prostitution is beset by obstacles." _Wall Street Journal_ 178:1+ September 17, 1971.

1898 New York. Association for Moral and Social Hygiene. _Results of vice suppression in New York City_.

1899 New York. Bureau of social hygiene. _Commercialized prostitution in New York city_. 1916. Another report issued 1917 compares 1912, 1915, 1916, 1917. 18 pages with charts.

1900 New York. Bureau of Social Hygiene. _Recommendations of the laboratory of social hygiene affiliated with New York state reformatory for women at Bedford Hills, N. Y., for disposition of first one hundred cases studied_. New York: Bureau of social hygiene, 32 pp.

1901 New York. The Committee of Fifteen. _The Social Evil with Special Reference to Conditions Existing in the City of New York_. New York: G. P. Putnam's Sons, and London: The Knickerbocker Press, 1902, 188 pp.

1902 New York City. Committee of Fourteen. _Annual report for 1914_. New York: Committee of Fourteen in New York city, 1915, 56 pp. The committee secured the passage of an injunction and abatement law, investigated department store conditions, worked to suppress disorderly houses and prostitution in tenements, and assisted in penalty cases.

1903 New York (city). Committee of Fourteen. _Annual reports, 1914-1916_. 3 volumes. New York: Committee of Fourteen, 1915-1917.

1904 New York (city). Committee of Fourteen. _Annual report for 1915_. Frederick H. Whittin, executive secretary. New York: 1916, 37 pp. Contains a report on the work of the committee, obstacles to vice repression, 1915, legislation and the courts, 1915, and the treasurer's report.

1905 New York (city). Committee of Fourteen. _Annual report for 1916_. New York: 1917, 94 pp.

1906 New York (city). Committee of Fourteen, F. H. Whitin, secretary, held a series of informal conferences during the national conference of charities and correction, Indianapolis, Indiana, May 10-17, 1916. The special meetings considered law enforcement as related to prostitution, and other phases of social hygiene. The conferences had the active support of the American social hygiene association. No printed report was made.

1907 New York (city). Committee of Fourteen. Annual report for 1918. New York: 1919, 72 pp. Tables.

1908 New York. Committee of Fourteen. Social evil in New York city. Secretary of Committee of Fourteen, 1910.

1909 New York. The Social Evil, with special reference to conditions existing in the City of New York. Progressive Science Series. 1912, 303 pp.

1910 New York society for the suppression of vice. 42d annual report for the year 1915. New York: The Society, 1916, 27 pp.

1911 New York society for the suppression of vice. 44th annual report, 1917. J. S. Sumner, secretary. 1917, 28 pp.

1912 New York society for the suppression of vice. 45th annual report, 1918. 1918, 26 pp.

1913 New York society for the suppression of vice. 70th year book: 1943 report. 1944, 16 pp. Tables.

1914 "Open House in Terre Haute; State University President Asks City to Reduce Prostitution." Time 93:20-1, February 21, 1969.

1915 Oregon. Social Hygiene Society. Fourth Annual Report. The Society, 1915, 60 pp. State wide extension.

1916 Paducah, Kentucky. Morals commission has been appointed to continue the work of the vice commission, with Sanders E. Clay, commissioner of public safety, as chairman. October 1916.

1917 Pascale, V. "Study of the service for the control of venereal diseases among sex offenders in New York city." J Social Hyg 19:111-42, March 1933. Tables.

1918 Pate, J. R. "Story and the moral; crusade to abate vice conditions in Louisville." J Soc Hyg 26:208-11, May 1940.

1919 Peters, J. P. Story of The Committee of Fourteen. Committee of fourteen, 1918, pp.347-88. Reprinted from Social Hygiene July 1918.

1920 Philadelphia, Pennsylvania. Municipal court. "Misdemeanants division: work of probation department in charge of streetwalkers and incorrigible minors." Report, 1915, pp.104-16, 1916.

1921 Philadelphia, Pennsylvania. Municipal court. "Misdemeanant girls and women." 3rd annual report, 1916, pp.122-7, 248-69, 1917.

1922 Philadelphia. Vice commission. Report on existing conditions. Philadelphia Vice Comission, 1913.

1923 Picton-Turbervill, E. "America and the social evil." 19th Cent 86:153-63, June 1919.

1924 Pittsburgh, Pennsylvania. Morals and efficiency commission. Report and recommendations, 1913. 43 pp. This commission is a permanent commission acting under a city ordinance and later under a state law of 1913. The report opposes segregation and summarizes much valuable experience.

1925 Pittsburg's housecleaning." Lit Digest 47:1232, December 20, 1913.

1926 Portland, Oregon. Vice commission. Report to the mayor and city council of Portland, January 1913. L. L. Levings, secretary. Portland: Vice commission, 1913, 216 pp.

1927 Powell, H. Ninety times guilty. New York: Arno Press, 1974. New York City.

1928 "Prostitution banished in Norwich, New York." Survey 30: 158-9, May 3, 1913.

1929 "Prostitution in New York City." Nation 142:369, March 25, 1936. Reply, Nation 142:531, April 22, 1936.

1930 "Prostitution in New York City." New Republic 69:172, December 30, 1931. Reply, New Republic 69:245, January 13, 1932.

1931 Quisenberry, W. B. "Eight years after the houses closed." J Social Hyg 39:312-22, October 1953. Tables. Hawaii.

1932 Quisenberry, W. B. "Was 'controled' prostitution good for Hawaii?" J Soc Hyg 39:312-22, October 1953. Results of closing of house in 1944.

1933 Rappaport, M. F. "Towards a new way of life: a progress report on work with prostitutes and promiscuous girls in the city of Baltimore." J Soc Hygiene 31:590-9, December 1945.

1934 "Real estate agent convicted in disorderly case." Survey 31:341, December 27, 1913.

1935 "Recommendations for improving procedures in dealing with prostitution cases in N. Y. city; made by Committee on Prostitution and Women's court of Welfare Council of N. Y. City." J Social Hyg 28:372-382, October 1942.

1936 Reckless, Walter C. "Prostitution in the United States." In Successful Marriage, Part V, Chapter 2. Edited by Morris Fishbein and Ernest W. Burgess. New York: Doubleday, 1947.

1937 Reckless, W. C. Vice in Chicago. Sociological Series. Chicago: University of Chicago, 1933, 332 pp. Reprinted by Patterson Smith, 1969.

1938 Reichard, Gladys A. Navaho Religion. New York: Bollingen Foundation, 1950, p.384

1939 Rhode Island state grange, at a 1913 session, passed a resolution favoring the formation of a state police force under the control of the governor to suppress white slave traffic.

1940 Ross, N. W. "$1 a dance." In Westward the Women, pp.122-36. New York: Knopf, 1944. In the Northwest, Pacific.

1941 Sacramento. "Report concerning a relaxation of law enforcement by some of Sacramento's authorities." Official Gazette 5:1-5, October 7, 1918.

1942 St Louis. Committee of 100. Vice Report. 1913. St. Louis municipal reference branch.

1943 St. Louis. Committee of one hundred for the suppression of commercialized vice in St. Louis. Brief in support of citizens' memorial to the board of police commissioners of St. Louis, Missouri, on the illegality and inexpediency of segregating commercialized vice in Saint Louis. 1914.

1944 Salisbury, Harrison. (Article). The New York Times September 10, 1959, p.10.

1945 "San Francisco's experience in enforcing the law against prostitution." Soc Hygiene 5:621-4, October 1919.

1946 Sarlat, Noah, editor. America's cities of sin. New York: Lion Books, 1951, 128 pp.

1947 Scott, L. C. "Prostitution and venereal disease problem in Louisiana." Nat Munic R. 13:200-2, April 1924.

1948 "Shall Chicago legalize hell?" Am City 7:405-6, November 1912.

1949 Sheehy, Gail. "Cleaning up Hell's bedroom; the landlords of Hell's bedroom." N Y Mag 5:50-60+, November 13, 1972. And N Y Mag 5:67-72+, November 20, 1972.

1950 Sheehy, Gail. "More questions and some answers on Hell'sS bedroom." New York M 5:6+, December 18, 1972.

1951 Shepherd, C. R. "Chinese girl slavery in America." Miss R 46:893-8, November 1923.

1952 "Sin Center; Newport, Kentucky." Time 77:19-20, May 26, 1961.

1953 "Slave traffic in America." Outlook 93:528-9, November 6, 1909.

1954 Smith, C. B. "Closing the New Orleans District." Nat Munic R 11:266-8, Sep. '22.

1955 Smith, H. Allen. California Sexual Deviation Research; Final Report. Sacramento: California State Printing Office, 1954, 160 pp. Volume 20. Number 1.

1956 "Social evil with reference to New York." Munic Affairs 6:141-4, March 1902.

1957 "Sodom on the Hudson." Newsweek 78:77 June 26, 1971.

1958 "Some early stages of the Chicago fight against prostitution: a symposium." Social Hygiene 6:273-84, April 1920.

1959 South Carolina. Governor Manning asks the state legislature to define vagrancy, making it triable in the sessions courts. He believes this is a simple way to protect soldiers and civilians against the depredations of venereally diseased women.

1960 South Carolina. Governor Manning recommends passage of an abatement and injunction law, to provide means of dealing with persons who permit their property to be used for immoral purposes.

1961 South Carolina. Governor Manning recommends that a constitutional amendment be passed raising the age of consent to eighteen years.

1962 "Stamping out the vice evil." Toledo City J 3:242, May 11, 1918.

1963 "State vice Report in Massachusetts." Survey 31:736-7, March 14, 1914.

1964 Stearn, Jess. Sisters of the Night. The Startling Story of Prostitution in New York City Today. New York: Julian Messner, Inc., 1956, 182 pp.

1965 Steffens, Lincoln. "Pittsburg: A City Ashamed." McClure's 21(May 1903):24-39.

1966 Stoy, E. H. "Chinatown and its curse." Arena 38:360-5, October 1907.

1967 Sutherland, D. F. Black plague of the American Continent. Quitman, Texas: Sutherland and Goodwin, 1908.

1968 Symanski, R. "Prostitution in Nevada." Assn Am Geog Ann 64:357-77, September 1974.

1969 Syracuse, New York. Committee of Eighteen Citizens. The Social Evil in Syracuse Being The Report of an investigation of the Moral Conditions of the City. Syracuse: 1913, 127 pp.

1970 Syracuse moral survey committee. Social evil in Syracuse: report. Syracuse, New York: Moral survey committee, 1913.

1971 Taylor, G. "Fighting vice in Chicago." Survey 29:94-5, October 26, 1912.

1972 Taylor, G. "Recent advances against the social evil in New York." Survey 24:858-65, September 17, 1910.

1973 Taylor, G. "Routing the segregationists in Chicago." Survey 29:254-6, November 30, 1912.

1974 Taylor, G. "Story of the Chicago vice commission." Survey 26:239-47, May 6, 1911.

1975 Taylor, S. B. and Cain, H. P., editors. "Blitzing the brothels: Tacoma's anti-prostitution campaign." J Soc Hyg 29:594-600, December 1943.

1976 Tennessee. Governor Rye recommends regulation of white slave traffic supplementing **U.S. Law.**

1977 Texas. Granting authority to enjoin crime, as the keeping of a bawdyhouse, is in the power of the legislature and invades no right of property. Campbell v. Peacock.

1978 Tippett, E. H. Suppressing prostitution in Cleveland. Cleveland: Federated churches of Cleveland, 1915.

1979 "To rehabilitate Portland prostitutes." Survey 31:176, November 15, 1913.

1980 Turner, G. K. "Daughters of the poor; New York city and the white slave of the world, under Tammany Hall." McClure's 34:45-61, November 1909.

1981 Twombly, C. G. "City that has followed up its report on vice conditions (Lancaster, Pa.)." Social Hygiene 1:388-96, June 1915.

1982 "United States and the importation of vice." Outlook 92:250+, May 29, 1909.

1983 "U. S. Supreme Court rules that Mann Act applies in District of Columbia." J Soc Hyg 31:312-13, May 1945.

1984 Van Deventer, Betty. How New York Working Girls Live. Girard, Kansas: Haldeman-Julius Pub., 64 pp.

1985 Vice conditions in Cleveland, year ending April 30, 1916. Cleveland: Federated churches of Cleveland, 1916, 22 pp. Contains: A report of the committee; Information furnished by Mayor Davis; Extracts from the Cleveland Medical Journal.

1986 "Vice investigation by the Illinois senate." Survey 29:897, March 29, 1913.

1987 "Vice in New York." Fortune 20:48+, July 1939.

1988 Vilas, M. S. Barbary coast of San Francisco. Burlington, Vt.: M. S. Vilas, 1915.

1989 Virginia. Com. on training camp activities. Virginia laws for the suppression of vice. Virginia: Board of charities and corrections, 1917, 14 pp.

1990 Vogliotti, Gabriel R. The Girls of Nevada. Secaucus, New Jersey: The Citadel Press, 1975, 264 pp.

1991 "Wages of sin; Chicago's Everleigh Club." Time 52:27, September 27, 1948.

1992 Warner, A. R. "Result of closing segregated vice district upon the public health of Cleveland." Am J Urology and Sexology 12:313-16, July 1916.

1993 "Warnings to girls from San Francisco." Survey 34:39, April 10, 1915.

1994 "Warns Philadelphia mayor vice conditions are menace to U. S. soldiers and sailors." Official Bul 3:1, January 9, 1919.

1995 Warren, J. H. Thirty years battle with crime. New York: Arno Press (NY Times Co), 1970. About New York City.

1996 Washer, B. S. "Report of the Louisville, Kentucky, vice commission." A review in J Crim Law 7:474-6, September 1916.

1997 Washington law of 1913 imposing a tax of $300 on property used as a disorderly house on the rendition of a permanent injunction against the nuisance held not unconstitutional as a deprivation of property without due process of law. State v. Jerome, 141 P 753.

1998 Waterman, W. C. Prostitution and its repression in New York City, 1900-1931. AMS Press, 1968.

1999 Whitlock, Brand. "White slave in America." English R 16:379-400, February 1914.

2000 "White slavery, 1972; teen-age prostitutes in Greenwich Village." Time 99:26+, June 5, 1972.

2001 Whitin, F. H. "Cleaning up New York." Nat Munic R 12:655-62, November 1923.

2002 Whittaker, P. The American way of sex. Putnam, 1974.

2003 Williams, D. H. "Suppression of commercialized prostitution in the city of Vancouver." J Soc Hyg 27:364-72, October 1941.

2004 Williams, R. M. "Oldest profession in Nevada--and elsewhere." Sat R World 1:9+, September 7, 1974.

2005 Winick, Charles, and Kinsie, P. M. The Lively Commerce: Prostitution in the United States. Chicago: Quadrangle, 1971, 320 pp.

2006 Wisconsin. Legislative committee to investigate the white slave traffic and kindred subjects. Report and recommendations. Senator Teasdale, Chairman. 1914, 246 pp.

2007 Wisconsin. Only six out of nineteen anti-vice bills have been advanced. All of the others have been killed. (May 10, 1915).

2008 "Wisconsin's last segregated district closed." Survey 33:328, December 26, 1914.

2009 Women's cooperative committee. Virginia Blythe, Chairman, Minneapolis. Organized in September, 1915. It is composed of one representative of each of seven women's organizations of the city uniting. The work is simply extending the civic work of the various women's clubs interested. The committee has in its employ a paid women investigator. The membership includes also an advisory membership of prominent men and women in the city, and also a citizens' committee to include every woman who will join the work. This latter committee is organized in accordance with the political sub-divisions of the city, each ward having a chairman and a vice-chairman, and each precinct a chairman. Several women are assigned to each city block to see that only wholesome conditions exist in that block. Meetings are to be held of the different groups at which various phases of the social evil will be discussed and information and knowledge thereon disseminated.

2010 Wood, Clement. Bohemian Life in N. Y.'s Greenwich Village. Giard, Kansas: Haldeman-Julius, Co., 64 pp.

2011 Wood, Clemnt. The Truth About New York's White Light Region. Girard, Kansas: Haldeman-Julius, Co., 64 pp.

2012 Woodmansee, H. A. *How "Wicked" Is Hollywood*. Girard, Kansas: Haldeman-Julius, Co., 63 pp.

2013 Woods, R. A. "Race problem in Boston (Mass.)." *Nat Munic R* 12:706-12, December 1923.

2014 Woolston, H. B. *Prostitution in the United States*. Volume 1: Prior to the entrance of the United States into the World War. Bureau of Social Hygiene Publication. Century, 1921, 360 pp. Tables, charts. Reprinted by Patterson Smith, 1969.

2015 Worthington, G. E. "Night Clubs of New York." *Survey* 61:413-17, January 1, 1929.

2016 Worthington, G. E. "Vice in Atlantic City." *Nat Munic R* 13:515-22, September 1924.

2017 Yarros, R. S. "Moscow revisited; social hygiene, 1930-1936." *J Soc Hyg* 23:200-8, April 1937.

2018 Young, G. B. and others. "Some aspects of the vice problem in Chicago." *Chicago City Club Bul* 7:223-30, June 25, 1914. Addresses by Dr. G. B. Young, comr. of health; Major M. L. C. Funkhouser, second deputy supt. of police; and Harriet E. Vittum, on June 10, 1914.

2019 Zimmerman, J. T. *America's black traffic in white girls*. 8th edition. 1912.

2020 "Zones of safety; Texas cantonment cities made safe for health and decency." *Survey* 38:349-50, July 21, 1917.

2021 Babikov, Konstantin Ivanovich. Prodazhnyia Zhenshchiny. (Women for Sale). Moscow: Publishing House of Uri Knowleo, 1870.

2022 Brain-Chaninov, N. "La prostitution dans l'Union Sovietique." Mercure Fr 228:589-99, June 15, 1931.

2023 Bronner, V. La lutte contre la prostitution en URSS. Moscow: 1936.

2024 _______. Prostitution and the Means of Its Liquidation. Moscow: 1931, 47 pp.

2025 Carter, Herbert Dyson. Sin and science. 4th Indian edition. Bombay: Current Book House, 1957, 156 pp.

2026 _________. Sin and Society. New York: Heck Cattell, 1946.

2027 **Champley, Henry.** Doroga v Shankhai. (The Road to Shanghai). Shanghai, 1935. In Russian.

2028 Cluver, E. H. "Experiment in social hygiene; campaign against prostitution and venereal disease in U.S.S.R." Brit M J 1:1120-2, May 29, 1937.

2029 Field, A. W. "Prostitution in the Soviet Union." Nation 142:373-4, March 25, 1936.

2030 Fridland, L. S. From Different Sides. Prostitution in the USSR. Berlin: 1931, 180 pp.

2031 Hirschfeldt, L. "Nagra ord om ett besole i ett institut i Moskva for Kampla mot prostitutionen." Svenska Lakartidn 31:1342-6, 1934. Campaign against prostitution in USSR.

2032 Hindus, Maurice. The Great Offensive. New York: Smith and Haas, 1933. There was a condensation, "Russia Bans Mrs. Warren's Profession." Readers Digest February 1934. The book claims that Russia banished prostitution.

2033 Janda, J. "Campaign against prostitution and venereal diseases in Russia, before and during present regime." Ceska Dermat 17:91-98, 1937.

2034 **Kollotnay, Alexandra.** "Fight against prostitution." Soviet Russia 5:42-7, 118-22, August-September 1921.

2035 _________. Prostitution and the Means of Struggle with it. Moscow: 1921, 23 pp.

2036 Lemaitre, F. "Campaign against venereal diseases and prostitution; protection of mother and child in Russia." Prophylax antiven 9:386-92, July 1937.

2037 Lepinay. "Combat against prostitution in U.S.S.R." _Prophylax antiven_ 6:417-44, November-December, 1934.

2038 Nelson, M. "Curious institutions of Soviet Russia: Moscow prophylactorium." _Canadian Forum_ 14:261, April 1934.

2039 Rabut, R. "What has become of prostitution in U.S.S.R.?" _Hopital_ 24:113-6, February (B) 1936.

2040 Robinson, W. J. "Prostitution conditions in the U.S.S.R." _J Social Hyg_ 19:228, April 1933.

2041 Russia. The People's Commissariat of Social Security. _Documents of the Interadministrative Commission for the Struggle with Prostitution_. Moscow: 1921, etc.

2042 Stowe, L. "Sexual License: key Soviet strategy." _Reader's Digest_ 66:27-32, March 1955.

2043 Winter, Ella. _Red Virtue_. New York: Harcourt Brace, 1933. Chapter on ending prostitution.

2044 Yarros, R. S. "Moscow revisited; social hygiene." _J Social Hyg_ 23:200-8, April 1937.

2045 "Bibliography." Municipal Affairs 5:231-2, March 1901.

2046 Bruno, B., and Fontanesi, M. "Bibliopgrafia per uno studio sugli aspetti criminologici delle prostituzione." In Gli aspetti generale della criminalita femminile; presentazione di Nicola Reale. (Ser studi di Criminologia, no.3) pp. 119-40. Milan: Administrazione provinciale, 1968.

2047 Dominique, Pierre (Pierre Lucchini). "Pour la reoverture des maisons closes." Contre la reoverture des maisons closes, par Jean-Gabriel Mancuni (Pour ou contre, 5). Berger-Levault, 1967.

2048 Federation Abolitionniste. Library. In 1947 they had 7850 volumes in their libraries and 729 periodical volumes. They also had a card file of 18000 cards about other books, and so forth. Many of them are only of peripheral interest but many are valuable.

2049 Gay, J. Bibliographie des ourvrages relatives a l'amour, aux femmes, au marriage. Paris: 1864. Also Turin and London, 1871, and several other editions.

2050 Gnoli, Umberto. Cartigiane romane, note e bibliographia. Arezzo-Vasari, 1941.

2051 Goodland, Roger. A Bibliography of Sex Rites and Customs. London: George Routledge, 1931.

2052 Haight, Anne Lyon. Banned Books. 2d ed rev New York: R. R. Bowker, 1955.

2053 Hayn, Hugo. Bibleotheca Germanorum Erotica. Leipzig: 1885.

2054 Hayn, Hugo, and Gotendorf, Alfred N., compilers. Bibleotheca Germanorum Erotica et Curiosa. Munich: 1913.

2055 Illinois. "Vice," in Selected bibliographies. Illinois state party platforms, 1916, pp.39.

2056 Kinton, Jack F. "Sociology of prostitution: a bibliography of books and journal articles." Social Science and Sociological Resources March 1973, 3 pp.

2057 Library of Congress. List of references on the history and suppression of prostitution. Washington, D.C.: Library of Congress, 1917.

2058 Library of Congress. Select list of references on the social evil. Washington, D.C.: Library of Congress, 1910. Additional references, 1911.

2059 Library of Congress. White Slave Act. A list of bibliographical references. Washington, D.C.: Library of Congress, 1930.

2060 Munro, W. B. "Social Evil," in _Bibliography of municipal government in the U.S.._ 1915, pp.318-21.

2061 "Protective Measures Program for the Community." _J Soc Hygiene_ 19:510-12, Dec. '33.

2062 "Readings and references of current and historical value." _J Social Hyg_ 22:437-8, December 1936.

2063 "Readings and references of current and historical value on social hygiene protective measures, prostitution and law enforcement." _J Social Hyg_ 21:294-8, June 1935.

2064 "Readings and references on prostitution and law enforcement." _J Social Hyg_ 19:541-2, December 1933.

2065 Seligman, E. R. A., editor. _List of books on the social evil, including pamphlets and leaflets published in the United States and foreign countries._ American social hygiene association.

2066 Semper Idem, pseudonym. _The "Blue Book." A bibliographical attempt to describe the guide books to the houses of ill fame in New Orleans as they were published there._ Heartman's Historical Series. 1936, 77 pp.

2067 Seruya, Flora C., et al. _Sex and Sex Education: A Bibliography._ New York: Bowker, 1972.

2068 "Tentative outline for a talk on social hygiene legal and protective measures." (bibliography) _J Social Hyg_ 22:415-18, December 1936.

2069 Adams, Martha. Martha Adams. Montreal: Editions du Jour, 1972, 220 pp.

2070 Adler, Polly. A House is Not a Home. New York: Rinehart Books, 1953. The best seller of its day.

2071 Aikman, Duncan. Calamity and the Lady Wildcats. New York: Henry Holt and Co., 1927.

2072 Alceim, Rachel. Washington Call Girl, as told to Richard Hofheimer. New York: Zebra Books, Kensington Pub. Corp., 1975. Another confessional; how much truth is debateable.

2073 Alciphron. Letters of Courtesans, no.15, ed. by Allen Rogers Benner and Frances H. Fobes. London: William Heinemann, 1962. Many other translations of this classic.

2074 Andrews, Allen. The Royal Whore. Philadelphia: Chilton Book Co., 1970.

2075 Anderson, Kristin and Dubreuil, Linda. The Wholesome Hooker. New York: Leisure Books, 1972 and Nordon Pub., 1973.

2076 Annie X. Moi Une Putain. Paris, M. Concorde, 1970, 157 pp.

2077 Anonymous, The Prostitutes of Quality or Adultery a-la-mode. Being Authentic and Genuine Memoirs of Several Persons of the Highest Quality. London: printed for J. Cooke and J. Coote, 1757, 223 pp. Poor man's Casanova.

2078 Anonymous, Street Walker. London: The Bodley Head, 1959 and New York: The Gramercy Publishing Co., 1962.

2079 Armand, E. Libertinaje y prostitucion--Grandes prostitutas y famoso libertinos. Tr. and rev. by the author. Valencia: Biblioteca Orto, n. d.

2080 Asbury, H. "Loose Ladies of New Orleans; excerpt from The French Quarter." American Mercury 39:235-43, Oct. '36.

2081 Asbury, H. "Penn's Greatest Rogue" American Mercury 53:738-46, Dec. '41.

2082 Autobiography of Sally Stanford: The Lady of the House. New York: G. P. Putnam's Sons, 1966, 255 pp.

2083 Barnes, Ruth. Pleasure was My Business, by Madame Sherry (pseud.) as told to S. Robert Tralins. New York: L. Stuart, 1961, 220 pp.

2084 Barth, Karl Heinz. Pension Anita; aus dem Tagebuch Einer Bordellmutter. Bayreuth: Hestia, 1971, 250 pp.

2085 Bax, Clifford. Pretty Witty Nell: the Story of Nell Gwyn and Her Times. New York: William Morrow Co., 1933.

2086 Beaujoint, Jules. Secret Memoirs of a French Royal Mistress. Girard, Kan.: Haldeman-Julius Pub.

2087 Bell, E. Moberly. Flame of Fire: Josephine Butler. London: A new biography authorized by the Josephine Butler Society. The woman who alerted the public about prostitution and its evils. An official biography.

2088 Bellocq, E. J. Storyville Portraits. New York: Graphic, 1970.

2089 Benalti, Alexander. Anrufgenugt. Stuttgart: Franz Decker Verlag, 1963, 181 pp. Account of a call girl.

2090 Bernardy, Francoise de. Talleyrand's Last Duchess. New York: Stein and Day, 1966.

2091 Best, Hillyer. Julia Bulette and Other Red Light Ladies. Western Printing and Publishing Co., Sparks, Nevada, 1959.

2092 Bizard, L. La Vie des Filles. 1934, 286 pp.

2093 Blanch, Lesley, The Game of Hearts: Harriet Wilson's Memoirs. New York: Simon and Schuster, 1955.

2094 Blanchard, Claude. Dames de Couer. Paris: Editions du Pre, 1946.

2095 Bleackley, Horace. Ladies Fair and Frail. London: The Bodley Head, 1925.

2096 Booker, Anton S. Wildcats in Petticoats. Girard, Kansas: Little Blue Books.

2097 Bradford, Gamaliel. Daughters of Eve. Reprinted New York: The New Home Library, 1942.

2098 Brantome, The Seigneur de. Lives of the Fair and Gallent Ladies, Tr. by A. R. Allenson. New York: Liveright Pub. Co., 1933 and Warburg, Ltd., 1955. Other editions.

2099 British Social Biology Council, Women of the Streets. London: Secker and Warburg, Ltd., 1955.

2100 Brooks, Virginia. My Battles with Vice. New York: The Macaulay Co., 1915, 248 pp. Prostitution in Chicago.

2101 Brown, A. J. "LoMo of San Francisco; Donaldina Cameron and her work for the rescue of Chinese girls." Missionary Review of the World 55:263-6, May '32.

2102 Bulliet, C. J. The Courtezan Olympia: an intimate survey of artists and their mistress-models. New York: Covici, Friede Pub., 1930 and McLeod, 1934.

2103 Burford, E. Queen of the Bawds; or the True Story of Madame Britannica Hollandia and her House of obscenitie. London: Spearman, 1973.

2104 Burgess, Ann Marie. Neither Sin Nor Shame. New York: Belmont Books, 1961.

2105 Burns, Elizabeth. The Late Liz: a Woman's Frank Confession of Sin and Salvation. New York: Popular Library, 1959.

2106 Butler, Arthur Stanley George. Portrait of Josephine Butler. London: Faber and Faber, 1954, 222 pp.

2107 Butler, Josephine. Avant l'Aurorre. XXII. Geneva: Federation Abolitionniste Internationale. Several times reprinted, not sure of first publication date.

2108 _______. Eine Stimme in der Wuste. (A Voice in the Desert). Paris: Library Sandoz and Fischbacher, 1875, 35 pp. unbound.

2109 _______. A Letter to the Mothers of England. Liverpool: Brakell, 1881.

2110 _______. Personal Reminiscences of a Great Crusade. London: Horace Marshall and Sons, 1896.

2111 _______. Index to "Personal Reminiscences of a Great Crusade". 1935.

2112 _______. Recollections of George Butler. Bristol: Arrowsmith, 1892, 282 pp.

2113 _______. Souvenirs Personnels d'Une Grande Croisade. Geneva: Federation Abolitionniste Internationale, n. d. (before 1902).

2114 _______. Sursum Corda. An address to the National Association for Repeal of the Contagious Diseases Act. Liverpool: T. Brakell, 1871.

2115 _______. The Voice of One Crying in the Wilderness: First appeal to continental nations against the system of regulated vice. Bristol: 1913, 78 pp.

2116 _______. "Moj Pochod Krzyzowy." Warsaw, 1904, 131 pp.

2117 _______. Josephine Butler; an autobiographical memoir. Bristol, 1911, 322 pp.

2118 Campbell, Jean. The Oldest Profession. New York: Belmont Books Pub., 1958.

2119 Cope-Meadows, M. Death Watch. Jarrolds, 1930.

2120 Choisy, Maryse. A Month Among the Girls. Tr. by G. Blochman. New York: Pyramid Books, 1960. First published in 1928.

2121 Coleman, K. "Carnal Knowledge: a portrait of four hookers." Kamp Magazine 10:16-26, Dec. '71.

2122 Corbin, C. E. Letters from a Chimney-corner. Fergus Printing, 1886.

2123 Cottle, T. J. "Matilda Rutherford, she's what you would call a whore." Antioch Review 31:519-43, Winter 1971-72.

2124 Cousins, S. To Beg I Am Ashamed. New York: Vanguard Press, 1938, by Kitabistan, 1940; by Richards Press, 1953; Paris: Oblique Press, 1955; New York: Lancer Books, 1962. An autobiography of a prostitute.

2125 Crawford, M. C. One Hundred Years of Work with the Girls in Boston. 1919.

2126 Cromwell, Helen. Dirty Helen. Los Angeles: Sherbourne Press.

2127 Cunningham, Peter. The Story of Nell Gwyn. Reprinted Edinburgh: John Grant, 1908, pp.132, 203-205.

2128 Daniels, Zeke. The Life and Death of Julia C. Bulette. Virginia City: Lamp Post, 1958.

2129 Day, Lillian. Ninon--a courtesan of quality. London: Jarrolds, 1958, 279 pp.

2130 Dean, Nancy with Jack Powers. Twenty Years Behind Red Curtains. Chicago: Newsstand Library, 1959. One of the better autobiographies.

2131 De Leeuw, H. Fallen Angels. Arco, 1954

2132 Denisa, Lady Newborough. Fire in My Blood. London: Elek Books, 1958.

2133 Devi, Manada. Autobiography of an Educated Fallen Woman. Calcutta: 1931, 165 pp.

2134 Diehl, Charles. Theodora. Paris: Eugene Rey, Libraire,n.d.

2135 Dinwiddy, J. R. "Unpublished Recollections of Mary Anne Clarke." Notes + Quer 21:328-30 S'74.

2136 Drago, Harry Sinclair. Notorious Ladies of the Frontier. New York: Dodd, Mead and Co., 1969.

2137 Edwardes, Allen. The Royal Whore. New York: Chilton Books, 1970.

2138 Erwin, Carol. The Orderly Disorderly House. Garden City, New York: Doubleday, 1960.

2139 Fawcett, Millicent. Josephine Butler. London: The Assn. for Moral and Social Hygiene, 1927.

2140 Felsek, Rudolf. Tagebuch Einer Andern Verlorenen. Leipzig: W. Fiedler, 1906, 246 pp.

2141 Fichte, Hubert. Interviews aus dem Palais d'Amour. Hamburg: Rowohlt-Tashenbush-Verl., 1972, 203 pp.

2142 Fille de Joie. Grove, 1967.

2143 Des "Filles" vous Parlent. Clichy, France: 1955, 63 pp. Prostitutes speak.

2144 Finmore, Rhoda Lee. Immoral Earnings or Mr. Martin's Profession. London: M. H. Publications, 1951.

2145 Fleischmann, Hector. Madame de Polignac et la Cour Galante de Marie-Antoinette. Paris: 1910.

2146 Forneron, Henri. Louise de Kerouaille: Duchess of Portsmouth. London: Sonnenschein, 1887.

2147 Gastineau, Benjamin. Les Courtisanes de l'Eglise. Paris, 1870.

2148 Gentry, Curt. The Madames of San Francisco. New York: Doubleday and Co., 1964, pp.30-31.

2149 Genuine and Authentic Memoirs of a Well-known Woman of Intrigue. London: 1787.

2150 George, W. R. Bed of Roses. Reprinted New York: Modern Library, 1928.

2151 Gerson, Noel Bertram. Neither Sin Nor Shame. New York: Belmont Books, 1961.

2152 Gibbs, Philip. King's Favorite, the love story of Robert Carr and Lady Essex. London: Hutchinson and Co., London, n.d. new edition, 320 pp.

2153 Gleason, A. "Story of Rosalinda." Collier's 51:16+, May 10, 1913.

2154 Glueck, Sheldon and Eleanor T. Five Hundred Delinquent Women. New York: Alfred A. Knopf, 1934.

2155 Goldberg, Issac. Queen of Hearts: The Passionate Pilgrimage of Lola Montez. New York: John Day Co., 1936.

2156 "Golden Girl." Time 61:20, Feb. 2, 1953.

2157 Goodnow, E. "Rosa: the true story of a sacrifice." Harper's Weekly 53:16-17, Sep. 4, 1909.

2158 Greenwald, H. Call Girl. Ballantine, 1958.

2159 Groetzinger, Leona Prall. Stories of Unfortunate Girls. Chicago(?): 1910(?), 47 pp.

2160 Hall, S. Ladies of the Night. Trident Press, 1973.

2161 Hamel, Frank. Famous French Salons. New York: Brentano, 1908.

2162 Hardwick, Mollie. Emma, Lady Hamilton. New York: Holt, Rhinehart, Winston, 1969, 312 pp.

2163 Harris, Sara. Nobody Cries for Me. New York: New American Library, 1959.

2164 Hartmann, Cyril Hughes. La Belle Stuart. London: George Routledge, 1924.

2165 Hayward, C. Dictionary of Courtesans. University Books, 1962.

2166 "Heart of a Magdalene." Public 15:1201-2 Dec. 20, 1912.

2167 Henderson, G. "Josephine Butler; her fight against the system of state regulated prostitution." Journal of Social Hygiene 14:193-7, Apr. '28.

2168 Herold, J. Christopher. Mistress to an Age; a life of Madame de Stael. Indianapolis: Bobbs-Merrill Co., 1958, 500 pp.

2169 Hibbert, Eloise Talcott. Embroidered Gauze; portraits of famous Chinese Ladies. New York: E. P. Dutton, n. d.

2170 Hillman, Fanny. Memoirs of a Jewish Madam. New York: Kantom, Inc., 1965.

2171 Hoekendijk, A. M. Deze Vrouw. Hague: 1949. A collection of 23 biographies, 22 of them of "lost" women.

2172 Holdridge, Helen. Mammy Pleasant. San Carlos, Calif.: Nourse Pub. Co., 1953.

2173 ________. The Woman in Black: the Life of Lola Montez. New York: G. P. Putman's and Sons, 1955.

2174 Hollender, Xaviera. The Happy Hooker. New York: Dell Pub. Co., 1972. Ms. Hollander made herself into a literary industry.

2175 Hollander, Xaviera. Letters to the Happy Hooker. Ed. by Bob Abel and Michael Valenti. New York: Warner Paperback Library, 1973.

2176 ________. On the Best Part Of a Man. New York: Signet--New American Library, 1975.

2177 Holt, Hilary E. The Diary Of Mata Hari. No. Hollywood, Calif.: Brandon House, 1967.

2178 ________. The Memoirs of Josephine Mitzenbacher. Vol.2. Tr. by Rudolf Schleifer. No. Hollywood, Calif.: Brandon House, 1967.

2179 Hunter, Diana and Alice Anderson. Jack Ruby's Girls. Atlanta, Ga.: Hallux, Inc. Publ., 1970.

2180 "James Bronson Reynolds; pioneer in the fight against commercialized prostitution." J Soc Hygiene 40:120-7, Mar. '54.

2181 Janney, O. E. "Influence of Josephine Butler in the United States." Journal of Social Hygiene 14:205-6, Apr. '28.

2182 Jarrett, Kay. Sex is a Private Affair. New York: The Hearst Corp. 1966.

2183 Jeannel, Julien Francois. De la Prostitution les Grandes Villes au Dux-neuviene Siecle et de l'Extinction des Maladies Veneriennes. Paris: Bailliere, 1874, 647 pp.

2184 Joelson, Annette. Courtesan Princess; Catherine Grand, Princess de Talleyrand. Philadelphia: Chilton Books, 1965, 279 pp.

2185 Johnson, R. D. "Folklore and Women: a social interactional analysis of the folklore of a Texas madam." Journal of American Folklore 86:211- 24, Jun. '73.

2186 Julie (pseud.). My Days and Nights. Putnam, 1974.

2187 Kale, Susan. The Fire Escape. New York: Doubleday, 1960.

2188 Kay, F. George. Lady of the Sun; the Life and times of Alice Perrers. New York: Barnes and Noble, Inc., 1873.

2189 Kendall, Sidney C. (Rev.). The Queen of the Red-Lights--a Story Founded Upon Fact. Los Angeles: W. J. Phillips, 1906.

2190 Kern, E. Wie Sie Dazu Kamen. Munich: Reinhardt, 1928, 182 pp. Life histories of 35 inmates of houses of prostitution and how they came to that.

2191 Kimball, Nell. Nell Kimball: Her Life as an American Madam, by Herself. Ed. with intro. by Stephen Longstreet. New York: Macmillan, 1970, 286 pp.

2192 Knapp, Bettina and Myra Chipman. That was Yvette; the biography of a great diseuse. London: Frederick Muller Ltd., London, 1966.

2193 Knox, Cleone. The Diary of a Young Lady of Fashion--in the Year 1784-1765. New York: D. Appleton and Co., 1926.

2194 Kornfeld, Robert. The Young Cats. Woodside, N. Y.: Zil, Inc., 1967.

2195 Kuhn, F. C. "Birdie's Book About Her Brothel." American Mercury 77:16-19, Oct. '53.

2196 "Ladies of the Night." Nation 188:466, May 23, 1959.

2197 Laidlaw, H. B. "My Little Sister." Survey 30:199-202, May 3, 1913.

2198 Lany, Olga. La Vie Chine. Paris: Hachette, 1950.

2199 League of Nations. Advisory Committee on Social Questions. Prostitutes: their early lives. New York: United Nations, Sales Section, 1938.

2200 Leah. Leah. Old Tappan, N. J.: F. H. Revell Co., 1973, 90 pp.

2201 Leathem, Harvey T. Daughters of Joy. Venice Publ. Corp., 1967.

2202 Lederer, William J. The Story of Pink Jade. New York: W. W. Norton and Co., Inc., 1966.

2203 Leroy-Boy, Magdeleine. De Josephine Butler aux Nations Unies. Geneva: Fed. Abol. Inter., 1950, 12 pp.

2204 Leslie, Anita. Mrs. Fitzherbert. New York: Ch. Scribner's Sons, 1960.

2205 Levaillant, Maurice. The Passionate Exiles; Madame de Stael and Madame Recamier. New York: Farrar, Straus and Cudahy, 1958, 354 pp.

2206 Lewis, Arthur H. La Belle Otero. New York: Trident Press, 1967.

2207 Lewis, Gladys Adelina. Call House Madam; the story of the career of Beverly Davis, as told by Serge G. Wolsey (pseud.). San Francisco: Martin Tudordale Co., 1942, 422 pp.

2208 Lewis, L. L. "Man Who Saved Chicago." American Mercury 20:178-84, Jun. '30.

2209 Lewis, Paul. Lady of France; a biography of Gabrielle d'Estress. New York: Funk and Wagnalls Co., Inc., 1963.

2210 The Life and Sufferings of Cecelia Mayo; founded on incidents in real life. Boston: M. Aurelius, 1843, 36 pp. The fall of an heiress through deception--parents take note et al.

2211 "The Life of a Los Angeles Sporting Girl". Ken (mag) May 5, 1938.

2212 Lockenstosser, Maria. Die Erinnerungen der Maria Lockenstosser, von ihr aufgezeichnet. Der offentlich keit ubergeben von Carl Borro Schwerla. Munich: K. Desch, 1972, 222 pp.

2213 Lofthouse, W. F. "Josephine Butler: Commemoration of a Reform." London Q R 150:101-4, Jun. '28.

2214 Loomis, Stanley. DuBarry: a biography. Philadelphia: J. B. Lippincott, 1959.

2215 Lowag, Dr. Leonard A. Confessions of a Hollywood Callgirl. Los Angeles: Sherbourne Press, Inc., 1964.

2216 Lucia, Ellis. Klondike Kate; the life and legend of Kitty Rockwell, the Queen of the Yukon. New York: Hastings House Pub., 1962.

2217 Ludovicus, M. (John Campbell). A Particular but Melancholy Account of the Great Hardships, Difficuties, and Miseries That Those Unhappy and Much To-Be-Pitied Creatures, the Common Women of the Town, are Plung'd into at this Juncture. The Causes of Their Misfortunes Fully Laid Down; and the Bad Effects that too much Rigour against Them will Produce. London: printed for the author, 1752, pp.6-16.

2218 Lynda. The Merry Madam. Pyramid Paperback, 1973.

2219 MacIner, Joyce. The Frog Pond. New York: Bantam/George Braziller, Inc., 1961.

2220 "Madame Again." Newsweek 43:40 Jun. 21, 1954.

2221 Madame Sherry (Ruth Barnes) with S. Robert Tralins. Pleasure was My Business. New York: Lyle Stuart, 1961.

2222 Madeleine: an autobiography. New York: Harper, 1919. An early 20th century autobiography which was a cause celebre in the book publishing world.

2223 Mahoney, Irene. Royal Cousin. Garden City: Doubleday, 1970.

2224 Mani, M. S. The Pen Pictures of the Dancing Girls. Madras: 1926, 127 pp.

2225 Markun, Leo. Mistresses of Today. Girard, Kan.: Little Blue Books.

2226 Marlowe, Kenneth. Cathouse Mother. Agoura, Calif.: Pad Library, 1966.

2227 Marx, Samuel. Texas Guinan; The Ace of (Night) Clubs. Girard, Kan.: Haldeman-Julius Pub.

2228 Marx, Samuel. Wild Women of Broadway. Girard, Kan.: Little Blue Books.

2229 Maurois, Simone Andre. Miss Howard and the Emperor; the story of Napolean III and his mistress. New York: Alfred A. Knopf, 1957.

2230 Ma Vie de Prostituee. Tr. from the English by Henri Descarmes. Paris: Buchet Chastel, Correa, 1960, 207 pp. A streetwalker in Picadilly.

2231 McGowan, Helen "Rocking Chair." Big City Madam. New York: Lancer Books, 1965.

2232 McManus, Virginia. Not for Love. New York: G. P. Putnam's Sons, 1960.

2233 "Memoirs of a Prostitute." London M II:626.

2234 Merlin, Lina, ed. Lettre Dalle Case Chuise. Milan: Edizioni Avanti, 1955, 203 pp.

2235 Messina, Alfredo. The Trial of Alfredo Messina. Ed. from the report by J. F. Whitcomb. London: 1956, 160 pp.

2236 Mestral-Combremont, J. de. Josephine Butler. Geneva: Fed. Abol. Inter., 1944. In German. In French: La noble vie d'une femme, Josephine Butler, published in 1942. An earlier short memoir by G. d'Avolio, "Giuseppina Butler", 18 pp., n. d.

2237 Michelson, H. Sportin' Ladies...confession of the bimbos. Chilton Book Co., 1975.

2238 Mirsky, Jonathan. The Jasper Gate Jonathan Quayne. New York: Lancer Books, 1967.

2239 Mitford, Nancy. Madame De Pompadour. London: The Reprint Society, 1954.

2240 Mitsuko, Iolana. Honolulu Madam. Los Angeles: Holloway House, 1969.

2241 Montespan, Madame. Memoirs of Madame la Marquise de Montespan. London: Grover Society, 1904, 2v.

2242 Moore, Robin. The Making of the Happy Hooker. New York: Signet, 1975.

2243 "Murrow and the Girls." Time 73:53-4 Feb. 2, '59.

2244 Murtagh, Judge John M. and Sara Harris. Who Live in the Shadow. Belmont Productions, Inc., 1959.

2245 Nell (pseud.). I Had No Choice; the diary of an "unfortunate." Chapman and Hall, 1940, 156 pp.

2246 Neumann, R. 23 Women; the story of an international traffic. New York: Dial Press, 1940, 316 pp.

2247 Notes for Speakers on the Works and Principles of Josephine Butler. London: Assn. for Moral and Social Hygiene, 1928, 16 pp.

2248 O'Higgins, H. J. "Case of Fanny." Collier's 48:11 Mar. 2, '12.

2249 Oppenheim, Ralph. The Splendors and Miseries of a Courtesan. Girard, Kan.: Haldeman-Julius Co.

2250 O'Sullivan, Frank Dalton. In the Orchard of Forbidden Fruit. Chicago: The National Publicity Bureau, 1915, 185 pp.

2251 Other Kind of Girl. Huebsch, 1914.

2252 O. W. (Marjorie Smith). God Have Mercy on Me. New York: Sheridan House, 1931.

2253 ___________. No Bed of Roses. New York: Macaulay Co., 1930.

2254 __________. *With My Eyes Wide Open*. New York: Sheridan House, 1949.

2255 "Pat and Minot." *Newsweek*. Feb. 16, 1953.

2256 Payne, Edward F. and Henry H. Harper. *The Charity of Charles Dickens, His Interest in the Home for Fallen Women and a History of the Strange Case of Caroline Maynard Thompson*. Boston: printed for members of the Bibliophile Society, 1929.

2257 Payton, Barbara. *I Am Not Ashamed*. Los Angeles: Holloway House Pub. Co., 1963.

2258 Pearl, Cyril. *The Girl with the Swansdown Seat*. Indianapolis: Bobbs-Merrill, 1955. Reviewed in *Saturday Review* 39:11 Apr. 7, '56.

2259 Peyrefitte, R. *Manouche: her life and times*.

2260 Phillips, Ary Caldwell. *Memoirs of a Harem Girl*. Tower Pub., Inc. 1968.

2261 "Pioneers and Later Progress." *Journal of Social Hygiene* 14:207-13, Apr. '28.

2262 Premoisan, Alain. *Les Cahiers de Cecile; confidences of a prostítute*. Mulhouse: Editions Salvator, 1965, 199 pp.

2263 "Primrose Pat." *Newsweek* 41:29 Feb. 23, '53.

2264 "Prostitutes Progress." *Newsweek* 21:28+ May 3, '43.

2265 Randall, Terri. *Hooker*. New York: Award Books, 1969.

2266 Reid, Ed. *The Mistress and the Mafia*; the Virginia Hill story. New York: Bantam Books, 1972. Bugsy Siegel and his girl.

2267 Reitman, Ben L. *Sister of the Road*; the autobiography of Boxcar Bertha. New York: Sheridan House, 1937.

2268 Rheine, T. V. *Der Sadismus in Einzeldarstellungen*. Bd. I: "Sadismus and Prostitution." Berlin: Sexualins Verl Anst, 1932, 96 pp. (*Sadism in autobiography*. Vol I: "Sadism and Prostitution").

2269 Rice-Davies, Marilyn. *My Life and Lovers*. Chicago: Novel Books, Inc.

2270 Rippey, S. C. "Case of Angeline." *Outlook* 106:252-6 Jan. 31, '14.

2271 Roberts, F. Fifteen Years with the Outcast. Gospel Trumpet Co., 1912.

2272 Rodocanachi, E. Courtisanes et Bouffons. Paris: 1894, 199 pp.

2273 Rolph, C. H. "Known Immoral Character." New Statesmen and Nation 41: 92-3 Jan. 27, '51. Gt. Britain.

2274 Root, Waverly. "Women Have Nothing to Kick About." American Mercury 68:400-40, Apr. '49.

2275 Rubin, Theodore Issac. In the Life. New York: Macmillan, 1961, 166 pp.

2276 _________. Sweet Daddy. New York: Ballantine Books, 1963.

2277 Salva, Anne. Je n'en Rougis Pas, etc. (Reminiscences). Paris: 1949, 246 pp.

2278 Sam, Gilbert A. The Confession of Abena Gyantra. Accra: Gillsam Pub. Syn., 1956, 15 pp.

2279 Sanders, Joan. La Petite; the life of Louise de la Valliere. Boston: Houghton Mifflin Co., 1959.

2280 Sanford, Jeremy. Prostitutes: Portraits of People in the Sexploitation Business. London: Secker and Warburg, 1976.

2281 Saunders, Edith. Napoleon and Mademoiselle George. New York: E. P. Dutton and Co., 1959.

2282 Scott, Geoffrey. The Portrait of Zelide. New York: Charles Scribners's Sons, 1959. Orig. pub 1927.

2283 Scott, Valerie X. and Herbert d'H. Lee. Surrogate Wife. New York: Dell Pub. Co., Inc., 1971.

2284 Seward, Desmond. The First Bourbon. Boston: Gambit, 1971.

2285 Shackleford, William Yancey. Belle Starr; the Bandit Queen. Girard, Kan.: Little Blue Books.

2286 Shaen, M. J. William Shaen; a brief sketch. Longmans, 1912, 93 pp.

2287 Sheehy, G. Hustling. Delacorte Press, 1973.

2288 Sichel, Walter. Emma Lady Hamilton. 3d ed rev New York: Dodd Mead and Co., 1907.

2289 Simpson, Jay. Secrets of Famous Mistresses. New York: Wisdom House, Inc., 1961.

2290 Slade, Caroline. Sterile Sun. New York: The Macaulay Co., 1936.

2291 Smith, Mary F. Baba of Karo: A Woman of the Muslim Hausa. London: Faber and Faber, Ltd., 1954.

2292 Snell, Joseph W. Painted Ladies of the Cowtown Frontier. Kansas City, Mo.: Kansas City Posse of the Westerners, 1965.

2293 Solano, Susan, Impresiones de Viaje; Bethsabe Hurtado, Josefina Butler, una mujer admirable; Mathilde Hildebrant de Perez Trevino Algunos aspectos de los sistemas reglamentarista y abolicionista. A 15 page pamphlet which was designed to highlight prostitution at the 4th Conference Internationale des Avocats in 1952.

2294 Spencer, A. G. "Josephine Butler and the English Crusade." Forum 49:77-81, Jun.-Jul. '13.

2295 ______. "A Memorial of a Great Woman." Journal of Social Hygiene 4:193-213, Apr. '28.

2296 Spencer, A. G. "Scarlet Woman." Forum 49:276-89, Mar. '13.

2297 Stafford, A. The Age of Consent. Hodder, '64.

2298 Stanford, Sally. The Lady of the House; the autobiography of Sally Stanford. New York: Putnam, 1966, 255 pp. Good autobiography.

2299 Stein, M. L. Lovers, Friends, Slaves. Berkley Pub. Corp., 1974.

2300 Stocks, Mary. Josephine Butler and the Moral Standards of Today. London: Alison Neilans Memorial Lecture, 1961, 15 pp.

2301 Stone, L. A. Woman of the Streets. Burton Pub., 1917, 1919.

2302 Strachey, Ray. "The Centenary of Josephine Butler: an interview with Dame Millicent Garrett Fawcett." Social Service Review 2:1-23 Mar '28.

2303 Streetwalker. London: Bodley Head, 1959 and New York: Viking Press, 1960. Low-priced call girl, excellent.

2304 Strickland, C. J. Hard to Believe. Charlotte, N. C.: Elizabeth Pub. Co., 1939.

2305 Tabor, Pauline. Pauline's. Louisville, Ky.: Touchstone, 1971, 295 pp. Autobiography of the owner-operator of a house of prostitution.

2306 Thirkell, Angela. Tribute For Harriette; the suprising career of Harriette Wilson. New York: Random House, 1936.

2307 Thompson, B. Sister of the Road; the autobiography of Box-Car Bertha. New York: Macaulay, 1937.

2308 Tomalin, N. "Happy Hooker." New Statesman 84:509 Oct. 13, '72.

2309 "Tomlinson and Diggs," Survey 30:655 Aug. 30, '13.

2310 Tomkinson, Constance. Les Girls--Something for the Boys. New York: Avon Pub., Inc., 1956.

2311 Tozer, Basil. The Story of a Terrible Life; the amazing career of a notorious procuress. London: T. Werner Laurie, Ltd., 1928.

2312 Tralins, Robert. Cairo Madam. New York: Paperback Library, 1968.

2313 Trelawney-Ansell, E. C. Traders in Women. Long, 1940.

2314 Trowbridge, W. R. H. Seven Splendid Sinners. New York: Brentano's, 1787.

2315 True Life Stories of Crooks, Con Men and Courtesans. Hong Kong: Octopus Books, 1973.

2316 Tuleda, Mariano. Biografia de la Prostitucion, una Lacra Social. Barcelona, R. Borras, 1960, 164 pp.

2317 Turner, E. M. Josephine Butler: an appreciation. London: The Assn. for Moral and Social Hygiene, 1928.

2318 _____. Josephine Butler: her place in history. London: 1945, 24 pp.

2319 Turner, G. K. "Strange Woman." McClure 41:25-33, May '13.

2320 Twenty Tales by Twenty Women; from real life in Chicago. Chicago: Novelty Pub. Co., 1903, 316 pp.

2321 Tzaut, Helene, comp. Filles Perdues et Retrouvees--Qulques Sauvetages; twenty years of work at "La Bienvenue" 1946-1966. Paris: La Bienvenue, 1966, 22 pp.

2322 Van Deventer, Betty. Lines of Chorus Girls. Girard, Kan.: Little Blue Books.

2323 Vaneer, William. Diary of a Geisha Girl. New York: Avon Pub., Inc., 1959.

2324 Washburn, Charles. Come into My Parlor. New York: Arno Press, 1974, 225 pp. About Chicago.

2325 Watts, Martha. The Men in My Life. New York: Lyle Stuart, 1960. Also published in France as Les Hommes dans Ma Vie. Paris: Buchet-Chastel, 1961.

2326 Williams, H. Noel. Memoirs of Madame duBarry of the Court of Louis XV. New York: P. F. Collier and Son, 1910.

2327 ________. Rival Saltanas: Nell Gwyn and Louise de Keroualle. London: Hutchinson and Co., 1915.

2328 Wilson, John Harold. All the Kings Ladies. Chicago: Univ. of Chicago Press, 1958.

2329 ________. Nell Gwyn Royal Mistress. New York: Pellegrini and Cudahy, 1952. Reprinted same year by Dell.

2330 Winn, D. Prostitutes. Hutchinson, 1974. About London.

2331 Wolsey, Serge G. Call House Madam. San Francisco: Martin Tudordale Corp., 1942. Another biography which ran into difficulty with the censors.

2332 Woodhill, Victoria C. The Elixir of Life. New York: Woodhull and Claflin, 1873.

2333 Wright, F. A. Letters of the Courtesans. Girard, Kan.: Little Blue Books.

2334 Ziegler, Philip. The Duchess of Dino. New York: John Day Co., 1963.

2335 Acuna, C. M. _Women for Sale_. Godwin, 1931.

2336 "Are Low Wages Responsible for Women's Immorality?" _Current Opinion_ 54:402 May '13.

2337 Baker, Lewis J. _The High Cost of Loving_. New York: Tower Pub., Inc., 1966.

2338 Barley, Stephan. _Bondage; the slave traffic in women today_. Funk, 1968. pp.261-3.

2339 _______. _Sex Slavery; a documented report on the international scene today_. Heinemann, 1968, pp.261-3.

2340 Bingham, T. A. "Girl that disappears." _Hampton_ 25:559-73, Nov. '10.

2341 Boyle, C. A. _The Traffic in Women_. Women's Freedom League, 1913, 8 pp.

2342 Bunting, M. H. L. "White Slave Traffic Crusade." _Contemp_ 103:49-52, Jan. '13.

2343 Burgess, Anne Marie and Michael Burgess. _The Girl Market_. Derby, Conn.: Monarch Books, Inc., 1963.

2344 Center, R. I. "Halt of Racketeering." _Atlantic Monthly_ 160:447-57, Oct. '37.

2345 Chase, F. W. "White Slave Traffic in Boston." _New Eng Mag_ ns 41:531-9, Jan. '10.

2346 Chrysler, C. B. _White Slavery_. Chicago: 1909, 1911, 251 pp.

2347 "Commercialized Prostitution as a Community Problem." _Journal of Social Hygiene_. Dec. '36 (entire issue).

2348 "Conference on the White Slave Trade." _Survey_ 24:714-5 Aug. 20, '10.

2349 Crad, J. (pseud.). _Traders in Women; a comprehensive survey of white slavery_. Long, 1940, 287 pp.

2350 Creel, H. G. _Prostitution for Profit_. National Rip-saw Publ., 1912.

2351 _Crimes of the White Slavers_. Regan Pub. n. d.

2352 Cross, Harold H. U. _The Lust Market_. New York: Citadel Press, 1956, 1963. Cross traveled--described brothels, etc. Mostly Barbary Coast, France, Australia.

2353 Davis, F. "Biggest Racketeer Falls." Sat Eve Post 210:12-13+ Oct. 30, '37.

2354 Deutsch, A. "Prostitution Racket is Back." American Mercury 63:270-7, Sep. '46. Discussion: 63:636, Nov. '46; 63:761, Dec '46; 64:382, Mar. '47.

2355 "Devilish Traffic." Literary Digest 101:33, Apr. 20, '29.

2356 "Do Americans Commercialize Sex?" symposium. Ladies' Home Journal 73:68-9+, Oct. '56.

2357 Dyer, A. S. European Trade in English Girls. London: 1885, 41 pp.

2358 "Economics of Hell." Spectator 108:261-2, Feb. 17, '12.

2359 "Financing a City by Returns From Vice." Survey 31:512-4, Jan. 31, '14.

2360 "Five White Slave Trade Investigations." McClure 35:346-8, Jul. '10.

2361 "France, proxenetisme." Economist 244:45, Sep. 16, '72.

2362 "Free Enterprises; Messina Brothers." Time 73:18-19, Apr. 27, '59.

2363 Fry, Monroe. Sex, Vice, and Business. New York: Ballantine Books, 1959, 159 pp. Popular.

2364 "Futility of the White Slave Agitation." Current Opinion 56:287-8, Apr '14.

2365 Gault, R. H. "Relation of Women's Wage to the Social Evil." J of Crim Law 4:323-5, S '13.

2366 Gerson, Noel Bertram. The Girl Market. Derby, Conn.: Monarch Books, 1963, 156 pp.

2367 Goron, M. F. El Mercado de Mujeres. Appleton, '12.

2368 "Hard Luck, Jellicoe--but it Served Lambton Right." Economist 248:16, Jun. 14, '73.

2369 Harris, H. W. Human Merchandise; a study of the international traffic in women. Benn, 1928, 272 pp.

2370 Harris, Sara. They Sell Sex; the call girl and big business. Greenwich, Conn.: Fawcett Pub., 1960. Pimps and others.

2371 Hodder, A. "Alliance Between Puritan and Grafter: New York City." Outlook 73:251-60, Jan. 31, '03.

2372 Holmes, J. D. "Vice and Wages." Survey 26:701-2, Aug. 12, 1911.

2373 "How to Make Money in Germany with the Oldest Profession in the World." American Druggist 166:21-2, Jun. 10, '72.

2374 "Is Commercializd Prostitution Returning." Journal of Social Hygiene 33:53-56, Feb. '47. Six charts analyzing results of ASHA community studies.

2375 "Is White Slavery Nothing More Than a Myth?" Current Opinion 55:348, Nov. '13.

2376 James, Donald H. Sex and Business. New York: Macfadden, 1971, 192 pp.

2377 Jeffers, Harry Paul. Sex in the Executive Suite. Chicago, Playboy Press, 1972, 279 pp.

2378 Joesten, Joachim. Vice, Inc.. New York: Ace, 1954, 159 pp.

2379 Kinsie, P. M. The Prostitution Racket. New York: American Social Health Assn., 1945.

2380 ______. "Sex Crimes and the Prostitution Racket." Journal of Social Hygiene 36:250-2, Jun. '50.

2381 ______. "To Combat the Return of Commercialized Prostitution: the 'Business' Stages a Comeback From Its Wartime Low; New Trends in an Old Racket." American City 64:102-3, Aug. '49.

2382 Kneeland, G. J. "Commercialized Prostitution and the Liquor Traffic." Social Hygiene 2:69-90, Jan. '16.

2383 _______. "Commercialized Prostitution and the Use of Property." Social Hygiene 2:561-72, Oct. '16.

2384 _______. "Commercialized Vice." Proc Am Acad Pol Sci 2:601-3, Jun. '12.

2385 "Landlord of Flat Living on Earnings of Prostitution." L Q Rev 73:297, Jun. '57.

2386 Law, E. N. Shame of a Great Nation; the story of the white slave trade. Detroit: privately pub., 1909.

2387 Legrand-Falco, ____, General Secretary of L'Union Temporaire contre la Regulation de la Prostitution et la Traite des Femmes. History of the Abolition of State Regulation of Prostitution, with Special Relation to France and the Position Today. London: Assn. for Moral and Social Hygiene, 1946, 30 pp.

2388 Lehman, F. M. and Clarkson, N. K. White Slave Hell. Christian Witness, n. d.

2389 "Living on the Earnings of Prostitution." L Q Rev 72:319, Jun. '56.

2390 Loewenherz, J. Prostitution oder Production, Eigentum oder Ehe?. Neuwied, 1895, 209 pp.

2391 "Lucrative Feudalism." Time 64:20, Jul. 26, '54.

2392 "Madame Again." Newsweek 43:40, Jun. 21, '54.

2393 Marshall, C. "Racketeering in Vice." Woman's J ns 16:18-19+, May '31.

2394 McInnes, N. "Tired Businessman's Risk? The World's Oldest Profession Has Gone Public." Barron's 53:9+, Jul. 9, '73.

2395 _____. "Wages of Sin; Investors in Bordellos Have Lost Their Shirts." Barron's 54:11+, Oct. 7, '74.

2396 Merriam, E. "Sex as a Selling Aid; Mr. Murrow Lifts the Lid." Nation 188:239-42, Mar. 21, '59.

2397 "Milestones in the March Against Commercialized Prostitution in the United States." Journal of Social Hygiene 22:431-4, Dec '36.

2398 "More Private Vices." (Wolfenden Report on homosexuality and prostitution.) Economist 184:735-6, Sep. 7, '57.

2399 "Murrow Broadcast Recalls '54 Account of Oldest Profession." (Sex as selling tool in business.) Adv Age 30:2+, Feb. 2, '59.

2400 Niemoeller, A. F. The Business Side of the Oldest Business; a survey of the organization, management, and earnings of prostitution from antiquity to the present. Girard, Kan.: Haldeman-Julius Pub., 1945.

2401 "Not Importunate." Economist 202:506, Feb. 10, '62.

2402 O,Brien, J. A. Can We Crush Commercialized Vice. Assn. Press, 1939.

2403 O'Callaghan, ____. The Slave Trade Today. New York: Crown Pub. 1961.

2404 __________. Damaged Baggage. New York: Roy Pub., 1969.

2405 __________. The Yellow Slave Trade. London: Anthony Blond, 1968.

2406 Ostwald, H. Prostitutionsmarket. Leipzig: 1907, 90 pp.

2407 Paz, M. Femmes a Vendre. 1936, 158 pp.

2408 Phillippon, Odette. L'Esclavage de la Femme dans le Monde Contemporain; ou la prostitution sans masque, etc. Paris: 1954, 234 pp.

2409 ________. Le Trafic des Femmes. Paris: 1956, 139 pp.

2410 Plante, R. B. "Bordello Bonds get SEC Red Light." Comm and Fin Chr 219:1+, Mar. 11, '74.

2411 "Prostitutes in Legalized Brothels Prove Value of Progonasyl as VD Prophylactic." Am Druggist 165:50, May 15, '72.

2412 "Policy of Business Folly." Journal of Social Hygiene 10:104-6, Feb. '24.

2413 "Punishment of a White Slave Trader." Outlook 98:567-8, Jul. 15, '11.

2414 "Radio Report on Sex and Business." America 100:513, Jan. 31, '59.

2415 Reitman, Ben L. The Second Oldest Profession--the Study of the Prostitute's Business Manager. New York: Vanguard Press, 1931.

2416 Murray, V. "Relation of Prostitution to Economic Conditions." Journal of Social Hygiene 18:314-21, Jun. '32.

2417 Reynolds, J. B. "Commercialized Vice." Survey 31:354, Dec. 27, '13.

2418 Roe, C. G. Horrors of the White Slave Trade. 1911, 448 pp.

2419 Ross, I. "Sex in the Boom Towns." American Mercury 55:606-13, Nov. '42.

2420 "Sex for Sale ; Business of Sex." Newsweek 53:94, Jan. 26, '59.

2421 Shayon, R. L. "Sorry, Wrong Number; Business of Sex." Saturday Review 42:28, Feb. 7, '59.

2422 Sheehy, Gail. "The Economics of Prostitution." Ms. 1:58-61+, Jun. '73.

2423 Shuler, Robert Pierce. Millionaires and Hired Girls. Los Angeles: 192(?), 64 pp.

2424 Simmel, Georg. Gesammelte Werke. vol I: Philosophie des Geldes. Berlin: Dunker and Hublot, 1958, 585 pp. section on prostitution and money.

2425 "State of the Union Regarding Commercialized Prostitution: a 10 year survey"; an analysis of 3,402 studies made by the American Social Hygiene Assn., Jan. 1, 1940 to Dec. 31, 1949, in 1,224 communities. Journal of Social Hygiene 36:50 F '50.

2426 "Story Behind the Book: The Lively Commerce." Pub W 199:53, May 24, 1971.

2427 "Trade in White Slaves." R of Rs 39:371-2, Mar. '09.

2428 "Trade Routes of White Slavers." Survey 59:486-8, Jan. 15, '28.

2429 "Traffic in Women and Children in the East." Nature 139:663, Apr. 17, '37.

2430 "Unhappy Hookers; Strike by Prostitutes." Time 105:33, Jun. 16, '75.

2431 "Unhappy Hookers; Strike in Marseilles." Newsweek 81:43 Feb. 12, '73.

2432 United States. White Slave Act of June 25, 1910. Supt. of Doc., 1910.

2433 "Vice Racketeers Lose Ground." Journal of Social Hygiene 38:186-7, Apr. '52. Chart entitled "Prostitution Conditions in the U. S. A.: a 12 year survey."

2434 "Wages and Sin." Lit Digest 46:621-4, Mar. 22, '13.

2435 Watt, Thelma. "Victorian But Not Bourgeois (Urania Cottage)." Guardian pp.4, Dec. 20, '67.

2436 "What is Your Reaction to the Ed Murrow Broadcast?" Symposium. Sponsor 13:521+, Feb. 14, '59.

2437 "White Slave." Survey 30:311-4, May 31, '13.

2438 "White Slave Revelations." Cur Lit 47:594-8, Dec. '09.

2439 White Slavery. Int. Purity Assoc.

2440 "White Slavers Routed." Outlook 103:569-71, Mar. 15, '13.

2441 "White Slaves." Outlook 94:131-2, Jan. 22, '10.

2442 "White Slave Trade." Contemp 82:735-40, Nov. '02 and Missionary Review 26:149, Feb. '03.

2443 The White Slave Traffic. P. S. King, 1912, 27 pp.

2444 *The White Slave Traffic*. C. A. Pearson, 1916, 126 pp.

2445 "White Slave Traffic." *Outlook* 95:545-6, Jul. 16, '10.

2446 Whitlock, B. "White Slave." *Forum* 51:193-216, F. '14.

2447 Adams, Samuel Hopkins. Tenderloin. Random House, 1959, 372 pp. New York City in the Gay 'Nineties.

2448 Aidoo, Ama Ata. "In the Cutting of a Drink," in Aidoo, No Sweetness Here. Doubleday, 1971 (1970).

2449 Aiken, Conrad. "West End," in Aiken, Collected Short Stories of Conrad Aiken. World Pub., 1960.

2450 Albee, Edward. Edward Albee's Everything in the Garden. Dramatists, 1968.

2451 Aldiss, B. W. "Lambeth Blossom," in Scortia, T. N. Strange Bedfellows: Sex and Science Fiction. Random House, 1973 (1972).

2452 Aldrich, Ann. Carol in a Thousand Cities. Greenwich, Conn.: Fawcett Pub., Inc., 1960.

2453 Algren, N. "Beasts of the Wild," in Best American Short Stories, 1957. Houghton, 1957.

2454 ____. "The House of the Hundred Grass Fires," in Algren, The Last Carousel. Putnam, 1973.

2455 ____. The Man With the Golden Arm. New York: Doubleday and Co., 1949.

2456 ____. "Police and Mama-sans Get It All," in Algren, The Last Carousel., Putnam, 1973.

2457 ____. A Walk on the Wild Side. New York: Farrar, Straus, 1956.

2458 ____. "Watch Out for Daddy," in Algren, The Last Carousel. Putnam, 1973.

2459 Amado, Jorge. "How Porciuncula the Mulatto Got the Corpse Off His Back," in Howes, B., ed., The Eye of the Heart; short stories from Latin America. Bobbs, 1973.

2460 Andersen, Sherwood. "White Spot," in Sherwood Andersen Short Stories. Hill and Wong, 1962.

2461 Andrezel, Pierre. The Angelic Avengers. Random House, 1947, 402 pp.

2462 Andric, Ivo. "Anika's Times," in The Vizier's Elephants; three novellas. p.55-130. tr. from the Serbo-Croatian by Drenka Melen. Harcourt, 1962, 247 pp.

2463 Arden, John. "The Waters of Babylon," in Arden, Three Plays. Grove, 1964.

2464 Aretino, Pietro. Letters and Sonnets. Tr. into English by Samuel Putman. Reprinted New York: Covici Frede, 1933.

2465 Arlen, Harold. House of Flowers. Book by Truman Capote, lyrics by Truman Capote and Harold Arlen, music by Harold Arlen. Random House, 1968.

2466 Asbury, H. "Hatrack." American Mercury 7:479-83, Apr. '26. Story of a small town prostitute. Reprinted in Stories of Scarlet Women and in American Mercury Reader, Blakiston, 1944.

2467 Aurell, Tage. "True Confessions," in Aurell, Rose of Jericho and Other Stories. Tr. from the Swedish by Martin S. Allwood. Univ. of Wisconsin Press, 1968.

2468 Austin, Mary Hunter. "House of Offence," in Austin, Lost Borders. Harper, 1909.

2469 Babel, Issac. "The Chinaman," in Babel, You Must Know Everything Stories, 1915-1937. Tr. from the Russian by Max Hayward. Farrar, Straus, 1969.

2470 ______. "A Hard-working Woman," in Babel, You Must Know Everything Stories, 1915-1937. Tr. from the Russian by Max Hayward. Farrar, Straus, 1969.

2471 ______. "Through the Fanlight," in Babel, Collected Stories. Criterion Books, 1955.

2472 Bahr, Jerome. "Hello, Lover!" in Bahr, All Good Americans. Scribner, 1937.

2473 Balzac, H. de. "The Succubus," in Tenn, W. and Westlake, D. E., ed., Once Against the Law. Macmillan, 1968.

2474 Barbey d'Aureville, Jules Amedee. "A Woman's Vengence," in The She Devils. Tr. by Jean Kimber. Oxford, 1964.

2475 Bart, Lionel. Fings Ain't Wot They. A play by Frank Norman, lyrics by Lionel Bart. Grove, 1962.

2476 Bataille, Georges. "Madame Edwards," in Evergreen Review Reader, 1957-1967. Grove, 1968.

2477 Behan, Brendan. The Hostage; a play. Methuen and Co., 1958. Set in a brothel, humorous.

2478 Benefield, Barry. "Daughters of Joy," in Benefield, Short Turns., Century, 1926.

2479 Bock, Jerry. Tenderloin. Based on the novel by Samuel H. Adams. Book by Jerome Weidman and George Abbott, music by Jerry Bock, lyrics by Sheldon Harnick. Random House, 1961.

2480 Borchert, Wolfgang. "The Crows Fly Home at Night," in Borchert, The Man Outside. Tr. from the German by David Porter. New Directions, 1971.

2481 ________. "Do Stay, Giraffe," in Borchert, The Man Outside. Tr. from the German by David Porter. New Directions, 1971.

2482 Bottome, Phyllis. "Droles de Gens." in Walls of Glass. Vanguard, 1958.

2483 Boyle, Patrick. "Square Dance," in Boyle, At Night All Cats Are Grey, and Other Stories. Grove, 1969 (c1966).

2484 Bowles, Paul. "The Story of Laheen and Idir," in Bowles, The Time of Friendship. Holt, 1967.

2485 Bremont, M. "Youth." American Vanguard, 1953. New School for Social Research by Dial Press, 1953.

2486 Brister, Bob. "Professor Tequila Joe," in Brister, Moss, Mallards, and Mules, and Other Hunting and Fishing Stories. Winchester Press, 1973.

2487 Brocchi, V. "The Illusion," in Best Continental Short Stories of 1923-24, 1924-5, 1926, 1927, and the Yearbook of Continental Short Stories, 1924-28. Dodd.

2488 Brooks, V. Little Lost Sister. Macaulay Co., 1914.

2489 Brown, George MacKay. "Celia," in Brown, A Time to Keep and Other Stories. Harcourt, 1969.

2490 Brown, Wenzell. The Kept Man. New York: Lancer Books, 1964.

2491 Browning, Norma Lee. City Girl in the Country and Other Stories. Chicago: Henry Regnery Co., 1955.

2492 Bulgakov, Mikhail. "Zoya's Apartment," in Bulgakov, The Early Plays of Mikhail Bulgakov. Tr. by Ellendia Proffer and Carl C. Proffer. Ind. Univ. Press, 1972.

2493 Bukowski, Charles. "Trouble With a Battery," in Erections, Ejaculations, Exhibitions and General Tales of Ordinary Madness. City Lights Books, 1972.

2494 ________. "The Way the Dead Love," in Bukowski, South of North, Stories of the Buried Life. Black Sparrow Press, 1973.

2495 ________. "The White Beard," in Erections, Ejaculations, Exhibitions and General Tales of Ordinary Madness. City Lights Books, 1972.

2496 Bullins, Ed. "The Excursion," in Bullins, The Hungered One; early writings. Morrow, 1971.

2497 Burke, Thomas. "Berye, the Croucher and the Rest of England," in Burke, Limehouse Nights. Horizon Press, 1973.

2498 _______. "Little Flowers of Frances," in Burke, More Limelight Nights. Doran, 1921.

2499 _______. "The Flu and the Pansy Greers," in Limehouse Nights. Horizon Press, 1973.

2500 Burley, W. J. Death in Stanley Street. New York: Walker and Co., 1974.

2501 Caldwell, Erskine. "Clementine," in Caldwell, Certain Women. Little, 1957.

2502 Capote, Truman. "Breakfast at Tiffany's," in Capote, Breakfast at Tiffany's. Random House, 1958.

2503 Carco, Francis. Les Malheurs de Fernande. Paris: L'Edition, 1918.

2504 Carlino, Lewis John. "Snowangel," in Carlino, Cages: Snowangel [and] Epiphany. Random House, 1963.

2505 Carter, Herbert Dyson. Sin and Science. New York: Heck-Cattell Pub. A novel dealing with male prostitution.

2506 Carson, Daniel Goodman. Hagar Revelly. New York: M. Kennerly, 1913.

2507 Carver, George. "Scarlet One," in The Midland; stories from the Midland. Knopf, 1924.

2508 Chekov, Anton. The Chourus Girl and Her Lover's Wife and Other Stories. Girard, Kan.: Little Blue Books.

2509 Chickamatsu, Monzaemon. "The Girl From Hakata; or Love at Sea," Tr. by Donald Keene in Chickamatsu, Major Plays of Chickamatsu. Columbia Univ. Press, 1961.

2510 Cliff, Ruth. The Followers. Evans, 1970.

2511 Cobb, Irving S. "Field of Honor," in Cobb, Local Color. Doran, 1916.

2512 Cocteau, J. "The Fantom of Marseilles," in Orlovitz, G. ed., The Award Avantgarde Reader. Award Books, 1965.

2513 Colton, John and Randolph, Clemence. "Rain." (based on W. Somerset Maugham's short story "Miss Thompson"), in Gassner, J., ed., Best American Plays; supplementary volume 1918-1958. Crown, 1961.

2514 Cooper, Giles. Everything in the Garden. Evans, 1963.

2515 Coppie, Françoise. "Poet and the Courtesan," in Coppie, Tales for Christmas, and Other Seasons. Tr. by Myrta Leonora Jones. Little, 1900.

2516 Cortazar, Julio. "The Other Heaven," in All Fires the Fire, and Other Stories. Tr. from the Spanish by Suzanne Jill Levine. Pantheon Books, 1973.

2517 The Courtesan's Jewel Box--Chinese Stories of the Xth-XVIIth Centuries. tr. by Yang Hsien-Yi and Gladys Yang. Peking Foreign Language Press, 1957.

2518 Coward, Noel Pierce. "Aunt Tittie," in Coward, To Step Aside. Doubleday, 1939.

2519 Crane, S. "Adventures of a Novelist," in Crane, The Red Badge of Courage, and Selected Prose and Poetry. Holt, 1968.

2520 ____. Maggie: a Girl of the Streets, in The Complete Novels of Stephan Crane. Doubleday, 1967, 821 pp. Also Oxford, 1960, (The World Classics).

2521 Curley, Daniel. "The Fugitive," in Curley, The Marriage Bed of Procrustes, and Other Stories. Beacon Press, 1957.

2522 _______. "A Story of Love, etc.," in Best American Short Stories, 1964. Houghton, 1964.

2523 Defoe, Daniel. The Fortunes and Misfortunes of the Famous Moll Flanders. Harcourt, Oxford, Dutton ed. available; first pub. 1722.

2524 ______. Roxanna. Various editions.

2525 Dobie, Charles C. "Pietro Galli--Scavenger," in Dobie, San Francisco Tales. Appleton, 1937.

2526 Dolan, Harry. "Crazy Nigger," in Schulberg, B. ed., From the Ashes: Voices of Watts. New American Library, 1967.

2527 Donoso, Jose. "Hell Has No Limits," in Triple Cross. Dutton, 1972.

2528 Dorr, Lawrence. "Curfew," in Dorr, A Slow, Soft River. Eerdmans, 1973.

2529 Dumas, Alexander. Camille. Modern Library, 1970, 270 pp. Other editions.

2530 Duprey, P. "Elisa the Hustler," in Howes, B., ed., From the Green Antilles: Writings of the Caribbean. Macmillan, 1966.

2531 Durrell, Lawrence. Tunc. New York: E. P. Dutton and Co. Reviewed in New York Times Book Review, Apr. 14, 1968, p.4.

2532 The Dutch Courtesan--Marston. Ed by M. L. Wine. Regents Renaissance Drama Series, Bison Books ('67-'68 catalogue), University of Nebraska Press.

2533 Dyer, Charles. Rattle of a Simple Man. London: French, 1963.

2534 Eyen, Tom. "The White Whore and the Bit Player," in Eyen, Sarah B. Dinnel and Other Plays." Winter House, 1971.

2535 Eastlake, W. "Unhappy Hunting Grounds," in Best American Short Stories, 1957. Houghton, 1957.

2536 Eldridge, Paul. "Birds of a Feather," in Eldridge, Men and Women. Acherman, 1946.

2537 _______. "Ingratitude Begins at Home," in Eldridge, Tales of the Fortunate Isles. Yoseloff, 1959.

2538 _______. "Madamoiselle Apertif," in Eldridge, One Man Show. Liveright, 1933.

2539 _______. "Santita," in Eldridge, Tales of the Fortunate Isles. Yoseloff, 1959.

2540 Ellison, Harlan. "The Very Last Day of a Good Woman," in Ellison, Alone Against Tomorrow; stories of alienation in speculative fiction. Macmillan , 1971.

2541 _______. "What I Did On My Vacation This Summer, by little Bobby Hirschorn, age 27," in Ellison, Love Ain't Nothing But Sex Misspelled. Trident Press, 1968.

2542 Evans, Max. "The Returning," in Evans, Southwest Wind. Naylor, 1958.

2543 "The Faithful Harlot," (Yu T'ang Ch'un). Tr. by Josephine Huang Hung in Hung, Classic Chinese Plays. Drama Book Specialists Pub., 1971.

2545 Faulkner, William. "The Bordello," in Watkins, A., Taken at the Flood. Harper, 1946.

2546 ________. The Reivers; a reminiscence. New York: Random House, 1962. Set in a house of prostitution in Memphis run by Miss Reba who also appeared in Sanctuary.

2547 ________. Sanctuary. New York: Random House, 1931.

2548 ________. "Uncle Bud and the Three Prostitutes," in Faulkner, The Portable Faulkner. Ed. by Malcolm Cowley. Viking, 1946.

2549 Ferber, Edna. "Woman Who Tried to be Good," in Ferber, One Basket. Doubleday, 1957.

2550 Ferbleman, Peter S. "Fever," in Ferbleman, Strangers and Graves. Atheneum Press, 1966.

2551 Ferraretti, Salvatore. Maisons Closes (Chase Chiuse); a drama in three acts. Naples, 1953, 45 pp.

2552 Fielding, Henry. "The Covent Garden Tragedy," in Trussler, S., ed., Burlesque Plays of the Eighteenth Century. Oxford, 1969.

2553 Filippo, Eduardo de. "Filumena Marturano," tr. by Eric Bentley in Corrigan, R. W., Masterpieces of Modern Italian Theatre. Collier Books, 1967.

2554 Franklin, Benjamin. Satires and Bagatelles. Ed. by Paul McPharlin. Detroit: Fine Book Circle, 1937.

2555 Friedman, Bruce J. "Let Me See Faces," in Friedman, Black Angels. Simon and Schuster, 1966.

2556 Galsworthy, John. "Defeat," in Galsworthy, The Apple Tree and Other Stories. Scribner, 1925; Tatterdemalion. Scribner, 1920; and Caravan. Scribner, 1925.

2557 Gardner, Gary. "A Train Going Somewhere," in Best Short Plays, 1968. Dadd, 1968.

2558 Gary, Romain. Lady L.. Simon and Schuster, 1959.

2559 Gautier, Theophile. "The Dead Lemon," in Caillois R., ed., The Dream Adventure. Orion, 1963.

2560 Genet, Jean. The Balcony. Tr. by Bernard Frechtman. Rev. ver. Faber, 1966 (c1958).

2561 Gerber, Merrie J. "Miss Mosh," in Gerber, Stop Here My Friend. Houghton, 1965.

2562 Glaze, Eleanor. "This Certainly Day," in Glaze, The Embrace and Stories. Bobbs, 1970.

2563 Glynn, Thomas. "Luz," in Voices of Brooklyn. ALA, 1973.

2564 Gold, Michael. Jews Without Money. An autobiographical novel. Reprinted Garden City, New York: Sun Dial Press, 1946.

2565 Gold, Ivan. "Change of Air," in Best American Short Stories, 1954. Houghton, 1954.

2566 _____. "Kimoko's Tale," in Nickel Miseries. Viking, 1963.

2567 Gover, Robert. One Hundred Dollar Misunderstanding. New York: Grove Press, 1962. Gover did several other novels with the same heroine.

2568 Graham, R. B. C. "Signalled," in Graham, Rodeo. Doubleday, 1934.

2569 _______. "Un Autre Monsieur," in Graham, Rodeo. Doubleday, 1936.

2570 Greene, Graham. "Jubilee," in Greene, 21 Stories. Viking, 1962.

2571 Grushenka, or Three Times a Woman. USSR, limited edition, 1928. Book published to call attention to abuses to women by the Czarist regime. Various English editions.

2572 Hammond, J. Hell Raisers of Wycombe.

2573 Hamp, Pierre. "Fried Potato Sisters," in Benjamin, L. S., and Hargreaves, R., eds., Great French Short Stories. Liveright, 1928.

2574 Hyashi, F. "Bones," in Saeki, S., ed. The Shadow of Sunrise; selected stories of Japan and the war. Kodansha, 1966.

2575 Haycox, Ernest. "Stage to Lordsburg," in Blacker, I. R., ed., The Old West in Fiction. Obolensky, 1961.

2576 Hemingway, Ernest. "Light of the World," in Hemingway, Hemingway Reader. Scribner, 1953.

2577 Heyward, Louis M. Grandpa and the Girls. New York: Permabooks, 1960.

2578 Himes, Chester. "A Nigger," in Himes, Black on Black: Baby Sitter and Selected Writings. Doubleday, 1973.

2579 Hippius, Zinaida. "Humility," in Hippius, Selected Works of Zinaida Hippius, tr. by Temira Pachmuss. Univ. of Illinois Press, 1972.

2580 Hoch, Edward D. "The Ripper of Storyville," in Mystery Writers of America, Dear Dead Days; the 1972 Mystery Writers of America anthology. Walker and Co., 1972.

2581 Hughes, Langston. "Soul Gone Home," in Hughes, Five Plays. Indiana Univ. Press. 1963.

2582 Huie, W. B. The Revolt of Mamie Stover. New York: Duell, Sloan and Pierce, 1951. A fictionalized prostitute heroine.

2583 Hunt, Hugh Allyn. "Acme Rooms and Sweet Marjorie Russell," in Best American Short Stories, 1967. Houghton, 1967.

2584 Hyams, Edward. "The Lover," in Turner, J., ed., Thy Neighbor's Wife. Stein and Day, 1968.

2585 Isherwood, Christopher. The Berlin Stories. New York: James Laughlin, 1946.

2586 Jackson, Charles Reginald. "Old Men and Boys," in Jackson, Earthly Creatures. Farrar, Straus, 1953.

2587 Jamieson, Morley. "Madame X," in Reid, J. M., ed., Scottish Short stories. Oxford, 1963.

2588 Jones, J. From Here To Eternity. New York: Scribner, 1951.

2589 Jones, Leroi. "Experimental Death Unit No. 1," in Four Black Revolutionary Plays. Bobbs, 1969.

2590 ______. "The Heretics," in Allen, D. M. and Creeley, R., eds., New American Story. Grove, 1965.

2591 Jouve, P. J. "In a Certain House," in Lehmann, J., ed., Modern French Stories. Faber, 1956.

2592 Kanin, Garson. "All Through the House," in Kanin, Cast of Characters; Stories of Broadway and Hollywood. Atheneum Pub., 1969.

2593 ______. "Define the Word Wife," in Kanin, Cast of Characters; Stories of Broadway and Hollywood. Atheneum Pub., 1969.

2594 ______. The Rat Race. New York: Dramatist Play Service, 1950. Girl who won a dance contest falls on hard times--about how to become a call girl.

2595 Karlen, Arno. "Serantha and the Boys," in Short Stories, 2. Scribner, 1959,

2596 Karlin, Wayne. "R and R," in Karlin, et al, Free Fire Zone; short stories from Viet Nam veterans. McGraw, 1973.

2597 Kauffman, R. W. House of Bondage. Moffat, 1910.

2598 Kawabata, Yasunari. "House of the Sleeping Beauties," in Yasunari, House of the Sleeping Beauties and Other Stories, tr. by Edward G. Seidensticker. Kodansha, 1969.

2599 Kerouac, J. "Billowy Trip in the World," in New Directions in Prose and Poetry, 16. New Directions, 1957.

2600 _____. "October in the Railroad Earth," in Evergreen Review Reader, 1957-67. Grove, 1968. Same as "The Railroad Earth."

2601 Kiki. The Education of a French Model; memoirs introduced by Ernest Hemingway. New York: Belmont Books, 1962.

2602 Kluge, Alexander. "Anita G.," in Kirkbride, Attendance List for a Funeral, tr. from the German by Leila Venneintz. McGraw, 1966.

2603 Konstantinov, Konstantin. "Day By Day," in Kirilov, N. and Kirk, F. eds., Introduction to Modern Bulgarian Literature. Twayne, 1969.

2604 Kuprin, A. Yama. New York: Bernard Guilbert Guerney, 1922.

2605 Lagerkvist, P. The Death of Ahasuerus, tr. from the Swedish by Naomi Walford. Random, 1962, 118 pp.

2606 _____. "The Philosopher's Stone," tr. by Thomas R. Buckman in Lagerkvist, Modern Theatre. Univ. of Neb. Press, 1966.

2607 La Guma, Alex. "Slipper Satin," in Rive, R., ed., Quartet: New Voices From South Africa. Crown, 1963.

2608 Landau, Mark Aleksandrovich. "The Ruby," in Landau, Night at the Airport. Scribner, 1949.

2609 Lauckner, Rolf. "Cry in the Streets," tr. by Maurice Edwards and Valerie Reich, in Solhel, W. H., ed., Anthology of German Expressionist Drama. Anchor Books, 1963.

2610 Leskov, Nikolai. "Deception," in Leskov, Satirical Stories of Nikolai Leskov. Pegasus, 1969.

2611 Lessing, Doris. "Mrs. Fortescue," in Winter's Tales, 9. St. Martins, 1963.

2612 _____. "A Road to the Big City," in Lessing, African Stories. Simon and Schuster, 1965, and in Lessing, Habit of Loving. Crowell, 1957.

2613 Lewis, Sinclair. Elmer Gantry. New York: Harcourt Brace, 1927.

2614 Loos, A. Gentlemen Prefer Blondes. London: Brentano, 1926.

2615 Loury, Robert James Collas. "New York Call Girl," in Loury, New York Call Girl. Doubleday, 1958.

2616 Luce, C. Booth. "Blyss Girl," in Luce, Stuffed Shirts, Liveright, 1931.

2617 Lynds, Dennis. "Just Once More," in New Voices, 2: American Writing Today. Hendricks House, 1955.

2618 Malamud, Bernard. "God's Wrath," in Best American Short Stories, 1973. Houghton, 1973.

2619 Mallet-Joris, Françoise. "The Ashtray," in Mallet-Joris, Cordelia and Other Stories, tr. by Peter Green. Farrar, Straus, 1965.

2620 ________. "Jimmy," in Mallet-Joris, Cordelia and Other Stories, tr. by Peter Green. Farrar, Straus, 1965.

2621 Manhoff, Bill. The Owl and The Pussycat. French and Doubleday editions, 1965.

2622 Mankowitz, Wolf. "The Last Cheesecake," in Mankowitz, Five One-act Plays. Evans, 1964., (c1956).

2623 Mason, R. The World of Suzie Wong. New York: Signet, 1957.

2624 Maupassant, Guy de. "Ball of Fat," in Maupassant, Complete Short Stories. Hanover House, 1955.

2625 ________. "Florentine," in Maupassant, Complete Short Stories. Hanover House, 1955.

2626 ________. "Graveyard Sirens," in Maupassant, The Tales of Guy de Maupassant, tr. by Lafcadio Hearn and others. Heritage, 1964.

2627 ________. "In Port," in Maupassant, Portable Maupassant. Viking, 1947. Also in Useless Beauty.

2628 ________. "Madame Tellier's Establishment," in Bercovici, K. ed., Best Short Stories of the World. Stratford, 1917 and in Maupassant, Madame Tellier's Establishment and Short Stories. Pearson, 1910

2629 ________. "Madame Tellier's Excursion," in Maupassant, Complete Short Stories. Blue Ribbon Books, 1941.

2630 ________. "Mademoiselle Fifi," in Maupassant, Complete Short Stories. Blue Ribbon Books, 1941 and in Mademoiselle Fifi and Other Stories, tr. by Ernest Boyd. Knopf, 1922 (Collected Novels and Stories, v.2).

2631 ________. "Odyssey of a Prostitute," in Maupassant, Olive Orchard and Other Stories. Knopf, 1925 (collected Novels and Stories, v.4). Same as "Poor Girl."

2632 ________. "Poor Girl," in Maupassant, Complete Short Stories, Blue Ribbon Books, 1941. Same as "Odyssey of a Prostitute."

2633 ________. "The Port," in Maupassant, Complete Short Stories. Blue Ribbon Books, 1941. Same as "In Port."

2634 ________. "Roly-Poly," (Boule de Suif), in Maupassant, The Tales of Guy de Maupassant, tr. by Lafcadio Hearn and others. Heritage, 1964. Same as "Ball of Fat."

2635 Mayer, Paul Avila. "Eternal Triangle," in Mayer, Three Hand Reel. Dramatists, 1967.

2636 McCleary, Dorothy. "Winter," in Burnett, W. and Burnett, H., eds., The Modern Short Story in the Making. Hawthorn Books, 1964.

2637 McPherson, James Alan. "An Act of Prostitution," in McPherson, Hue and Cry. Little, 1969.

2638 McWhirter, G. "The Harbinger," in New Canadian Stories, '72. Oberon Press, 1972-3.

2639 Mokuami, Kawatake. The Love of Izayoi and Sheishin. Tr. by Frank T. Motofugi. Tuttle, 1966.

2640 Monteilhet, H. Andromache; or The Inadvertent Murder. New York: Simon and Schuster, 1970, 175 pp.

2641 Moorsi, George. "The Hat," Moorsi, A Duck May Be Somebody's Mother. Delacorte Press, 1967.

2642 Mortimer, Chapman. Amparo. London: Weidenfeld and Nicolson, 1971, 175 pp.

2643 Morang, Alfred. "A Quarter For The Gas," in Morang, The Works of Alfred Morang. Ker-Ban Enterprises, 1965.

2644 Moravia, Alberto. "Confusion," in Moravia, Bought and Sold, Tr. by Angus Davidson. Farrar, Straus, 1973 (c1971).

2645 ________. "Consumer Goods," in Moravia, Bought and Sold, tr. by Angus Davidson. Farrar, Straus, 1973 (c1971).

2646 ________. "Home is a Sacred Place," in Moravia, The Wayward Wife and Other Stories. Farrar, Straus, 1960.

2647 Morrien, Adriaan. "Hijo de Puta," in Literary Review, Modern Stories From Many Lands. Maryland Books, 1963.

2648 Moseley, William. "The Preacher and Margery Scott," in The Best American Short Stories, 1968. Houghton, 1968.

2649 Nakamoto, Takako. "The Only One," in Gluck, J. ed., Ukiyo: Stories of the "Floating World" of Postwar Japan. Vanguard, 1963.

2650 Nathan, Robert. One More Spring. First published 1933.

2651 Newman, G. F. Three Professional Ladies. Dell.

2652 Oates, Joyce Carol. "Love and Death," in Matthews, J., ed., Archetypal Themes in the Modern Story. St. Martins, 1973.

2653 O'Casey, Sean. The Plough and the Stars. A play. Rosie Redmond is a prostitute.

2654 O'Hara, John. "Barred," in O'Hara, Barred and Other Stories. Random House, 1968.

2655 ______. Butterfield 8. New York: Harcourt Brace, 1935.

2656 ______. "Ninety Minutes Away," in O'Hara, The Hat on the Bed. Random House, 1963.

2657 O'Neill, Eugene. "Anna Christie," in O'Neill, The Emperor Jones, Anna Christie, The Hairy Ape. Modern Library, 1964 (c1937).

2658 _______. "The Web," in O'Neill, Ten "Lost" Plays. Random House, 1964.

2659 Ostaijen, Paul Van. "The Loch's Brothel," in Ostaijen, Patriotism, Inc. and Other Tales, tr. by E. M. Beckman. Univ. of Mass. Press, 1971.

2660 O'Sullivan, Laurence. "Madonna and Metronome," in O'Sullivan, An Hour After Requiem and Other Stories. Doubleday, 1966.

2661 Ovid, Amores, ed. and tr. by Grant Showerman. Loeb Classical Library. London: WH, 1921. Many editions.

2662 Ovid, The Art of Love, tr. by Charles D. Young. New York: Liveright Pub. Corp., 1931. Many editions.

2663 Paquet, B. T. "Warren," in Karlin, W., et al, Free Fire Zone; short stories by Viet Nam veterans. McGraw, 1973.

2664 Parker, James Reid. "Welcome to Aunt Kitty's," in London, E., The World of Law, v.1. Simon and Schuster, 1960.

2665 Patrick, Vincent. "Ramon," in New Voices 4: American Writing Today. Hendricks House, 1960.

2666 Plautus. "Poenulus; or the little Carthaginian," tr. by Janet Burroway, in Bovie, P. ed., Five Roman Comedies. Dutton, 1970. Many othe52r editions.

2667 Petrakis, Harry Mack. "Rosemary," in Petrakis, The Waves of Night, and Other Stories. McKay, 1969.

3100 Phillips, Robert. "Obsession," in Phillips, The Land of Lost Content. Vanguard, 1970.

2668 Pincherle, Alberto. "Tired Courtesan," in Pincherle, Bitter Honeymoon and Other Stories. Farrar, Straus, 1956.

2669 Pirandello, Luigi. "Chee-Chee," tr. by William Murray in Pirandello, Pirandello's One Act Plays. Anchor Books, 1964.

2670 ________. "All Passion Spent," in Pirandello, Short Stories, tr. by Frederick May. Oxford, 1965.

2671 ________. "Yesterday and Today," in Pirandello, Short Stories, tr. by Lily Duplaix. Simon and Schuster, 1959.

2672 Porter, Katherine Anne. "Magic," in Porter, Old Order. Harcourt, 1955.

2673 Premchand. "The Road to Hell," in Premchand, The World of Premchand, tr. by David Rubin. Ind. Univ. Press, 1969.

2674 Prevost, Abbe. Manon Lescaut. 1964.

2675 Rechy, J. City of Night. New York: Grove Press, 1963. Male prostitution in the U. S.

2676 Reiter, Charles Jules. This Night in Sodom. Grove, 1962.

2677 Ribnikar, Jara. "She," in Ribnikar, I and You and She, tr. by Eva Tucker. McGraw, 1972.

2678 Rice, Cale Young. "No News," in Rice, A. C. H. and Rice C. Y., Passionate Follies: Alternate Tales. Appleton, 1936.

2679 Rich, R. First Victorian; or, Sweet Celandine. London: Hale, 1971, 240 pp.

2680 Robins, E. My Little Sister. Dodd, 1913.

2681 Rosenfeld, Isaac. "Alpha and Omega," in Rosenfeld, Alpha and Omega. Viking, 1966.

2682 Rumaker, Michael. "Gringos," in Rumaker, Gringos and Other Stories. Grove, 1967 (c1966).

2683 Sallis, James. "The Fevors of His Heart," in Sallis, A Few Last Words. Macmillan, 1970.

2684 Samuels, Gertrude. "The Corrupters," in Best Short Plays. Dodd, 1969.

2685 Sender, Rumon. "The Red Light," in Sender, Tales of Cibola, tr. by Florence Sender and Others. Los Americas Pub., 1964.

2686 Shadbolt, Maurice. "Maria," in Shadbolt, The New Zealanders. Antheneum Pub, 1961, (c1959).

2687 Shapiro, Lamed. "Principles," in Shapiro, The Jewish Government, and Other Stories, tr. by Curt Leviant. Twayne, 1971.

2688 Sharma, Partap. A Touch of Brightness. Grove, 1968.

2689 Shaw, Bernard. "Mrs. Warren's Profession," in Shaw, Plays Unpleasant. Penguin, 1961.

2690 Schoenfeld, Abraham H. The Joy Peddler. New York: privately printed.

2691 Singer, Issac Bashevis. "In the Poorhouse," in Singer, Selected Short Stories of Issac Bashevis Singer. Modern Library, 1966.

2692 ___________. "Yanda," in Singer, The Seance and Other Stories. Farrar, Straus, 1968.

2693 Sitati, Paul. "Jane," in Angoff, C. and Povey, J., eds., African Writing Today. Manyland Books, 1970 (c1969).

2694 Slade, C. Mrs. Party's House. New York: Vanguard, 1948.

2695 ____. Sterile Sun. New York: Vanguard, 1934.

2696 Slauerhoff, Jan Jacob. "Larrio's," in Greshoff, J., ed., Harvest of the Lowlands; an anthology in English translation of creative writing in the Dutch language. Querido, 1945.

2697 Smith, W. Bessie Cotter.

2698 Sterling, Thomas. "Bedlam's Rent," in Prize Stories, 1969; the O. Henry awards. Doubleday, 1969.

2699 Stinetorf, Louise A. La China Poblana. Indianapolis: Bobbs Merrill, 1960. A recreation of the life of Myrrha Pagus who was sold as a white slave in Mexico.

2700 Stories of Scarlet Women. New York: Avon Books, 1955.

2701 Taggart, John. "They Fell Thunderously, and His Armour Clattered Upon Him," in The Great Lakes Anthology, 1. Antioch Press, 1964.

2702 Taylor, Peter. "The Fancy Woman," in Contemporary American Short Stories. Fawcett, 1967 and in Taylor, The Collected Stories Of Peter Taylor. Farrar, Straus, 1969.

2703 Theroux, Paul. "Memories of a Curfew," in Theroux, Sinning with Annie and Other Stories. Houghton, 1972.

2704 Thousand Nights. Various translations: John Payne, Richard Burton, et al.

2705 Thurman, Wallace. "Cordelia the Crude," in Turner, D. T., ed., Black American Literature; essays, poetry, drama, fiction. Merrill, 1970.

2706 Trevisan, Dalton. "Dear Old Girl," in Trevisan, The Vampire of Curitiba and Other Stories, tr. from the Portuguese by Gregory Rabassa. Knopf, 1972.

2707 ______. "The Girl From Normal School," in Trevisan, The Vampire of Curitiba and Other Stories, tr. from the Portuguese by Gregory Rabassa. Knopf, 1972.

2708 ______. "Passion Night," in Trevisan, The Vampire of Curtiba and Other Stories, tr. from the Portuguese by Gregory Rabassa. Knopf, 1972.

2709 Tuohy, Frank. "A Survivor in Salvador," in Tuohy, The Admiral and the Nuns, and Other Stories. Scribner, 1962 and in Publisher's Choice. Scribner, 1967.

2710 ______. "Two Private Lives," in Winter's Tales. St. Martins, 1955.

2711 Uhnak, D. Ledger. New York: Simon and Schuster, 1970; Pocket Books, 1972.

2712 Vargas Llosa, Mario. The Greenhouse, tr. from the Spanish by Gregory Rabassa. Harper, 1968, 405 pp.

2713 Villiers de I'Isle, Adam. "Maryelle," in Villiers de I'Isle, Cruel Tales. Oxford, 1963. (The Oxford Library of French Classics).

2714 Villiers de I'Isle, Adam. "Maryelle," in Cruel Tales. Oxford, 1963. (The Oxford Library of French Classics).

2715 Villon, François. The Complete Works, tr. by Anthony Bonner. New York: David McKay, 1960. Other editions.

2716 ______. Poems, tr. by John Payne. London: Villon Society, 1892. Other editions.

2717 Vynnychenko, Volodymyr. "A Strange Episode," in Luckyi, G. S. N., ed., Modern Ukrainian Short Stories. Ukrainian Academic Press, 1973.

2718 Wallace, Irving. The Nympho and Other Maniacs. New York: Simon and Schuster, 1971.

2719 Waltari, Mika Toimi. "Goldilocks," in Waltari, Moonscape, and Other Stories, tr. by Naomi Walford. Putnam, 1954.

2720 Walters, Michael. *Horns Up*. No. Hollywood, Calif.: Dominion Pub. Co., 1969.

2721 Ward, Douglas Turner. *The Reckoning*. Dramatists, 1970.

2722 Warren, Robert Penn. "Statement of Ashby Wyndham," in Lytle, A., ed. *Craft and Vision*; the best from *Sewanie Review*. Delacorte Press, 1971.

2723 Weidman, Jerome. *Asterisk!*. Dramatists, 1969.

2724 Wharton, Edith. "New Years Day," in Wharton, E. *Old New York*, v.4. Scribner, 1952.

2725 "The Whore With the Pure Heart," in Bauer, W. and Franke, H., ed., *The Golden Casket*; Chinese novellas of two millennia, tr. by Christopher Levenson. Harcourt, 1964.

2726 Williams, T. "Hello From Bertha," in Williams, T., *27 Wagons Full of Cotton, and Other One-act Plays*. New Directions, 1953.

2727 Williams, T. "Yellow Bird," in Williams, *One Arm, and Other Stories*. New Directions, 1954.

2728 Williamson, J. C. "Swede Nelson, All-American," in Williamson, *The Deep Treasure: Tales of the Oilfields*. Crown, 1960.

2729 ________. "You Know Tom McLain," in Williamson, *The Deep Treasure: Tales of the Oilfields*. Crown, 1960.

2730 Wilson, Lanford. "Balm in Giliad," in Wilson, *Balm and Giliad, and Other Plays*. Hill and Wang, 1965.

2731 Winslow, Thyra Samter. "Ruby Moon," in Winslow, *My Own Native Land*. Doubleday, 1935.

2732 Wolfe, Bernard. "Marcianna and the Naturae Carpaine in Papaya," in Gold, D., ed., *The Human Committment*. Chilton Books, 1967.

2733 Wolfe, Thomas. "Face of the War," in Thorp, W., ed., *Southern Reader*. Knopf, 1955.

2734 Woollcott, Alexander. "Entrance Fee," in *Bedside Tales*. Penn, 1945. Same as "Histoire de France."

2735 __________. "Histoire de France," in Cain, J. M., ed., *For Men Only*. World Pub., 1944. Same as "Entrance Fee."

2736 Wright, Richard. "Big, Black Good Men," in *Best American Short Stories, 1958*. Houghton, 1958.

2737 Wynne, John Huddleston. The Prostitute; a poem. London: J. Wheble, 1771, 44 pp.

2738 Yordan, P. Anna Lucasta. Dramatists, 1950.

2739 Zola, Emile. Nana. New York: Pocket Books, Inc., 1941. Other editions.

2740 Zweig, Stefan. Kaleidoscope. Tr. by Eden and Cedar Paul. Viking, 1934.

2741 Zweig, Stefan. "Moonbeam Alley," in Haydn Hand Cournos, J., ed., World of Great Stories. Crown, 1947.

2742 Adam, J. R. The Pretty Girls of London, Their Little Love Affairs, Playful Doings, etc.. Depicted in 12 spirited lithographic drawings by Quiz. Cited in Pisanus Fraxi.

2743 Almanach des Adresses des Demoiselles de Paris de Tout Genre et Toutes les Classes. Paris: de l'Impreimerie de l'Amour, 1791. Cited in Fleishmann, Les Demoiselles.

2744 Almanach Nouveau des Citoyennes Bien Actives de Paris; consacrees aux plaisirs de la Republique contennant la notice exacte des femmes devouees a la paillardise par temperament, part interet et par besoin, leurs noms, qualites, ages, demeures, et le tarif de leurs appas, tout a prix fixe qu'au caseul.... Paris: Impremire de Blondy, 1793.

2745 L'Amour a l'Encan; ou la tactique secrete de la Galanterie devoilee, Revue semi-morale, semi-folatre des serails patentes de la Capital, et. Paris: Librairie Française et Etrangere, 1829.

2746 Les Bordels de Paris Avec Leurs Noms, Demeures et Prix. Paris, 1790.

2747 Boyhood Photos of J. H. Lartique: The Family Album of A. G. Hedaye. Time-Life Books, 1950, 1966. Includes photos of famous prostitutes.

2748 Cahier des Representations et Doleances due Beau Sexe; adresse au Roi, au moment de la tenue des Etats Generaux. Paris: 1789, BN, Lb 39, 7090.

2749 The Cheats of London. London: 1766.

2750 Commenge, O. La Prostitution Clandestine a Paris. Paris: 1897.

2751 Cuissin, P. Les Nymphes du Palais Royal. Paris: 1815.

2752 Les Dames de Maison et les Filles d'Amour Avec des Notions Sur les Differens Bordels de Paris et les Maisons de Passe. Paris: c1830.

2753 Defrance, E. La Maison de Madame Gourdan. Paris: 1908.

2754 Les Demoiselles du Palai-Royal aux Etats-Generaux. Paris, 1789, BN, Lb 39, 1750.

2755 Les demoiselles Chit-Chit du Palais-Royal et des differenes Quartiers de Paris; traitees selon leur merite, leur age, leur beaute, leur taille, leur caractere. Paris: de L'Impremiere de Caillot et Courcier, 1793.

2756 Le Depart des Belles Femmes en Grand Costume pour Embellir Longchamps Pendant Trois jour; avec la liste de leurs noms. Se trouve a Paris sour le vestible due theatre de la

Republique. 8 pp.

2757 Dictionnaire Anecdotique des Nymphes du Palais-Royal et Autres Quartiers de Paris; par un Homme de Bien. Paris: Marchands de Nouveautes, 1826.

2758 L'Espion Libertin ou le Calendrier du Plaisir; contenant le list des joiles femmes de Paris, leur noms, demeures, talents, qualites et savoir-faire, suivie des prix de leurs charmes. 1803, reprinted Brussels: 1882. Cited in Flieshmann, Les Demoiselles.

2759 d'Estoc, Marchal. Paris-Eros. Paris: 1903.

2760 The Everleigh Club. (Views of the exterior and interior.) Chicago: n. t. p., 1902, 31 pp.

2761 Les Fastes Scandaleux ou Galerie des Plus Aimables Conquines de Paris, etc. 2d edition, revised and corrected 1796, 32 pp.

2762 Fleishmann, Hector. Les Demoiselles d'Amour du Palais-Royal. Paris: 1911.

2763 The Ghost of Moll King, or a Night at Derry's; an exact description of the most celebrated Ladies of Pleasure who frequent Covent-Garden and Other Posts likewise those in keeping their keepers. London: 1785.

2764 Harris List of Covent-Garden Ladies or a New Atlantis for the Year. or variation on the title Harris List of Covent-Garden Ladies: or Man of Pleasure's Kalender; containing an exact description of the most celebrated Ladies of Pleasure who frequent Covent Garden and Other Parts of this Metropolis. London: H. Ranger, Temple Exchange, many editions beteen 1760-1793.

2765 Hervez, Jean. Maisons d'Amour et Filles de Joie. Paris: 1911.

2766 Hibbeler, Ray. Upstairs at the Everleigh Club; the inside story of Chicago's famed mansion of Sex where Millionaires, Princes and Playboys filled the Beds. Volitant Books, n. d., 127 pp.

2767 The Humours of Fleet-Street and the Strand. London: Printed for A. Wright, 1748, 97 pp. Descriptions of the houses.

2768 Joli Peches des Nymphes du Palais-Royal; rues et faubourgs de Paris. Paris: 1801. Reprinted several times in Geneva and Brussels. Cited in Gay.

2769 Liste Complete des Plus Belles Femmes Publiques et des Plus Saines du Palais de Paris; leurs gout et caprices, le prix de leurs charmes et les roles que remplissoient quelques-unes dans plusiers theatres. Paris: 1793. Cited by Fleishmann,

Les Demoiselles.

2770 The Midnight Sky or a View of the Transactions of London and Westminster From the Hours of Ten in the Evening till Five in the Morning. London: 1766.

2771 New Orleans. (Guidebooks to the Houses of Prostitution). 1. The Green Book; or Gentlemen's Guide to New Orleans, announced as published in 1895. Do not know of any existing copies; 2. The Lid. 8 unnumbered pages. New Orleans: before 1900; 3. HELL-O. 8 unnumbered pages. New Orleans: about 1900; 4. Sporting Guide, of the Tender-loing District of New Orleans, La., where the four hundred can be found. 24 unnumbered pages. New Orleans: very early 1900's; 5. Blue Book; Tenderloin 400. 40 unnumbered pages and despite its title, it has a greenish cover. New Orleans: 1895; 6. A Directory of the Tenderloing; being a comprehensive and accurate record of the addresses of the sporting Ladies in that portion of the town commonly known as Storyville. Give them a call, boys, and you'll get treated right. 24 pp., red cover. New Orleans: 1903; 7. Blue Book. Gray cover, 92 unnumbered pages. 6th ed New Orleans: 1905; 8. Blue Book. Lavender cover, 7th ed, 1906; 9. Blue Book. 104 unnumbered pages, blue cover, 8th ed, 1907; 10. Blue Book. 96 unnumbered pages, red cover, 9th ed New Orleans; 11. Blue Book. 96 unnumbered pages, gray cover, 10th ed, 1909; 12. Blue Book. 96 unnumbered pages, gray cover, New Orleans: 1910-1911; 13. Blue Book. 96 unnumbered pages, gray cover, New Orleans: 1911-1912; 14. Blue Book. 96 unnumbered pages, blue cover, New Orleans: 1915.

2772 Nouvelles Liste des Plus Jolies Femmes Publiques de Paris; leurs demeures, qualites et savoir faire, dediee aux amateurs par un connoiseur jure de l'Academie des f----. Paris: 1801. A new edition published in 1805. Cited in Fleishmann, Les Demoiselles.

2773 Observations Critiques d'un Flaneur sur la Promenade de Longchamps ou Examen Joyeus dex Voitures Qui Doivent s'y Rendre Pendant Trois Jours. Impreimerie Aubry, 1790.

2774 La Parc au Cerf; ou l'Origine de l'Affreux Deficit, par un zelepatriote. Paris: 1790.

2775 Les Plaisirs de Longchamps pour l'an IX; noms et qualites de toutes les dames qui doivent s'y trouver avec leurs amiables favoris, details de leurs costumes, couplets acet egard. Paris: an IX (1803), 4 pp.

2776 Porzellanfuhre. A guide to prostitution in Berlin. Various editions.

2777 "Die Prostitution in Berlin und ihre Opfer." Berlin: 1846.

2778 _Le Putanisme d'Amsterdam._ Amsterdam: 1681 and Brussels: 1883 (?).

2779 _Revue de Boudoirs en Vaudevilles ou Liste des Jolies Femmes de Paris; leurs noms et leurs demeures._ Paris: Palais des Plaisirs, year eight, 1802.

2780 Saint-Marc, B. and Marquis de Bourbonne. _Les Chroniques du Palais-Royal._ Paris: 1881.

2781 _Les Serails de Londres._ 1802. New printing, Brussels: (?).

2782 _Les Serails de Paris._ 1802. New printing, Paris: 1885.

2783 Scharold, D. G. "Das Frauenhaus," in _Kuriositaten der Physisch-literarisch-artistisch-historischen Vor-und-Mitwelt._ Weimar: 1822, v.9.

2784 _The Sporting House and Club Directory, Chicago; containing a full and complete list of all strictly finest class club and sporting houses._ Chicago: Ross and St. Clair, 1889, 64 pp.

2785 _Tarif des Filles du Palais-Royal; lieux circonvoisins et autres quartiers de Paris, avec leurs noms et demeures._ Paris: 1790. Cited by Fleishmann, _Les Demoiselles._

2786 _Tres Selrieuses Remonstrances des Filles du Palais-Royal et Lieux Circonvoisins a Mm. de la Nobelsse._ Paris, 1789, BN, Lb 39, 1073.

2787 Acton, W. Prostitution. London: 1857. 2d ed., 1870. Reprinted London: Macgibbon Kee, 1968.

2788 An Essay towards a General History of Whoring From the Creation of the World, to the reign of Augustulus. (1698).

2789 Baldwin, F. D. "Invisible Armour." Am Q 16:432-44, Fall '64.

2790 Bassermann, Lujo. The Oldest Profession; the history of prostitution. New York: Stein and Day Pub., 1968.

2791 Bauer, Max. Liebesleben in Deutscher Vergangenheit. Berlin: P. Langenscheidt, 1924. 75 illustrations.

2792 Bauer, Max. Weih und Sittlichkeit: die sittengeschichte der Deutschen Frau. Berlin: Eigenbrodler Verlag, 1927.

2793 Bauer, Willi. Geschichte und Wesen der Prostitution. Stuttgart: Weltspiegel-Verlag, 1956. rev. ed. pub. in 1960.

2794 Bloch, Iwan. Der Ursprung der Syphilis. 2 v. Jena: Gustav Fischer, 1911. Much on prostitution.

2795 Bloch, Iwan. Die Prostitution. Berlin: Marcus, 1912. (Handbuch der Gesamten Sexualwissenschaft in Einzeldar-steilungen. Bd.1).

2796 Bloch, Iwan and Georg Loewenstein. Die Prostitution. Bd.2. Berlin: Louis Marcus Verlagsbuchhandlung, 1925, 728 pp.

2797 Boiron, N. M. La Prostitution dans le'Histoire--Devant la Droit--Devant l'Opinion. Nancy: 1926. 190 pp.

2798 Brachwitz, Richard. "Die Sittlichen Verhaltnisse im Alten Berlin. Eine Kulturhistorische Betrachtung." Sudhoffs Arch Gesch Med 1942(35):339-347. General pre-20th century history.

2799 Briffault, Robert. The Mothers. London: George Allen and Unwin, 1952. 3v.

2800 Brinton, Crane. A History of Western Morals. New York: Harcourt Brace and Co., 1959.

2801 Bullough, Vern L. The History of Prostitution. New Hyde Park, N. Y.: University Books, 1964, 304 pp. Historical survey from primitive and ancient times to the present.

2802 Bullough, Vern L. The Subordinate Sex: A History of Attitudes Towards Women. Urbana: Univ. of Ill. Press, 1973.

2803 Burgess, William. The World's Social Evil: A Historical Review and Study of the Problems Relating to the Subject. Chicago: Saul, 1914, 413 pp.

2804 Bussy-Rabutin, ____. **Histoire Amoureuse des Gaules.** Ed. by A. Poitevin. Paris: 1858.

2805 Caffarena, Angel. Apuntes Para la Historia de la Mancebias de Malaga. Malaga: Juan Such Libreria Antiquaria El Guaalhorce, 1968. Malaga.

2806 Calhoun, Arthur W. A Social History of the American Family. 3v. Cleveland: Arthur H. Clarke, 1917-19.

2807 Carboneres, Manuel. Picaronas y Alchauetas o la Mancebia de Valencia. Valencia: 1876.

2808 Clarkson, F. A. "History of Prostitution." Canad M A J 41:296-301, Sep. '39.

2809 Compston, Herbert Fuller Bright. The Magdalen Hospital: the Story of a Great Charity, with foreward by the Archbishop of Canterbury. 8v. London: S. P. C. K., 1917.

2810 Damiani, B. M. "Un Aspecto Historico de la Lozana Andaluza." MLN 87:178-92, Mar. '72.

2811 Debray, Th. F. Histore de la Prostitution et de la Debauche Chez Tous les Peuples du Globe Depuis l'Antiquite la Plus Reculee Jusqu'a Nos Jours. Paris: Lambert et Gie, 1880.

2812 Dingwall, Eric John. The Girdle of Chastity. New York: The Macaulay Co., n. d.

2813 Das Dirnentum und der Dirnengeist in der Gesellschaft. Leipzig: Verlag von Max Spohr, 1893, 1918. 119 pp. unbound.

2814 Dufour, Pierre (Paul Lacroix). Historie de la Prostitution Chez tous les Peuples du Monde Depus l'Antiquite la Plus Reculee Jusqu'a nos Jours. 6v. Paris: Lire, 1851-53. 6v. Brussels: Librairie Encyclopedique de Perichon, 1851-54. 7v. Brussels, 1861.

2815 Duhren, Eugen. Englische Sittengeschichte. Berlin: 1912.

2816 Edwardes, Allen. The Jewel in the Lotus: A Historical Survey of the Sexual Culture of the East. New York: The Julian Press, 1960.

2817 Entschleierte Geheimnisse der Prostitution in Hamburg. Leipzig:Julius Koffka, 1847, 103 pp.

2818 Epton, Nina. Love and the English. London: Cassell, 1960.

2819 Epton, Nina. Love and the French. London: Cassell, 1959.

2820 Epton, Nina. Love and the Spanish. Cleveland: World Books, 1962. Reviewed in New York Times, Oct. 14, 1962.

2821 Fournier, Francisque-Michel et Edouard. Histoire des Hotelleries, Cabarets, Courtilles, et des Anciennes Communautes et Confreries d'Hoteliers, de Taverniers, de Marchands de Vin. Paris, 1859.

2822 Fridland, L. From Different Sides. (In Russian) Petropolis: c1931.

2823 Greer, J. H. Prostitution, its History, Cause And Cure. Crucible Pub., 1920.

2824 Guardia, J. M. De La Prostitution en Espagne. This is a supplement to the third edition of Parent-Duchatelet.

2825 Guyot, Yves. La Prostitution. Paris: G. Charpentier, 1882.

2826 Hanauer, W. "Geschichte der Prostitution in Frankfurt a. m.," in Festschrift zum 1. Kongress der Deutschen Gesellschaft zur Bekampfung der Geschlectskrankheiten. Frankfurt a. m., 1903.

2827 Harkness, Georgia. The Sources of Western Morality. New York: Scribner's Sons, 1954.

2828 Harriet, W. Geschichte der Prostitution Aller Volker. Berlin: Schoneberg, Jawerstahl, 1912.

2829 Hartmann, Grethe, Boliger og Bordeller. Copenhagen: 1949. 128 pp.

2830 Hayward, C. Dictionary of Courtesans--an Anthology, Sometimes Gay, Sometimes Tragic, of the Celebrated Courtesans of History From Antiquity to the Present Day--Arranged in Alphebetical Order. New York: University Books, 1962., 491 pp.

2831 d'Henri, ____. Geheimnisse der Prostitution; Enthullungen aus dem Leben der Boheme aller Lander. Leipzig: 1871.

2832 Heywood, Thomas. Nine Books of Various History Concerning Women. London: 1624.

2833 Henriques, Fernando. Prostitution and Society: A Survey. London: MacGibbon, 1962-68. 3v. Contents: Vol.1: Prostitution and Society. Vol.2: Prostitution and the New World. Vol.3: Modern Sexuality.

2834 Hervas, Ramon. Historia de la Prostitution. Barcelona: Telestar, 1969.

2835 Himes, Norman E. "History of the Condom" and, with Randolph Cautley, "Condom," in Encyclopedia Sexualis. New York: Dingwall-Rock, 1936.

2836 "History of Government Control of Prostitution." Westm 93:119.

2837 Hugel, F. Zur Geshichte, Statistik und Regelung der Prostitution. Vienna: 1865.

2838 Hunt, Morton M. Natural History of Love. New York: Alfred A. Knopf, 1959.

2839 Ignacio dos Santo Cruz, Francisco. Da Prostitution na Cidaede de Lisboa. Lisbon: 1841.

2840 Jeanselme, E. Histoire de la Syphilis. Paris: G. Doun et Cie, 1931.

2841 Journaux et Canards Erotiques du Temps Passe. Paris: Les Yeux Ouverts, 1970. France.

2842 Kinsie, Paul M. "Prostitution--Then and Now." Reprinted from J Soc Hygiene. New York: Jun. '53, 10 pp.

2843 Lacroix, Paul (Pierre Dufour). History of Prostitution Among All the Peoples of the World, From the Most Remote Antiquity to the Present Day. tr. from the French by Samuel Putnam. New ed New York: Covici, 1926, 1931, 1932. 2v.

2844 Lecky, W. E. H. A History of European Morals. Reprinted New York: George Braziller, 1955.

2845 Le Pileur, Louis. La Prostitution du XIIIe au XVIIe Siecle. 8v. Paris: H. Champion, 1908.

2846 Lewinsohn, Richard. A History of Sexual Customs. New York: Harper and Bros., 1958. p.26.

2847 Lowe, ____. Die Prostitution Aller Zeiten and Volker. Berlin: 1852.

2848 Lucka, Emil. Eros: The Development of the Sex Relation Through the Ages. New York: G. P. Putnam's Sons, 1915.

2849 Ma, Hs-t'ien. Chinese Agent in Mongolia. Tr. by John de Frances. Baltimore: The John Hopkins Press, 1949, pp.128-29.

2850 Martell, P. "Zur Geschichte der Prostitution der Staadt Berlin." Zsch f Sex.-wiss u Sex Pol 26:133-145. Berlin.

2851 McCabe, Joseph. The Story of the World's Oldest Profession: Protitution in the Ancient, Medieval and Modern Worlds. Girard, Kan.: Haldeman-Julius, 1932, 123 pp.

2852 Meissner, M. I. "Zur Geschichte des Frauenhauses in Altenburg," in Neues Archiv fur Sachsische Geschicte und Alterumskunde. ed. by Hubert Ermisch, II. Dresden: 1881.

2853 Morel de Rubempre,-_____. La Pornologie ou Historie Nouvelle Universelle et Complete de la Debauche de la Prostitution et Autres Depravations. Terry: Palais Royal, Galerie de Valois, n. d., 2v.

2854 Nevill, Ralph. The Romantic Past. London: Chapman and Hall, 1912. History of love.

2855 Parmlee, Maurice. The History of Modern Culture. Ch. 51, "The Function of Prostitution." New York: Philosophical Library, 1960.

2856 Partridge, Burgo. A History of Orgies. New York: Crown Pub., 1960.

2857 Peters, E. Prostitution und Geschlectskrankheiten. Ihre Gesundheitlichen, Sittlichen, Wirtshaftliche und Gesellschaftlichen Schaden und Ihre Bekampfung. Berlin: Kraft und Schonheit, 1908, 104 pp.

2858 Rabutaux, A. P. E. De la Prostitution en Europe Depuis l'Antiquite Jusqu'a la Fin du XVI Siecle. Paris: Lebigre-Duquesne Freres, 1851. p.54.

2859 "Readings and References of Current and Historical Value." J Soc Hygiene. 22:434-8, Dec. '36.

2860 Regnault, F. L'Evolution de la Prostitution. 1906, 354 pp.

2861 Reitman, B. C. Second Oldest Profession. Vanguard, 1931.

2862 Robinson, W. J. Oldest Profession in the World, Prostitution. New York: Eugenics Pub. Co., 1929. Reviewed by B. Reitman in Am J Soc 36:316-17, S '30.

2863 Rosenbaum, Julius. The Plague of Lust. Reprinted New York: Frederick Pub., 1955. Bk. II, pp.187-223. This is a classic work.

2864 Sanger, William W. History of Prostitution: Its Extent, Causes, and Effects Throughout the World. New York: Harper, 1858, 685 pp. Reprinted 1910, '13, '19, '21 by Medical Pub. Co. A new edition (dated 1897) reprinted by Eugenics Pub. Co. in 1937 and by Arno Press in 1972.

2865 Schlegel, Gustave. _Histore de la Prostitution en Chine_. Rouen: Lemonnyer, 1881.

2866 Schreiber, Hermann (Lujo Bassermann). _The Oldest Profession_. New York: Stein and Day, 1968, 300 pp.

1400 Scott, George Ryley. _A History of Prostitution from Antiquity to the Present Day_. Rev. and enl. London: Torchstream, 1952, 320 pp. Reprinted by Medical Life Press, 1954. Original edition, Werner Laurie, 1936.

2867 Servais, Jean-Jacques and Jean-Pierre Laurend. _Histoire et Dossier de la Prostitution_. Paris: Planete, 1967, 45 pp.

2868 Seymour-Smith, Martin. _Fallen Women_. London: Thomas Nelson, 1969. Good survey.

2869 Simha, S. N. and Vasu, N. K. _History of Prostitution in India_. Calcutta, 1933.

2870 Sorge, Wolfgang. _Geschichte der Prostitution_. Berlin: Potlhof and Co., 1919.

2871 Stern, B. _Geschichte der Offentlichen Sittlichkeit in Russland_. Berlin: 1907.

2872 Taylor, G. Rattray. _Sex in History_. New York: Vanguard Press, 1954.

2873 Thomas, K. "Double Standard (History of an idea deeply rooted in England for centuries)." _J Hist Ideas_ 20:195-216, Apr. '59. Bibliography.

2874 Turner, E. S. _A History of Courting_. New York: E. P. Dutton and Co., 1955.

2875 Urquhart, Margaret M. _Women of Bengal_. London: Student Christian Movement, n. d. Not particularly good.

2876 Villefosse, Rene Heronde. _Histoire et Geographie Galantes de Paris_. Paris: les Edition de Paris, 1957.

2877 Wachsmuth, Wilhelm. _Europeisch Sittengeschichte_. Leipzig: 1838.

2878 Waldegg, Richard and Werner Heinz. _Geschichte und Wesen der Prostitution_. Stuttgart: Weltspiegel Verlag, 1956. p.95.

2879 Walker, J. _Review of White Slavery_. Chicago: by the author, 1912.

2880 Westermarck, Edward. _The History of Human Marriage_. 5th ed., 3v. London: Macmillan, 1922. Also New York: Allerton Book Co., 1922.

2881 Westermarck, Edward. *A Short History of Marriage*. London: Macmillan, 1926.

2882 Whitwell, J. R. *Syphilis in Earlier Days*. London: H. K. Lewis and Co., 1940.

2883 Zeledon, Joaquin. "Estudio de Cien Historias de Prostiucion," in *Memoria del Cuarto Congresso Centroamericano de Venereologia*. Jun. '52, pp.139-148.

2884 Altekar, A. S. The Position of Women in Hindu Civilization. Banaras: Motilal Banarsidass, 1956.

2885 Ckaklader, H. C. Social Life in Ancient India; a study in Vatsyayana's Kamasutra. 2d ed Calcutta: Susil Gupta, 1954.

2886 Crawley, Ernest. The Mystic Rose; a study of primitive thought in its bearing on marriage. New York: Meridian Books, 1960. Reprinted from 2d ed, 1927.

2887 Dupouy, Edmond. La Prostitution dans l'Antiquite. Paris: Librairie Meurillon, 1887. Cinquieme ed Paris: 1906.

2888 Fitton, J. W. "That Was No Lady, That Was..." Classical Q 64(1970):56-66.

2889 Flaceliere, R. Love in Ancient Greece. New York: Crown, 1962.

2890 Frichet, Henry. Fleshpots of Antiquity: The Lives and Loves of Ancient Courtesans. Tr. from the French with fwd., intro., essays, and notes by A. F. Niemoeller. New York: Panurge, 1934, 249 pp.

2891 Friedlander, Ludwig. Roman Life and Manners Under the Early Empire. 7th ed London: George Routledge and Sons, 1940.

2892 Jacob, P. L. Les Courtesanes de l'Ancienne Rome. Brussels: 1884, 222 pp.

2893 Kiefer, O. Sexual Life in Ancient Rome. London: Routledge and Kegan Paul, 1934.

2894 Le Gal, Joel. "Metiers de Femmes au Corpus Inscriptionum Latinarum." Revue des Etudes Latines 47 5d(1970): 123-30.

2895 Licht, Hans (Paul Brandt). Sexual Life in Ancient Greece. New York: American Anthropological Society, 1934. Also London: Routledge and Kegan Paul, 1932. pp.329-332.

2896 Markun, Leo. Prostitution in the Ancient World. Girard, Kan.: Haldeman-Julius Co., 64 pp.

2897 Meyer, Johann Jacob. Sexual Life in Ancient India. New York: Barnes and Noble, 1953.

2898 Meyer, Paul. Der Romische Konkubinat Nach den Rechtsquellen und den Inschriften. Leipzig: 1895.

2899 Montifaud, Marc de (Madame Leon Quivogne). Les Courtesanes de l'Antiquite. Paris and Brussels: 1870.

2900 O'Hara, Albert Richard, S. J. The Position of Women in Early China; according to the Lieh Nu Chuan dissertations. Washington: Catholic University of America, 1945. Also in

Catholic University of America, Studies in Sociology, v.XVI.

2901 Patai, Raphael. Sex and Family in the Bible. New York: Doubleday, 1959, 282 pp.

2902 Paulys Real-Enzyklopadie der Klassischen Altertumswissenschaft. Various articles: "Lupa," "Acca Laurentia," "Flora," "Hetairai," "Prostitution," et al.

2903 Pomeroy, Sarah B. Goddesses, Whores, Wives, and Slaves: Women in Classical Antiquity. New York: Schocken Books, 1975. In spite of the title this mainly is a history of women.

2904 Randone, M. and Alberti, C. "Prostitution and Venereal Diseases in Antiquity," Minerva Med 52: Varia 1874-8, Oct. 17, '61.

2905 Savage, Charles Albert. The Athenian Family. Baltimore: John Hopkins Univ., 1907.

2906 Van Gulik, R. H. Sexual Life in Ancient China. Leiden: E. J. Brill, 1961, p.182.

2907 Van Selms, A. Marriage and Family Life in Ugaritic Literature. London: Luzac and Co., 1954.

2908 Wilkinson, H. P. The Family in Classical China. Shanghai: Kelly and Walsh, 1926. Not very good.

2909 Brundage, James. "Prostitution in the Medieval Canon Law." Kalamazoo, Mich.: Western Michigan Univ., 1972. Paper read and published in _Signs_, 1976.

2910 Bullough, Vern L. "Changing Attitudes Toward Prostitution in Early Medieval Period." _Studies in Medieval Culture_ X(1976).

2911 Fort, George F. _History of Medical Economy During the Middle Ages_. New York: J. W. Bouton, 1883.

2912 Fregier, Honore Antoine. _Des Classes Dangereuses de la Population dans les Grandes Villes et des Moyens de les Rendre Meilleures_. Paris: J. B. Bailliere, 1840. 2v. Parent-Duchatelet more complete for same period.

2913 Fuchs, Eduard. _Illustrierte Sittengeschichte vom Mittelalter bis zur Gegenwart_. Munich: 1909.

2914 Grisostomi, E. _Notizie Storiche Sui Lasciti de Donna Amante da Fermo e di Paolo de Sasso Ferrato at Grand Hospitals di Trevigi_. Biennale della Marca per la Storia della Medicina IV AHI, 1961. Flagellation in the 15th c.

2915 Hamdani, Abbas. _The Huhtasib as Guardian of Public Morality_. Unpublished paper given at the Western Michigan Medieval Conference at Kalamazoo, Michigan, 1972.

2916 Hervez, Jean. _Ruffians et Ribaudes au Moyen Age_; d'apres l'histore de la prostitution. Paris: Bibliotheque Des Curieux, n. d., 349 pp.

2917 Koukoules, P. _The Private Life of the Byzantines_. 8v. Athens: 1947-57. II,2,117-162. In Greek.

2918 Lehman, Andree. _Le Role de la Femme dans l'Historie de France, au Moyen Age_. Paris: 1952.

2919 Laignel-Lavistine and Galland, Pierre. "Louis IX et la Prostitution." _Bull Soc Franc Hist Med_ 28(1934):174-7.

2920 Markun, Leo. _Prostitution in the Medieval World_. Girard, Kan.: Haldeman-Julius Co., 63 pp.

2921 Meroni, Ubaldo. "Cremona Fedelissima," in _Annali della Biblioteca Governativa e Libreria Civica di Cremona_ III, 1950. Contains a short section on lupanars and prostitutes in the Middle Ages.

2922 Pansier, P. "Histoire des Pretendus Statuts de la Reine Jeanne et de la Reglementation de la Prostitution a Avignon au Moyen Age." _Janus_ '02.

2923 Robert, U. "Les Signes d'Infamie au Moyen Age. Filles Publiques." Paris: Societe des Antiquaires. _Memoires_ ser.5, t.6. Also Paris: Honore-Champion, 1891. Includes insignias and clothing that medieval prostitutes were supposed to wear.

2924 Salusbury, G. T. Street Life in Medieval England. 2d ed Oxford: Pen-in-Hand, 1948.

2925 Stefanutti, Ugo. "Cortigiane in Venezia d'Altritempi Aspecti Medici e Sociali." Rass Medica 35(5):158. Illustrations in color include old quarter of Venice.

2926 Stefanutti, Ugo. "Venetian Courtesans of Bygone Times." Rass Med (Int. ed.) 36(3):153-168, '59.

2927 Westerhout, A. R. Het Geslachtsleven Onzer Voorouders in de Middeleeuwen. Amsterdam: 1899, 134 pp.

2928 Besant, Sir Walter. London in the Time of the Stuarts. London: Adam and Charles Black, 1903. Part of a multi-volume set dealing with London in different centuries.

2929 Bousset de Missy, J. Histoire Publique et Secrete de la Cour de Madrid Depuis l'Avenement du Roi Phillip V. Liege: 1719.

2930 Calza, Carlo. Documenti Mediti sulla Prostituzione, Tratti Cagli Archivi della Republica Veneta. Milan: Societa Coop, 1869.

2931 Casagrande di Villaviera, Rita. La Cortigiane Veneziano nel Cinquecento. Milan: Longanesi, 1968, 321 pp.

2932 Crosby, Alfred W. The Columbian Exchange: Biological and Cultural Consequences of 1492. Westport, Conn.: Greenwood Pub. Co., 1972.

2933 Desjardins, Albert. Les Sentiments Moraux au XVIe Siecle. Paris: 1887.

2934 d'Henri, Dr. Geheimnisse der Prostitution: Enthullungen aus dem Leben der Boheme Galante Aller Lander. Leipzig: Verlags-Anstalt, 1871, 159 pp.

2935 Fabretti, Ariodante. La Prostituzione in Perugia nei Secoli 14th, 15th, 16th: Document Mediti. Torino: T. Dell 'Editore, 1885, 1890.

2936 Fuchs, Edward. Illustrierte Sittengeschichte. Vol.1: "Renaissance." Munich: Albert Langen Verlag fur Literatur und Kunst, 1909.

2937 di Giacomo, S. La Prostituzione a Napoli nei Secolo XV, XVI e XVII. Naples: 1899.

2938 God's Judgement Against Whoring. Being an Essay Towards a General History of it, from the Creation of the World to the Reign of Augustulus and thence down to the present year 1697. London: R. Baldwin, 1697, 318 pp.

2939 Keene, Wallis. Some Polite Scandals of Parisian Life. Girard, Kan.: Little Blue Books. Discussion with much data.

2940 Morgan, Edmund S. "The Puritans and Sex." New Eng Q 15(1942).

2941 Mulzer, P. "Report of Regulations on Control in Italy, Athens and Constantinople." Dermat Wchnschr 97:1628-35, Nov. 18, 1933.

2942 Munger, Robert S. "Guaiacum the Holy Wood From the New World." J Hist Med Allied Sci IV(1949):196-229. 16th c.

2943 Nelson, John Charles. Renaissance Theory of Love. New York: Columbia Univ. Press, 1958.

2944 Oberholzer, Emil. Delinquent Saints. New York: Columbia Univ. Press, 1956.

2945 Pallavicino, Ferrante. The Whore's Rhetorick in Two Dialogues. Reprinted New York: Ivan Oblensky, Inc., 1961, 160 pp.

2946 Panormitae, Antonii. Hermaphroditus. Frieder, Carol, Forbergius-Cobugri Sumtibus Meuseliorum, 1894, p.138.

2947 Petherick, Maurice. Restoration Rogues. London: Hollis Carter, 1951.

2948 Pike, Ruth. Aristocrats and Traders; Sevillian Society in the Sixteenth Century. Ithaca: Cornell Univ. Press, 1972, pp.204-211.

2949 Le Pileur, L. La Prostitution du XIIIe au XVIIe Siecle. Documents Tires des Archives d'Avignon, du Comtata Venaissin, de la Principaute d'Orange et de la Ville Libre Imperiale de Besancon. Paris: 1908.

2950 Pogge,________. Les Bains de Bade aux XVe Siecle. Tr. by A. Meray. Paris 1868 and 1876.

2951 La Procedure Faite Contre Les Filles de Joye, a la Requete des Bourgeois de Paris. (In verse). Paris: 1619, 13 pp.

2952 Rabutaux, A. P. E. De la Prostitution en Europe Depuis l'Antiquite Jusqu'a la Fin du XVIe Siecle. Paris: Sere, 1851. Ancient to 16th century.

2953 Rodriguez-Solis, E. Historia de la Prostitucion en Espana y America. 2v in 1. Madrid: F Cao y Domingo del Val, 1890(?) and Biblioteca Nueva, 1931.

2954 Shell, George. The Whore's Rhetorick, Calculated to the Meridian of London and Conformed to the Rules of Art in Two Dialogues. London : 1683.

2955 Stow, John. The Survey of London Contayning the Originall, Increase, Moderne Estate, and Government of that City. London: 1633.

2956 Valaquer, Anastaio Marcellino. La Obligaciois Prevenida Con Su Primera y Segunda Respuesta a un Papel Manuscrito, 2 June 1677. Pozzuoli: G. Fasulo, 1678, 146 pp.

2957 La Vita et Miserande Fine della Puttana: Riproduzione de XII Rarissime Stampe Popolari Veneziane della Prima Meta del Secolo XVII. Rome: 1922.

2958 Wilson, John Harold. *All The Kings Ladies: Actresses of the Restoration*. Chicago: University of Chicago Press, 1958.

2959 Adams, G. and Hutton, E. "Sex in Old New York; story of the birth and death of the Magdalen Society." Am Mercury 52 :550-7, May '41.

2960 Bleackley, Horace. Ladies Fair and Frail: Sketches of the Demimonde During the Eighteenth Century. London: John Lane, The Bodley Head, 1909.

2961 Bloch, Iwan. 120 Days of Sodom and the Sex Life of the French Age of Debauchery. Tr. and ed. by Raymond Sabatier. New York: Falstaff Press, 1934, pp.80-83.

2962 Bournand, François. L'Amour sous la Revolution. Preface by Victorien Sardou. Notices et Documents Historiques de Jules Claretie et Georges Cain. Paris: 1909.

2963 Brosses, Ch. de. L'Italie Galante et Familiere au XVIIIe Siecle. New ed. Paris: 1885. Originally published 1752, 30 pp. Some defense of prostitution.

2964 Capon, G. Les Maisons Closes au XVIIIe Siecle: Academies de Filles et Courtiere d'Amours, Maisons Clandestines, Matrones, Mares-Abbesses, Appareilleuses et Proxeenetes. Rapports de Police, Documents Secrets. Notes Personneles des Tenancieres. Paris: 1903.

2965 Capon, Gaston. Les Petites Maisons Galantes de Paris au XVIIIe Siecle. Folies Maisons de Plaisance et Vide-Bouteilles d'Apres des Documents Inedits et des Rapports de Police. Preface by R. Yve-Plessis. Paris: 1902.

2966 Letter to the Author of 'Thelyphthora' (i. e. Martin Madan) Intended as a Supplement to Mr. Hill's Address 'The Blessing of Polygamy'. Bound with Gally, H. Some Considerations Upon Clandestine Marriages. 1750. London: J. Matthews, 1781.

2967 Cohen, H. Guide de l'Amateur de Livres a Fogires et a Vignettes du XVIII Siecle. 3d ed Paris: 1896.

2968 Curti, Merle. "Human Nature in American Thought." 2 parts. I: The Age of Reason and Morality. II: Retreat From Reason in the Age of Science. Pol Sci Q LXVIII(1953):354-75, 492-510.

2969 DeFrance, E. La Maison de Madame Gourdon. Documents Inedits, 1908, 237 pp.

2970 d'Estree, Paul. Les Infames Sous l'Ancient Regime. Documents Historique Inedit. Paris: 1902.

2971 Dodd, William. The Magdalen or History of the First Penitent Received into that Charitable Asylum. London: W. Lane, 1780. Series of letters signed M. S. to a lady, with anecdotes of other penitents.

2972 Doleances des Femmes Publiques. An eight page pamphlet, supportive of prostitutes, issued in April, 1789, in Paris.

2973 Fielding, John. An Account of the Origin and Effects of a Police Set on Foot by His Grace the Duke of Newcastle in the Year 1753, upon a Plan Presented to his Grace by the late Henry Fielding, Esp.; To Which is Added a Plan for Preserving those Deserted Girls in this Town, who become Prostitutes from Necessity. London: A. Millar, 1753, p.32.

2974 Fleischmann, Hector. Les Filles Publiques sous la Terreur; D'apres les rapports de la police secrete, des documents nouveaux et des pieeces inedits tirees des Archives Nationales. Paris: 1908.

2975 Fleury, Comte. Louis XV Intime et les Petites Maitresses. Paris: Librairie Plon, 1899.

2976 Handbuch Aller Unter der Regierung Kaiser Joseph II Fuer die K. K. Erblander Ergangenen Verordungen und Gesetze. 18v. Vienna: 1785-1790. Vol.4 has section on Joseph II's attempts to elevate fallen women, of considerable number. Vol.1, p.163-4 has section on abolishing concept of illegitimacy and disabilities, treatment of unmarried mothers, etc.

2977 Hanway, Jonas. Letter V. to Robert Dingley, Esp.; Being a Proposal for the Relief and Employment of Friendless Girls and Repenting Prostitutes. London: R. and J. Dodsley, 1758.

2978 Hanway, Jonas. Letters Written Occasionally on the Customs of Foreign Nations in Regard to Harlots, the Lawless Commerce of the Sexes, the Repentance of Prostitutes, the Great Humanity and Beneficial Effects of Magdalene Charity in London, and the Absurd Notions of the Methodists. London: Rivington, 1761, 597 pp. In a sense, he urges charity.

2979 Herold, J. Christopher. Love in Five Temperments. Antheneum, 1961. High class eighteenth-century prostitutes.

2980 Herold, J. Christopher. Mistress to an Age; a life of Madame de Stael. New York: The Bobbs-Merrill Co., Inc., 1958.

2981 Herve-Piraux, F. R. Les Temples d'Amour aux XVIIIe Siecle. Paris: 1910.

2982 Hervez, Jean. La Galanterie Parisienne sous Louis XV et Louis XVI. D 'Apres le Memoires, les Rapports de Police, les Libelles, les Pamphlets, les Satires, Chansons du Temps. Paris: 1910.

2983 Hervez, Jean. Societes d'Amour au XVIIIe Siecle. Paris: 1909.

2984 Hill, Richard. The Blessings of Polygamy Displayed. London: J. Mathews, 1781. Says polygamy won't solve problem since a man may continue to lust after women even though he has several wives.

2985 Horne, Charles. Serious Thoughts on the Miseries of Seduction and Prostitution with a Full Account of the Evils that Produce Them. London: Swift and Son, 1783. Pamphlet arguing against prostitution.

2986 Lacour, Louis. Le Parc aux Cerfs du Roi Louis XV. Paris: 1859.

2987 Lewis, W. H. The Splendid Century. New York: William Sloane, 1953.

2988 London. Lock Hospital. A Short History of London Lock Hospital and Rescue Home, 1746-1906. 1906, 32 pp.

2989 McAdam, E. L. "Dr. Johnson and Saunders Welch's Proposals (to remove the nuisance of common prostitutes)." R Engl Stud ns 4:337-45, Oct. '53.

2990 Madan, Martin. An Account of the Triumphant Death of F. S., a Converted prostitute who died April 1763, aged 26. Reprinted London: Z. Fowle, n. d.

2991 Madan, Martin. Thelyphthora or a Treatise on Female Ruin. British Museum lists editions for 1780 and 1781. Also printed for J. Dodsley, 3v.

2992 Mandeville, Bernard. A Modest Defence of Public Stews: or an Essay Upon Whoring, as it is Now Practis'd in These Kingdoms. London: A. Moore, 1724, pp.1-10.

2993 Mannix, Daniel P. The Hell Fire Club. New York: Ballantine Books, 1959.

2994 Martin's Hobby Houghed and Pounded or Letters on Thelypthora. London: printed for J. Buckland, 1781. An answer to Madan whose aim was laudable but polygamy is not the solution to prostitution.

2995 Moers, Ellen. The Dandy: Brummel to Beerbohm. New York: The Viking Press, 1960.

2996 Nocturnal Revels: or the History of the King's Place. London: 1779, 2v.

2997 Nutzbares, Galantes und Curiouses Frauenzimmer-Lexicon. Frankfurt and Leipzig: 1739.

2998 Penn, James. Remarks on Thelyphthora. London: printed for the author, 1781.

2999 Petition des Femmes du Tiers l'Etat au Roi. Jan. 1, 1789. BN, LB39, 920. Pamphlet dealing with prostitution.

3000 Pilkington, Iain D. B. The King's Pleasure. London: Jarrolds, 1957.

3001 Poussin, Father. Pretty Doings in a Protestant Nation Being a View of the Present State of Fornication, Whorecraft and Adultery, in Gt. Britain, and the Territories and Dependencies there unto belonging. London: printed for J. Roberts, 1734.

3002 Restif de la Brentonne, Nicholas Edme. Le Pornographe; ou, Idees d'un honnete-homme sur unprojet de relegment pour les prostituees propre a prevenir les malheurs qu occasionne le publicisme des femmes. London: J. Nourse, La Haie, Gossejunior and Pinet, 1770, 368 pp. and Brussels: Gay and Douce, 1879.

3003 Russell, Philips. The Glittering Century. London: Charles Scribner, 1936.

3004 Schreiber, S. Etta. The German Woman in the Age of Enlightenment. New York: King's Crown Press, 1948.

3005 Schulz, Fredrick. Ueber Paris und die Pariser. Berlin: 1791. pp.1, 451-55, 467-74, 501.

3006 Secret History of the Green Room. London: 1795.

3007 Shorter, Edward. The Making of the Modern Family. New York: Basic Books, 1975.

3008 Stiles, Henry Reed. Bundling. Reprinted New York: Book Collectors Assn., 1934. Originally published 1871.

3009 Stunnon, J. "Episodes of Medicine in Liege: Prostitution Under the Empire." Rev Med Liege 6:827-841. Dec. 15, 1951.

3010 Taxil, Leo. La Prostitution Contemporaine. Paris: 1884.

3011 Towers, John. Polygamy Unscriptural; or Two Dialogues Between Philalethes and Monogamus in which the Principal Errors of the First and Second Edition of the Revd. Mr. M-D-W's "Thelyphthora" are Detected. London: printed for the author by Alex Hogg and J. Trapp, et al, 1781. Says he would not give ladies same freedom as men.

3012 Turgon, A. "Prostitution and Venereal Disease During the French Revolution." Progres Med (supp) 67:29-32, Apr. 1, 1939.

3013 Veze, Raoul. _La Galanterie Parisienne au XVIIIe Siecle_. Paris: 1905.

3014 _Vies et Actions des Coquettes, Maitresses...les plus Celebres d'Angleterre_. London: 1721.

3015 Waugh, M. A. "Attitudes of Hospitals in London to Venereal Disease in the 18th and 19th centuries." _Br J Vener Dis_ 47(2):146-50, Apr. '71.

3016 Welch, Saunders. _A Proposal to Render Effectual a Plan, to Remove the Nuisance of Common Prostitution from the Streets of the Metropolis_. London: C. Henderson, 1758.

3017 Williams, A. L. "Pope's 'Duchesses and Lady Mary's'." _R Engl Stud_ n s 4:359-61, Oct. '53.

3018 Willim, John. _The London Bawd with Her Character and Life Discovering the Various Subtile Intrigues of Lewd Women_. 4th ed London: 1711.

3019 Acton, William. *Prostitution, Considered in its Moral, Social, and Sanitary Aspects;* in London and other large cities and garrison towns; with proposals for the control and prevention of its attendent evils. Cass, 1912. Originally published London: John Churchill and Sons, 1857, 1870.

3020 Andrew, E. W. and Bushnell, K. C. *The Queen's Daughters in India*. London: 1898, 127 pp.

3021 *An Appeal to the People of England on the Recognition and Superintendence of Prostitution by Governments*. Nottingham: F. Banks, 1869, 36 pp.

3022 Bancroft, Caroline. *Six Racy Madams of Colorado*. Boulder: Johnson Pub. Co., 1965, 63 pp.

3023 Banks, Olive and J. A. Banks. *Feminism and Family Planning in Victorian England*. New York: Schocken Books, 1964, p.116.

3024 Barcroft, W. *The Contagious Diseases Acts*. London: 1883, 16 pp.

3025 Bebel, A. *A Revolting Injustice*. What Deputy Bebel Says on the State Regulation of Vice. London: 1896, 4 pp.

3026 Behrend, F. J. *Die Prostitution in Berlin*. Erlangen: J. J. Palm und Ernst Enke, 1850, 294 pp.

3027 Bentinck, Right Hon. G. C. *The Government and the Contagious Diseases Acts*. London: 1883, 14 pp.

3028 Beraud, F. F. A. *The Public Women of Paris: Being An Account of the Causes of Their Depravation, Their Several Classes, Their Means and Ways of Living, Their Arts, Their Habits, and Practices*. New York: Dewitt and Davenport, 1849, 293 pp. Originally published in 1839, Paris: Desforge et Compagnie. Supplement to Parent-Duchatelet.

3029 Bertani, A. *La Prostituzione Patentata e il Regolamento Sanitario.* Milan: 1881, 93 pp.

3030 Bevan, William. *Prostitution in the Borough of Liverpool*. Liverpool: B. Smith, 1843. A pamphlet based upon a lecture delivered in the Music Hall. Lecture was response to request from the Benevolent Society for Reclaiming Unfortunate Females. Cites other authorities, then gives his own theories and an analysis of extent in Liverpool based upon the report of the head constable.

3031 Bewes, W. A. *Manual of Vigilance Law*. London: 1888, 71 pp.

3032 Blaschko, Alfred. "Die Prostitution im 19 Jahrhundert," in Anfang des Jahrhunderts. Berlin: Verlag d. Socialist Monatshifte, 1902.

3033 Bochard, J. De la Prostitution a Brest. 1856, 35 pp.

3034 Booth, C. The Iniquity of State Regulated Vice. London: 1884, 14 pp.

3035 Das Bordella als Staadtsanstalt. Leipzig: 1851.

3036 Borel, Pastor T. The White Slavery of Europe. Ed. by Joseph Edmondson. 2d ed London: Dyer Bros., 1880. I think this is where the term "white slave" developed; says on p.6 if the traffic in Negroes has finally been abolished so must the "white slave trade be similarly treated." Borel says he got the term from Mrs. Butler who told it to Countess Agenor de Gasparin.

3037 Boyer, Paul S. Purity in Print. New York: Charles S. Scribner, 1968.

3038 Brown, Dee. The Gentle Tamers; women in the old Wild West. New York: G. P. Putnam's Sons, 1958, 317 pp.

3039 Budberg, Roger Baron. "Chinesische Prostitution." Globus 97 (1910).

3040 Burnham, J. C. "Medical Inspection of Prostitutes in America in the Nineteenth Century: The St. Louis Experiment and its Sequel." Bull Hist Med 45 (3):203-18, May-Jun. '71.

3041 Butler, Josephine E. A Grave Question. London: 1886, 7 pp.

3042 Butler, Josephine E. Principles of the Abolitionists. London: 1885, 14 pp.

3043 Butler, Josephine E. Revival of the Abolitionist Cause. Winchester: 1887, 55 pp.

3044 Butler, Josephine. Simple Words About the Repeal of the Contagious Disease Acts. Bristol: 1886, 7 pp.

3045 Butler, Josephine E. Woman's Work and Woman's Culture. London: Macmillan, 1869.

3046 Calcutta. The Social Evil in Calcutta. Calcutta: 1886, 112 pp.

3047 Chesney, Kellow. The Victorian Underworld. 8v. London: Temple Smith, 1970.

3048 Charrington, Frederick Nicholas. The Battle of the Music Halls. London: Dyer Bros., 1885(?), 15 pp.

3049 Chevalier, Louis. Classes Laborieuses et Classes Dangereuses a Paris Pendant la Premiere Moitie au XIX a Siecle. Paris: Plon, 1958. pp.380-397.

3050 Chicago's Dark Places; investigations by a corps of specially appointed commissioners. 5th ed Chicago: The Craig Press, and Women's Temperance Publishing Assn., 1891, 224 pp.

3051 Commenge, J. R. V. Oscar. La Prostitution Clandestine a Paris. Paris: 1897, 567 pp.

3052 Corbin, Mrs. Caroline Elizabeth (Fairfield). Letters from a Chimney-corner. A Plea for Pure Homes and Sincere Relations Between Men and Women. Chicago: Fergus Printing Co., 1886, 50 pp. Really an anti-suffrage tract. Wants women to use their moral fervor in the home.

3053 Corlieu, A. La Prostitution a Paris. Paris: 1887, 127 pp.

3054 Cruz, Francisco Ignacio do Santos. Da Prostituicao na Cidade de Lisboa. Lisbon: 1841, 457 pp.

3055 Cutrera, A. Storia della Prostizuione in Sicilia. Mainland, 1903.

3056 Dalton, H. Der Sociale Aussatz. Ein Wort Uber Prostitution. Hamburg: 1884, 64 pp.

3057 Dauthendey, Max. Die Geflugelte Erde. Munich: 1910. Has considerable material on prostitution including a discussion of prostitution in Yoshiwara.

3058 Despres, A. La Prostitution en France. Paris: J. B. Bailliere et Fils, 1883.

3059 Drago, H. B. Notorious Ladies of the Frontier. New York: Dodd, 1969.

3060 Duchesne, E. A. De la Prostitution dans la Ville d'Alger. Paris: J. B. Bailliere et Garnier Freres, 1853. Deals primarily with French period but also combs sources for material before and has several pages on male prostitution.

3061 Dyer, Alfred. The European Slave Trade in English Girls. London: Dyer Bros., 1880.

3062 Dyer, Alfred. Six Years Labour and Sorrow: The Fourth Report of the London Committee for Suppressing the Traffic in British Girls for the Purposes of Continental Prostitution. London: Dyer Bros., 1885, p.2.

3063 Dyer, A. S. Slave Trade in European Girls in India. Bombay: 1893, 4 pp.

3064 Fiaux, F. L. La Police des Moeurs. Paris: 1888, 1010 pp. Also a 1907 ed.

3065 Fiaux, F. L. La Prostitution en Belgique. Paris: F. Alcan, 1892, 72 pp.

3066 France, Hector. Les Van-Nu-Pieds de Londres. Paris: 1884.

3067 Fricke, C. Die Frauenfrage in Ihrer Bezihung zur Prostitution. Berlin: 1885, 52 pp.

3068 Gentry, Curt. The Madams of San Francisco; an irreverent history of the city by the Golden Gate. Garden City, N. Y.: Doubleday, 1964, 323 pp.

3069 Die Geschichte der Prostitution und der Verfalls der Sitten in Berlin. Altona, Verlagsbureau, U. Prinz, 1871. Pamphlet, 114 pp.

3070 Giersing, O. M. Tangs Forslag til en Saedelighedslov. Kjobenh.: 1889, 20 pp.

3071 Glascow. The Glascow System for the Repression of Vice. London: 1883, 8 pp.

3072 Gladstone, J.P. Observations on the Committee with Reference to the Moral Section of the Majority Report. London: 1886, 20 pp.

3073 Gledstone, J. P. Observations on the Recent Select Committee of the House of Commons. London: 1884, 20 pp.

3074 Goldman, M. "Prostitution and Virtue in Nevada; Virginia City 1860-80's." Society 10:32-8, Nov. '72.

3075 Gozzoli, G. La Prostitution in Italia. Roma: 1886, 47 pp.

3076 Gt. Britain. Royal Commission on Contagious Diseases Acts. A Critical Summary of the Evidence Before the Royal Commission upon the Contagious Diseases Acts 1866-1869. Prepared by D. Kingsford. 8v. London: Tweedie, 1869(?). Ch. 4-6 only.

3077 The Greatest of Our Social Evils: Prostitution as it Now Exists in London, Liverpool, Manchester, Glascow, Edinburgh, and Dublin. London: H. Bailliere, 1857. Some good figures.

3078 Guillot, A. La Lutte Contre l'Exploitation et la Reglementation du Vice a Geneve Jusqu'au 22.3.1896, Histore et Documents. Geneva, 1899.

3079 Guyot, Y. La Traite des Vierges a Londres. Paris: 1885, 285 pp.

3080 H., J. C. Babylon; or the "Pall Mall Gazette" and Salvation Army on the Corruption, Cruelties, and Crime of London. Comp. by J. C. H. London: Publishing Depot of the Salvation Army, 1885.

3081 H., S. State Legalization of Vice. London: 1882, 20 pp.

3082 Haas, Alex de. De Minstreel van de Mesthoop; Liedjes, leven en achtergronden van Eduard Jacobs, pionier van het Nederlandse cabaret, 1867-1914. Behalve met vele fotografieen geillustreerd met prenten en tekningen, etc. Amsterdam: 1958, 152 pp.

3083 Harris, G. Le Prostitute nel Secolo XIX. Milan: 1886, 201 pp.

3084 Harrison, Michael. Fanfare of Strumpets. London: W. H. Allen, 1971, 271 pp.

3085 Heikel, R. Uttalande i Prostitutionsfrajan. Helsingfors: 1888, 6 pp.

3086 Hemyng, Bracebridge. "Prostitution in London," in Henry Mayhew, London Labour and the London Poor. 4v. Reprinted New York: Dover Books, 1968. Vol. IV, pp.210-72.

3087 Hermanides, S. R. Reglementeering der Prostitutie, Hygienisch Gerechtvaardigd?. s' Gravenhage, 1883, 144 pp.

3088 Hill, S. The Antagonism of State Regulation of Vice to Christian Teaching. London: 1884, 14 pp.

3089 "Historic Notes on Prostitution and Venereal Disease." Urol and Cutan R 52:113-116, Feb. '48.

3090 Holder, C. F. "Chinese Slavery in America." N Amer R 165: 288-94 , Sep. 1897.

3091 Holmes, Kay Ann. "Reflections by Gaslight: Prostitution in Another Age." Issues in Criminology 7(1):83-101, Win. '72. History of law enforcement against prostitution in the U. S. during the late 19th and early 20th centuries.

3092 Hoyois, J. Liberte, Tolerence ou Repression en Matiere de Mouers. Brussels: 1883, 122 pp.

3093 Hyde, H. Montgomery. The Cleveland Street Scandal. London: W. H. Allen, 1976, 266 pp. 1899 scandal involving boy prostitution.

3094 Jeannel, Julien François. Memoire sur la Prostitution Publique et Parallelé Complet de la Prostitution Romaine et de la Prostitution Contemporaine. 8v. Paris: G. Germer-Bailliere, 1862, 241 pp. Tables. 2d ed the same, 1863.

3095 Jeannel, J. F. de. Die Prostitution in den Grossen Stadten im Neunzehten Jahrhundert und die Vernichtung der Venerischen Krankheiten. Tr. by F. W. Muller. Erlangen, 1869. French title is De la Prostitution dans les Grandes Villes au Dix-neuvieme Siecle. 2d ed Paris: 1874.

3096 Just-Nielsen, L. Prostitutionssporgsmaalet. Straf eller Sundhedsforholdsregal?. Kjobenh.: 1897, 15 pp.

3097 Kaehler, G. Beitrage zur Geschichte der Prostitution in Hamburg. 1897, 274 pp. (Zeitschrift fur Social- und Wirtschaftsgeschichte, Erganzungsheft 2).

3098 Kellen, Betty. The Mistresses; domestic scandals of nineteenth century monarchs. New York: Random House, 1966, 341 pp.

3099 Koch, W. D. Hvad Skal der Saettes i Stedet for den Autoriserede Prostitution?. Kjobenh.: 1888, 47 pp.

3100 Kuhn, Julius. Die Prostitution im Neunzehnten Jahrhundert. Leipzig: Verlag von Ed. Wartig, 1871, 220 pp., unbound. Also 1892 edition.

3101 Lecour, C. J. La Prostitution a Paris et a Londres 1789-1877. 3d ed Paris: P. Asselin, 1877, 474 pp.

3102 Leggi Ememorie Venete sulla Prostituzione Finocella Caduta della Republica. Venice: M. Visentini, 1870-72, 399 pp. Only 150 copies.

3103 Leonowens, Anna H. Siamese Harem Life. Reprinted New York: E. P. Dutton, 1953. First ed 1873.

3104 Lippert, H. Die Prostitution in Hamburg. Hamburg: 1848.

3105 Lloyd, Benjamin E. Lights and Shades in San Francisco. San Francisco: A. L. Bancroft, 1876.

3106 Logan, William. An Exposure From Personal Observations of Female Prostitution in London, Leeds, Rochdale, and Especially in the City of Glascow. Glascow: G. Gallie and R. Fleckfield, 1843, 48 pp. Numerical and cost accounting of prostitution. One of the better statistical studies.

3107 Logan, William. The Great Social Evil. London: Hodder and Stoughton, 1871. An extension of his earlier study.

3108 London. Moral Reform Union. History of the Contagious Diseases Acts. London: 1892, 8 pp.

3109 Lorenzi, G. Legge e Memorie Venete sulla Prostituzione. Venice: 1870-1872.

3110 Lowndes, F. W. Prostitution in Liverpool. London: 1886. 56 pp.

3111 Luchetti, Valya. "The Fate of Julia Bulette." Westways Sep. '76, pp.31-33, 69-70.

3112 Ludecke, Hugo. "Deutsche Bordellgassen," in Beiwerke zum Studium der Anthropophyteia. 4v. Leipzig: 1911, 270 pp.

3113 Luke, Sir Henry. "Echoes of La Belle Epoque." Listener 75:16-17, Jan. 6, '66.

3114 MacGlashan, W. England on Her Defence! Reply to "The Maiden-Tribute". Newcastle: 1885, 14 pp.

3115 MacLaren, D. C. D. Acts in India. London: 1889, 23 pp.

3116 Maedchen, Die Gefallen Madchen und die Sittenpolizei. Berlin: 1886, 59 pp.

3117 Mammoli, T. La Prostituzione Cousiderata ne' Suoi Rapporti Con la Storia. Rocca S. Casciano, 1881, 179 pp.

3118 Marcus, Steven. The Other Victorians. New York: Basic Books, 1966.

3119 Maroni, P. Die Gesetzliche Prostitution. Hildesheim: 1884, 40 pp.

3120 Martineau, Louis. La Prostitution Clandestine. Paris: A. Delahaye, 1883, 216 pp.

3121 Martineau, Louis. Die Clandestiene Prostitutie. Amsterdam: 1888, 218 pp.

3122 Mayhew, Henry. London Labour and the London Poor. 4v. London: Griffin, Bohn, and Dover Pub., 1968. Vol. 4 is devoted to the study of prostitution throughout Europe and the rest of the world.

3123 Mayhew, Henry. London's Underworld; being selections from 'Those That Will Not Work,' the fourth volume of "London Labour and the London Poor." Ed. by Peter Quennell. London: W. Kimber, 1950, 434 pp.

3124 Mazzulla, F. M., and J. Brass Checks and Red Lights. Privately published. Western Federal Savings Bank, Denver, Colorado, 1966.

3125 Melendy, R. L. "The Saloon in Chicago." Am J Soc 6(1900):289-306, 433-464.

3126 Miller, Ronald Dean. Shady Ladies of the West. Los Angeles: Westernlore Press, 1964, 224 pp.

3127 Miller, James. Prostitution Considered in Relation to Its Cause and Cure. Edinburgh; 1859.

3128 Mireur, Hippolyte. La Prostitution a Marseille: Histoire, Administration et Police, Hygiene. 8v. Paris: E Dentu, 1882, 404 pp.

3129 Morris, J. Our Sin and Shame. Wimbleton: 1885, 8 pp.

3130 Mueller, F. W. Die Prostitution in Deutschland. Regensburg: 1892, 64 pp.

3131 Munchheimer. "Die Prostitutionsfrage in der Literatur des Jahres 1896." Ztsch f Criminal-Anthrop I:53-74, 1897.

3132 Nasher, I. L. "Prostitution in 1886 and 1916." Am J Urology and Sexology 12:501-7, Nov. '16.

3133 Newman, F. W. Remedies for the Great Social Evil. London: 1889, 21 pp.

3134 Nield, Keith. Prostitution in the Victorian Age; debates on the issue from 19th century critical journals. Germany: Gress International Pub., 1973.

3135 Norway. Sedelighedsforeninger. Etudes sur la Repression de la Prostitution en Norvege. Christiania: 1899, 70 pp.

3136 Die Offentiche Sittenlosigkeit mit Besonderer Beziehung auf Berlin, Hamburg und die Andern Groszen Stadte des Nordlichen und Mitteren Deutschlands. Berlin: Th. Chr. Fr. Enslin, 1869, 40 pp.

3137 Ostwald, Hans. Berliner Bordelle. Leipzig: Verlaq von Ernst Muller, c1850, 84 pp. bound.

3138 P. P. London. "The Maiden Tribute of Modern Babylon." Pall Mall Gazette. July, 1885, by William Stead. London: 1885.

3139 P. P. London. Les Scandales de Londres Devoiles par la 'Pall Mall Gazette'. Traduction litterale. Paris: 1885, 314 pp.

3140 P. P. London. Os Escandalos de Londres. Lisbon: 1886, 161 pp.

3141 P. P. London. Pall Mall-Babylonier im Deutschen Reich. Leipzig: 1885, 63 pp.

3142 Parent-Duchatelet, A. J. B. De la Prostitution Dans la Ville de Paris. 2v. Paris: J. B. Bailliere, 1836.

3143 Paris Dansant ou les Filles d'Herodiade Folles Danseuses des Bals Publiques Attrib. to l'Abbe Constant. Paris: Chez Tous les Marchands de Nouve Aules, 1845, 112 pp.

3144 Pearsall, Ronald. Public Purity Private Shame. London: Weidenfeld Nicolson, 1976.

3145 Pearsall, Ronald. The Worm in the Bud; the world of Victorian sexuality. 2v. New York: Macmillan, 1969, 560 pp. Ch. 6 in Pt. II deals with various aspects of prostitution (including the Stead case and Whitechapel murders) during the Victorian era.

3146 Pearson, Michael. The Age of Consent: Victorian Prostitution and Its Enemies. London: Newton Abbott, 1972. Also David and Charles, 1972. History of Prostitution in Gt. Britain.

3147 Pearson, Michael. 5 Virgins. Saturday Review Press, 1972.

3148 Petrie, Glen. A Singular Iniquity; the campaigns of Josephine Butler. New York: The Viking Press, 1971, 317 pp.

3149 Picton-Turbervill, E. "America and the Social Evil." Nineteenth Century 86:153-63, Jul. '19.

3150 Pierrot, A. Essai d'Etude sur l'Attenuation de la Prostitution par la Modification de la loi sur les Cafes. Montmedy, 1895, 29 pp.

3151 Pini, Della Prostituzione. Milan: 1887, 45 pp.

3152 Pivar, David. Purity Crusade Sexual Morality, and Social Control 1868-1900. Westport, Conn.: Greenwood Press, 1973.

3153 Pradier, F. H. Histoire Statistique, Medicale et Administrative de la Prostitution dans la Ville de Clermont-Ferrand. Clermont-Ferrand, 1859.

3154 Die Prostituion in Berlin. Berlin: 1846.

3155 Die Prostitution in Leipzig. Leipzig: 1854.

3156 Prostitution Onder de Oude en Nieuwe Volken. Amsterdam: 1885, 158 pp.

3157 Rabutaux, A. P. E. De la Prostitution en Europe. Paris: 1881, 303 pp.

3158 Reglement et Ordonnances sur la Prostitution de Bruxelles. V.M. D. P. Brussels: Imprime aux Frais des Filles d'Amour, 1873. Since syphilis is inherent, regulation essential. Divides prostituion into four classes depending upon cost. Includes some police ordinances.

3159 Rey, Dr. L. (preface G. Hartmann). Die Offentliche und Heimliche Prostitution und die Prostituirten Frauen. Grimma und Leipzig: Druck und Verlag des Verlags Comptoirs, 1851, 134 pp. unbound.

3160 Rey, J. L. Ueber Prostituirte und Prostitution in Alegemeinen. Grimma: Verlags-Comptoirs, 1847, 136 pp. unbound.

3161 Richard, C. La Prostitution Devant le Philosophe. Paris: 1881, 176 pp.

3162 Richard, Emile. La Prostitution a Paris. Paris: J. B. Bailliere et Fils, 1890, 295 pp.

3163 Richardson, Joanna. The Courtesans; the demi-monde in nineteenth-century France. Cleveland and New York: The World Pub. Co., 1967.

3164 Richelot, Gustave Antoine. The Greatest of Social Evils: Prostitution as it Now Exists in London, Liverpool, Manchester, Glascow, Edinburgh, and Dublin. London, New York: H. B. Bailliere, 1857, 344 pp.

3165 Richelot, S. La Prostitution en Angleterre et en Ecosse. Paris: 1857.

3166 Riegel, R. E. "Changing American Attitudes Towards Prostitution (1800-1920)." J Hist Ideas 29:437-52, Jun. '68.

3167 Reizenstein, Franzeska (Nyss) von (pseud. Franz von Nemmersdorf). Der Kampf des Geschlechter: Eine Studie aus dem Leben und fur das Leben. Leipzig: M. Spohr, 1892, 188 pp.

3168 Rohrmann, Carl. Der Sittliche Zustand von Berlin Nach Aufhebung der Geduldeten Prostitution des Weiblichen Geschlechts. Leipzig: Rohrmann's Verlags-Expedition, 1847, 238 pp. unbound.

3169 Ryan, Michael. Prostitution in London; with comparative view of that of Paris and New York. London: Bailliere, 1839, 447 pp.

3170 Schlesinger, W. Die Prostitution in Wien und Paris. Wien: Verlag von Tendler and Comp. (Julius Grosser), 1868, 24 pp. unbound.

3171 Schonfeldt, G. Beitrage zur Geschichte des Pauperismus und der Prostitution in Hamburg. Weimar: 1847.

3172 Scholz, Fridrich. Prostitution und Frauenbewegung. (Prostitution and Feminist Movement). Leipzig: Eduard Heinrich Mayer, 1897, 88 pp. unbound.

3173 Schrank, Joseph. Die Amtlichen Vorschriften, Betreffend die Prostitution in Wien. Vienna: J. Safar, 1899.

3174 Schrank, Joseph. Die Prostitution in Wien. 2v. Vienna: 1886.

3175 Scott, B. Is London More Immoral Than Paris or Brussels? London: 1884, 14 pp.

3176 Scott, B. State Regulated Vice as it Existed in London. London: 1886, 12 pp.

3177 Scott, Benjamin. A State Iniquity: Its Rise, Extension and Overthrow. Republished New York: Augustus M. Kelley Pub. 1968, 401 pp.

3178 Scott, Craig. The House They Lived In. North Hollywood, Ca.: Brandon House, 1963, 160 pp.

3179 Shorter, Edward. "Middle-Class Anxiety in the German Revolution of 1848." J Soc Hist 2(1969):189-215.

3180 Sigsworth, E. M. and T. J. Wyke. "A Study of Victorian Prostitution and Venereal Disease," in Martha Vicunis, Suffer and Be Still. Bloomington: Univ. of Indiana Press, 1972, p.97.

3181 Snell, Joseph W. Painted Ladies of Cowtown Frontier. New York: Dodd, Mead and Co., 1969.

3182 The Social Evil in Calcutta. 3d ed Calcutta: Thomas S. Smith, 1886(?). Says number of prostitutes difficult to determine but says there were at least 525 who professed Christianity, mostly at the lower levels. Not particularly sophisticated.

3183 Spoelstra, C. Teedere Zaken. Open Brief (on prostitution in the Transvaal). Pretoria: 1896.

3184 The Sporting and Club House Directory, Chicago; containing a full and complete list of all strictly first class club and sporting houses. Chicago: Ross and St. Clair, 1889, 64 pp.

3185 Stansfeld, Right Hon. J. Repeal of the Contagious Diseases Acts. Speech. London: 1884, 15 pp.

3186 Stieber, W. J. C. E. Die Prostitution in Berlin und Ihre Opfer. 2d ed Berlin: 1846.

3187 Storia della Prostituzione Press o Tutti I Popoli del Mondo. Compiled from the work of Petro, Dufour, Beraud, Rabataux, Esquiros, Parent-Duchatelet, Sabatier, Acton, Ryan, Rosenbaum, Callisto, Sacchi. 4 pts. Milan: Emilio Croci, 1865. No citations.

3188 Stuermer, C. L. V. "Die Prostitution in den Stadten Russlands," in _Dermatologische Zeitschrift_, Bd.6. Enganzungsheft. 1899.

3189 Stumcke, Heinrich. "Die Theaterprostitution im Wandel der Zeiten." _Archiv fur Frauenkunde_, ed. by Max Hirsch. I (1914).

3190 Tait, William. (surgeon). _Magdalenism: An Inquiry into the Extent, Causes, and Consequences of Prostitution in Edinburgh_. Claims one prostitute for every 8 adult males in Edinburgh, compared to one for every 60 in London, one for every 15 in Paris, and one for every 6 or 7 in New York. Obviously some far fetched figures. Does have age of prostitutes admitted to the Lock Hospital. Says there are natural and accidental causes.

3191 Talbot, James Beard. _The Miseries of Prostitution_. 3d ed London: Madden, 1844, 80 pp.

3192 Tarnowsky, B. _Prostitution und Abolitionismus_. Hamburg: 1890, 222 pp.

3193 Taxil, L. _La Corruption Fin de Siecle_. Paris: 1891, 425 pp.

3194 Taxil, L. _La Prostitution Contemporaine_. Paris: 1884, 508 pp.

3195 Terrot, Charles. _The Maiden Tribute_; a study of the white slave traffic of the nineteenth century. London: Muller, 1959, 230 pp.

3196 Touraine, A. and P. Renault. "Close Relationship Between Prostitution and Economic Activity; study of years 1814-1932." _Bull Soc Franc de Dermat et Syph_ (Reunion Dermat, Strasbourg) 40:995-1002, Jul. '33.

3197 Tristan, Mme. Flora. _Promenades dans Londres_. Paris: 1840.

3198 Turanov, N. M. "Progressive Ideas in the Control of Social Diseases in the Pre-October Period (Russian)." _Vestn Derm Vener_ 43: Aug. 3-9, 1969.

3199 Universitaetslehrer. _Ex Malis Minimal Reflexionen zur Prostitutionsfrage_. Berlin: 1891, 15 pp.

3200 Untitled. A Pamphlet, 52 pp. No frontspiece. Printed by P. P. Carpenter, Oberlin Press, Warrington. After 1844.

3201 Verax. _The Social Evil in South Calcutta_. Calcutta: 1895, 20 pp.

3202 Vermorel, Auguste Jean Marie. Ces Dames. Paris: Chez Tous les Libraires, 1860, 216 pp.

3203 Vestal, Stanley. Queen of Cowtowns, Dodge City. New York: Harper and Bros., 1952.

3204 Vilas, Martin Samuel. The Barbary Coast of San Francisco. Burlington, Vt.: Free Press Assn., 1915.

3205 Vintras, Achille. On the Repressive Measures Adopted in Paris Compared With the Uncontrolled Prostitution of London and New York. London: Hardwicke, 1867, 86 pp.

3206 Virmaitre, C. Paris Documentaire. Trottoirs et Lupanars. Paris: 1893, 282 pp.

3207 Virmaitre, C. Paris-impur. Paris: 1889, 302 pp.

3208 Voorhoeve, H. C. Brieven Over Het Congres Tegen de Prostitutie. d'Haag: 1883, 32 pp.

3209 Vox Clamantis. Public Morality. Our Streets. London: 1890, 7 pp.

3210 Wardlaw, Ralph. Lectures on Magdalenism: Its Nature, Extent, Effects, Guilt, Causes and Remedy. Reprinted New York: J. S. Redfield, 1843, p.166.

3211 Warren, John H. Thirty Years Battle With Crime. Arno Press, 1970. (1874). Prostituton in New York City.

3212 Westerberg, O. M. Prostitutionens Reglementering. Stockholm: 1890, 144 pp.

3213 Wilson, Jackson Stitt. The Harlots and the Pharisees or The Barbary Coast in a Barbarous Land. Printed by the author, 1913, 35 pp.

3214 Wilson, Samuel Paynter. Chicago by Gaslight. Chicago: 191-, 148 pp.

3215 Wodehouse, John (Lord Kimberley). Lord Kimberley's Defence of the Government Brothel System at Hong Kong. London: National Assn. for Repeal of Contagious Diseases Act, 1882, 76 pp.

3216 Woodward, C. Vann. The Strange Career of Jim Crow. New York: Oxford Univ. Press, 1966, 2d ed p.102..."A New Orleans ordinance segregated white and Negro prostitutes in separate disticts."

3217 "The Wren." Pall Mall Gazette. London: Tinsey Bros., 1867.

3218 Yedo. *Notes on the History of the Yoshiwara of Yedo*. Yokohama: 1894, 22 pp.

3219 Addams, J. A New Conscience and an Ancient Evil. New York: 1912. 219 pp.

3220 Armand, Ernest. Libertinage et Prostitution. Paris: Editions Prima, 1932.

3221 Asbury, H. Barbary Coast; an informal history of the San Francisco underworld. Knopf, 1933; Jarrolds, 1934.

3222 Asbury, Herbert. The French Quarter. New York: Knopf, 1936. Chapters XII and XIV.

3223 Asbury, Herbert. Gem of the Prairie; an informal history of the Chicago underworld. Knopf, 1940.

3224 Barnes, Claude Teancum. White Slave Act: History and Analysis of its Words, Other Immoral Purpose. Salt Lake City, Utah: Claude T. Barnes, 1946, 49 pp.

3225 Beck, J. "History of Legalized Prostitution 1984-2004." Nat R 26:748-9+, Jun. 5, 1974.

3226 Bell, E. A. ed. War on the White Slave Trade. C. C. Thompson and J. L. Nichols.

3227 Bell, E. A. White Slavery Today. Chicago: L. W. Walter Co., 1917.

3227A Benjamin, Harry. Prostitution and Morality; a definative report on the prostitute in contemporary society and an analysis of the causes and effects of the suppression of prostitution. New York: Julian Press, 1964, 495 pp.

3228 Bierhoff, Frederic. "Die Prostitutionsfrage in New York," in Zeitschrift fur Bekampfung der Geschlechtskrankheiten, X (1910).

3229 Billington-Grieg, T. "Truth About White Slavery." English R 14:428-46, 1913.

3230 **Bloch, Iwan.** Sexual Life in England. London and New York: 1934.

3231 Burgess, W. World's Social Evil: Historical Review and Study of the Problems Relating to the Subject; with supplementary chapter on a Constructive policy, by Harry Olson. Chicago: Saul Bros., 1914. Contains a vast amount of information relative to prostitution and its social and economic effects, including social hygiene and diseases, license and regulation systems and white slave traffic. Appendix contains copies of the U. S. injunction and abatement, pandering, white slave, and regulation of immigration laws and a chart of prostitution laws by state.

3232 Chicago. Vice Commission. *The Social Evil in Chicago;* a study of existing conditions. Chicago: Gunthorp-Warren Printing Co., 1911.

3233 Coote, W. A. *A Romance of Philanthropy: Being a Record of the Work of the National Vigilance Association.* By the Assn., 1916, 235 pp.

3234 Decante, R. *La Lutte Contre la Prostitution.* Paris: Girard and Briere, 1909, 234 pp.

3235 "Devilish Traffic." *Literary Digest* 101:33, Apr. 20, 1929.

3236 Ditzion, Sidney. *Marriage Morals and Sex in America.* New York: Bookman Associates, 1953.

3237 Eslava, R. G. *La Prostitution en Madrid.* Madrid: 1900, 100 pp.

3238 Feldman, E. "Prostitution, the Alien Woman and the Progressive Imagination, 1910-1915." *Am Q* 19:192-206, Sum. '67.

3239 Fiaux, F. L. *La Police des Moeurs.* 2v. 1907.

3240 Filler, Louis. "House of Bondage," in *Crusaders for American Liberalism*, pp.285-95. Harcourt, 1939 and Antioch, 1961.

3241 Flexner, Abraham. *Prostitution in Europe.* New York: The Century Co., 1914. pp.138-139.

3242 Gerling, A. W. *Die Leibliehe und Geistige Prostitution Unserer Zeit.* Leipzig: E Thiele, n. d., 24 pp.

3243 Gould, George. *Twenty Years' Progress in Social Hygiene Legislation: 1925-1944.* American Social Hygiene Assn., 1944. An extract.

3244 Gray, J. H. *Red Lights on the Prairies.* New American Library, 1973 and Toronto: Macmillan of Canada, 207 pp. Canadian prairie provinces.

3245 Haemerling, Konrad. (pseud. Curt Moreck). *Kultur- und Sittengeschichte der Neusten Zeit.* Dresden: Aretz, c1928.

3246 Hall, G. M. *Prostitution in the Modern World;* a survey and a challenge. Emerson, 1936.

3247 Halperin, S. E. *(Prostitution).* Moscow: Okhrana Materinstva i Meadenchestva, 1927, 32 pp.

3248 Hartmann, Grethe. *The Girls They Left Behind.* Copenhagen: Ejnar Munksgaard, 1946, 207 pp. Aftereffects of German occupation.

3249 Hepburn, K. H. Woman Sufferage and the Social Evil. National Woman Suffrage Pub.

3250 Hirschfeld, Magnus, et al. The Sexual History of the World War. Tr. into English. New York: Panurge Press, 1943.

3251 "An Historical Vignette: from House of Infection to Hospital for Control of Venereal Disease." J Am Vener Dis Assoc 2(1):31-2, Sep. '75.

3252 Kent, Victoria. "Prostitucion." Rev Mex Social 13:45-54, 1951. Discussion of evolution of prostitution since early 20th century.

3253 Kneeland, G. J. Commercialized Prostitution in New York City. New York: Bureau of Social Hygiene. Publications, 1913, 333 pp. Also by The Century Co., 1931, 251 pp.

3254 Knight, G. K. The White Slaves of England. Denham, 1910, 22 pp.

3255 La Croix, History of Prostitution, with supplements on Brazil by D. Amancio Peratoner. Brazil (in Portuguese), 1885-1887.

3256 Lubove, R. "The Progressive and the Prostitute." Historian 24(1962):308-330.

3257 Ludecke, Hugo. "Deutsche Bordellgassen," in Das Geschlectleben des Deutsches Volkes, pp.260-93. 430 pp. Lots of illustrations.

3258 Madras Vigilance Assn. Various tracts written in the 1930's against prostitution.

3259 Markun, Leo. Prostitution in the Modern World. Girard, Kan.: Haldeman-Julius Co, 63 pp.

3260 Markun, Leo. Prostitution in the United States. Girard, Kan.: Little Blue Books, 61 pp.

3261 Markun, Leo. The White Slave Traffic. Girard, Kan.: Little Blue Books, 32 pp.

3262 Miller, Max. Holladay Street. New York: New American Library, 1962, 222 pp. Also Signet Books. Prostitution in Colorado.

3263 Miner, Maude E. Slavery of Prostitution; a plea for emancipation. New York: Macmillan Co.: 1916, 308 pp. Dissertation at Columbia University, 1971.

3264 Murphy, U. G. The Social Evil in Japan. 2d ed Tokyo: Methodist Pub. House, 1904.

3265 Neher, Anton Otto. Die Geheine und Offentlich Prostitution in Stuttgart, Karlsruhe und Munchen, mit Berucksichtigung des Prostitutionsgewerbes in Augsburg und Ulm Soure die Ubrigen Grosseren Studten Wurttembergs. Paderborn: F. Schoning, 1912.

3266 Neumann, Robert. 23 Women; the story of an international traffic. New York: The Dial Press, 1940, 316 pp.

3267 New York. Committee of Fifteen. The Social Evil. New York: G. P. Putnam, 1902, 188 pp. William H. Baldwin, Jr., chairman; Edwin R. A. Seligman, Secretary.

3268 New York. Committee of Fourteen. The Social Evil in New York City: A Study of Law Enforcement. New York: Andrew H. Kellogg, 1910.

3269 Niemoeller, Adolph F. Sexual Slavery in America. New York: Panurge Press, 1935, 255 pp.

3270 Nocturnal Revels. Introduction by Pol Andre. Paris: A. Michel, c1910, 379 pp.

3271 O'Callaghan, Sean. The Slave Trade Today. New York: Crown, 1962, 191 pp.

3272 O'Callaghan, Sean. The White Slave Trade. London: New English Library, 1967, 159 pp.

3273 O'Callaghan, Sean. The Yellow Slave Trade: A Survey of the Traffic in Women and Children in the East. London: Blond, 1968, 140 pp.

3274 Oestereich, Heinrich. Gegenwartsaspekte der Prostitution. Koln-Klettenberg: Volkswartbund, 1956, 26 pp.

3275 Orth, Penelope. An Enviable Position; the American mistress from slightly kept to practically marriage. New York: David McKay Co., Inc., 1972, 303 pp.

3276 O'Hara, Barratt. Lieutenant-Governor of Illinois. Report of the Senate Vice Committee. Chicago: Allied Printers, 1916, 979 pp.

3277 Parkhill, F. Wildest of the West. Holt, 1951.

3278 "Prey of the Blind Tigers." Literary Digest 103:22-3, Nov. 2, '29.

3279 The Prostitute and the Social Reformer; Comercialized Vice in the Progressive Era. Arno Press, 1974. Reprint of the Report of the Vice Committee of Minneapolis to his Honor, James C. Hayes, Mayor. Originally published 1911. Report on existing conditions with recommendations to Hon. Rudolf Blankenburg, Mayor of Philadelphia. Originally published

1913.

3280 Reckless, Walter C. *Vice in Chicago*. Univ. of Chicago Press, 1933.

3281 Rees, Seth Cook. *Miracles in the Slums; or, Thrilling Stories of Those Rescued From the Cesspools of Inequity*. Chicago: S. C. Rees, c1905, 301 pp.

3282 Regan, John, comp. *Crimes of the White Slavers and the Results*. Chicago: J. Regan and Co., 1912, 182 pp.

3283 Reid, Ed. *The Mistress and the Mafia; the Virginia Hill story*. National General Co., 1971, 211 pp.

3284 Riegal, Robert E. "Changing Attitudes Toward Prostitution." *J Hist Ideas* 19(1968):437-452.

3285 Roe, Clifford Griffith. *The Girl Who Disappeared*. Chicago: American Bureau of Moral Education, 1911, 352 pp.

3286 Roe, Clifford Griffith. *The Great War on White Slavery or Fighting for the Protection of Our Girls*. Clifford G. Roe and S. S. Steadwell, 1911, 448 pp.

3287 Roe, Clifford Griffith. *Horrors of the White Slave Trade*. New York(?): c1911, 448 pp.

3288 Roe, Clifford Griffith. *Panders and Their White Slaves*. New York: Fleming H. Revell Co., c1910, 224 pp.

3289 Rose, A. *Storyville, New Orleans*. Univ. of Alabama Press, 1974.

3290 Roydan, M., ed. *Downward Paths*. London: G. Bell and Sons, 1916.

3291 "Satelliks, Oldest Profession." *Time* 69:34, May 20, '57.

3292 Shepherd, C. R. "Chinese Girl Slavery in America." *Miss R of the World* 46:893-8, Nov. '23.

3293 Stern, Michael. *The White Ticket: Commercialized Vice in the Machine Age, From the Official Records at the New York District Attorney's Office*. New York: National Library Press, 1936, 255 pp.

3294 Tamburro, Giuseppe. *Il Problema del Meretricio Nella Storia, Nella Legislazione Attuale, nei Progetti all'esame del Parlamento*. Rome: Edizion i Scientifiche dell' Azienda Editoriale Italiana, 1948, 72 pp. In Italy. 3d ed revised, edited, amplified 1950, 84 pp.

3295 Teeters, N. K. "Early Days of the Magdalen Society of Philadelphia." Soc Serv R 30:158-67, Jun. '56.

3296 Terrot, Charles. Traffic in Innocents; the shocking story of White Slavery in England. New York: E. P. Dutton and Co., 1960.

3297 Thery, J. "De Saint Louis a Gaston Doumergue la Condition des Femmes Folles de Leur Corps." Mercure Fr 184:249-53 Nov. 15, 1925.

3298 Touraine, A. and P. Renault. "Prostitution and Syphilis in France from 1900 to 1932." Bull Soc Franc de Dermat et Syph (Reunion Dermat., Strasbourg) 40:1002-1008, Jul. '33.

3299 The Traffic in Girls: White Slavery as Now Practiced in America. Chicago: 1910(?), 31 pp. "Dangers of a large city."

3300 Turner, George Kibbe. "The Daughters of the Poor." McClure's 24:45-61, Nov. '09.

3301 Turner, G. K. "The Daughters of the Poor," in Weinberg, A. M. and Weinberg, L., eds., The Muckrakers. Simon and Schuster, 1961, pp.408-29.

3302 "Twenty-two Year's Progress in Social Hygiene Legislation in States." J Soc Hygiene 32:360, Nov. '46.

3303 Upson, A. T. "Purity Movement in Chicago." Miss R of the World 43:29-33, Jan. '20.

3304 "Wages of Sin; Chicago's Everleigh Club." Time 52:27, Sep. 27, 1948.

3305 Walker, Edwin C. Marriage and Prostitution: An Address at the Dinner of the Sunrise Club--May 19, 1913. Manhatten: Edwin C. Walker, 1913, pamphlet unbound, 28 pp.

3306 Walker, James. Walker's Review of White Slavery. Chicago: J. Walker, 1912, 62 pp. U. S.

3307 "Warnings to Girls from San Francisco." Survey 34:39, Apr. 10, 1915.

3308 Washburne, Charles. Come Into My Parlor. New York: Knickerbocker Pub. Co., 1934, and National Library Press, 1936. Reprinted by Belmont Books, 1961.

3309 Waterman, W. C. Prostitution and its Repression in New York City. New York: 1932, 164 pp. Reprinted 1968, Columbia Univ., Columbia Studies in the Social Sciences, no.352. New York: AMS Press.

3310 Wendt, Lloyd, and Herman Kogan. Lords of the Levee. Garden City: Garden City Pub. Co., 1944.

3311 "White Slave Trade." Contemporary R 82:735-40, Nov. '02 and Miss R of the World 26:149, Feb. '03.

3312 The White Slave Traffic. London: C. A. Pearson, 1913, 115 pp.

3313 "White Slavery in the Argentine." Literary Digest 106:22, Jul. 19, 1930.

3314 Whitlock, Brand. "The White Slave." Forum 51:193-216. Feb. '14.

3315 Whitlock, Brand. "The White Slave in America." English R 16:379-400, Feb. '14.

3316 Willis, W. N. Western Men with Eastern Morals. Intro. by R. A. Bennett. London: S. Paul, 1913, 264 pp.

3317 Willis, W. N. White Slave Market. Anglo-Eastern Pub. Co, 1933.

3318 Willis, W. N. The White Slaves of London. Boston: Richard G. Badger, 1913, 176 pp. and Anglo-Eastern Press, 1932. Account of Slave Trade in England. Somewhat exaggerated.

3319 Wilson, Jackson Stitt. The Harlots and the Pharisees. Berkeley: by the author, 1913. A Socialist pamphlet naming capitalism as the real evil.

3320 Wilson, Samuel Paynter. "Chicago" and its Cess-pools of Infamy. Chicago: 1909. White Slave traffic.

3321 Wisconsin. Legislative Committee to Investigate the White Slave Traffic and Kindred Subjects. Reports and Recommendations. Madison, Wis.: R. H. Hillyer, 1914, 246 pp.

3322 Wood, Clive, and Beryl Scutters. The Fight for Acceptance. Aylesbury, Eng.: Medical and Technical Pub. Co., 1970.

3323 Woolston, Howard B. Prostitution in the United States. New York: Century Co., 1921 and by the New York Bureau of Social Hygiene. Reprinted 1960 by E. P. Dutton and Co. An important pioneering sociological study.

3324 Yamamuro, G. "Social Evil in Japan." Miss R of the World 46:801-4, Oct. '23.

3325 Zahorova-Nemcova, M. "The Organization of Anti-prostitutional work in the Czechoslovak Republic." J Soc Hygiene 11:407-416, 1925.

3326 "Zones of Safety; Texas Cantonment Cities Made Safe for Health and Decency." Survey 38:349-50, Jun. 21, '17.

3327 Additon, Henrietta Silvas. City Planning for Girls: A Study of the Social Machinery for Case Work with Girls in Philadelphia. Social Service Monographs, No. 5. Chicago, Ill.: University of Chicago Press, 1928, 150 pp.

3328 Aronovici, G. Unmarried Girls with Sex Experience. Philadelphia: Bureau of Social Research of the Seybert Institute, 1915.

3329 Barbagallo, A., et al. "Environmental Factors in Juvenile Delinquency." Minerva Med 66(59):2949-53, September 12, 1975.

3330 Bell, Ernest A. Fighting the Traffic in Young Girls; or War on the White Slave Trade. G. S. Ball, 1910, 481 pp.

3331 Bell, M., editor. "Social correctives for delinquency." Yearbook National Probation Association 39, 1946, 328 pp.

3332 Bergeron, M., et al. "Deux Ans de Fonctionnement d'un Centre d' Observation pour Vagabonds Juveniles." Annee Med-psycholgique 108:612-15, 1950.

3333 Berkowitz, H. "Education the largest factor in the awakening of a new conscience." in, National conference of charities and correction. Proceedings, 1914, pp.205-11.

3334 Bingham, A. T. "Determinants of Sex Delinquency Among Adolescent Girls." Journal of Criminal Law and Criminology 13 (1923):494-586.

3335 Bingham, T. A. Girl that diappears: the real facts about the white slave trade. R. G. Badger, 1911.

3336 Bizard, L. "Vagabondage, prostitution and judicial statutes concerning vagabond minors." Paris med (annexe) 1:v-xiii, March 3, 1934.

3337 Bowen, L. De K. Road to destruction made easy. Chicago: Juvenile protective association, 1915.

3338 Bryan, James H. "Apprenticeships in Prostitution." Social Problems 12(3):287-97, Winter 1965. Also in Delinquency, Crime and Social Problems, pp 500-14. Edited by D. R. Cressey and D. A. Ward.

3339 Carlebach, Julius. Juvenile Prostitutes in Nairobi. East African Studies, No. 16. Kampala, Uganda: Applied Research Unit,East African Institute of Social Research, 1962, 50 pp.

3340 Cooper, C. R. Designs in scarlet. Boston: Little, Brown, 1939, 372 pp. Study of juvenile delinquency and organized prostitution.

3341 Curth, W. "Social problems of venereal diseases among New York youth." Arch Klin Exp Dermatol 227(1):637-40, 1966.

3342 Deardorff, N. R. "Unmarried girls with sex experience." National Municiple Review 5:529-10, July 1916.

3343 Doka, V., et al. "Analysis of juvenile delinquency in Bratislava in 1964." Cesk Gynekol 31(8):603-5, October 1966.

3344 Edholm-Sibley, M. G. Traffic in girls and Florence Crittenton missions. National purity association.n.d.

3345 Ekstrom, K. "One hundred teenagers in Copenhagen infected with gonorrhoea. A socio-psychiatric study." British Journal of Venereal Disease 42(3):162-6, September 1966.

3346 Farmer, R. D. and Harvey, P. G. "Alienated youth--a preliminary study of rootless young people--social and personality characteristics." Social Science Medicine 8(4):191-5, April 1974.

3347 Gane, E. M. "Community safeguards in the protection of childhood and youth." J Soc Hygiene 26:200-7, May '40.

3348 _____. "Why childrens' workers want law enforcement against prostitution." J Soc Hygiene 29:429-33, Oct. '43.

3349 Gardner, George E. "Sex Behavior of Adolescents in Wartime." Annals of American Academy of Political and Social Science, November 1944.

3350 Gibbens, T. C. N. "Juvenile Prostitution." British Journal of Delinquency 8(1):3-12, July 1957.

3351 Gray, Diana. "Turning-Out: A Study of Teenage Prostitution." Urban Life and Culture 1(4):401-425, January 1973.

3352 Hardar, Salem. La prostitution el la traite des femmes et des infants; pref de Louis Hugueny. Paris: Domet-Montchrestien, 1937. pp.409-24.

3353 Hatch, Willard Paukard. Prostitution and Sex Education. San Francisco, 1910, 320 pp.

3354 Heagerty, J. J. "Education in relation to prostitution." Journal of Social Hygiene 10:129-38, March 1924.

3355 Hodder, J. D. "What is being done for girls who go wrong." Pedagog Sem 16:361-6, September 1909.

3356 Holsopple, F. Q. Social Non Conformity in 420 Delinquent Girls. Philadelphia: United States Interdepartmental Social Hygiene Board, 1919.

3357 Imker, Henning and Rossner, Lutz. "Jugendliche im Einflussbereich der Prostitution." Die Deutsche Schule (October 1969), 61st year.

3358 Kagan, Herman. Prostitution and sexual promiscuity among adolescent female offenders. Dissertation, University of Arizona, 1969.

3359 Kammerer, P. G. Unmarried mother. Little, 1918.

3360 Kauffman, R. W. Girl that goes wrong. Moffat, 1911.

3361 Kirkendall, Lester A. "Circumstances associated with teenage boy's use of prostitution." Marriage and Family Living 22(2):145-49, May 1960.

3362 Koska, W. "Comparative analysis of harlotry acts committed with juveniles and adults." Prezegl Lek 30(4):401-5, 1973.

3363 Krishnaswamy, Shrimathy A. "A study of the responses of sex-delinquents, prostitutes and non-delinquent girls." Int J Sexol 8:97-9, 1954.

3364 League of Nations. Advisory committee for the protection and welfare of children and young people. Traffic in women and children committee. Report on the work of the 5th session. World peace foundation, April 17, 1926, 10 pp.

3365 League of Nations. Traffic in women and children committee. Conference of central authorities in eastern countries, Bandoeng (Java), February 2-13, 1937. Minutes. Internatational Document Service, 1937, 115 pp.

3366 League of Nations. Traffic in women and children committee. Conference of central authorities in eastern countries. Report. International Document Service, 1937, 115 pp.

3367 League of Nations. Traffic in women and children committee. Position of women of Russian origin in the Far East. World Peace Foundation, 1935, 16 pp.

3368 Le Clec'h, Jules. La prostitution des mineurs. Paris: Collection du Bulletin, 1910. Commentaire des lois nouvelles et secrets.

3369 LeMoal, Paul. Etude sur la prostitution des mineures. Paris: Editions sociales francaises, 1965, 216 pp.

3370 Lethbridge, Henry. "Girls in danger." Far Eastern Econ R 53:583-7, September 22, 1966.

3371 Lindsay, Mary K. "Prostitution: Delinquency's time bomb." Crime and Delinquency 16(2):151-7, April 1970. Suggests sufficiency of long sentences and utilization of halfway houses.

3372 London. Committee for suppressing the traffic in British Girls. _Six Years' Labour and Sorrow_. London: 1886, 111 pp.

3373 Luther, M. "Girls in the New York higher courts." _J Crim Law_ 6:126-8, May 1915.

3374 Marien, Kate. _Kinder von Prostituierten; eine sozialhygienische Analyse_. Hamburg: W. Bertelsmann, 1966, 100 pp. Socially handicapped children.

3375 Martin, P. _Les mineures vagabonds et prostitutes_. (Adolescent vagrant girls and prostitutes.) Dissertation at Lyon: 1939, 216 pp.

3376 Miner, M. E. "Problem of Wayward Girls and Delinquent Women." _Proceedings_ Am. Acad. Pol. Sci. 2:604-12, Jun. '12.

3377 Ness, Eliot. _What about girls?_ 3rd revised edition. New York: Public Affairs Commission, 1960. Originally published 1947, reprinted 1951.

3378 Nichols, J. L. _Fighting the Traffic In young Girls_.

3379 Niederhoffer, E. "Referat Dr. Cimbal (Altona) auf der Reichsconferenz evangelischer 1931 uber Heilpadagogik." _Zentbe P Psychotherap_ 4:533-37, 1931. Importance of childhood experiences emphasized.

3380 Oestereich, Heinrich. _Jugendschutz vor allem! Zur Jugendgefahrdung durch Prostitution und Bordelle_. Koln: Klettenberg, 1954, 15 pp.

3381 Padilla Pimentel, Manuel de J. "Prostitution in adolescence." _Revista de la clinica de la Conducta_ 6(13):10-8, December 1973.

3382 Philippon, Odette. _La jeunesse coupable vous accuse: les causes familiales et sociales de la delinquance juvenile; Enquete Mondiale_. Paris: Recueil Sirey, 1950, 276 pp.

3383 Pongratz, Liselotte. _Prostituiertenkinder_. Stuttgart: Gustav Fischer Verlag, 1964, 23 pp. Socially handicapped children.

3384 "Protection and welfare of children and young people." _League of Nations Monthly Summary_ 13:90-2, April 1933.

3385 Rappaport, M. F. "A protective service for promiscuous girls." _Fed Probation_ pp.32-6, January 1945. Also in _Baltimore Health N_ 23:25-35, April 1946.

3386 Reelfs, J. D. _La traite des femmes et des enfants et la maison de tolerance_. Geneva: Federation Abolitionniste Internationale, 1933, 93 pp.

3387 Risler, Marcelle. "Enquete sur la condition des prostituees mineures a Paris en 1960." L'hopital en l'aide sociale a Paris July-August, 1960, pp.515-9.

3388 Roe, C. G. Girl who disappeared. Saul Brothers, 1914.

3389 _____ Panders and their white slaves. Revell, 1910.

3390 _____ Prodigal daughter: the white slave evil and the remedy. Walter, 1911.

3391 Roosevelt, T. "Cause of decency." J Educ 74:367-8, October 12, 1911.

3392 Seagrove, M. "Causes underlying sex delinquency in young girls." J Soc Hyg 12:523-9, December 1926.

3393 Schachter, M. and Cotte, S. "Etude de la Prostitution Juvenile a la Lumiere du Test de Rorschach." Archives Internationales de Neurologie 70(1951):4-18. Young girl and boy prostitutes compared.

3394 _____. "Juvenile male prostitution. Clinico-psychological study of a megalosomic adolescent under age 14." Osp Psichiatr 37(1):123-44, January-June 1969.

3395 Seybert Institution. Bureau for social research. Unmarried girls with sex experience. Philadelphia: Bureau for social research of the Seybert Institution, 1916.

3396 Sipova, I. and Nedoma, K. "Family setting and childhood in socially and sexually depraved women." Ceskoslovenska Psychiatrie 68(3):150-3, June 1972.

3397 Spina, R. "La sensibilita general nei delinquenti e nelle prostitute." Rev Quind d Psicol I:65-70, 1897.

3398 Stanciu, E., et al. "Study of the etiology of criminal behavior disorders in a group of 61 juvenile delinquents." Neurol Psihiatr Neurochir 19(1):59-66, January-February 1974.

3399 Sumner, W. T. "Child protection and the social evil." Nat Educ Assn 1911:1110-6.

3400 Tappan, Paul Wilbur. Delinquent Girls in Court. New York: Columbia University Press, 1947. Reprinted by Patterson Smith, 1969.

3401 Terrot, Charles. Traffic in innocents, maiden tribute (a study of white slavery trafic of the nineteenth century). Muller, 1959, 230 pp.

3402 Thomas, W. I. The Unadjusted Girl. Boston: Little Brown, 1923.

3403 "Traffic in women and children inquiry concerning the system of state licensed houses in so far as it concerns the traffic." League of Nations Official Journal 6:1284-96, September 1925.

3404 Towne, A. W. "Community program for protective work with girls." Soc Hygiene 6:57-71, January 1920.

3405 United States. Children's bureau. Laws relating to sex offences against children. U. S. Children's Bureau, Supt. of documents, 1925.

3406 Uschi, Bob. Onderwerp: Jeugd prostitutie. Amsterdam: De Bezige Bij, 1971, 172 pp.

3407 Wessel, Rosa, editor. A case work approach to sex delinquents. Philadelphia: Pennsylvania School of Social Work, 1947, 132 pp. Collection.

3408 Wilson, V. W. "A Psychological study of juvenile prostitutes." Int J Soc Psychiat 5(1):61-73, Summer 1959.

3409 Young, T. S. "Girl guides." China W R 78:343, November 7, 1936.

3410 "Abatement act is dead: the New Jersey court of appeals declares act unconstitutional." Am Issue 13:1, June 28, 1919.

3411 Abbott, L. "Care of vicious women." Outlook 104:101-2, May 17, 1913.

3412 "The abolition of licensed or tolerated houses of prostitution." J Soc Hyg 21:109-17, March 1935.

3413 Addams, J. "Efforts to Humanize Justice." Survey 63:275-8, December 1, 1929.

3414 ____. "Plea for a new legislature to make and enforce laws against vice." J Crim Law 4:304-6, June 1913.

3415 Additon, H. S. "Work among delinquent women and girls." Ann Am Acad 79:152-60, September 1918.

3416 "Age of Consent." Harpers Weekly 47:732, May 2, 1903.

3417 "Against nature: Wolfenden report." Economist 185:844, December 7, 1957.

3418 "Agreement against White Slavery to come into force in July." United Nations Bulletin 10:498, May 15, 1951.

3419 Aimee, Lucas. Des Dander de la Prostitution. Paris: Chez l'author, 1841. Gives ordonnances de 1832, brief synopsis-sort of essay.

3420 Alphonso, R. M. La Reglamentacion de la Prostitutcion. Breves apuntes sobre como debe ser en Cuba. Havana, 1912, 174 pp.

3421 "All out war on prostitution called best way to curb crime."Newsweek 18:58, September 29, 1941.

3422 Ambrosini, Giuseppe. "La casa di prostituzione nel conetto della legge Merlin." Guistizia penale (June 1960):466-79.

3423 Amelunxen, Clemens. Der Zuhalter. Hamburg: Kriminalistik Verlag, 1967, 119 pp. Prostitution in Federal Republic.

3424 American social hygiene association. Case against the red light district. The association, 1920.

3425 ________________. Forms and Principles of State Social Hygiene. 1944, 16 pp. Reprinted from the Journal of Social Hygiene.

3426 ________________. Law enforcement. The Association, 1919.

3427 ________________. Segregation of prostitution and the injunction and abatement law against houses of prostitution. The Association, 1916.

3428 ________________. Social hygiene legislation manual, 1921. The Association, 1921.

3429 ________________. Standard forms of laws. In six parts. The Association, 1919.

3430 ________________. Why let it burn: the case against the red light district. New York: The Association, 1919, 16 pp.

3431 Anderson, E. "Prostitution and social justice: Chicago, 1910-15." Soc Serv R 48:203-28, June 1974.

3432 Anderson, V. V. "Immoral woman as seen in court: a preliminary report." Med Rec 93:78, January 12, 1918. Also in J Crim Law 8:902-20, March, 1918. Reprinted from Boston Medical School and Surgical Journal December 27, 1917.

3433 Anslinger, Harry, and Oursler, Will. The murderers: the story of narcotic gangs. New York: Farrar, Straus and Cudahy, 1961, 307 pp.

3434 "Application of the Mann Act." Law Guild Rev 6: 652, November-December 1946.

3435 "Application of the Mann Act." Yale Law R 56:718-30, April 1947.

3436 Archdale, Richard Latham. Prostitution and Persecution. London: Pall Mall Press, 1960, 30 pp.

3437 Arendt, Sisiter Henriette. Menschen, die den pfad verloren erlebnisse aus meiner funfjahrigen tatigkeit als polizei-assistentung Stuttgart. Stuttgart: M. Kielmann, 1907, 115 pp.

3438 Arizona. Act making it a misdemeanor for any person who, being the owner or lessee of any building or place, permits the same to be used for purposes of prostitution, assignation, etc., and providing punishment therefore. A referendum has been filed against this act and therefore it must be submitted to the electors of the state at the next general election in November, 1918. (Ch. 62. P. L. 1917)

3439 Arkansas. Act to prohibit prostitution, lewdness, and assignation. (No 240, Acts 1943)

3440 Arkansas. Act to suppress houses of prostitution, punish the keepers thereof, and welfare inmates thereof, and for other purposes. (Act 361, Acts 1941)

3441 Arleff, Wilfried Peter. Die Prostitution im geltenden und zukunftigen Strafrecht; zugleich ein Beitrag zur Bestimmung der Grenzen Staatlicher Strafbefgnis. Koln, 1973, 142 pp.

3442 "Assembly action on White Slave traffic." *United Nations Bulletin* 5:1019, December 15, 1948.

3443 Association for Moral and Social Hygiene. *An Injustice to be Remedied: The Law and the Prostitute*. London, 1950, 7 pp.

3444 ________________. *Case against the report of the street offences commission*. The Association, 1929.

3445 ________________. *Compulsory repatriation of Prostitutes*. The Association.

3446 ________________. *No regulation, no traffic in women*. The Association.

3447 ________________. *Present day opinion on regulation*. The Association, 1929.

3448 Attribution Des Moeurs. *Police Municipale-Le 16 Juillet Rapport*. France, 32 pp.

3449 Avril de Sainte-Croix, G. *Traffic in women and children*. World Peace Foundation, 1925.

3450 Babcock, B. *With claw and fang*. Indianapolis: Clean Politics Pub. Co., 1911.

3451 Bacharach, A. *Der Begriff der Kuppelei*. Breslau, 1911, 106 pp.

3452 Bailay, Stephen (pseud.). *Bondage: sex slavery*: a documentary report on the international scene today. Heinemann, 1968.

3453 Bailey, Derrick Sherwin, editor and compiler. *Sexual Offenders and Social Punishment*. London: Westminster Church Information Board, 1956.

3454 Balfour of Burleigh, Lord. *The Relation Between State Regulation of Prostitution and the Traffic in Women and Children*. 1944, 4 pp. Reprinted in 1958. A Paper given at a Conference of the British Medical Association.

3455 Ballard, J. "Prostitution and the law." *Spec* 182:398+, March 25, 1949. Reply by Hardwick, K. B. *Spec* 182:478, April 8, 1949.

3456 Barber, R. W. "Application of the Mann Act." *Geo L. J.* 35:407-10, March 1947.

3457 Barnes, C. T. *White Slave Act*. Private, 1946. Salt Lake City.

3458 Barnes, Harry Elmer, and Negley, K. Teeters. New Horizons in Criminology. 3rd edition. Englewood Cliffs: Prentice Hall, 1954.

3459 Bartsch, Gerog. Prostitution, Kuppelei und Zuhalterei. Hamburg: Deutsche Polizei, 1956, 93 pp.

3460 Batria, Puran. "The Criminal aspect of prostitution." Internat'l Crim Pol R 206:80-8, March 1967.

3461 Bauer, W. "Freie Prostitution oder Reglementierung." OTV-Presse, Zentralorgan der Gewerschaft offentliche Dienste, Transport und Verkehr Polizeidienst August 1:246-8, and November 1:342-4, 1956. A brief history of the measures and current status of prostitution in Deutchland.

3462 Beavers, J. L. "Suppression preferable to segregation." Am City 9:22-4, July 1913.

3463 Beck, J. J. Tractatus de eo quo justum est circa struprum. Nuremberg, 1743.

3464 Becker, W."Gesetzliche Bestimmunger im Kamp gegen moderne Formen der Prostitution." Polizei-Praxis April 1957:85-8. Pro reglementation.

3465 Bell, Ernest Albert. Fighting traffic in young girls. Chicago, 1910, 481 pp. Also issued under title War on the White Slave Traffic. Chicago: Charles C. Thompson, 1909.

3466 Bell-Taylor, Ch. Dangers de la reglementation. Geneva: Federation abolitionniste internationale, [N.D. before 1902].

3467 "Bemerkungen des Chefarztes zur Regelung der Prostitution." Oesterr San.-Wes. (Vienna) 13:225-227, 1901.

3468 Benedetto, Guglielmo di. "Il capitolo del meretricio nel T.U. leggi di P.S." Rivista di Polizia Rome, February 1958:57-82.

3469 Beotra, B. R. The Suppression of Immoral Traffic in Women and Girls, Act 1956, with State Rules. 2nd edition. Allahabad, India: Law Book Co., 1970, 390 pp. Deals with prostitution in India.

3470 Beraud, F. F. A. and Beraud, Albert Montemont. Les filles publiques de Paris la police qui les regit; precidees d'une notice historique sur la prostitution chez les divers peuples de la terre. 2 volumes. Paris and Leipzig: Chez Desforge et Compagnie, 1839.

3471 Berger, R. Un Aspect de l'active sociale de la Societe des Nations. La traite des femmes. Montpellier, 1926, 151 pp.

3472 Bertani, A. La prostituzione patenta e il regolamento sanitaria Lettera ad A. De Pretis Milano. Librerieggalleria, 1881.

3473 Berthelsen, C. P. The Civil Regulation of Morality and Prostitution; a critical enquiry into the question of prostitution. Copenhagen: 1896.

3474 Blackwell, A. S. "State regualtion of the social evil." Woman Citizen 3:227+, August 17, 1918.

3475 Bliem, M. J. "Where shall we drive the prostitute?" Social Hygiene Bul 5:1,7, January 1918.

3476 Blocq-Mascart, Maxime. La lutte contre la prostitution et la debauche. Paris:1945, 28 pp. A pamphlet.

3477 Blom-Cooper, Louis. "Prostitution: a socio-legal comment on the case of Dr. (Stephen) Ward." British J Soc 15:65-71, March 1964.

3478 "Blow at Freedom? Jelke trial." Time 61:84, February 16, 1953.

3479 Blum, P. "Applications of laws of April 13 and April 24, 1946 and sanitary control." Ann de dermat et syph Bull. Soc. franc de dermat et syph. 1) 7:34-8, February 1947.

3480 Blumer, Herbert, and Hauser, Philip. Movies, Delinquency and Crime. New York: MacMillan, 1933.

3481 Boldt, J. Prostitutionens reglementering och Lakaresallskapet. Helsingfors, 1897, 24 pp.

3482 Booth, B. "The White Slave Traffic Act." Calif. S. B. J. 20:102-5, March-April 1945.

3483 Borel, Thomas. The White Slavery of Europe. Translated by Joseph Edmondson. London: Dyer Bros. N. D. , 1876.

3484 Bovet, Felix. Les limites de l'intervention de l'Etat en matiere de prostitution. Geneva: Federation abolitionniste internationale, [n.d. before 1902].

3485 ______. La prostitution au point de vue legal. Geneva: Federation abolitionniste internationale, [n.d. before 1902].

3486 Braden, F. "Steady pressure on the prostitution racket; a police cheif needs support." J Social Hyg 38:193-203, May 1952.

3487 Brazao, Arnaldo. Abolicionismo. 1945, 14 pp.

3488 Bridel, Louis. La question des moeurs et l'Etat. Geneva: Federation abolitionniste internationale. [n.d. before 1902].

3489 ______. Mesures legales propres a restreindre la prostitution. Geneva: Federation abolitionniste internationale, [n.d. before 1902].

3490 **Brintzer, C. Stra'frechtliche Massnahem** zur Bekampfung der Prostitution. Eine rechtshistorische Untersuchung. Kiel, 1933, 127 pp.

3491 British parliamentary committee, Sir John Wolfenden, chairman. Reposrt of the Committee on Homosexual Offences and Prostitution. London: H. M. S. Stationery Office, 1957.

3492 Bryant, A. "Wolfenden Report." Illus Lond News 231:496, September 28, 1957.

3493 Burkhardt, Rudolf. Der Strum bricht los. Der Streit um den Wolfenden Report in England. Ein Report uber einen Report. Kommentare und Ubersetzungen. Zurich, 1957, 16 pp.

3494 Butte, L. "Le Projet de loi concernant la prostitution et la prophylaxie des maladies veneriennes adopte par la commission extra-parlementaire du regime des moeurs." Ann de Therap Dermat et Syph 7:49-60, 1907.

3495 Butte, L. "La question des maisons de tolerance appreciee par les maires des principales villes de France." Ann de Therap Dermat et Syph (Paris) 5:73-77, 1905.

3496 Buxton, E. O. "Prostitution and its Remedy." Am J Pol 3:39.

3497 Caldrone, M. S. "'Pornography'as a public health problem." Am J Public Health 62(3):374-6, March 1972.

3498 California. "Red light abatement law." Cal Comwealth Club Transac 9:469-503, September, 1914. Issued as a separate report. Gives majority and minority reports on the law which came before the voters of California in the November election. Much information is included. Adopted in November 1914 by the voters: Yes-402,629, No-352,821.

3499 "California red-light law still in doubt." Survey 33:167, November 14, 1914.

3500 "The campaign against the white slave traffic, prostitution, and venereal diseases." Rev Prat(Paris) 11:Suppl.VIII-XVIII, January 21, 1961. In French.

3501 "Campaign against vice." Outlook 66:874-6, December 8, 1900.

3502 Campbell, S. Samuel. Sex and Blackmail Rackets Exposed. Girard, Kansas: Haldeman-Julius Pub, 31 pp.

3503 Caprio, Frank, and Brenner, Donald. Sexual Behavior: Psycho-Legal Aspects. New York: Citadel Press, 1961. See 249-52.

3504 Carrasco Canalis, Carlos. "Consideraciones en torno a la policia de la moralidad en Espana." Ponencias espanolas (IV Congress internacional de derecho compardo[In Hamburg]), pp 223-72. Barcelona, 1962. A study of the moral police and prostitution and the law in Spain.

3505 Casalinuovo, Aldo. "Un nuovo capitolo nella storia del diritto Haliano. Le norme penali della legge Merlin." La Calabria Giudizaria XXXII 1958(Milan):137-57. A study following the law abolishing tolerated houses in Italy.

3506 Catlin, G. E. G. "Moral offences and the criminal law." Outlook (London) 60:807-9, December 17, 1927.

3507 Cecil, R. H. "One law for men...." Spec 185:380, October 13, 1950.

3508 "Chart of laws to suppress prostitution." In World's social evil, pp 392-3. By W. Burgess. 1914.

3509 Chaterlon, Lis. En 1963 Aun Existe la Trata de Blancas. Barcelona: Ediciones Rodegar, 1963. Some fictionalized cases of individuals based on undercover agents dealing with prostitutes.

3510 Chesser, E. Live and let live. London: Heinemann, 1958. Also Philosophical Library, 1958.

3511 Chicago. City council. Creation of a health safety commission: and ordinance creating a health and safety commission, recommended for passage by the Comittee on judiciary, November 20, 1922. Pamphlet no. 1270. Municiple reference library, 1922.

3512 Chopman, John. Prostitution: Governmental Experiments in Controlling It. Reprinted from Westminister Review n.s. LXXIII, January 1870. London: Trubner and Co., 1870. Description of various attempts at regulation. Concludes repression a failure-need for regulation. British governmental indifference and repression of contient.

3513 Choveronius, Bermondus. Comentarri...untitulum de publicis concubinarcias. Nunc primium germania excusi. Speyer B. Albinus, 1598, 883 pp.

3514 Chrysler, Charles Byron. White Slavery. Chicago, 1090, 251 pp.

3515 Clarke, W. "Postwar Social Hygiene Problems and Strategy." *J Soc Hygiene* 31:4-15, Jan. '45.

3516 "Clause 79 of the Page law." *Survey* 25:276-80, November 19, 1910.

3517 "Clause 79 of the Page law is held unconstitutional." *Survey* 25:416-7, December 10, 1910.

3518 Cloete, Stuart. *Abductors*. New York: Simon and Schuster, 1966, 433-7 pp.

3519 Close, K. "In May Act areas." *Survey* 79:67-70, March 1943.

3520 "Closing a vice district by strangulation." *Survey* 35:299, December 4, 1915.

3521 Cogiart, P. J. *La prostitution. Etude de science criminelle* 1939, 269 pp.

3522 Colcord, J. C. "Fighting prostitution." *Survey* 78:214-5, August 1942.

3523 Cole, W. E. "Delinquent women-the prostitutes." *Tenn L Rev* 13:71-8, February 1935.

3524 Colmet-Daage, F. *La reglementation de la prostitution ou l'organisation du desordre*. Geneva: Federation Abolitionnist Internationale. [n.d. before 1942], 29 pp.

3525 Colorado, Illinois, Indiana, and Michigan legislatures, at their 1915 sessions, passed abatement and injunction laws; Ohio had a bill; Missouri had a bill which would probably have passed had it come to a vote; Wisconson had nineteen social hygiene bills recommended by the vice commission besides other bills on the subject.

3526 "Columbia, S. C. adopts new ordinance." *Social Hygiene Bulletin* 4:3, September 1917.

3527 Comite Abolicionista Perua. (Pamphlet). Contents: "Legislacion abolicionista en Vigencia." by S. Solano; "Enfermedades venereas," by A. Higginson; "Josefina Butler una mjuer admirable," by B. Hutardo. Lima: 1959.

3528 Commenge, ____. "La question de la prostitution devant le Senat." *Bull Med* (Paris) 9:659-663, 1895.

3529 Committee of 14. *Annual report for 1930*. 1931, 66 pp, tables.

3530 *Compilation of laws on age of consent*. American social hygiene association, October 1916, 72 pp.

3531 Compilation of laws on injunction and abatement. American social hygiene association, October 1916, 163 pp.

3532 Compilation of laws on keeping disorderly houses. American social hygiene association, October 1916, 71 pp.

3533 Compilation of laws on white slavery. American social hygiene association, October 1916, 175 pp.

3534 "Concerning the situation in the Chicago morals court." J Social Hyg 19:170-1, March 1933.

3535 Connecticut. Act concerning houses of assignation, lewdness and prostitution. Declared to be nuisances; abatement provided for. (Ch. 362, P. L. 1917)

3536 Constant, Jean. "Reglementation administrative et repression penale en matiere de prostitution et de proxenetisme." Rapports belges au VI Congress international de droit compare (Hamburg, 1962), pp. 417-36. Brussels, 1962.

3537 Contagious Diseases Acts (Women). "Tables." Westminister Review 152:249-60, September 1899; 152:397-443, October 1899; 152:488-509, November 1899; 152:609-27, December 1899.

3538 "Convention on traffic in persons adopted by [U. N. general] assembly." United Nations Bulletin 8:56-9, January 1, 1950.

3539 Convention pour la repression de la trait des etres humains et de l'exploitation de la prostitution d'autrui. Lake Success, 1950. Text in English, French, Chinese, Spanish and Russian.

3540 Cook, F. J. "Corrupt Society." Nation 196:478, June 1, 1963.

3541 Cooper, Courtney Ryley. Designs In Scarlet. Reprinted. Garden City: Blue Ribbon, 1942.

3542 __________. Here's To Crime. Boston: Little, Brown and Co., 1937.

3543 Cosson, George. Iowa injunction and abatement law. Government printing, 1912.

3544 _____. "Why an abatement and injunction law?" Am City 16:44, January 1917. Synopsis of an address delivered at the annual meeting of the St. Louis social hygiene society, held in St. Louis, Mo., November 19-21, 1916.

3545 Costa Manso, Odilon da. Prostitucao e poder da policia. Sao Paulo, 1952, 13 pp. Criticizes the police for not Enforcing the law.

3546 Costello, Mary. "Legalization of prostitution." Editorial Research Reports August 25, 1971:653-70.

3547 Cowan, Rex. "The Female Prostitute." Criminal Law Review September 1956:611-14. A London Journal.

3548 Cowley, M. "Vice squad carries on."New Republic 63:147-9, June 25, 1930; and 63:177-80, July 2, 1930.

3549 Creel, G. "Where is the vice fight?" Harper's Weekly 59:340-2, October 10, 1914.

3550 "Criminal law admendent(white slave traffic)." Spec 108:747-9, May 11, 1942.

3551 "Criminal code-Bill of rights-whether offence of vagrancy by common prostitute constitutes discrimination by sex." U B C L Rev 6:442, December 1971.

3552 "Criminal law-conspiracy by women to violate Mann Act." Ga B J 14:372-3, February 1952. U.S. vs. Martin.

3553 "Criminal law--Conspiracy to corrupt public morals." Camb L J 1961:144, November 1961. Shaw vs. D.P.P.

3554 "Criminal law-placing female in house of prostitution." Wash Law Rev 24:67, February 1949. State vs. Basden.

3555 "Criminal law-Mann Act-dominant purpose test." Wayne L Rev 9:369, Winter 1963. U.S. vs. Hon.

3556 "Criminal law: one act-one crime? two crimes? three? or 84?" Ga B J 17:270-5, November 1954. Bill vs. U.S.

3557 "Criminal law-the principle of harm and its application to laws criminalizing prostitution." Denver L J 51:235-62, 1974.

3558 "Criminal law-White Slave Traffic Act-several offences arising from a single transaction." Minn L Rev 30:124-5, January 1946. U. S. vs. St. Claire.

3559 "Criminal law-white slave traffic-other immoral acts." Loyola L Rev 10:268, 1960-61. U. S. vs. McClung.

3560 Cross, H. H. U. Lust market. New York: Citadel Press, 1958.

3561 Crowdy, R. E. "The Humanitarian activities of the League of Nations, with discussion." Royal Inst Internat'l Affairs J 6:153-69, May 1927.

3562 ______. "League of Nations; international position with regard to prostitution and the suppression of traffic in women and children." J Social Hygiene 10:549-59, December 1924.

3563 Crown, S. "Pornography and sexual promiscuity." Med Sci Law 13(4):239-43, October 1973.

3564 "Cry Wolfenden[committee at odds on prostitution]." Economist 183:1136+, June 29, 1957.

3565 Dallagrac, Dominique. Dossier prostitution. Translated by Antonio Vlaiente. Paris: Robert Laffront, 1966, 316 pp. Barcelona: Ayma, 1968. A collection of documents dealing with prostitution.

3566 "Dangerous legislation again." Woman Citizen 4:59, June 21, 1919.

3567 Delahaye, Jean. L'Orient, quartier reserve. Fed. Ab Int, 1949, 32 pp.

3568 Deloynes, ____. "Sur un projet de reglementation de la prostitution." Rev San de Bordeaux 5:73-76, 1888.

3569 Demiere, Lise. L'interement administratif des prostitutees dans le Canton de Vaud. Geneva, to obtain the diploma, March 1953, 73 pp. A study presented to the School of Social Studies.

3570 Denmark. Justitsministeriet. Udvalget til Overvejelse af Foranstaltninger prostituerede Kuinder og Aendring af de gaeldende Bestemmelser til Modarbejdelse af Prostitutionen. Betaenking om foranstaltninger til bekaempelse af prostitutionen, etc.. Copenhagen, 1955, 145 pp.

3571 Denning, Alfred Thompson, Lord. Lord Denning's report. London: H. M. Stationery Office, 1963, 113 pp. Great Critian Parliment.

3572 Denver. Morals commission. Report concerning licensed cafes and restaurants. Denver: Commisssioners of the city and county of Denver, 1913.

3573 Despres, A. "Sur la prostitution reglementee et ses rapports avec la depopulation." Bull Soc d'Anthrop de Paris 12:158-161, 1877, 2, s. Discussion: 161-166.

3574 Devine, T. "Weapons for the cities war on prostitution." Am City 61:85-6, January 1946.

3575 Dickey, Anthony. "Soliciting for the purposes of prostitution." Crim Law Review October 1969:538-44.

3576 Dieckhoff, Albr. Zur Rechtslage im derzeitigen Sittenstrafrech. Hamburg, 1958, 112 pp. Laws in Germany and in Switzerland dealing with moral legislation, including prostitution.

3577 "Difficulty in prostitution control." Am City 57:11, October 1942.

3578 "Discussion of the construction, applicability and effect of the federal 'white slave traffic act'." L R A 1915 A 862. Case-note to Johnson vs. U. S.

3579 Disney, John. A view of Ancient Laws Against Morality and Profanity. Cambridge: C. Crownfield, 1724.

3580 "Disorder in the streets." Law Times 164:309, October 22, 1927.

3581 District of Columbia supreme court has affirmed the Kenyon "red-light" law, modeled after the Iowa abatement and injunction act(Press rept July 10,1915).

3582 Dolleans, E. La Police des moeurs. Paris, 1903, 262 pp.

3583 Dominique, Pierre. Pour la reouverture des maisons closes. And Mancini, Jean-Gabriel. Contre la reouverture des maisons closes. Collection Pour ou Contre. Nancy: Berger-Levrault, 1967, 160 pp. The pros and cons of tolerated prostitution.

3584 Donato di Migliardo, Francesco. "Della prostituzione." Giustizia penale (May 1961):138-50.

3585 D'Orban, P. T. "Female narcotic addicts: a follow-up study of criminal and addiction careers." Brit Med J 4(1888):345-7, November 10, 1973.

3586 Dosch, A. "Extinguishing the red-light; operation of abatement laws on the Pacific coast." Sunset 37:38-40, August 1916.

3587 "Do the contagious disease acts suceed?" Westminster Review 152:608-27, December 1899, and 153:135-58, February 1900.

3588 Douglas, Ariz. "Ordinance defining certain ofences against public morals, and providing for the punishment of the same."(Ord. no. 177 passed July 23, 1917). U. S. War dept. Comm. on training camp activities pp. 12-3, 1917. What some communities of the West and Southwest have done for the protection of the morals and health of soldiers and sailors.

3589 Dragotti, G. "Reform of the Merlin law." Policinico [Prat] 72(41):1409-11, October 11, 1965.

3590 Drake, B. "Criminal law (amendment) bill." New Statesman 16:336, December 18, 1920.

3591 "Dramatizing vice." Lit Digest 47:577-8, October 4, 1913.

3592 Drummond, Isabel. The Sex Paradox. New York: G. P. Putnam's Sons, 1953. Deals with the law.

3593 Drysdale, C. R. "On Prostitution." Med Press and Circ (London) 7:411, 1869.

3594 Drysdale, C. R. "La Reglementation de la Prostitution." Cong Period Internat d Sc Med Compt Rend (Amsterdam, 1879) 6:88-92, 1880.

3595 Dufflin, Marie. "So you can't do anything about prostitution?" Prison World March 1944:+.

3596 Easley, E. T. "The present state of the argument in favor of a contagious diseases act." Richmond and Louisville M J (Louisville) 22:297-327, 1876.

3597 Edger, H. "Prostitution and International Women's League." Radical R 1:397.

3598 Edmondson, R. J. "Legal meaning of prostitution." Justice of the Peace 107:483-4, October 9, 1943.

3599 Egbert, James Thomas. Prostitution and the Law. London: Heinemann, 1951.

3600 "Eliminate the vice district." Soc Hygiene 3:107-9, January 1917.

3601 Elliott, Mabel A. Crime in Modern Society. New York: Harper and Brothers, 1952.

3602 Ellis, Havelock. "White Slave Crusade." In Essays in war time pp 116-26. London: Constable, 1917.

3603 Elster, A. "Die absolute Kriminalitat des Zuhalters." Krim M 11: 52-4, 1936. Essential criminality of the procurer. Parasitic existence is contrary to Nazi ideal of manly honor.

3604 "End of Clause 79." Survey 26:552-3, July 8, 1911.

3605 England. British Social Hygiene Council. Joint Standing Committee of the British Social Hygiene Council and the Conference of British Missionary Societies. Traffic in Women. Official and non-official co-operative action in combating the traffic in the East. 1934, 95 pp.

3606 England. Commons, House of. Report to the Select Committee appointed to inquire into the Contagious Diseases Act. London, 1882, 750 pp.

3607 England. Home Office. Committee on Homosexual Offences and Prostitution. Report of the Committee on Homosexual Offences and Prostitution. Presented to Parliament by the Secretary of State for the Home Department and the Secretary of State for Scotland, etc.. London, 1957, 155 pp.

3608 "Erie puts out the red lights." Survey 50:97, April 15, 1923.

3609 Everett, R. H. "Can We Regulate Prostitution?" Federal Probation 11(1947):39-42.

3610 ______. "International traffic in women and children." J Soc Hyg 13:269-88, May 1927.

3611 ______. "Program emphases for preparedness condition." J Soc Hyg 26:364-6, November 1940.

3612 Fabre de Morlhon, J. "Measures regarding minor criminals and sex offenders." Ann Med Leg (Paris) 47(6):665-9, November 1967.

3613 "Failure of charge of encouraging prostitution(Rex vs. Parker)." Justice of the Peace 94:206, March 29, 1930.

3614 Fairchild, F. H. "Suppression of prostitution and allied vice." J Soc Hyg 37:322-31, October 1951.

3615 Falconer, M. P. "Segregation of Delinquent women and girls as a war problem." Ann Am Acad 79:160-6, September 1918.

3616 "Farwell to the Committee of Fourteen." Literary Digest 114:15, December 17, 1932.

3617 Federationa abolitionniste internationale published several documents before 1902. Statuts de la Federation. Simple expose du but et des principes de la Federation. Actes du Congres de Geneve 1877. Materiaux recueilis pour les sections du Congres de Geneve 1889. Situation Abolitionniste mondiale Geneva:1853. Souvener de la Conference de Geneve (1899).

3618 Federal Probation for April, 1943 is devoted to a symposium dealing with a general survey of the problem; some aspects of venereal disease prevention, control, and treatment; the repression of prostitution; and the redirection of the prostitute.

3619 Federal Security Agency. Social Prostection Division. Techniques of Law Enforcement Against Prostitution. Washington: Government Printing Office, 1943.

3620 ____________. Techniques of Law Enforcement in the Use of Police Women, with Special Reference to Social Protection. Washington: Goverment Printing Office, 1945.

3621 Fiaux, Louis. *L'Armee et La Police des Moeurs*. Paris: Felix Alcan, 19??.

3622 ______. *Le delite penal de contamination intersexualle*. Geneva: Federation Abolition, [n.d.], 261 pp.

3623 ______. *Les maisons de tolerance, leur femeture*. Geneva: Federation abolitionniste internationale, [n.d. before 1902].

3624 ______. *La police des moeurs en France et dans les principaux pays dex l'Europe*. Paris:1888.

3625 ______. *La prostituion "cloitree", Les maisons de femmes autorisees par la police devant le medecine publique*. Brussells: Lamertin, 1902?.

3626 ______. *La prostitution reglementee et les pouvoirs publics dans les principaux Etats des deux Mondes*. 3 volumes. Paris: Alcan, 1902.

3627 Fielding, Sir John. *An Account of the Origin and effects of a police, set on foot by the grace of the Duke of Newcastle in the year 1753. To which is added a plan for preserving those deserted girls in this town who become prostitutes from necessity*. London: A. Millar, 1958, 64 pp.

3628 "Fighting the world traffic in women and children." *Review of Reviews, American* 69:102, January 1924.

3629 Figueiredo Ferraz, Esther de. *A prostituicao remanescente de escravatura femina*. Sao Paulo, 1952, 16 pp. A speech given at a conference, Centre academique de criminologie de l'Ecole de police.

3630 File, K. N. "NArcotics involvement and female criminality." *Addict Dis* 1(2):177-88, 1974.

3631 "Les 'filles' victimes des hommes." Numero special of *Moissons nouvelles* No. 27 Clichy, 1958, 88 pp. Le Nid' 4th brochure.

3632 Finch, S. W. *Federal campaign against the white slave traffic*. New York probation and protective association, December 1912, 16 pp. Reprinted from the Fourth annual report of the New York probation association.

3633 "Flatfoot floozies; police technique in Washington, D. C.." *Time* 95:44+, May 18, 1970.

3634 "Flatfoot floozies; police women arrest customers in Washington, D. C.." *Newsweek* 75:99, May 18, 1970.

3635 Flexner, Abraham. "Legal and administrative phases of the social hygiene problem." J of the Soc of Sanitary and Moral Prophylaxis 5:215-23, October 14, 1914.

3636 ________. "Next steps in dealing with prostitution." National Conference of Charities and Correction. Proceedings 1915:253-60.

3637 ________. Regulation of prostitution in Europe. American social hygiene association, 1914, 15 pp.

3637A Flodin, F. Det nya italienska Prostitutionsreglementet. Finska Lakaresallskapet: Handlingar, 1892.

3638 Foix, Pedro. Problemas sociales de dercho penal. Mexico: Ediciones de la sociedad mexicana de Eugenesia, 1942, 272 pp. Deals with Spanish laws of the second republic in 1931.

3639 Foril, A. Zur Frage der staatlichen Regulierung der Prostitution. Tages-und Lebensfragen, 1892, 31 pp.

3640 Fosdick, R. B. "Prostitution and the police." Social Hygiene 2:11-19, January 1916. Also published seperatly by the American Social Hygiene Association, 1916. Presented at the Central states conference on the problems of social hygiene, Chicago, October 26, 1915.

3641 "For the suspicion of an intention." Woman Citizen 4:114-4, July 5, 1919.

3642 "Fourtune survey: is legalized prostitution best way to cure the national evil of venereal disease?" Fourtune 15:164+, January 1937.

3643 Fowler, William. Speech on the Contagious Disease Act. London: W. Tweedie and Company, 1870. Says French system failed because not all women registered.

3644 Frankignoul, Louis. Proces moral de la prostitution et de sa reglementation. Geneva: FAI, 1952.

3645 Franklin, Z. C. "Report on prostituion asks local law enforcement officers to maintain 'the same degree of vigilance in this **important** task as **manifest** the past year'." Nat Munic R 32:83-5, February 1943.

3646 "Free choice under 40D." New Statesmen 11:406-7, August 24, 1918.

3647 French, S. "Prostitution and the law; a late eighteenth century view." Justice of the Peace 119:129-30, February 26, 1955.

3648 Frenkel, F. E. "Sex Crime and its Socio-historical background." J Hist Ideas 1964 25:333-52.

3649 Friedrich, O. "Reflections on the sad profession; Time essay." Time 98:34-5, May 23, 1971.

3650 Fujita, Taki. "Prostitution prevention law." Contemporary Japan

3651 Gans, H. S. "Consequences of unenforceable legislation." Pro Am Acad Pol Sci 1:563-89, June 1911.

3652 Gautier, Alfred. "La femme dans le projet de Code penal suisse." Revue penale Suisse 1912 pp 231-95.

3653 Gay, Margherita. "Intorno alla Legge Merlin." ALi (July-August, 1964):99-103. Nos. 7-9, 24:484-97, 1956.

3654 Gemaehling, P. Verso un Nuovo Ordine di Costume (Con quali mezzi legali si puo lottare contro la prostituzione). Geneva: FAI, 1950, 15 pp.

3655 General Assembly Against Vice. Dept. of Social Prevention. "Report: concept of vice." Arch Mex Ven.-Sif y Dermat 3:59-72, Mar.-Apr. '44.

3656 George, B. J., jr. "Delimitation of Administrative Regulation and Penal Sanctions in the Field of Prostitution Proxenetism." Report given at the VIth Congress International de droit compare held in Hamburg, 1962. 15 pp. Available at Ann Arbor, Michigan.

3657 George, B. J. "Legal, Medical and Psychiatric Considerations in the Control of Prostitution." Mich Law R 60:717, Apr. '62.

3658 Georgia. Act declaring houses of lewdness, prostitution and assignation nuisances. No.230, P. L. 1917.

3659 Gerstlacher, J. A. Tractatus Medico-legalis de Stupro in Usum Eorum qui Jurisprudentiae et Medicinae Opera dan Praecipue Eroum qui in Foro Versantur. Erlangen, 1772.

3660 Ghadialli, D. P. F. Railroading a Citizen. 2v. Malaga, N. J.: Spectro-Chrome Inst., 1926.

3661 Gibbens, T. C. "Female Offenders." Br J Psychiatry spec. no. 9:326-33, '75.

3662 Gibbons, H. "Should prostitution be licensed?" Pacific M and S J (San Francisco) ns 1:294-299, 1867-8.

3663 Gihon, A. L. "Government regulation of prostitution." Md M J (Balt.) 8:518-521, 1881-2.

3664 Gihon, A. L. "The prevention of venereal disease by legislation." Sanitarian (New York) 10:321-343, 1882.

3665 Gilman, Mrs. CPS. "Parasitism and Civilized Vice," in Schmalhausen, S. D., and V. F. Calverton, eds., Women Coming of Age, pp.110-126. Liveright, 1931.

3666 Glassford, P. D. "Prostitution Legalized." Am Mercury 41:455-60, Aug. '37.

3667 Glover, Edward. The Roots of Crime; selected papers on psycho-analysis. Vol. II. New York: International University Press, 1960, 422 pp.

3668 "G Men Center Upon White Slaves." Lit Digest 122:26+, Aug. 29, '36.

3669 Goodhart, A. L. "Shaw Case: the law and public morals." L Q Rev 77:560, Oct. '61.

3670 Gordon, M. L. Penal Discipline. Dutton, 1922.

3671 Gotoin, P. L. "The Potential Prostitute." J Crim Psychopathology 3:359-367, Jan. '42.

3672 Gouges, Olympe de. Le Bonheur Primitif de l'Homme. Paris: 1789. De Gouges was an ex-courtesan who looked forward to repression of common prostitution.

3673 Gould, George, and R. E. Dickerson, comps. Digest of State and Federal Laws Dealing with Prostitution and Other Sex Offenses, with Notes on the Control of the Sale of Alcoholic Beverages as It Relates to Prostitution Activities. Amer. Social Hygiene Assn., Pub. no. A-22. New York: Amer. Social Hygiene Assn., 453 pp.

3674 Gould, G. "Laws Against Prostitution and Their Use." J Soc Hygiene 27:335-43, Oct. '41.

3675 Gould, G. "Twenty Years' Progress in Social Hygiene Legislation; developments in adoption of state laws for prevention and control of venereal diseases and for repression of prostitution from year 1925 to November 1, 1944." J Soc Hygiene 30:456-469, Nov. '44.

3676 Gt. Britain. Colonial Office. Report of a committee appointed by the secretary of state for the colonies to examine and report on Straits Settlements ordinance no.15 of 1927 (women and girls protection amendment ordinance) and Federated Malay States enactment no.18 of 1927 (women and girls protection amendment enactment). H. M. stationary office, 1929, 19 pp. Tables.

3677 Gt. Britain. Committee on Homosexual Offenses and Prostitution. _The Wolfenden Report_; authorized American edition. Lippincott, Stein and day editions, 1963, 243 pp.

3678 Gt. Britain. Foreign office. _International Convention for the Suppression of the Traffic in Women and Children_. Opened for signature at Geneva, from Sep. 30, 1921 to Mar. 31, 1922. H. M. stationary office, 1923, 18 pp. Table. (Treaty ser. no.26 (1923), Cmd. 1986). Text in French and English.

3679 Gt. Britain. Home Office. committee on Homosexual Offenses and Prostitution. _Report_. Sep. 1957, 155 pp. Wolfenden Report.

3680 Gt. Britain. Parliament. Joint Select Committee on the Criminal Law Amendment Bill (H. L.), the Criminal Law Amendment (no.2) Bill (H. L.), and the Sexual Offenses Bill (H. L.). _Report_; together with the proceedings of the committee, minutes of evidence, and appendices. H. M. stationary office, 1920, 135 pp. The same report, ordered by the House of Commons to be printed, bears the number 222.

3681 Greenland, C. "Patterns of Prostitution Following the Wolfenden Report." _Crim L Q_ 4:202, Aug. '61.

3682 Griffith, Hester T. "California's Red Light Abatement and Injunction Act." _Our West_ ns 8:117-21, Sep. '14.

3683 Guillot, A. _La Lutte Contre l'Exploitation et la Reglementation du Vice a Geneve_. Geneva: 1899, 326 pp. hie." _Arch f Krim.-Anthrop u Kriminalistik_ 48:135-181, '12.

3684 Haft, Marilyn G. "Hustling for Rights." _Civil Liberties R_ 1:8-26, Win./Spr. '74.

3685 Hafiz-Nouir, Achene D. _Adultery_. Aribee, 1971.

3686 Halleck, Charles W., et al. "Should Prostitution be Legalized." _Med Aspects of Hum Sexuality_ 8(4):54-83, Apr. '74.

3687 Hales-Toohe, J. "Benefactor or Menace." 123:264, Apr. 25, '59.

3688 Hammer, W. _Zehn Lebenslaufe Berliner Kontrollmadchen_. 1905, 103 pp.

3689 Harding, T. S. "Endless War on 'Vice'." _M Rec_ 147:20 (adv. paging) Apr. 20, '38.

3690 Hatch, D. P. _Underworld and Its Women_. Roger Bros, 1910.

3691 Hattak, Nizi. Crimes of prostitution. Aribec, 1971.

3692 Haupe, Theodore. Crime and Punishment in Germany. New York: E. P. Dutton and Co., 926. p.85.

3693 Heald, R. L. "Interstate Transporation of Prostitutes on a Purely Vacation trip, Unconnected with Their Profession, is not Transportation with such a Purpose as to be Criminal Within the Meaning of the Mann Act, construed in the light of legislative intent." Geo L J 33:114-19, Nov. '44.

3694 Heeren, J. J. "The League of Nations and the International Traffic in Women and Children." Chinese Soc and Pol Sci R 12:251-8, Apr. '28. Bibliography.

3695 Hefner, H. "Laws of Prostitution." Playboy 13:69+, May '66.

3696 Henne-am-Rhyn, O. Die Gebrechen der Sittenpolizei aller Zeiten. Leipzig: 1893.

3697 Henne am Rhyn, Otto. Die Gebrechen und Sunden der Sittenpolizei aller Zeiten, Vorzuglich der Gegenwart...2. Verbesserte Auflage. Leipzig: 1897, 169 pp.

3698 Hepburn, K. H. "Page Bill." Survey 25:79-80, Oct. 1, '10.

3699 Hill, C. J. "White Slave Traffic Act--intent and purpose within the meaning of the Act." N C L Rev 23:147-52, Feb. '45. Mortensen v. U. S.

3700 "Home Office on the Defensive." Economist 180:19, Jun. 7, '56.

3701 Hooker, E. H. "Page Bill." Survey 24:710-1, Aug. 13, '10.

3702 Hoopington, A. "Street Offenses." Outlook (London) 60:780-1, Dec. 10, '27. Discussion 60:824-5, 853, Dec. 17-24, '27.

3703 Hoover, J. E. "White Slave Traffic." J Crim Law 24:475-82, Jul. '33.

3704 Hopf, G. "Das Bordellwesen in der Heutigen Gesetzgebung." Zeitschrift fur Haut- und Geschlechtskrankheiten 12(1952):10. German Legislation.

3705 Hubbard, E. "Abolition of Vice." Hearst's Mag 23:663-4, Apr. '13.

3706 Hugel, Franz Seraph. Zur Geschichte, Statistik und Regelung der Prostitution. Vienna: Typographisch Literarisch-artistiche Anstalt, 1865.

3707 Husain, Mazhai. The Suppression of Immoral Traffic in Women and Girls Act, 1956. Eastern Book Co., 1958, 103 pp.

3708 Hutzel, E. L. "Policewoman's Role in Social Protection." J Soc hygiene 30:537-44, Dec. '44.

3709 "Illinois Abatement Law Held Constitutional." Survey 37:173, Nov. 18, '16. (Bill: HB 164) Provides terms of restraint for prostitutes to houses of shelter, or to hospitls for treatment. (Press report July 29, 1916).

3710 Illinois General Assembly. Senate. Vice Committee. Report Chicago: 1916, 979 pp.

3711 "Immoral Purposes." Sol J 71:905, Nov. 26, '27.

3712 India. (Republic). (Laws, Statutes, etc.) Prevention of Immoral Traffic in Women and Girls Act. Eastern Books, 1958.

3713 Indiana. Act to Enjoin and Abate Houses of Lewdness, Assignation and Prostitution, to Declare the Same to be Nusances, etc. (Acts of 1915, Chap. 122). Indiana Char and Corr 100 Quar, pp.32-5, Mar. '15.

3714 "Injunction and Abatement Acts: legislation in 1915." Soc Hygiene 2:248, Apr. '16. Summarizes bills which became laws and bills introduced but not passed.

3715 International Bureau for the Suppression of Traffic in Persons. Introductory Notes on the Legislative Development of the International Conventions for the Suppression of the Traffic in Persons (1899-1949). London: 1955, 22 pp. With notes by Wanda Grabinska and Rachael Crowdy-Thornhill.

3716 International Bureau for the Suppression of Traffic in Persons. Report. London: annual.

3717 "International Congress on Prostitution." Internat R Crim Policy pp.125-8, Jan. '54.

3718 International Federation of the Amies de la Jeune Fille. Report for 1927. World Peace Foundation, 1927.

3719 "International Legislation for the Protection of Girls." Charities and the Commons Oct. 4, 1902.

3720 "International Prostitution; on part II of the report of the expert committee on the traffic of women and children." Nation (London) 42:445-6, Dec. 17, '27.

3721 International Review of Criminal Policy. Prostitution. International Review of Criminal Policy, no.13. Paris: United Nations, Oct. 1958, 184 pp.

3722 "Interstate Immorality: the Mann act and the Supreme Court." Yale Law J 56:718-[illegible]), Apr. '47.

3723 Iowa. "Red Light Law. (S F no.329)," in Iowa. Recent Temperance Legislation, p.26-32, 1915.

3724 Jacob, H. D. "White Slavery." Case and Comment 23:20-2, Jun. '16.

3725 James, T. E. Prostitution and the Law. London: William Heinemann, 1951, 160 pp. Tables. A study of the law in various countries, especially England, relating to factors considered basic in precipitating prostitution.

3726 Japan. Ministry of Justice. The Administration of the Anti-prostitution Law in Japan. Tokyo: 1960, 65 pp.

3727 Japan. How the Social Evil is Regulated in Japan. Tokyo: 1904.

3728 "Japan's Dangerous Flowers (anti-prostitution law)." Economist 185:599-600, Nov. 16, 1957.

3729 Jersild, Jens. "Prostitutionsudvalgets Betaekning." Politiet pp.17-21, May '56. Proposes ratification of the International Convention of Dec. 2, 1949.

3730 Jimenez Asenso, E. Abolicionismo y Prostitucion. Madrid, 1963, 358 pp.

3731 Johnson, Bascom. "The Attitudes of Governments Toward Foreign Prostitutes." J Soc Hygiene 14:129-38, Mar. '28.

3732 Johnson, Bascom. "Good Laws....Good Tools: injunctions and abatements versus houses of prostitution (review of legislation in the various states)." J Soc Hygiene 38:204-11, May '52.

3733 Johnson, Bascom. "International Efforts for the Prevention of Traffic in Women and Children." J Soc Hygiene 9:200-15, Apr. '23.

3734 Johnson, Bascom. "International Traffic in Women and Children." J Soc Hygiene 14:65-75, Feb. '28. Report of the special body of experts on traffic in women and children, appointed by the Council of the League of Nations.

3735 Johnson, Bascom. J Soc Hygiene for Feb. '47 devoted to: Postwar progress against prostitution. Contents are: Is commercialized prostitution returning?; Are we holding our own against prostitution; Milestones in the march against prostitution.

3736 Johnson, Bascom. "Law Enforcement," in International Conference of Women Physicians. Proceedings, 1919. Vol.6: Conservation of health of women in marriage, pp.176-83, 1920.

3737 Johnson, Bascom. Law Enforcement Against Prostitution from the Point of View of the Public Official. Am Soc. Hygiene Assn., 1920. Also in Nat Munic R 9:427-34, Jul. '20.

3738 Johnson, Bascom. "Social Hygiene Laws in Action." J Soc Hygiene 32:353-6, Nov. '46.

3739 Johnson, Bascom. "Vice Problem and Defense." Survey 77:140-3, May '41.

3740 Johnson, Bascom. What Some Communities of the West and Southwest Have Done for the Protection of the Morals and Health of Soldiers and Sailors. Am Soc. Hygiene Assn., 1917.

3741 Johnson, Bascom. "Women Sex Offenders in New York Courts." J Soc Hygiene 35:374-83, Nov. '49.

3742 Johnstone, A. "Law and Social Hygiene." J Soc Hygiene 29:225-8, Apr. '43.

3743 Jones, A. E. "Law vs. Prostitution." Crim Law R 1960:704, Oct. '60.

3744 Journal des Inspecteurs de M. de Sartines. Premier Serie 1761-1764. Brussels-Paris: 1863.

3745 Kanowitz, Leo. Sex Roles in Law and Society. Albuquerque: Univ. of New Mexico Press, 1973.

3746 Karishka, P. The Underworld and Its Women. New York: Roger Bros., 1910, 15 pp.

3747 Kemble, H. S. "A Medico Legal Aspect of Prostitution." Justice of the Peace 112:465-6, Jun. 24, '48.

3748 King, William. Los Angeles Police Dept. Los Angeles: 1944, 14 pp.

3749 Kingsford, Douglas. A Critical Summary of the Evidence Before the Royal Commission upon the Contagious Diseases Acts 1866-69. 8v. 126 pp.

3750 Kinsie, P. M. "Commercialized Prostitution." The Police Chief 26:19, Jun. '59.

3751 Kinsie, P. M. "Communities vs the Prostitution Racket." J Soc Hygiene 36:45, Jan. '50.

3752 Kinsie, P. M. "Law Enforcement Progress During 1947." J Soc Hygiene 33: 445-447, Dec. '47.

3753 Kinsie, P. M. "Sex Crimes and the Prostitution Racket." J Soc Hygiene 36:250-2, Jun. '50.

3754 Klingler, H. "Das Problem der Prostitution." Die Polizei Polizei-Praxis pp.111-114, May '56. An argument for regulation.

3755 Koch, R. A. "The San Francisco Separate Women's Court." J Soc Hygiene 30:288-295, May '44.

3756 Krassel, Franz W. Privatrecht und Prostitution; eine sozial-juristische studie. Leipzig and Vienna: 1894.

3757 Kreuzer, A. "Parasitare Erscheinungsformen der Delinquenz Drogenabhangige. I. Aus Einer Kriminologischen Untersuchung Uber 'Drogen und Delinquenz." Kriminalistic 28(6):269-273, '74.

3758 "Kriminalrat" Michalke. "Prostitution und Abolitionismus." Polizei Praxis pp.227-230, Sep. '56. Pro-regulation.

3759 Kronhausen, Eberhard and Phyllis. Pornography and the Law. New York: Ballantine Books, 1959.

3760 Kross, A. M. "New Techniques for Handling Prostitution Cases." Am City 50:87, Apr. '35.

3761 Kubicek, Earl C. "Soldiers and Sinners at Loma Parda." Smithsonian J Hist 2(1), Spr. '67.

3762 Ladame, P. Les Maisons de Tolerence Geneva: FAI. n. d., before 1902.

3763 Ladame, . L'Institution de la Police des Moeurs au Point de Vue de l'Hygiene. Geneva: FAI, before 1902.

3764 Ladame, P. De la Prostitution dans ses rapports Avec l'Alcoolisme, le Crime et la Folie. Geneva: FAI, before 1902.

3765 Lade, J. H. "Legal Prosecution of the Master Saboteur." N Y S Health N 19:201-2, Nov. 30, '42.

3766 Lafitte, Francois. Homosexuality and the Law: The Wolfenden Report in historical perspective." Brit J Delinq 9:8-9, '58.

3767 Landesco, John. "The Exploitation of Prostitution," in Ill. Assn. for Criminal Justice. Illinois Crime Survey, pp.845-63, 1929.

3768 Landmann, Hermann. "Aussenseiter als Prostituiertenmorder." Kriminalistik (Hamburg) pp.302-303, Aug. '57. Recounts a case of the sadistic murder of a prostitute.

3769 Larremore, T. A. "Nevada Outlaws Houses of Prostitution; legal aspects of developments which ended the reign of licensed prostitution."

3770 Lasserre, Jean. Comment les Maisons Furent Fermees. Geneva: FAI, 1954, 144 pp.

3771 "Law Enforcement and Legislation." (various authors). J Soc Hygiene 29:277-305, May '43.

3772 League of Nations. Abolition of Licensed Houses. Geneva: FAI, 96 pp.

3773 "League of Nations and Traffic in Women." Educ R 74:11-12, Jun. '27.

3774 "League of Nations and Traffic in Women and Chidren." Justice of the Peace 91:293, Apr. 16, '27.

Note: League of Nations material is arranged in chronological rather than in alphabetical order.

3775 League of Nations. Advisory Com. on the Traffic in Women and Children. Minutes of the first session, held at Geneva from Jun. 28-Jul. 1, 1922. World Peace Foundation, Jul., 31, 1922, 70 pp. C 445 M 265 1922 IV.

3776 League of Nations. Advisory Committee on Traffic in Women and Children. Summary of Annual reports for 1922 Received from Governments Relating to the Traffic in Women and Children. World Peace Foundation, 1924.

3777 League of Nations. Advisory Committee on Traffic in Women and Children. Minutes of the First-Second Sessions; held at Geneva, 1922-23. 2v. World Peace Foundation, 1922-23.

3778 League of Nations. Advisory Committee on the Traffic in Women and Children. Minutes of the Second Session; held at Geneva, From March 22nd to 27th, 1923. World Peace Foundation, Mar. 31, 1923. C 225 M 129 1923 IV.

3779 League of Nations. Traffic in Women and Children: reports of the work of the Advisory Committee, during Its Second Session, held at Geneva, March 22nd-27th, 1923. (Adopted by the Council on April 19th, 1923). World Peace Foundation, Aug. 16th, 1923, 12 pp. A 36 1923 IV.

3780 League of Nations. Advisory Committee on Traffic in Women and Children. Minutes of the Third Session; held at Geneva from April 7 to 11th, 1924. World Peace Foundation, 1924.

3781 League of Nations. Traffic in Women and Children: summary of annual reports, for the year 1924. World Peace Foundation, 1925, 16 pp. CTFE250(1).

3782 League of Nations. Advisory Committee on Traffic in Women and Children. Report on the Work of the Third Session Adopted by the Committee on April 11th, 1924. World Peace Foundation, 1924.

3783 League of Nations. Traffic in Women and Children: summary of annual reports for the year, 1924. World Peace Foundation, Dec. 19, 1925.

3784 League of Nations. Advisory Committee on Traffic in Women and Protection of Children. Minutes of the Fourth Session; held at Geneva, May 20-27, 1925. World Peace Foundation, 1925.

3785 League of Nations. Advisory Committee on the Traffic of Women and Children. Report of the Fourth Session, Geneva, May, 1925. World Peace Foundation, 1925.

3786 League of Nations. Advisory Committee for the Protection and Welfare of Children and Young People. Traffic in Women and Children Committee. Minutes of the Fifth Session; held at Geneva, March 22-25, 1926. World Peace Foundation, 126, 105 pp.

3787 League of Nations. Traffic in Women and Children: summary of annual reports for 1926. World Peace Foundation, Jan. 31, 1928, 23 pp. 1928 IV 1.

3788 League of Nations. Traffic in Women and Children: summary of annual reports for 1927. World Peace Foundation, Feb 15, 1929, 32 pp. 1929 IV 1.

3789 League of Nations. Advisory Commission for the Protection and Welfare of Children and Young People. Traffic in Women and Children Committee. Minutes of the 1st-5th Session; held at Geneva, 1922-1926. 5v. World Peace Foundation, 1922-26.

3790 League of Nations. Advisory Committee on Traffic in Women and Children. Report on the Work of the Third-Fifth Session; held at Geneva, 1924-26. 3v. World Peace Foundation, 1924-26.

3791 League of Nations. Advisory Commitee for the Protection and Welfare of Children and Young People. Traffic in Women and children Committee. Minutes of the Sixth Session; held at Geneva, April 25-30, 1927. World Peace Foundation, Jun. 24, '27, 225 pp.

3792 League of Nations. Advisory Committee for the Protection and Welfare of Children and Young People. Traffic in Women and Children Committee. Minutes of the Seventh Session; held at Geneva, Mar. 12-17, 1928. World Peace Foundation, 1928, 148 pp. 1928 IV 15.

3793 League of Nations. Advisory Committee for the Protection and welfare of Children and Young People. Traffic in Women and Children Committee. Seventh Session: report of the Jewish association for the protection of girls and women, for the year ending December 31, 1927. World Peace Foundation, Feb. 8, 1928. 1928 IV 5.

3794 League of Nations. traffic in Women and Children Committee. Seventh Session: report. World Peace Foundation, Feb. 11, 1928, 12 pp. 1928 IV 7.

3795 League of Nations. Advisory Committee for the Protection and Welfare of Children and Young People. Traffic in Women and Children Committee. Minutes of the Eighth Session; held at Geneva, April 19-27, 1929. World Peace Foundation, Aug. 1, 1929, 140 pp. 1929 IV 6.

3796 League of Nations. Traffic in Women and Children: summary of annual reports for 1929, prepared by the secretariat. World Peace Foundation, Feb. 16, 1931, 34 pp. 1931 IV 2.

3797 League of Nations. Advisory Committee for the Protection and Welfare of Children and Young People. Traffic in Women and Children Committee. Report of the Eighth Session adopted by the Committee, April 26, 1929. World Peace Foundation, April 29, 1929, 10 pp. 1929 IV 3.

3798 League of Nations. Advisory committee for the protection and welfare of children and Young People. Traffic in women and Children Committee. Minutes of the Ninth Session; held at Geneva, April 2-9, 1930. World Peace Foundation, Jul. 20, 1930, 220 pp. Tables. 1930 IV 6.

3799 League of Nations. Traffic in Women and Children Committee. Summary of Annual Reports for 1930. World Peace Foundation, 1932, 29 pp.

3800 League of Nations. Advisory Committee for the Protection and Welfare of children and Young People. Traffic in Women and Children Committee. Report on the Ninth Session; adopted by the Committee on April 9, 1930. World Peace Foundation, April 16, 1930, 12 pp. 1930 IV 2.

3801 League of Nations. Traffic in Women and Children Committee. Minutes of the 10th Session; held at Geneva, April 21-27, 1931. World Peace Foundation, May 29, 1931, 92 pp. 1931 IV 8.

3802 League of Nations. Traffic in Women and Children: Obscene Publications; summary of annual reports for 1931. World Peace Foundation, 1933, 38 pp.

3803 League of Nations. Traffic in Women and Children Committee. Minutes of the Eleventh Session, April 4-9, 1932. World Peace Foundation, 1932, 8 pp.

3804 League of Nations. Traffic in Women and Children Committee. Report on the Work of the Eleventh Session. Geneva, April 4-9, 1932. World peace Foundation, 1932, 10 pp.

3805 League of Nations. Advisory Committee for the Protection and Welfare of Children and Young People. Report of the Work of the Commission in 1933. World Peace Foundation, 1933, 31 pp.

3806 League of Nations. Traffic in Women and Children Committee. Summary of Annual reports for 1932-33; prepared by the secretariat. World Peace Foundation, 1934, 36 pp.

3807 League of Nations. Traffic in Women and Children Committee. Summary of Annual reports for 1933-34; prepared by the secretariat. World Peace Foundation, 1935, 41 pp.

3808 League of Nations. Traffic in Women and Children Committee. Summary of Annual Reports for 1934-5; prepared by the secretariat. World Peace Foundation, 1936, 37 pp.

3809 League of Nations. Advisory Commission on Social Questions. Summary of Annual reports for 1936/37. Internat. Doc. Service, 1938, 7 pp.

3810 League of Nations. Advisory Commission on Social Questions. summary of Annual Reports for 1937/38. International Document Service, 1939, 41 pp.

3811 League of Nations. Advisory Commission on Social Questions. Summary of Annual Reports for 1938/39: traffic in women and children. International Document Service, 1940, 39 pp.

3812 League of Nations. Advisory Commission on Social Questions. Summary of Annual reports for 1939/40: traffic in women and children. International Document Service, 1941, 23 pp.

3813 League of Nations. Advisory Commission and Social Questions. Summary of Annual Reports, for 1940-41: traffic in women and children. International Document Service, Nov. 5, 1942, 32 pp. Tables. 1942 IV 2.

3814 League of Nations. Advisory Commission on Social Questions. Summary of Annual Reports, for 1943/44: traffic in women and children. International Document Service. Nov. 15, 1945, 15 pp. Table. 1945 IV 2.

3815 League of Nations. Advisory Commission on Social Questions. Summary of Annual Reports, for 1944-45: traffic in women and children. International Document Service, April, 20, 12 pp. Tables. 1946 IV 1.

3816 League of Nations. Committee on Traffic in Women and Children. Abolition of Licensed Houses. Geneva: 1934, 96 pp.

3817 League of Nations. Advisory Commission for the Protection and Welfare of Children and Young People. Traffic in Women and Children Committee. Abstract of the Reports from Governments on the System of Licensed Houses as Related to Traffic in Women and Children. World Peace Foundation, Dec. 9, 1927, 51 pp. Tables. 1927 IV 14.

3818 League of Nations. Advisory Commission for the Protection and Welfare of children and Young People. Traffic in Women and Children Committee. Licensed Houses; abstract of the reports from governments on the system of licensed houses as related to traffic in women and children; additional information received from governments of countries where the system of licensed houses has been abolished. World Peace Foundation, Feb. 28, 1929, 91 pp. Tables. 1929 IV 2.

3819 League of Nations. Traffic in Women and Children Committee. Central Authorities. World Peace Foundation, 1932, 20 pp.

3820 League of Nations. Traffic in Women and Children Committee. Concise Study of the Laws and Penalties Relating to Souteneurs. World Peace Foundation, 1931, 30 pp. Also in League of Nations Journal 12:1850-77, Sep. '31.

3821 League of Nations. Traffic in Women and Children Committee. Conference of Central Authorities in Eastern Countries. Bandoeng, Java, Feb. 2-13, 1937. Minutes of the Meetings. Geneva: 1937, 115 pp.

3822 League of Nations. Advisory Commission on Social Questions. Enquiry into Measures of Rehabilitation of Prostitutes; pt.3-4: Methods of rehabilitation of adult prostitutes, conclusions and recommendations. Geneva: International Document Service, 1939, 157 pp.

3823 League of Nations. Advisory Commission on Social Questions. Traffic in Women and Children Committee. Position of Women of Russian Origin in the Far East. Geneva: 1935, 16 pp.

3824 League of Nations. Advisory Committee on Social Questions. Prevention of Prostitution. Geneva: 1943, 182 pp. U. N. t. 46.

3825 League of Nations. Advisory Committee on Social Questions. Suppression of the Exploitation of the Prostitution of Others; observations of various governments on the second draft convention. Geneva: 1938.

3826 League of Nations. Traffic in Women and Children: 1, Rapporteur's report adopted by the Council on June 5, 1928; 2, Report to the Council of the traffic in women and children committee. World Peace Foundation, 1928, 11 pp. 1928 IV 18.

3827 League of Nations. Traffic in Women and Children: report of the fifth committee to the Assembly. World Peace Foundation, Sep. 17, 1927, 2 pp. 1927 IV 11.

3828 League of Nations. Traffic in Women and Children: report of the fifth committee to the Assembly. World Peace Foundation, Sep. 17, 1929, 2 pp. 1929 IV 9.

3829 League of Nations. Traffic in Women and Children Committee. Report of the Fifth Committee to the Assembly. World Peace Foundation, Sep. 27, 1930, 2 pp. 1930 IV 9.

3830 League of Nations. Traffic in Women and Children: report of the fifth committee to the Assembly. World peace Foundation, 1932, 4 pp.

3831 League of Nations. Reports of the Special Body of Experts on Traffic in Women and Children. Pt.1. World peace Foundation. Feb. 17, 1927, 50 pp.

3832 League of Nations. Traffic in Women and Children: resolutions adopted by the Assembly, the Council and the Traffic in Women and Children Committee, 1920-1929. World Peace Foundation, Nov. 20, 1929, 15 pp. 1929 IV 10.

3833 League of Nations. Traffic in Women and Children Committee. Study of the Laws and Regulations with a View to Protecting Public Order and Health in Countries Where the System of Licensed Houses Has Been Abolished. World Peace Foundation, Jun. 20, 1930, 93 pp. Tables. 1930 IV 5.

3834 League of Nations. Traffic in Women and Children: draft protocol for the suppression of traffic in women of full age. World Peace Foundation, 1933, 5 pp.

3835 League of Nations. Advisory Commission for the Protection of Children and Young People, (afterwards the Advisory Committee on Social Questions). Digest of the Comments by Private Organisations on the Repor of the League of Nation Commission of Enquiry into Traffic in Women and children in the East. Geneva: 1934, 20 pp.

3836 League of Nations. Advisory Committee on Social Questions. The Work of the Bandoeng Conference. Geneva: 1938, 86 pp.

3837 League of Nations. Advisory Commission for the Protection and Welfare of Children and Young People. Work of the Commission for the protection of Women and children in the

Near East. World Peace Foundation, 1923.

3838 League of Nations. Commission of Enquiry into Traffic in Women and Children in the East. Report to the Council. Geneva: 1933, 556 pp. Summary of the report published in 1934 by the World Peace Foundation. 41 pp.

3839 League of Nations. International Convention for the Suppression of the Traffic in Women and Children; opened for signature at Geneva, from Sep. 3oth, 1921, to Mar. 31, 1922. World Peace Foundation, Mar. 31, 1922, 7 pp. A 125 (2) 1921 IV.

3840 League of Nations. Records of the International Conferences on Traffic in Women and Children; meetings held from Jun.30-Jul.5, 1921. World Peace Foundation, 1921, 137 pp. C 484 M 339 1921 IV.

3841 League of Nations. Traffic in Women and Children: report on the international women's associations. Avril de Sainte-Croix. World peace Foundation, 1925, 6 pp. CTFE234.

3842 League of Nations. Report of the Special Body of Experts on Traffic in Women and Children. World peace Foundation, Nov. 27, 1927, 226 pp. Tables, chart map. 1927 IV 2. 2 pts.

3843 League of Nations. Secretariat. Traffic in Women and children: summary of annual reports for 1922-1924. 3v. World Peace Foundation, 1924-25.

3844 League of Nations. Suppression of the White Slave Traffic in Women and children. Assem. Doc. 8. 2 pts. Geneva: Nov. 17, 1920.

3845 Lefroy, Muriel. The Solicitation Laws. London: Assn. for Moral and Social Hygiene, 1948. Alison Neilans Memorial Lecture, no.3.

3846 "Legalizing Prostitution; the great social war." Lond Q 46:452.

3847 "Legalizing Prostitution; resolition for Ohio legislature." Newsweek 80:88, Sep. 4, '72.

3848 Legnani, M. Discurso Contra la ley de Represion del Proxenetismo; el aboligionismo y el reglamenarismo. San Jose, Santa Lucia: 1924, 58 pp.

3849 Legrand-Falco, M. La Convention de 1949 des Nations Unies sur la Repression et l'Abolition de la Traite des Etres Humanis. Conference held at Paris in 1953. UNESCO, 15 pp.

3850 "Legislation in Iowa Compared With the Law Proposed for the Suppression of Vice in Illinois." J Crim Law 3:920-9, Mar. '13.

3851 Legislation sur la prostitution. Clichy: Mar. '66, 19 pp. A brief survey.

3852 "Legislative Year; legislation for repression of prostitution," J Soc Hygiene 17:52-5, jan. '31.

3853 Leigh, L. H. "Vagrancy, Morality and Decency, Indecency and Obscenity--Indecent Exposure." Crim Law R 1975:381-90; 413-20, Jun./Aug. '75.

3854 Leopardi, G. "Lights and Shadows of the Merlin Law. Medico-social aspects." Attual Ostet Ginecol 12(1):137-44, Jan.-Feb. '66.

3855 Leppington, E. Le Neo-reglementarisme. Geneva: FAI, n. d., 58 pp.

3856 Liagre, _____. (Regulation). Liege Med 29:1347-1364, 22, '36.

3857 Licensing of Sin in India. London: 1887, 7 pp.

3858 Lodovici, E. Samek. Un Medico a la Legge Merlin. Rome: G. Bardi, 1965, 108 pp. A study of Merlin's Law.

3859 London. Committee for the Exposure and Suppression of the Traffic in English Girls. Second (Third) Report of the London Committee for the Exposure and Suppression of Traffic in English Girls for Purposes of Continental Prostitution. London: Effingham Wilson. 1882, 1883.

3860 London. International Bureau for the Suppression of the White Slave Traffic. Preparatory Conference, Oct. 1923. report. 1924, 63 pp.

3861 Lombroso, Cesare. Female offender. New York: Philosophical Press, 1958, 313 pp.

3862 Lombroso, Cesare, and G. Ferrero. La Femme Criminale et la Prostituee. Paris: Alcan, 1896, 679 pp.

3863 Lombroso, Cesare, and G. Ferrero. Das Weib als Verbrecherin und Prostituirte. Hamburg: Verlagsanstalt, 1894(?), 590 pp.

3864 Lukas, E. J. "Digging at the Roots of Prostitution." Probation 22:97-100, 109-112, '44.

3865 Lyttelton, E. "League's Big Little Jobs." Outlook 138:448-50, Nov. 19, 1924.

3866 MacDonald, John M. Rape; offenders and their victims. Springfield, Ill.: Charles C. Thomas, 1971, 342 pp.

3867 "Mann Act Conviction Requires Finding That Only One Purpose For Transportation Need be Immoral." J Pa L Rev 99:423-5, Dec. '50. Dargle v. U. S.

3868 "Mann Act--limited in the second circuit?" Wash and Lee Law Rev 16:282, Fall '59. U. S. vs. Ross.

3869 "Mann Act--visit to foreign jurisdiction and return--dominant purpose test." J B A Kan 19:186-90, Nov. '50.

3870 "Mann Law Upheld." Outlook 115:179-80, Jan. 31, '17.

3871 Mannes, M. "Let's Face It." McCalls 92:18+, Jun. '65.

3872 Marsh, M. Prostitutes in New York City: Their Apprehension, Trial, and Treatment, July 1939-June 1940. New York: Welfare Council of New York, 1941.

3873 Marsh, N. J. "Treatment of Cases of prostitution in New York City." Soc Hygiene 2:517-25, Oct. '16.

3874 Maryland. Act providing for the revocation of any business license operated in connection with a place of prostitution. Ch.406, Laws 1920.

3875 Massachusetts. Commission for Investigation of White Slave Traffic, Boston. Report; February, 1914.

3876 Maurer, D. W. "Prostitutes and Criminal Argots." Am J Soc 44:545-50, Jan. '39.

3877 "May Bill Becomes Law; text of measure to prohibit prostitution in military and naval establishment zones." J Soc Hyg 27:344-5, oct. '41.

3878 Mayer, Joseph. Regulation of Commercialized Vice: an analysisof the transition from segregation to repression in the United States. National Industrial Conference, 1922, 55 pp. Bibliography, tables, chart. PhD. dissertation, Columbia Univ.

3879 Mayer, Joseph. "Social Legislation and Vice Control." Soc Hygiene 5:337-48, Jul. '19. Table.

3880 McManus, Martin J. "Comments." So Cal Law Rev 19:250-56, Mar. '46.

3881 McMurdy, Robert. "The Use of the Injunction to Destroy Commercialized Prostitution." Am Inst Crim J pt.1 19:513-17, Feb. '29.

3882 McQuaid, Elizabeth. "Polls Open, Brothels Close: San Antonio (Tex.) breaks with tradition (1951 law-enforcement campaign and the eradication of vice)." J Soc Hygiene 38:250-60, Jun. '52.

3883 Mead, F., and A. H. Bodkin. The Criminal Law Amendment Acts, 1885 and 1912. Butterworth, 1913, 215 pp.

3884 Mead, m. "Should Prostitution be Legalized." Redbook. 136:50+, Apr. '71.

3885 "Meaning of 'House of Prostitution'." Mich Law Review 27:469-70, Feb. '29. (Calif.) People vs. Barrett. 270 Pac 1010.

3886 "Meaning of the White Slave Act as Shown by Federal Decision." J Crim Law 4:738-40, Jan. '14.

3887 Meersch, Maxence van der. Femmes a l'Encan: un es lavagisme patente. Paris: A. Michel, 1945, 157 pp.

3888 Meier, Eugen. Die Behandlung der Prostitution im Schweizerischen Strafrecht. Zurich: 1948, pp.10-12. A doctoral thesis about the Swiss legislation about prostitution.

3889 Mendoza, Jose Rafael. "Los Limites Entre la Reglamentacion Administriva y la Regresion Penal en Material de Prostitucion y de Proxenetismo." Ponencias Venenezolanas para el VI Congreso Internacional de Derecho Comparado. Caracas: 1962. The Congress was held in Hamburg.

3890 Menken, A. D. "Law Enforcement in relation to the Treatment of Sex Offenders in New York City." J Soc Hygiene 19:143-50, Mar. '33.

3891 Mercier, L. S. Le Tableau de Paris. New ed Paris: 1889. Police inspector.

3892 Merlin, Lina. Giu la Maschera del Lenocino. Rome: 1960, 18 pp. A speech given to the Italian Parliament by the promoter ofthe abolitionist law.

3893 Meuron, Alf. de. L'Influence Morale et Social du Regime de la Police des Moeurs. Geneva: FAI, n. d., before 1902.

3894 Micklewright, F. H. Amphlett. "A Legal Layman and the Street Offenses Bill." Plain View 12:193-9, Winter '59.

3895 "Milestones in March Against Prostitution." J Soc Hygiene 33:65-72, Feb. '47.

3896 Milliken, R. J. "The Role of the Police Woman's Bureau in Combatting Prostitution." Federal Probation. 7(1943):20-22.

3897 Miner, M. E. "Probation Work for Women." Ann Am Acad 36:27-36, Jul. '10.

3898 Miner, M. E. "Two Weeks in the Night Court." Survey 22:229-34, May 8, '09.

3899 Mireur, Docteur H. La Prostitution a Marseille; histoire administration et police hygiene. Paris: E. Dentee, 1882.

3900 Missouri--Act to enjoin and abate houses of lewdness, assignation and prostitution; to declare the same to be nusances; to enjoin the person or person(s), who conduct or maintain the same and the owner or agent of any building used for such purpose; and to assess a penalty against the person maintaining said nuisance and the ground, the building and owner thereof. H. B. 314, Laws 1924.

3901 Monroe, D. G. "Questions and Answers on Prostitution and the Law." J Crim Law 33:404-8, Jan. '43.

3902 Montana--Act declaring all houses where acts of assignationor prostitution are held or occur nuisances, and providing for abatement and prevention of such nuisances, by injunction and otherwise. Ch.95, P. L. 1917.

3903 Moraglia, G. B. "Nuove Ricerche su Criminali, Prostitute e Psicopatiche."Archivo di Psichiatria 16:305-327.

3904 "More Private Vices (recommendations of the Wolfenden Committee)." Economist 184:735-6, Sep. 7, '57.

3905 Morland, N. An Outline of Sexual Criminology. Hart, 1967.

3906 Moreno, H. "Prostitution and Crime; medico-legal study of case." Rev Med Leg y Jurisp Med 8:220-223, Aug.-Dec. '44.

3907 Morrison, L. D. "Prostitution and the Police; a crime that can be prevented." J Soc Hygiene 37:365-72, Nov. '51.

3908 Morsier, Emilie de. La Mission de la Femme Geneva: FAI, n. d., before 1902.

3909 Morsier, A. de. La Police des Mouers en France et la Campagne Abolitionniste. Geneva: FAI, n. d., before 1902.

3910 Mueller, Gerhard. Legal Regulation of Sexual Conduct. New York: Oceana Publications, 1961.

3911 Murphy, U. G. The Social Evil in Japan. 4th ed rev Tokyo: Methodist Pub. House, 1909.

3912 Murtagh, Judge John M. (Chief magisitrate of thr city of New York), and Sara Harris. Cast the First Stone. New York: Pocket Books, Inc., 1957, 262 pp.

3913 National Advisory Police Committee to the Federal Security Administrator. Techniques of Law Enforcement Against Prostitution. Washington, D. C.: 1943, 75 pp.

3914 National Advisory Police Committee to the Federal Security Administrator. Techniques of Law Enforcement in the Treatment of Juveniles and the Prevention of Juvenile Delinquency. Washington, D. C.: 1944, 60 pp.

3915 National Conference of Charities and Correction. Proceedings, 1914. Contents: "Treatment of Prostitution. Iowa Injunction Law." by H. S. Holligsworth; "Hotels and the social evil." by F. H. Whitin; "Atlanta crusade." by J. C. Logan; "Closing of Houses of Prostitution in Kansas City." by K. L. Schreiber; "Progress in Baltimore." by J. W. Magruder; "Reform in Little Rock." by Rabbi L. Witt; "Progress Against Vice in St. Louis." by R. N. Baldwin.

3916 "Nations Act Against the White Slave Trade." Char 21:979-90, Feb. 20, 1909.

3917 "Nation's Infamy; report of the League of Nations Commission on the White-Slave Traffic." Lit Digest 93:32, May 14, '27.

3918 Neilans, A. "Abolitionist Movement Against Prostitution." Int R Missions 22:81-93, Jan. '33.

3919 Neilans, A. International Movement Against Prostitution. Edinburgh House Press, 1933.

3920 Neilans, A. "Persecution of Prostitutes." New Statesman 20:200-1, Nov. 18, '22.

3921 Nelson, L. C. "Application of the Mann Act." Geo Wash Law r 15:214-25, Feb. '47.

3922 Nelson, L. C. "A Re-examinatin of the Purpose of the White slave Traffic Act." Geo Wash Law R 15:214-25, Feb. '47.

3923 Ness, E. "Federal Government's Program in Attacking the Problem of Prostitution." Federal Probation 7(1953):17-19.

3924 Neumann, Robert. 23 Women: the story of an international traffic. New York: Dial Press, 1940, 316 pp.

3925 "New French Law for Reppression of Prostitution goes Into Effect." J Soc Hygiene 32:383-5, Nov. '46.

3926 "New Law of Ohio for Abatement of Houses of Prostitution." Ohio Pub Halth J 8:290-5, Jul. '17.

3927 "New Legislation Dealing with Prostitution and the Venereal Diseases." Soc Hygiene 5:625-8, Oct. '19.

3928 New Mexico. Act for the repression of prostitution. SB 47, Laws 1921.

3929 "A New Technique for Handling Prostitution Cases." Am City p.87, Apr. '35.

3930 New South Wales. Act to make provision for the closing of disorderly houses; and for purposes connected therewith. No.6, Statutes 1943.

3931 New York (city). Bureau of Social Hygiene. Recommendations of the Laboratory of Social Hygiene Affiliated With New York State Reformatory for Women at Bedford Hills, N. Y., for Disposition of First One Hundred Cases Studied. New York: Bureau of Social Hygiene, 1915.

3932 New York (state). Act to Amend the Public Health Law; in relation to the suppression of certain nuisances. Ch.670, Laws 1927.

3933 New York (state). Library. Legislative Reference Section. Analysis of the Laws of the Various States Dealing With Prostitution. M. B. Csontos, comp. Albany: 1937, 114 pp.

3934 New York (state). Library. Legislative Reference Section. Digest of State Laws Relating to the Regulation and Supervision of the Social Evil. C. E. Hathaway, comp. Albany, Dec. '24, 36 pp.

3935 New York (state). Library. Legislative Refernece Section. Digest of the Injunction and Abatement Laws of the Various States That Relate to the Social Evil. Arlene Dilts and C. E. Hathaway, comps. Albany: Dec. '24, 53 pp.

3936 New York (state). Library. Legislative Reference Section. Evaluation of Methods Used to Repress or Regulate Prostitution in the United States and Foreign Countries. M. B. Csontos, comp. Albany: 1937, 75 pp.

3937 Niles, A. S. Police Department and the Social Problem. National Conference of Charities and Corrections reprint 1915, no.46, 11 pp. Address before the National Conference in Baltimore, Md., May 12-19, 1915. pp.421-33.

3938 "No Dirty Compromise." Ind 74:1117, May 22, '13.

3939 "Nostrums for Vice." Ind 52:2942-3, Dec. 6, 1900.

3940 O'Callaghan, Sean. Damaged Baggage: the white slave trade and narcotics trafficking in the Americas. New York: Roy, 1970, 191 pp.

3941 "Offenses Contra Bonos Mores; consideration of Shaw v. D. P. P." Sol J 105:897, 922, 942, Oct. 27-Nov. 10, '61.

3942 O'Hare, K. R. Law and the White Slaver. National Rip-saw Pub., 1912.

3943 Oliva, Silvestre. "Proyecto de la Ordenza Reglamentaria d la Prostitucion," in, Pan American Scientific Congress, Procedings, 1915 9:518-25, '17.

3944 "On the Local front: report on prostitution asks local law enforcement officers to maintain vigilance; excerpts." Natl Munic R 32:83-5, Feb. '43.

3945 Orapsey, Edward. The Nether Side of N.Y. or the Vice, Crime and Poverty of the Great Metropolis. Montclair, N. J.: Patterson Smith, 1969, 185 pp.

3946 "Organized Vice as a Vested Interest." Cur Lit 52:292-4, Mar. '12.

3947 Orr, C. Bruce. The Sexual Offenses Act. Butterworth, 1956, 164 pp. Gt. Britain.

3948 Osborne, F. J. "Law Enforcement Program Applied." Soc Hygiene 5:83-96, Jan. '19.

3949 Ottolenghi, S., and V. Rossi. Duecento Criminali e Prostitute Studiate nei Laboratore di Clinica Psichiatrica di Torino. Turin: Booc, 1898, 316 pp.

3950 "Page Bill; a symposium." Survey 24:868-70, Sep. 17, '10.

3951 Paleolog, Stanislawa. The Women Police of Poland 1925-39. London: Assn. for Moral and Social Hygiene, n.' d.

3952 "Pandering--successful procurement not necessary for conviction of completed crime." Santa Clara Law 14:180-8, Fall '73.

3953 Parent-Duchatelet, A. J. B. De la Prostitution dans la Ville de Paris. 2d ed rev and corr Paris: J. B. Bailliere, 1837. 2v.

3954 Paris. Police. Reglementation de la Prostitution a Paris. Clermont, 1887, 48 pp.

3955 Parker, Daniel, and Helene Tzaut. Comment Entreprendre la Lutte Pratique Contra l'Immoralite Publique sur le Plan Municipal. Paris: Cartel d'Action Morale, c1945, 30 pp.

3956 Parker, V. H. "Segregated District." Woman's Citizen ns 10:26, Sep. '25.

3957 Pennington, L.R. "Challenge to Law Enforcement; FBI experience with the white slave traffic." J Soc Hygiene 30:530-7, Dec. '44.

3958 Pennsylvania. Act for repression of Prostution and assignation; making it unlawful to solicit, aid, or permit prostitution, or to use or permit the use of any place for the purpose of prostitution or assignation; making certain evidence admissible in proceedings under this act; authorizing the committment of prostitutes to private institutions; providing for their parole; and prescribing penalties. No.403, Laws 1923.

3959 Pennsylvania. Act relating to prostitution. No.43, Laws 1931.

3960 Peto, D. O. G. "Kaleidoscope." Crim Law R 1958:793, Dec. '58.

3961 Peyton, D. C. "Prostitution; its nature and cure." J Crim Law 4:466-8, Sep. '13.

3962 Pfeiffer, T. N. "Matter and Method of Social Hygiene Legislation." Soc Hygiene 3:51-73, Jan. '17.

3963 Pfeiffer, T. N. Social Hygiene Legislation in 1915. Am. Social Hygiene Assn.

3964 Philippon, Odette. Le Trafic des Femmes. 2d ed Paris: 1956, 139 pp.

3965 Pinard, M. "Inefficacy of Present Regulation in relation to Public Health." Prophylax Antiven 9:344-355, Jun. '37.

3966 Piltzer, David S. "Mazza v. Cavicchia Revisited." N J Law J 96:1+, Mar. 1, '73.

3967 Pinney, J. B. "France Votes No; blocks efforts to reopen brothels." J Soc Hygiene 38:3228-33, Oct. '52.

3968 Pittsburgh, Pa. License court has refused licenses to a large number of saloons that have taken ovr the traffic in commercialized vice which was supposedly broken up by the elimination of the tenderloin. Notices are now being served on owners of the closed public houses to prevent their property from being reopened as common assignation houses. Steps are also being taken to secure some agency thru which the work of the defunct morals bureu can be re-established, and responsibility for moral conditions definitely localized. (May 27, '16).

3969 Plauzoles, Sicard de. "Illegality of Regulation in Regards to Human Rights." Prophylax Antiven 9:331-344, Jun. '37.

3970 Plauzoles, Sicard de. "Opinion of Alfred Fournier on Regulation of Prostitution and of Houses of Tolerance." Prophylax Antiven 9:580-603, Oct. '37.

3971 Ploscowe, Morris. Sex and the Law. New York: Prentice Hall, 1951. Reprinted by Ace Books, 1962.

3972 La Police des Moeurs: lettres adressees au Journal "La Lanterne" par un ex-agent de moeur et un medecen. 8v. Paris: La Lanterne, 1879. pp. viii, 92.

3973 "Policeman on Prostitution." Time 27:18, May 11, '36.

3974 Pollak, Otto. The Criminality of Women. Philadelphia: Univ. of Pa. Press, 1950.

3975 Popenoe, Paul. "Law Enforcement: a plan for organized action." Soc Hygiene 5:355-67, Jul. '19.

3976 Popkin, Z. "Vignettes From a Women's Court." Independent Woman 14:398-400+, Dec. '35.

3977 Powell, Hickman. Ninety Times Guilty. New York: Harcourt, Brace, 1939. Organized vice, prostitution, and drug addiction.

3978 "The Prevention and Repression of Prostitution in North America." International R of Crim Pol 13;15-25, Oct. '58.

3979 "Preventive Justice." Justice of the Peace 116:67-8, Feb. 2, '52.

3980 "Probation for Girls Who Err." Survey 23:349-50, Dec. 11, '09.

3981 "Problem of Vice and Graft." Lit Digest 46:61-2, Jan. 11, '13.

3982 "A Progress Report in Case of the People vs. the Prostitution Racket." (editorial). J Soc Hygiene 35:51-74, Feb. '49.

3983 "Proposal for the Legalization of Prostitution in Connecticut." Conn B J 49:162-78, Mar. '75.

3984 "The Proposal of the Delegation of the USA." Survey 51:515, Feb. 15, '24.

3985 Prostitutie en Strafrecht. Rapport van de commissie ingesteld bij besluit van de Minister van Justite. 's-Gravenhage: 1964, 67 pp.

3986 "Prostitution a Fifth Column." Science News Letter 38:260, Oct. 26, '40.

3987 "Prostitute in jail." J Crim Law 11:276-9, Aug. '20. Bibliography.

3988 Prostitution and Illicit Drug Traffic on the U. S.-Mexico Border. Ellwyn R. Stoddard, ed. Texas, Border-State University Consortium for Latin America, 1971.

3989 "Prostitution and the Law: emerging attacks on the 'woman's crime'." UNKC Law R 43:413-28, Spr. '75.

3990 "Prostitution: a non-victim crime? Women endorsing decriminalization." Issues in Criminology 8:137-62, Fall '73.

3991 "Prostitution: a penal or a medical problem." Part 1-2. Chi Law J 20:10-21, 119-51, Jan./Feb. '72.

3992 "Prostitution: (legislation in 1915). Soc Hygiene 2:242-8, Apr. '16. Summarizes bills which became laws and bills introduced but not passed.

3993 "Prostitution, regulation of vice." Munic Aff 5:376.

3994 "Prostitution: a survey of the present position." Justice of the Peace 125:59, Feb. 4, '61.

3995 "Prostitution Law Ruled Unconstitutional." Natl Cath Rep 10:8, Mar. 8, '74.

3996 Protetti, Ettore. Offesa al Pudore e all'Onore Sessule nella Giurisprudenza. Padova: Cedam, 1972, 410 pp. Italy.

3997 "Provisions of the Page Bill." Survey 24:499-501, Jun. 25, '10.

3998 "Public Order (legislation)." Law Times 162:43, Nov. 27, '26.

3999 "Pushed Off the Sidewalk; London." Time 73:21, Feb. 9, '59.

4000 "Putting Out the Red Lights." Lit Digest 51:1086-7, Nov. 13, '15.

4001 Rabut, R. "Campaign Against Prostitution." Prophylax Antiven 8:461-468, Sep. '36.

4002 Rainwater, Lee, and William L. Yancey. The Moynihan Report and the Politics of Controversy. Cambridge, Mass.: MIT Press, 1967. pp.39-124.

4003 Randolph, N. "Jelke? Jelke? Wasn't he the guy who..." Esquire 67:136-9+, Apr. '67.

4004 Rappaport, M. F. "After Ten Years." J Soc Hygiene 39(1953):209-215.

4005 Rappaport, M. F. "Toward a New WAy of Life." J Soc Hygiene 31(1945):590-599.

4006 Rapports Inedits du Lieutenant de Police Rene d'Argenson (1647-1715). Intro., notes and index by Paul Cottin. Paris: 1891. Considerable on Prostituion.

4007 Ratcliffe, W. A. "Street Offenses Bill; a Scottish Comparison." Crim Law R 1959:322, May '59.

4008 Raumer, Carl von. Die Gefallenen Madchen und die Sittenpolizei. Berlin: 1900, 63 pp.

4009 Ray, C. "Pre-Wolfenden." Spectator 199:389, Sep. 27, '57.

4010 Reasoner, M. A. "Contolled Prostitution in Coblenz, Germany." J Sexol and Psycholanal 2:199-205, '24.

4011 Reckless, Walter C. The Crime Problem. New York: Appleton-Century-Crofts, 1955, 1961. 1955 ed best on prostitution.

4012 Reckless, W. C. "The Impact of War on Crime, Delinquency, and Prostitution." Am J Sociol 48:378-386, '42. U. S. oriented, WWII.

4013 Reckless, W. C. Vice in Chicago. Montclair, N. J.: Paterson Smith, 1969, 314 pp.

4014 "Red Light for the Red Lights." Time 39:55, Apr. 27, '42.

4015 Reed, T. H. "Corruption of Politics by Organized Vice," in, Reed, Government for the People, pp.123-36. 1915.

4016 "Regulation 33B." New Statesman and Nation 25:10, Jan. 2, '43.

4017 "Regulation, Cure, and Prevention of Prostitution." Contemp 14:220.

4018 "Reinhardt, James Melvin. "A Critical Analysis of the Wolfenden Report." Fed Probation 23:36-41, Sep. '59.

4019 Renk, D. "Prostitution," in Handworterbuch der Staatswissenschaften von Conrad. Jena, 1901.

4020 "Rent From Immoral Earnings." Sol J 101:387, May 11, '57.

4021 Report and Recommendation of the Wisconsin Vice Committee. Madison: 1914.

4022 "Report of the Departmental Committee on Sexual Offenses Against Young Persons." Justice of the Peace 90:1-3, Jan. 2, '26; Sol J 7:279, Jan. 9, '26; Law Times 161:2-3, Jan. 2, '26.

4023 "Requirements of State Laws against Prostitution." J Soc Hygiene 30:470-71, Nov. '44. Tables.

4024 Reuiz de Linares, Jose L. "Notas Acerca del Problema de la Prostitucion." Investigacion (Madrid) pp.14-16, May '56.

4025 Reyes, F. "Results of New Federal Law on Prophylaxis of Venereal Diseases as Compared to Old Regulations on Practice of Prostitution." Arch Mex Ven.-Sif y Dermat 2:13-16, '43.

4026 Reynolds, J. B. "International Agreements in Relation to the Suppression of Vice," in Pan American Scietific Congress, Proceedings, 1915 9:496-502, '17. Also in Soc Hygiene 2:233-44, Apr. '16; and separately by the American Social Hygiene Assn.

4027 Reynolds, J. B. "International White Slavery." J Crim Law 3:134-7, May '12.

4028 Reynolds, J. B. "War Against the White Slave Traffic and Commercialized Vice," in National Conference of Charities and Correction, Proceedings, 1914, pp.211-7.

4029 Rice, J. L. "Application of the Mann Act." Rocky Mtn L R 20:221-4, Feb. '48.

4030 Rice, Wallace de Grooy Cecil. When "Whoppee" was a War Cry; moody reflections on a gaudy era. Series in The Chicagoan. Chicago: 1931.

4031 Richter, Hans Peter. "Prostitution." Kriminalistik pp.453-456, Dec. '57. Prostitution in 65 cities with 13 million inhabitants, of which 8,600 are classified by police as prostitutes.

4032 "Riotous or Indecent." Sol J 71:974, Dec. 24, '27.

4033 "Riotous Prostitution." Sol J 74:649 Oct. 4, '30.

4034 Robertson, E. G. B. "Traffic in Women and children Committee (of the League of nations)." Interdependence pp.-6, Jun. '29.

4035 Robinson, Victor. Morals in Wartime; 1. General survey from ancient times; 2. Morals in the first world war; 3. Morals in the second world war. New York: Publishers Foundation, 1943, 205 pp.

4036 Roby, Pamela A. "Politics and Criminal Law: revision of the New York state penal law in prostitution." Social Problems 17:83-109, Summer '69.

4037 Roby, Pamela A. "Politics and Prostitution: a case study of the revision, enforcement, and administration of the New York State Penal Laws on Prostitution." Criminology 9(4):425-47, '72.

4038 Roby, Pamela A. Politics and Prostitution: a case study of the formulation, enforcement and judicial administration of N. Y. State Laws, 1870-1970. New York Univ., 1971. Dissertation, available from Ann Arbor, Microfilm.

4039 Roby, Pamela, and V. Kerr. "Politics of Prostitution." Nation 214:463-6, Apr 10, '72.

4040 "Rockefeller Grand Jury Report." McClure 35:471-3, Aug. '10.

4041 "Rockefeller, Jr.'s, War on the the Social Evil." Lit Digest 46:283-4, Feb. 8, '13.

4042 "Rockefeller Report on Commercialized Vice." Survey 30:257-9, May 24, '13.

4043 Rogers, B. "The Mann Act and Noncommercial Vice." Law Notes 36(37):107-8(27-8), Jun. '33.

4044 Rolland, B., and H. Rebyeir. La Police Feminine: son role dans la lutte contre proxenetisme et la prostitution. Paris: 1947, 30 pp.

4045 Rolph, C. H. "Prostitution and the Law." New Statesman and Nation 33:330-1, 351, May 1-17, '47. Reply by K. B. Hardwick, 33:391, May 31, '47. Gt. Britain.

4046 Rolph, C. H. "Wolfenden Revisited." New Statesman 54:373-4, Sep. 28, '57.

4047 Rosenblatt, C. "Prostitution of the Criminal Law." Am Crim L Rev 11:373, Winter '73.

4048 Rotta, C. "Current Legislation Concerning Prostitution." Minerva Med 57(57):varia 945+, Jul. 21 '66.

4049 Saavedra, Alfredo M. Prostitucion, no Reglamentada. Mexico: Ediciones de la Sociedad Mexicana de Eugenesia, 1968, 63 pp.

4050 Sabatier, M. Histoire de la Legislation sur les Femmes Publique et les Lieux de Debauche. Paris: J. P Roret, 266 pp.

4051 Sacotte, Marcel.Les Limites Entre la Reglementation Administrative et la Repression Penale en Matiere de Prostitution et de Proxenetisme. Etudes de Droit Contemporain, ns (1962), 17 pp.

4052 Sacotte, Marcel. "Les Sanctions et Mesures Applicables aux Souteneurs." Revue Internationale de Criminologie et de Police Technique 15(1961):185-197.

4053 "Sailors and Sex; prostitution flourishes in Japan; Navy policy comes under attack." Newsweek 26:82+, Nov. 12, '45.

4054 St-John-Stevas, Norman. Obscenity and the Law. London: Secker and Warburg, 1956.

4055 Saint Louis, Mo. "Ordinance making it unlawful to engage in prostitution or aid or abet prostitution. (Ord.42599)." St. Louis City J pp.14-15, Apr. 20, '43.

4056 Satyendra-Natha Mukhopadhyaya. Murder of Prostitutes for Gain. Calcutta: 1935, 115 pp.

4057 Schmidt, F. "Studies on the Registration and Care of Socially Endangered Groups of Persons in a District." Z Gesamte Hyg 19(5):378-84, May '73.

4058 Schrank, Joseph. Die Regelung der Prostitution. Wien: Im Selbstverlage des Verfassers, 1892, 20 pp.

4059 Schreiber, L. Arias. "In Favor of Abolition." Cron Med (Lima) 53:132-135, Mar. '36.

4060 Schuppe. "Present Status of Problem." Monatschr f Krim.-Psychol 26:394-399, '35.

4061 Schur, Edwin M. Crimes Without Victimqs; deviant behavior and public policy; abortion, homosexuality, drug addiction. Englewood Cliffs, N. J.: Prentice-Hall, 1965, 180 pp.

4062 Scott, Benjamin. A State Inequity: Its Rise, Extension and Overthrow. London: Kegan Paul, Trench, Trubner and Co., 1890. Includes an appendix of literature on the repeal movement.

4063 Scott, G. R. Into Whose Hands. Reprinted Brooklyn, N. Y.: Waron Press, 1961.

4064 Seagle, William. "The Twilight of the Mann Act." Am Bar Assn J 55:641-7, Jun. '69.

4065 "Seek New Prostitution Code." Christian Century 81:151, Dec. 9, '64.

4066 "Segregation of Prostitutes: correspondence concerning U. S. Army policy." J Soc Hygiene 27:87, Feb. '41.

4067 Segregation of Prostitution and the Injunction and Abatement Law Against Houses of Prostitution. Am. Social Hygiene Assn. pub. no.73, 1916, 12 pp.

4068 Segregation of Prostitution. Am. Social Hygiene Assn. pub. no.50, 4 pp. Contains a list of cities of the U. S. having a population of 100,000 (1910) that are reported to have abandoned officially the policy of segregating prostitution.

4069 Selfridge, E. A. "Redlight Vote." Survey 33:344, Dec. 26, '14.

4070 "Senate Committee on Education and Labor Reports Favorably on S.1779 Authorizing Federal Security Administrator to Assist States in Matters Relating to Social Protection (including hearings on bill). J Soc Hygiene 32:230-232, May '46.

4071 Sennett, Mary Ware. Birth Control Laws. New York: Frederick H. Hitchcock, 1926.

4072 Sexual Offenders and Social Punishment--evidence submitted to Church of England Moral Welfare Council on Homosexual Offenses and Prostitution. Comp. and edited by Derrick Sherwin Bailey. Westminster: Church Information Board, 1956.

4073 Shanahan, L. "The Threat of Legalized Prostitution." Marriage 53:54-9, Oct. '71.

4074 Sheffield, A. E. "Page Bill." Survey 24:596, Jul. 9, '10.

4075 Sheffield, A. E. "Written Law and the Unwritten Double Standard." Int J Ethics 21:475-85, Jul. '11. Also R of Rs 44:242-3, Aug. '11.

4076 Sheldon, Amos. A Comparative Survey of Laws in Force for the Prohibition, Regulation, and Licensing of Vice in England and Other Countries. London: 1877.

4077 Sheldon, L. "Bad Woman's Vote." Overland ns 61:165-9, Feb. '13.

4078 Sherwin, Robert V. Sex and the Statutory Law. New York: Oceana Pub., 1949.

4079 Skousen, Willard Cleon. "The Chief's Responsibility for Vice Control." 6 pts. Pt.5: Prostitution. Law and Order 16:10, '68; 17:10, '69.

4080 Slovenko, R. "Everything You Wanted to Have in Sex Laws." J Forensic Sci 18(2):118-24, Apr. '73.

4081 Smashing the White Slave Trade. Chicago: Currier Pub. Co., 1909.

4082 Smith-Hurd. Illinois Annotated Statutes. Criminal Code of 1961. Chicago: Burdette Smith, 1961. First state to reform sex laws in accordance with American Law Institute recommendations.

4083 "Social Evil." Outlook 70:606-8, Mar. 8, 1902.

4084 "Social Evil in Chicago." J Crim Law 3:804-6, Jan. '13.

4085 "Social Evil--vice reports and investigations." Nat Munic R 5:698-702, Oct. '16.

4086 "Social Hygiene and the Problem of Prostitution," in, National Conference of Charities and Correction, Proceedings 1914:197-256.

4087 "Social Hygiene in Wartime; prostitution, social protection and the police. Symposium." J Soc Hygiene 28:365-429, Oct. '42.

4088 Solano, S. (In favor of abolition). Cron Med (Lima) 53:120-128, mar. '36.

4089 Solano, S. "Sexual Reform." Cron Med (Lima) 53:368-371, Oct. '36.

4090 Solano, S. "Two Years of Abolitionist Propaganda." Cron Med (Lima) 54:303-305, Sep. '37.

4091 "Solicitation to the Annoyance." Sol J 71:549, 964, Jun.9, Dec. 17, '29.

4092 "Soliciting in a Street." L Q Rev 76:487, Oct. '60. Smith v. Hughes.

4093 "Soliciting Without Annoyance." Sol J 72:2, Jan. 7, '28.

4094 South Africa. (Laws, Statutes, etc.) Commentary on the Immorality Act. (Act no.3 of 1957). Juta, 1960.

4095 South Carolina. Act prohibiting lewdness, assignation and prostitution and providing penalties for violation thereof. No.744, Acts 1942.

4096 South Australia. Act amending criminal law bill increases punishment for certain sexual offenses, and facilitate conviction of guilty persons. Maximum penalty for lewdness is made two years and whipping for firt offense, four years and whipping for second offense. To facilitate conviction of guilty jury may find against prisoner for lesser offenses where accusation is rape or attempted carnal knowledge. Maximum penalty for all sexual offenses is increased from two to seven years hard labor. Where offender is suffering from venereal disease he may be kept in confinement after expiration of sentance until pronounced cured. (Passed Assembly Oct. 3, passed Council Oct. 25, 1917.

4097 Spencer, A. G. "Age of Consent ond Its Significance." Forum 49:406-20, Apr. '13.

4098 Spencer, A. G. "Is the Page Bill All Right?" Survey 24:354-5, May 28, '10.

4099 Spencer, A. G. "State Regulation of Vice and Its Meaning." Forum 49:587-601, May '13.

4100 Spencer, A. G. "Word More on the Page Bill." Survey 24:514-5, Jun. 25, '10.

4101 Spingarn, A. B. Laws Relating to Sex Morality in New York City. Bureau of Social Hygiene, 1915. Also by New York: Century, 1926.

4102 "Spinster's Victory." Newsweek 51:54+, Feb. 10, '58.

4103 Stamatiades, Platon B. (Prostitution). 1959, 165 pp. In Greek.

4104 "State and Federal Laws Concerning White Slave Traffic, Keeping Disorderly Houses and Age of Consent, January, 1916." Am. Social Hygiene Assn. Bul 2:5, Jan. '16. Quality of laws tabulated by states under the following heads: White slave law, Keeping disorderly houses, Criminal law, Civil law, Age of consent.

4105 "State of the Union Regarding Commercialized Prostitution; a 1949 summary." J Soc Hygiene 35:146-61, Apr. '49. Bibliography.

4106 "State of the Union Regarding Commercialized Prositution--a ten year survey; analysis of 3402 studies made January 1, 1940 to December 31, 1949 in 1224 communities." J Soc Hygiene. 36:50, Feb. '50.

4107 Statement Respecting the Prevalence of Certain Immoral Practices in His Majesty's Navy. London: Ellerton and Henderson, 1821. Reprinted London: 189-. 42 pp.

4108 Stellung des Staates zur Prostitution. Hannover: 1883, 35 pp.

4109 Stevas, Norman St. John. Obscenity and the Law. London: Secker and warburg, 1956. pp.66-67.

4110 Stowe, L. B. "Vice, Crime, and the New York Police." R of Rs 48:73-8, Jul. '13.

4111 "Street Offences." Justice of the Peace 92:828, Dec. 22, '28 and Sol J 72:867-8, Dec 29, '28.

4112 "Street Offenses." Spectator 141:911, Dec. 15, '28.

4113 "Street Offenses Act." Sol J 103:687, Sep. 4, '59.

4114 Stringer, Hubert. Moral Evil in London. Chapman, 1925, 270 pp. Bibliography.

4115 Stuart, James. The New Abolitionists; a narrative of a year's work. Being an account of the mission undertaken to the continent of Europe by Mrs. Josephine E. Butler. 8v. London: Dyer, 1876.

4116 "Study and Treatment of Persons Charges With Prostitution," by Miriam Van Waters; "Survey of 100 May Act Violators Committed to the Federal Reformatory for Women (Alderson, W. Va)," by Helen Hironimus. Fed Probation pp.27-34, Apr. '43.

4117 Sullivan, G. D. "Interpretation of a Statute--consequence of absurdity." U Kan City L Rev 13:110-12, Dec. '44, Feb. '45. Beach v. U. S.

4118 "Superintendance of Prostitution by the State." Westm 92:556.

4119 "Suppressing Traffic in Persons: third committee (social, cultural and humanitarian committee, United Nations general assembly)'s progress on draft convention. U. N. Bull 7:538-44, Nov. 1, '49.

4120 "Supreme Court Upholds the White Slave Law; the New York situation." Survey 29:799-894, Mar. 8, '13.

4121 Sutherland, Edwin H. and Donald R. Cressey. Principles of Criminology. 6th ed. J. B. Lippincott, 1960.

4122 "Sweeping the Streets." Spec 199:291, Sep. 6, '57. Discussion 199:38, 368, 434, Sep. 13-20, Oct. 4, '57.

4123 Taft, Donald R. Criminology. 6th ed. New York: Macmillan Co., 1956. Ch.17 on Sex Delinquency.

4124 Talbot, James Beard. The Miseries of Prostitution. London: James Madden and Co., 1844. Rather far fetched estimates on London. Estimates one prostitute to every 60 adult males. Basic causes are neglect of parents, inadequate renumeration for female labor. Proposed brothels be purchase by municipalities and closed, making seduction a penal offense, some other interesting ideas.

4125 Tarnovskii, Veniamin Mikhaylovich. Prostitution und Abolitionismus. Hamburg und Leipzig: L. Voss, 1890.

4126 Taylor, G. "Morals Commission and Police Morals." Survey 30:62-4, Apr. 12, '13.

4127 Taylor, G. "Police Efficiency the First Effect of Vice Inquiries." Survey 28:136-41, Apr. 20, '12.

4128 Taylor, G. "War on Vice." Survey 29:811-3, Mar. 8, '13.

4129 Taylor, H. L. "Manhandling the Mann Act?" Nat B J 5:39-51, Mar. '47.

4130 Tennessee. Act to prohibit prostitution and assignation. Ch.157, Public Acts 1943.

4131 Tessmann, Gunter. Die Panurge: Volkerkindliche Monographie Eines West Africanischen Negerstammes. Berlin: Ernst Wasmuth, 1913. I, 108.

4132 The Theodosian Code. Tr. with commentary by Clyde Pharr in collaboration with Theresa S. Davidson and Mary B. Pharr. Princeton: Princeton U., 1952.

4133 Third Paulist de Estudo Policiais Promovida Pelo Centro Academico de Criminologia. Nov. 3-7, 1952. Sao Paulo: 1953. Devoted to prostitution and the police.

4134 Thornton, R. Y. "Controlled Prostitution--a myth." J Soc Hygiene 40:111-19, Mar. '54. Reprinted separately. Arguments against segregated vice districts.

4135 Thornton, R. Y. "Organized Crime in the Field of Prostitution." J Cri Law 46:775-9, Mar./Apr. '56.

4136 Thornton, R. Y. "You're in the Fight Against Prostitution." J Soc Hygiene 40(1954):111-116.

4137 Thoughts on the Plan for a Magdalen House. London: James Waugh, 1758, 59 pp. Some inaccurate surveys of earlier Magdalen houses, but regards them as essential to cure prostitution since there prostitutes could be trained in industry, and their morals could be reformed.

4138 Timewell, J. The Police and the White Slave. James Timewell, 1913, 14 pp.

4139 "Toleration of Vice." Ind 53:50, Jan. 3, '01.

4140 Touraine, A. "Some Reflections on the Recent Legal Texts on Prostitution, Proxenetism, Homosexuality and the Prevention of Venereal Diseases." Presse Med 69:871-3, Apr. 22, 1961. In French.

4141 "Towards Abolition of the Prostitute Registry." Prophyl Sanit Morale 32:305-12, Dec. '60. In French.

4142 "Traffic in Persons and Prostitution." J For Med 7:1, Jan.-Mar., '60.

4143 "The Traffic in Women Bill." Sol J 72:232, Apr. 7, '28.

4144 "Trusting the Police; street offenses bill." Economist 190:477-80, Feb. 7, '59.

4145 Union Belge Contre l'Exploitation de la Debauche. L'Esclavage de la Prostituee, ses aspects juridiques, moraux et sociau. Brussels: n. d., 31 pp.

4146 "United Against Social Vice." Ind 74:609-10, Mar. 20, '13.

4147 "United States Government Threatens Deportation of White Slavers in New Efforts to Combat Commercialized Prostitution." J Social Hygiene 22:425, Dec. '36.

4148 U. S. Immigration Commission (1907-1910). Importing Women for Immoral Purposes--Report in Response to Senate Resolution no.86. Washington: U. S. Government Printing Office, 1909.

4149 U. S. Immigration Commission. 1907- . Steerage Conditions, Importation and Harboring of women for Immoral Purposes. Washington: Sup't. of Docs., 1911.

4150 U. S. National Advisory Police Committee. Techniques of Law Enforcement Against Prostitution. Washington: GPO, 1943, 75 pp.

4151 U. S. Office of Community War Services. Division of Social Protection. Challenge to Community Action. GPO, 1945, 76 pp.

4152 U. S. Senate. Com. on the District of Columbia. Repression of Prostitution in the District of Columbia: hearings on S. 1616, a bill for the repression of prostitution in the District of Columbia, October 13, and 20, 1921. (U. S. 67th Congress, 1st sess.). 1921, 48 pp, Tables.

4153 U. S. Dept. of State. Suppression of White Slave Traffic. (61st Congress, 2d sess. Senate Doc. 214). Washington D. C.: Supt. of Doc, 1909.

4154 U. S. Supreme Court, Feb. 1, 1915, held that under the federal white slave law, a woman transported in violation of the law could be indicted as a co-conspirator with the person who caused her to be transported. The opinion intimated that a woman could also be indicted if she engaged in a conspiracy to have herself transported with a view to blackmail. The decision, it is believed, will make prosecutions very difficult. (Press report).

4155 U. S. Supreme Court held, April 24, 1916, in a white slave case, that the Mann Act is faulty and should be corrected, since it permitted a woman to fail to register an inmate of her house of ill fame, to protect herself from being convicted of violating the state law against prostitution. (Angeline Lombardo v. State of Washington; press report Apr. 25, 1916).

4156 U. S. Supreme Court held, Jan. 15, 1917, that prosecutions under the Mann white slave law for transporting women in interstate commerce are not limited to commercialized vice, and include personal immoral acts.

4157 "United Nations Assumes League (of Nations) Functions: conventions concern traffic in women, children, obscene publications." U N W Bul 3:558-9, Oct. 28, '47.

4158 United Nations. International Convention for the Suppression of the White Slave Traffic; signed at Paris on 4 May 1910; amended by the Protocol signed at Lake Success New York, 4 May, 1949. Lake Success: 1950, 9 pp.

4159 United Nations. International Convention for the Suppression of the Traffic in Women and Children; opened for signature at Geneva from September 30, 1921 to March 31, 1922; amended by the protocol, signed at Lake Success, New York, November 1, 1947. Internat. Doc. Service, Aug. 2, 1948, 9 pp. 1948 IV 4.

4160 United Nations. International Convention for the Suppression of the Traffic in Women of Full Age; signed at Geneva, October 11, 1933; amended by the Protocol, signed at Lake Success, New York, November 12, 1947. Internat. Doc. Service, Aug. 2, 1948, 8 pp. 1948 IV 3.

4161 United Nations. Protocol Amending the International Agreement for the Suppression of the White Slave Traffic of the 18th of May, 1904, and the International Convention for the Suppression of the White Slave Traffic of the 4th of May, 1910. Lake Success: May 4, 1949. London: H. M. Stationary Off., 1954, 28 pp.

4162 United Nations. The Suppression of the Traffic in Persons and of the Exploitation of Others. 1959. E/CN 5/338.

4163 United Nations. Suppression of the White Slave Traffic. Protocol, with annex between the United States of America and other governments amending Agreement of May 18, 1904, and Convention of May 4, 1910. Proclaimed by the President of the United States of America Aug. 9, 1951, entered into force with respect to the United States of America Aug. 14, 1950. Washington: GPO, 1952, 53 pp. U. S. Dept. of State pub. no.4436. Treities and other international acts series, 2332.

4164 United Nations. Social Commission. Draft Convention of 1937 for Suppressing the Exploitation of the Prostiution of Others. (Item 6b of the Draft agenda). Transfer to the United Nations of the functions exercised by the French government under the International agreement of 18 May 1904 and the International convention of 4 May, 1910 for the suppression of the white slave traffic, and the International agreement of 4 May, 1910 for the suppression of obscene publications (item 6c f the draft agenda). Lake Success: 1948. E/CN 5/41. ||~ 4710 United Nations. Secretariat. Observations Made by Governments and Organizations With Respect to the Draft Convention for the Suppression of the Traffic in Persons and of the Exploitation of the

Prostitution of Others. Lake Success: 1949, 38 pp.

4165 United Nations. Economic and Social Council. Social Committee. First Session, Lake Success, New York, January 20-February 5, 1947:note on prostitution, traffic in women and children and obscene publications; items 8 and 11 of the provisional agenda. Lake Success, New York: Jan. 18, 1947, 43 pp. 1947, E/CN 5/14. Not generally distributed.

4166 United Nations. Economic and Social Council. Secretary General. Transfer to the United Nations of the Functions and Powers Exercised by the League of Nations under the Conventions on the Traffic in Women and Children and in Obscene Publications. Lake Success: New York: Jun. 12, '47, 51 pp. Tables. 1947, E/444. Not generally distributed.

4167 United Nations. Economic and Social Council. Traffic in Women and Children; summary of annual reports for 1946-47 prepared by the Secretariat. Internat. Doc. Service, 1948, 20 pp. Tables. 1948 IV 2 (1948, E/TWC 1946-47/summary).

4168 United Nations. Economic and Social Council. Traffic in Women and Children; addendum to summary of annual reports, for 1947-48, prepared by the Secretariat. Internat. Doc. service, 1950, 32 pp. Tables. 1950 IV 5 (E/TWC 1947-48/Summary/Add 1 Apr.18, 1950).

4169 United Nations. Economic and Social Council. Traffic in Women and Children; summary of annual reports for the period 1948-1950. Internat Doc. Service, Aug. '52, 43 pp.

4170 United Nations. Economic and Social Council. Traffic in Women and Children; addendum to the summary reports for the period 1948-50. Internat Doc. Service, Mar. 1, 1953, 17 pp.

4171 United Nations. Dept. of Social Affairs. Social Defence; prevention of crime and treatment of offender, suppression of traffic in persons and of exploitation of the prostitution of others. 1950-. Annual. ST/SAO/ser E.

4172 United Nations. Dept. of Economic and Social Affairs. Study of Traffic in Persons and Prostitution. New York: Internat. Doc. Service. Columbia Univ. Press, 1959. ST/SOA/SD S 301.4243.

4173 Ursini, Simonis Christophi. Commentatio Juridica de Quaestu Merectrico. Halle, 1737.

4174 Van der Valk, M. H. Conservatism in Modern Chinese Family Laws. Leiden: E. J. Brill, 1952.

4175 Van Haecht, A. La Prostituee; statut et image. Brussels: Editions de l'Universite de Bruxelles, 1973, 212 pp.

4176 Vanhove, J. Essay de Droit Coutumier de Ruanda. (essay on the common law of Ruanda). Institut Royal Colonial Belge, Section des Sciences Morales et Politiques. Memoires, vol.10, pp.3-125. Brussels: Institut Royal Colonial Belge, 1941.

4177 Van Waters, M. "Study and Treatment of Persons Charged With Prostitution." Federal Probation. 7(1943):27-30.

4178 Varela, A. R. "Current Judicial Aspects of Prostitution." Sem Med (Buenos Aires) 121:1786-8, Nov. 12, '62.

4179 Veilland, M. La Prostitution; etude critique de droit compare. Lyon, 1918, 158 pp.

4180 Vella, G., and A. Petiziol. "Contributo alla Conoscenza del Comportamento della Prostituta." Quaderni di Criminologia Clinica (Rome) 3(1960), 30 pp.

4181 Venters, C. V. "Prosecution of Women under the Mann Act." Law Notes 38:29-31, S. '34.

4182 The Vice Commission of Philadelphia. Pub. by the Commission, 1913.

4183 "Vice Investigations: (list of reports of state and local vice conditions)." Am Soc Hygiene Assn Bul 2:3-4, Mar. '16.

4184 "Vice Laws in Prospect; Wolfenden Report." Economist 189:881, Dec. 6, '58.

4185 "Vice Racketeers Lose Ground; prostitution conditions in the USA: a 12 year survey." J Soc Hygiene 38:186-7, Apr. '52.

4186 "Victimless Crime Laws." N C Central L J 6:258-74, Spr. '75.

4187 "View From Curzon Street." Newsweek 53:43, Feb. 9, '59.

4188 Vintras, A. (M. D.) On the Repressive Measures Adopted in Paris Compared With the Uncontrolled Prostitution of London and New York. London: Robert Hardwicke, 1867.

4189 Virginia. Laws, statutes, etc. Virginia Laws for the Suppression of Vice. Richmond: State Board of Charities and Corrections, 1917.

4190 Vitray, L. "U. N. Blacks out the Red Lights." U N World 4:41-4, Jul. '50.

4191 "Votes for Women and Votes to Table the Hartford Vice Report." Survey 31:73, Oct. 18, '13.

4192 Wagner, Roland Richard. Virtue Against Vice: a study of moral reformers and prostitution in the progressive era. Univ of Wisconsin, 1971, 281 pp. (Dissertation).

4193 Ware, Helen R. E. The Recruitment Regulation and Role of the Prostitute in Britain from the Middle of the Nineteenth Century to the Present. London: 1969. (Dissertation).

4194 Warren, John H. Thirty Years Battle With Crime. New York: Arno Press, 1970, 400 pp.

4195 Washington Supreme Court decided, April 24, 1916, in a white slave case that the Mann Act is faulty and should be corrected, since it is permitted a woman to fail to register an inmate of her house of ill fame, to protect herself from being convicted of violating the state law against prostitution. (Angeline Lombardo v. State of Washington; press report Apr. 25, '16).

4196 Waterman, Willoughby C. Prostitution and Its Repression in New York City. New York: Columbia Univ. Press, 1932, pp.117-59.

4197 Watson, C. "Recent Changes in French Policy." Brit J Ven Dis 30:103-113, Jun. '54.

4198 Weil, A. L. "In the Hands of the Police; a plea for laws against vice." Survey 30:203-4, May 3, '13.

4199 Welch, Saunders. A Proposal to render effectual a Plan to Remove the Nuisance of Common Prostitutes from the Streets of This Metropolis. London; C. Henderson, 1758. Wants to transport keepers of bawdy houses on conviction; arrest and hold prostitutes, send those guilty to hospital or work houses, if they return to old life be transported.

4200 Werner, C. H. Die Lex Heinze und Ihre Geschichte. Dortmund, 1935, 44 pp.

4201 Wenzky O. "Sittenpolizeiliche Problem um Dirnenhauser." Die Polizei Aug. and Sep. '54, pp.143-145, 162-163. An account of some of the difficulties of police in Cologne in dealing with tolerated houses.

4202 West Virginia. Act declaring certain building and places used for purposes of prostitution to be nuisances, providing for suit inequity to enjoin the same, and to assess taxes thereon, and providing penalties for the violation of injunctions issued here-under. (Ch.19, Acts 1925).

4203 "What a City Should Know About Law Enforcement: legal experts frame questionnaire on technique of control of prostitution and venereal disease." Soc Hygiene Bul 7:10, Jan. '20.

4204 "What is a Brothel?" Aust L J 16:240, Dec. '42. (Rowarth v. Grace).

4205 "What is a Brothel?" Justice of the Peace 106:267. Jun. 6, '42.

4206 White, C. "What Law Enforcement Means to Us: the problem of prostitution." J Soc Hygiene 17:393-402, Oct. '31. Tables.

4207 White Slave Traffic. Offices of "M. A. P.", 1910, 115 pp.

4208 "White Slave Decision." Lit Digest. 46:500-2, Mar. 8, '13.

4209 "White Slave Traffic Before the Supreme Court." Cur Opinion 54:272, Apr. '13.

4210 Whitin, F. H. "The Enforcement of the Vagrancy-prostitution Law and the Proposed Amendment," in New York State Assn. of Magistrates, Proceedings, 1925, pp.54-63, 1926.

4211 Whitin, F. H. "Obstacles to Vice Repression." Soc Hygiene 2:145-63, Apr. '16. Presented at the annual meeting of the Am. Social Hygiene Assn., Boston, Oct. 8, '15. Also published separately by the Assn.

4212 "Why Let It Come Back? Case against commercialized prostitution and segregated vice districts." J Soc Hygiene 22:403-11, Dec. '36.

4213 "Why Our Police Fail." Cur Lit 53:669-71, Dec. '12.

4214 Wilke,____. "Zuhalterei und Ihre Bekampfung." Krim 8:274-276, '34. Procuring and its control.

4215 Williams, D. G. T. "Sex and Morals in the Criminal Law, 1954-1963." Crim L Rev 1964:253, Apr. '64.

4216 Williams, J. E. H. "Street Offenses Act, 1959." Modern Law R 23:173, Mar. '60.

4217 Williams, J. E. H. "The Wolfenden Report." Pol Q 29:134-43, Apr./Jun. '58.

4218 Wilson, Paul. The Sexual Dilemma; abortion, homosexuality, prostitution, and the criminal threshold. Queensland: Univ. of Queensland Press, 1971, 172 pp.

4219 Winde, E. de, et al. "Proposed Law for the Suppression of Official Regulation in France." Prophylax Antiven 9:69-87, Feb. '37.

4220 Wisconsin. Defines the word "roadhouses" and provides for their suppression. (Ch.401, Laws 1921).

4221 Wisconsin. Legislative Reform Dept. Synopsis of Laws of the Several States and of England and Canada relating to the Social Evil. Jan, '14, 34 pp.

4222 Wisconsin. Legislature. Report and Recommendations of the Wisconsin Legislative Committee to Investigate the White Slave Traffic and Kindred Subjects. Democrat Ptg. Co., 1914.

4223 Witherspoon, J. H. "Legal and Administrative Phases of Prostitution Control," in National Inst. of Munic. Law Officers, Proceedings, 1942, pp.417-22, 1943.

4224 "Wolfenden Report: user of premises." Sol J 101:741, Sep. 28, '57.

4225 Wolzendorff, Kurt. Polizei und Prostitution. Tubingen: 1911.

4226 Women and Girls in Moral and Social Danger. New Dehli Central Bureau of Correctional Services, 1971, 127 pp.

4227 Women Endorsing Decriminalization. "Prostitution: a non-victim crime?" Issues in Criminology 8(2):137-162. Argues for legalization and decriminalization.

4228 Wood, J. C. "Street Offenses Act, 1959." Crim Law R 1960:521, Aug. '60.

4229 Woods, R. A. "Prohibition and Social Hygiene." Soc Hygiene 5:137-45, Apr. '19.

4230 Worth, Thomas. A Second Letter to the Right Hon. W. Ewart Gladstone Opposing the Attempt Under the Title of a "Contagious Diseases Bill" to Introduce Into This Country the Continental System of Licensed Prostitution. Nottingham: F, Banks, 1870.

4231 Worthington, George E., and Ruth Topping. Study of Specialized Courts dealing With Sex Delinquency. 1: "The Morals Court of Chicago." New York: Am. Social Hygiene Assn., Inc., 1921. Reprinted from Social Hygiene 7(4):351-411, '21. 2:"Misdemeanants' Division of the Philadelphia Municipal Court." 1922; 3: "Second Sessions of the Municipal Court of the City of Boston." 1922. Am. Social Hygiene Assn.

4232 Worthington, G. E. "Summary and Comparative Study of the Special Courts in Chicago, Philadelphia, Boston and New York." J Soc Hygiene 9:348-75, Jun. '23. Also reprinted separately by the Association.

4233 Worthington, G. E., and Ruth Topping. Specialized Courts Dealing with Sex Delinquency. Hitchcock, 1925. Reprinted by Patterson Smith, 1969.

4234 Worthington, G. E., and Ruth Topping. "Standards for a Socialized Court for Dealing With Sex Delinquents." J Soc Hygiene 10:335-60, Jun. '24.

4235 "Wreck of Commercialized Vice." Survey 35:532-3, Feb. 5, '16.

4236 Wright, W. J. P. Regulated Vice and the Traffic in Women. International Abolitionist Federation, 1914.

4237 Wulffen, Erich. Woman as a Sexual Criminal. Tr. by David Berger. New York: Am. Ethnological Press, 1934. pp.493-522.

4238 Wyoming. Act declaring to be a nuisance any building, erection, or place used for the purpose of prostitution, gambling, or the unlawful keeping and sale of intoxicating liquor, together with the furniture, fixtures, musical instruments, gambling devices and other contents, and providing for the abatement thereof and punishment for the same. (Ch.87, Laws 1921).

4239 Wyoming. Act providing for the repression of prostitution. (Ch.98, Laws 1921).

4240 Zehnder, C. Die Gefahren der Prostitution und Ihre Gesetzliche Bekampfung. Zurich: 1891, 247 pp.

4241 Zimmerman, Jean Turner. Vere of Shanghai. Chicago: c1925, 136 pp.

4242 Zur Frage der Bekampfung der Prostitution in Bundesrepublik Deutschland. Frankfurt: Deutsches National Komitee zur Bekampfung des Madchenhandels, 1956. A summary of legislation in Germany.

4243 Alciphron. *Epistola Letters*. Ed. and tr. by Frances Forbes. Loeb Classical Library. London: W. H. Allen, 1949. Letters of courtesans.

4244 "Anthology of Prostitution." *Time* 81:34, Apr. 12, '63.

4245 Aretino, Pietro. *Dialogues*. Tr. by Raymond Rosenthal. New York: Stein and Day, 1971.

4246 Astour, M. C. "Tamar the Hierodule; an essay in the method of vestigal motifs." *J Bib Lit* 85:185-96, Jun. '66.

4247 Barnett, James H. *Divorce and the American Divorce Novel 1858-1937*. Philadelphia: Univ of Penn. Press, 1939.

4248 Beauvoir, Simone de. *Must We Burn De Sade?* Tr. by Annette Michelson. New York: Peter Nevill, 1953.

4249 _____. *The Second Sex*. Tr. and ed. by H. M. Parshley. New York: Knopf, 1953.

4250 Becker, W. A. *Charikles*. Leipzig: 1840.

4251 Borthwick, E. K. "Femme Fatale in Asclepiades." *Classical R* ns 17:250-4, Dec. '67.

4252 Braun, Sidney D. *The Courtesane in the French Theater From Hugo to Becque (1831-1885)*. Baltimore: John Hopkins Press and London and Paris: Humprey Milford-Oxford Univ. Press, 1947, 157 pp.

4253 Capellanus, Andreas. *The Art of Courtly Love*. Tr. by John Jay Parry. New York: Columbia Univ., 1941.

4254 Capon, Gaston and R. Yve-Plessis. *Les Theatres Clandestins*. Paris: 1905.

4255 Castiglione, Baldassare. *The Courtier*. Tr. by Thomas Hoby. National Alumori, 1907.

4256 Castiglione, Baldessare. *Il Libro del Cortegiano*. Florence: Sansani, 1947.

4257 *The City Madam*. Ed. by Cyrus Hoy. Regents Renaissance Drama Series, Bison Books, Univ. of Nebraska Press.

4258 Compiegne, Mercier. *Manuel des Boudoirs*. Brussels ed: n. d.

4259 Damodaragupta. *Eastern Love*; the lessons of a bawd and harlot's breviary. English versions of the Kuttanimatam of Damodaragupta and Samayamatrika of Kshemendra. 2v. Rodker, 1927.

4260 d'Almeras, Henri, and Paul d'Estree. Les Thetres Libertins au XVIIIe Siecle. Paris, 1905.

4261 Deegan, D. Y. The Stereotype of the Single Women in American Novels. New York: Columbia Univ., 1951.

4262 Dictionary of American Slang. Comp. and ed. by Harold Wentworth and Stuart B. Flexner. New York: Thomas Y. Crown, 1960.

4263 Duffet, Thomas. The Spanish Rogue.

4264 Feydeau, Ernest Aime. De luxe des Femmes des Moeurs de la Litterature et de la Vertu. Paris: M. Levy, 1866, 237 pp.

4265 Forjaz de Sampaio, Albino. O Livros das Cortesas; antologia de poetas Portuescses e Brasileiros. 2d ed Lisbon: Guimaes, 1920, 258 pp. Bibliography on prostitution, pp.45-49.

4266 Fracastor, Hieronymus. Syphilis. St. Louis: The Philmarto, 1911.

4267 Freilecher, L. P. "Story Behind the Book. 'The Lively Commerce'." Pub Weekly 199:53, May 24, '71.

4268 Greenwald, Harold, and Aron Krich. The Prostitute in Literature. New York: Ballantine Books, 1960. A good survey.

4269 Haag, H. Der Gestaltwandel der Kupplerin in der Franzosischen Literatur des 16. und 17. Jahrhunderts. Marburg, 1936, 75 pp. (Marburger Beitrage zur Romanischen Philologie).

4270 Hamel, Maurice and C. Tournier. De la Prostitution dans la Litterature. Nice: 1927.

4271 Harrison, Michael. Fanfare of Strumpets. London: W. H. Allen, 1971, 252 pp.

4272 Hauschild, C. H. Die Gestalt der Hetare in der Griechischen Komodie. Leipzig: 1933, 71 pp.

4273 Hayward, C. The Courtesan. London: Casanova Society, 1926.

4274 Hayward, C. Dictionary of Courtesans. Reprinted New York: University Books, 1962.

4275 Head, Richard. The English Rogue. London: 1665. Reprinted London: G. Routledge and Sons, 1928.

4276 Hogarth, William. "The Harlot's Progress," in Hogarth, Marriage a la Mode. New York: Lear, 1947.

4277 Huang, Hsueh-so. *Ch'in Lou Chi.* (Prostitutes in Literature). 1939, 12 pp.

4278 *L'Infortune des Filles de Joye Suivie de la Maigre par Adrien de Montluc, Comte de Cramail.* Paris: 1624. Cited in Gay.

4279 Jacob, P. L. *Les Courtesanes de l'Ancienne Rome.* Brussels: 1884, p.222.

4280 Johnson, S. "Misella Debauched (Saturday, 2nd November, 1751)," in Johnson, *The Rambler*, pp.257-60. Dutton, 1953.

4281 Johnson, S. "Misella Debauched (Tuesday, 5th November, 1751)," in Johnson, *The Rambler*, pp.260-64. Dutton, 1953.

4282 Krich, A. M. *The Anatomy of Love.* New York: Dell Pub. Co., 1960.

4283 Lambert, ____. *Les Amours et Galanteries des Grandes Dames;* des actrices et des cocottes celebres de Paris. Geneva: c1885, 64 pp.

4284 Laurence, D. H. *Sex Literature and Censorship.* Ed. by Harry T. Moore. New York: Twayne Pub., 1953.

4285 Laurent-Tailhade, Marie-Louise. *Courtesans, Princesses, Lesbians.* Paris: Editions de la Fontaine d'Or.

4286 Lewis, C. S. *The Allegory of Love.* Oxford: Galaxy, 1958.

4287 Lewis, D. B. Wyndham. *François Villon.* New York: Literary Guild, 1928.

4288 Loth, David. *The Erotic in Literature.* New York: Julian Messner, 1961.

4289 Lucian. *Dialogues.* Tr. by A. M. Harman. Loeb Classical Library. London: W. H. Allen, 1913. 8v planned, 5 so far.

4290 Lucian. "The Dialogues of Courtesans," in *The Works of Lucian.* Tr. by John Dryden. 4v. London: Sam Briscoe, 1711.

4291 Lucianus Samosatensis. (Lucian). *The Mimes of the Courtesans.* New York: privately printed, The Press of Classic Lore, 1928.

4292 Lundin, John Philip. *Mistresses.* New York: Lancer Books, Inc., 1968, 320 pp.

4293 Malleson, Mrs. W. T. *A Reply to Miss Garrett's Letter on the Contagious Diseases Acts in the "Pall Mall Gazette".* Bradford: J. Heinson and Co., 1871, 35 pp. National Society for Promotion of Social Purity.

4294 Marks, R. "Treatment of Delinquent Women: a nineteenth-century experiment reported in the letters of Charles Dickens." Soc Serv R 27:408-18, Dec. '53.

4295 Mather, E. Powys. Eastern Love, vol. II.

4296 Maurer, David. "Prostitutes and Criminal Argots." Am J Sociol 44:546-550, Jan. '39.

4297 Mazzulla, Fred and Jo. Brass Checks and Red Lights; prostitutes, parlor houses, professors, procuresses and pimps. Denver, Colo.: Fred and Jo Mazzulla, 1966, 56 pp.

4298 Mencken, H. L. The American Language. 4th ed (with suppl 1 and 2) New York: A. A. Knopf, 1955. Suppl.1, 1952; Suppl.2, 1956.

4299 Millett, Kate. The Prostitution Papers. New York: Aireu, 1973, 160 pp.

4300 Miu, Ch'uan-sun. Ch'in-Huai Kuang Chi. 4v. 1924. Prostitution in Nanking.

4301 Mozer, F. "Balzac et la Vie Galante de Son Temps." Mercure Fr 278:59-83, Aug. 15, 1947. France.

4302 Mullick, P. N. (Rai Promatha Nath Mullick Bahadur). The Mahabharata; a critical study. Calcutta: privately published, 1934.

4303 Nishio, Kunio. Nihon Bungakei to Yujo. 1972, 239 pp. Prostitution in Japanese literature to 1868.

4304 Ono, Susumu. Yujo Hyobanki Shu. 2v. 1965.

4305 Ouida. "Love versus Avarice: the causes which make for social evil." Lippincott's Magazine 83:712-7, Jun. '09.

4306 Pallavicino, Ferrante. The Whore's Rhetorick. New York: Ivan Obolensky, 1961. First published by George Shell in 1683.

4307 Passman, Hanns. Der Typus der Kurtisane im Elisabethanischen Drama. Borna-Leipzig-Noske, 1926.

4308 Payne, Edward F. and Harper, Henry H. The Charity of Charles Dickens, His Interest in the Home for Fallen Women and a History of the Strange Case of Caroline Maynard Thompson. Boston: printed for members of the Bibliophile Society, 1929.

4309 Philos, D. R. (Buhne und Prostitution). The Theatre and Prostitution. With an Introduction by Dr. B. Bentovin: "Prostitution as Reflected in the Modern Russian Theatre." St. Petersburg, 1910, 101 pp.

4310 Picardeau, Robert Fernand. Les Idees de Restif de la Bretonne. Paris: M. Vigne, 1929, 51 pp.

4311 Pizzorusso, A. "Situations and Environment in Margot la Ravauseuse." Yale French Stud 40:142-55, '68.

4312 Rawson, C. J. "The Phrase 'Legal Prostitution' in Fielding, Defoe and Others (Marriage Without Love)." Notes and Queries 7:298, Aug. '64.

4313 Real, J. "Brothel in O'Neill's Mansions." Mod Drama 12:383-9, Feb. '70.

4314 Rodocanachi, E. Courtesanes et Bouffons. Paris: 1894, 199 pp.

4315 Roy, Pratap Chandar. The Mahabharata. Tr. by Hiraldi Haldar. 7v. 2d rev ed Calcutta: Oriental Pub. Co., 1955-56.

4316 Seymour-Smith, Martin. Fallen Women; sceptical enquiry into the treatment of prostitutes, their clients and pimps. Nelson: 1969. Study of prostitutes in literature.

4317 Schwartz, K. "Whorehouse and the Whore in Spanish American Fiction of the 1960's." J Interam Stud. 15:472-87, Nov. '73. Bibliography.

4318 Seigel, J. P. "Jenny: the divided sensibility of a young and thoughtful man of the world." Stud Engl Lit 9:677-93, Autumn '69.

4319 Stendahl (Marie Henri Beyle). On Love. Reprinted New York: Doubleday Anchor, 1957.

4320 Stone, L. A., et al. Story of Phallicism. 2v. Ltd. ed. P. Covici, 1927.

4321 Ternant, A. de. "Courtesan on the French Stage." Westm 154:671-84, Dec. '00.

4322 'Tis a Pity She's a Whore. Ed. by N. W. Bawcutt. Regents Renaissance Drama Series, Bison Books, Univ. of Nebraska Press, 1967-68.

4323 Valency, Maurice. In Praise of Love. New York: Macmillan Co., 1958.

4324 Venice. (Appendix). Il Catalogo delle Principali e Piu Onorate Cortigiane di Venezia nel Cinquecento. Tratto da Una Copia Manuscritta del Civico Museo Correr di Venezia. Con Uno Studio su Il Libertinaggio sotto la Dominate di Fulvio Dittico, etc. Venice: 1956, 72 pp.

4325 Walker, Alexander. Sex in the Movies. Pelican ed. London: Penguin Books, 1968. Some insights.

4326 "White Slave Films." Outlook 106:120-2, Jan. 17, 1914.

4327 "White Slave Films: a review." Outlook 106:345-50, Feb. 14, 1914.

4328 Whitman, A. "Books; from art to avarice: the sad fate of America's upper-crust brothels." Harpers 244:102-4, May '72.

4329 Witkowski, G. J. and L. Nass. "Les Actrices et la Galanterie," in Le Nu au Theatre. Paris: 1909.

4330 Wyman, Margaret. "The Rise of the Fallen Woman." American Quarterly 3(1951):167-77.

4331 Anderson, Dora. *H. J. Wilson: Fighter for Freedom.* London, 1953. Henry Joseph Wilson (1833-1914) was one of the leaders in the fight for abolition of regulation.

4332 Angenent, H. L. "Characteristics of a Pimp." *Ned Tijdschr Psychol* 24(4):207-26, April 1969.

4333 Bloch, Iwan. *Marquis de Sade: His Life and Works.* Translated by James Bruce. New York: Brittany Press, 1948.

4334 Bluher, Hans. *The Role of the Erotic in the Male Society.* Stuttgart: Ernest Klett Verlag, 1962, 330 pp. In German.

4335 Bourne, Kenneth, editor. *The Blackmailing of the Chancellor.* London: Lemon Tree Press, 1975, 96 pp. One of the individuals (Brougham, Lord Chancellor) blackmailed by Harriette Wilson in order to keep him out of her memoirs. These are the previously unpublished letters between the two.

4336 Butts, William Harlen. "Boy Prostitutes of the Metropolis." *J Clin Psychopath* 8:673-68, April 1947. Statistical analysis of living conditions involving ten case histories.

4337 Call, H. "Male Prostitution on the West Coast." In *Prostitution and Morality.* By H. Benjamin, and R. E. L. Masters. New York: Julian Press, 1964.

4338 Casanova. *Memoirs.* Translated by Arthur Machen. New York: Putnam's Sons, N.D. Especially Book II, Chapter VII, pp 140-42.

4339 "Chickenhawks; young male hookers hunting homosexuals." *Newsweek* 81:42, April 30, 1973.

4340 Coombs, N. R. "Male Prostitution: a psychosocial view of behavior." *Am J Orthopsychiatry* 44(5):782-9, October 1974.

4341 Craft, M. "Boy Prostitutes and Their Fate." *Br J Psychiatry* 112(492):1111-4, November 1966.

4342 Deisher, R. W.; Eisner, V.; and Sulzbacher, S. I. "The young male prostitute." *Pediatrics* 43(6):936-41, June 1969.

4343 ______. "The young male prostitute." *Pediatrics* 45(1):153-4, January 1970.

4344 DeMente, Boye. *Some Prefer Geisha: the lively art of mistress-keeping.* Rutland: U. and C. E. Tuttle, 1966.

4345 Drtil, J. "Sex life of men during long term imprisonment." *Cesk Psychiatr* 65(4):245-50, August 1969.

4346 "Fly now, pay later; D. Caril murders and a boy-prostitute ring." *Newsweek* 82:22+, August 27, 1973.

4347 Fowler, W. S. A Study in Radicalism and Dissent: The Life and Times of Henry Joseph Wilson. London: Epworth Press, 1961. One of the leaders in the abolitionist campaign.

4348 Freyhan, F. A. "Homosexual Prostitution. A case report." Deleware State Medical Journal 19:92-94, May 1947.

4349 Gandy, P., and Deisher, R. "Young male prostitutes. The physician's role in social rehabilitation." JAMA 212(10):1661-6, June 8, 1970.

4350 Ginsburg, K. N. "The "meat-rack": a study of the male homosexual prostitute." Am J Psychother 21(2):170-85, April 1967.

4351 Gokhale, B. B.; Masters, R. S.; and Gokhale, T. B. "The Clients of the Common Prostitutes." Soc Defence 8(29):30-8, 43, '72.

4352 Gibbens, T. C. N. and Silberman, M. "The Clients of Prostitutes." British Journal of Venereal Diseases. 36(June 1960), 5 pp.

4353 _______. The Clients of Prostitutes. London: Josephine Butler Society, 1962, 14 pp.

4354 Hall, Susan. Gentlemen of leisure; a year in the life of a pimp. New York: New American Library, 1972, 189 pp.

4355 Hardy, Allison. The Autobiography of a Pimp. N.P., N.D., 128 pp.

4356 Harris, M. The Dilly boys: male prostitutes in Piccadilly. London: Croom Helm, 1973.

4357 Henstone, J. P. The Piccadilly Ambulator or Old Q(ueensberry) containing Memoirs of the private life of this evergreen votary of Venus. London, 1808.

4358 Hoffman, Martin. "The Male Prostitute." Sexual Behavior 2(8):16-21, August 1972.

4359 Hoffman, R. "Why men pay for love; interview." Cosmopolitan 136:124-7, July 1955.

4360 Hohman, Leslie B. and Schaffner, B. "The Sex Lives of Unmarried Men." American Journal of Sociology 52(May 1947):501-7.

4361 Jersild, Jens. Barnet og de homoseksuelle problem. Copenhagen, 1957, 79 pp. Only a small part deals with prostitution.

4362 ______. *Boy prostitution.* Translated by Oscar Bojesen. *Copenhagen:* G. E. C. Gad, 1956, 101 pp. An extension of his study on male homosexual prostitution (Den Mandlige prostitution). Jersild is a police inspector in Copenhagen.

4363 ______. *Den mandlije prostitution; arsager, omfang, rolger.* *Copenhagen:* Dansk videnskabs forlag, 1953, 148 pp. Homosexual prostitution.

4364 Kennedy, L. *The Trial of Stephen Ward.* London: V. Golancz, 1964. Accused of running a prostitution spy ring.

4365 Kester, Hermann. *Casanova.* Translated by James Stern and Robert Pick. New York: Harper and Brothers, 1955. A biography of Casanova.

4366 Kirkendall, L. A. "Circumstances Associated with Teenage Boys' Use of Prostitution." *Journal of Marriage and Family Living* 22(1960):145-9.

4367 Lloyd, Robin. *For Love or Money: Boy Prostitution in America.* New York: Vanguard, 1976, 236 pp. Called a sexploitation book.

4368 Lowag, Dr. Leonard A., as told to John O'Day. *Confessions of a Male Prostitute.* Los Angeles: Sherbourne Press, Inc, 1964, 136 pp.

4369 Mancini, Jean Gabriel. *Prostitutes and their parasites.* Translated by D. G. Thomas. London: Elek Books, 1963, 109 pp.

4370 MacNamara, D. E. J. *Male Prostitution in American Cities: A Socioeconomic or Pathological Phenomenon?* A paper presented to the March 1965 meeting of the American Orthopsychiatric Association.

4371 Mead, Margaret. *Male and Female: A Study of the Sexes in a Changing World.* New York: William Morrow, 1959.

4372 **Milner, Christina.** *Black players: the secret world of Black pimps.* Boston: Little, Brown, 1973, 329 pp. San Francisco Bay Region.

4373 Montani, L. C. "Agostino Bertani, physician and patriot; opponent of regulation of prostitution." *Clin Nuova* 10:382-4, March 4, 1950.

4374 Morin, Edgar. *Rumour in Orleans.* New York: Pantheon Books, 1971.

4375 *My Secret Life.* (2 Vols., reprinted, New York: Grove Press, 1966) XI, 2191-2.

4376 Nedoma, K. "Homosexual prostitution in adolescence." _Cesk Psychiat_ 58:312-4, October 1962. Czecheslovakia.

4377 Randoph, N. "Jelke? Jelke? Wasn't he the guy who...?" _Esquire_ 67:136-9+, April 1967.

4378 Reitman, Ben Lewis. "Pimps." In _Encylopaedia Sexualis_, pp. 605-13. Edited by Victor Robinson. New York: Dingwall-Rock, 1956.

4379 _________. _Second Oldest Profession: A Study of the Prostitute's Business Manager_. New York: Vanguard, 1931, 266 pp.

4380 Russell, D. H. "The psychopathology of boy prostitutes." _Int Off Ther_ 15:49-52, 1971.

4381 Slim, Iceberg. _Pimp: the story of my life_. 1969, 317 pp.

4382 Stein, Martha L. _Lovers, Friends, Slaves: Nine Male Sexual Types: Their Psycho-Sexual Transactions With Call Girls_. New York: Berkly Pub. Co. and P. T. Putnam's Sons, 1974. Outstanding study.

4383 Winick, C. "Prostitutes' clients' perception of the prostitutes and of themselves." _Int J Soc Psychiat_ 8:289-97, Autumn 1962.

4384 Accettella, F. Proposizioni Scientitiche e Pratiche per la Limitazione della Infezione Sifilitica. Caserta, 1875.

4385 Achscharumoff, D. D. On the Sanitary Relations of Tolerance and Supervision of Prostitutes. Poltava, 1886.

4386 Achten, M. G. "Syphilis Yesterday and Today." J Med Lyon 49(141):685-702, Apr. 20, 1968.

4387 Acton, William. The Functions and Disorders of the Reproductive Organs in Childhood, Youth, Adult Age, and Advanced Life Considered in Their Physiological, Social and Moral Relations. 5th ed London: J. and A. Churchill, 1871.

4388 Acton, William. Prostitution Considered in Its Moral, Social, and Sanitary Aspects. London: John Churchill, 1857, pp. v-vi.

4389 Acton, William. Prostitution in Relation to Public Health; forming the introductory chapter to the second edition of the treatise on syphilis. Reprinted by the author. London: 1851.

4390 Acton, William. Prostitution. Ed., with intro. and notes, by Peter Fryer. New York: Praeger, 1969, 251 pp.

4391 Adam, E., et al. "Type B Hepatitis Antigen and Antibody Among Prostitutes and Nuns: a study of possible venereal transmission." J Infect Dis 129(3):317-21, Mar. '74.

4392 Admiraal, D. J. "De Prostitutie en de Burgerlijke Overheid; een rapport en nog wat." Med Weekbl Amst 1896-7, iii, 369, 376.

4393 Agninaga, G. "Reflexiones Sobre la Prostitucion." Espana Med (Madrid) 4:476, 1859.

4394 Alcina, B. "Vigilancia Oficial de la Prostitucion." Gac de Hig y Climat (Cadiz) 2:353-357, 1881.

4395 Alcoba, ___. "La Prostitucion y su Profilaxis." Corresp Med (Madrid) 16:344, 355, 372, 378, 391, 1881.

4396 Alfaro, M. "Informe Sobre Prostitucion; segundo semestre de 1873." Observador Med (Mexico) 1879-80, v, 8, 23.

4397 Alhoy, Philadelphe Maurice. Physiologie de la Lorette. Nouvelle edition augmentee d'une notice sur la vie de l'auteur. Brussels: 1882, 78 pp.

4398 Allison, G. H. and J. C. Ullman. "The Intuitive Psychoanalytic Perspective of Galdos in Fortunata and Jacinta." Int J Psychoanal 55(3):333-43, '74.

4399 Alonzo Gonzalez, M. "Prophlaxis de las Enfermedades Venereas Sifiliticas Socialmente Considerada." Rev Esp de Oftal., Sif., etc. (Madrid) 8:317-329, 1884.

4400 American Social Hygiene Assn. The Case Against the Red Light District. Issued by the Treasury Dept., U. S. Public Health Service. VD no.54. Washington D. C.: Gov't. Printing Office, 1920, 7 pp.

4401 American Social Hygiene Assn. Community Prostitution and Venereal Diseases. 3 parts. 1919.

4402 American Social Hygiene Assn. Standard Statistics of Prostitution, Gonorrhea, Syphilis. 1919.

4403 American Social Hygiene Assn. Why Let It Burn? The Case Against the Red Light District. 1919.

4404 Anders, J. M. "The Role of the Medical Profession in Combating the Social Evil." Medicine 12:821-825, 1906.

4405 Andrews, E. "Practical Obstacles Confronting the Police Power in Dealing with Prostitutes and with Venereal Diseases." Bull Northwest Univ M Sch (Chicago) 1:242-244, 1899-1900.

4406 Andrews, Edmund. Prostitution and Its Sanitary Management. St. Louis: 1871, 31 pp.; Chicago M Exam 12:65-97, 1871.

4407 de los Angeles, S. "El Problem de la Prostitucion en Filipinas." Rev Filipina de Med y Farm (Manila) 1921, xii, 97-103.

4408 Aruin, M. "The Beginning of Venereal Disease Control in the USSR (V. M. Bronner, 1876-1938)." Vestn Dermatol Venerol 45(5):54-8, May '71.

4409 Assn. for Moral and Social Hygiene. Compulsory Methods and the Treatment of Venereal Diseases. Geneva: Federation Abolitionniste Internationale, 1942.

4410 Astruc, Jean. De Morbus Venereis. Paris: 1736.

4411 Asverus, ___. "Ueber Prostitution und Venerische Erkrankungen." Arch f Off Gsndhtspflg (Strassb.) 9:179-190, 1884, 1. diag.

4412 "Auch Ein Wort Uber Prostitution." Bern Cor.-Bl f Aerzte u Apoth 2:10-14, 1851.

4413 Augagueur, V. "La Prostitution, la Police des Moeurs et Quelques Ouvrages Recents Qui en Traitent." Lyon Med 43:507, 1883; 44:233; 45:100, 133.

4414 B., A. "The Social Evil." Med Press (Dublin) 12:302, 1865, 2, s.

4415 B., L. Gjenmaele mod Dr. Hornemann's Piece "Den Offentlige Sundhedspleie og Prostitutionen". Copenhagen: 1880.

4416 Babcock, H. P. "On the Only Practical Means of Limiting the Spread of Venereal Diseases." West Lancet (San Francisco) 1:3-14, 1872-3.

4417 Babou, A. F. Documents sur la Prostitution et les Maladies Veneriennes a Toulouse. Toulouse: 1904.

4418 Baccaredda-Boy, A. and A. Rebora. "Epidemiological and Theraputic Data on Gonorrhea in Genoa and Other Parts of Italy." Br J Vener Dis 47(5):378, Oct. '71.

4419 Baermann, G. "Die Gonorrhoe der Prostituierten." Ztschr f Bekampf d Geschlectskrankh 2:100, 133, 1903-4.

4420 Bakacs, T. (Prostitution). Orvosok Lapja 3:309-319, Mar. 9, 1947.

4421 Balina, P. L., et al. "Problems of Fight Against Venereal Diseases; suggestions for their solution in relation to question." Semana Med 2:669-681, Sep. 5, 1935.

4422 Baloff, A. "Supervision of Prostitution by the Medical Police." Feldscher (St. Petersburg) 10:486-473, 1900.

4423 Bandilla, O. and E. Gunther. "Incidence of Atypical Cornifying Epithelium in Portio Cervicalis of Prostitutes; possible relation to development of cancer." Zentralb f Gynak 60:722-724, Mar. 28, 1936.

4424 Bandler, V. "Ueber die Venerischen Affectionen Analgegend bei Prostituierten." Arch f Dermat u Syph 43:19-30, 1898.

4425 Bandler, V. "Zur Kenntniss der Elephantiastischen und Ulcerativen Verandegungen des Ausseren Genitales und Rectums bei Prostituirten." Arch f Dermat u Syph 48:337-348, 1899.

4426 Baratono, A. "I Fondamenti Biologici della Prostituzione." Quaderni di Psichiat (Geneva) 12:31-33, 1925.

4427 Barduzzi, D. "Sulla Profilassi Pubblica della Sifilde in Rapporto con la Prostituzione." Reforma Med (Rome) 5:326, 332, 1889.

4428 Barduzzi, D. "Sulla Regolamentazione del Meretrico." Rass d Stud Sess (Rome) 1921, i, 173-75.

4429 Bare, ____. "De la Syphilis dans ses Rapports avec la Prostitution, par une Commission Composee de MM. Moriceau, Marchand, Leroux, Hignard, Marce et Bare, rapporteur." J de la Sect, de Med Soc Acad Loire-Inf (Nantes) 22:129-161, 1846.

4430 Barret, W. L. "Prostitution in its Relation to Public Health." Rep Bd Health St. Louis 1871:22-43.

4431 Barreto Coutinho, S. "Venereal Diseases and Prostitution in Federal District." Folha Med 27:30, Feb. 26, 1946; 37, Mar. 5, 1946; 43, Mar. 25, 1946.

4432 Barros, J. M. de. "Serologic Diagnosis of Syphilis in Prostitution Area of Sao Paulo." Arq Fac Hig e Saude Pub 4:185-89, Dec. '50.

4433 Barthelemy, R. "Frequency of Syphilis and Role of Prostitution in Its Dissemination." Ann d Mal Ven 29:272-278, Apr. '34.

4434 Barthelemy, T. "Etat de Sante des Prostituees Clandestines au Moment de leur Arrestation; causes et consequences." Bull Soc Internat de Prophyl (etc.) 1:105-126, 1901.

4435 Barthelemy, T. "Prophylaxie Publique de la Syphilis." Ann de Dermat et Syph (Paris) 9:721-737, 1888, 2, s.

4436 Barthelemy and Augagneur. "Les Systemes de Reglementation Actuellement en Vigneur ont-ils eu Une Influence sur la Frequence et la Dissemination de la Syphilis et des Maladies Veneriennes?" (Report) Confer Internat p la Prophyl de la Syph et d Mal Ven (Brussels) 1899, i, fasc.1, 1.quest., 1-71. Discussion: 1900, ii, compt. rend. d seances, 17-141, 10 ch., 1 diag.

4437 Bauer, A. C. "The Regulation of Prostitution as a Hygenic Measure." Cincin Lancet-Clinic ns 33:411-416, 1894.

4438 Bayet. "Prostitution et Maladies Veneriennes en Belgique." Confer Internat p la Prophyl de la Syph et d Mal Ven. Brussels: 1899. 1(2):763-768.

4439 Bazzoni, C. "Relazione sull' Ufficio Sanitario di Sorveglianza alla Prostituzione in Milano." Atti Accad Fis.-Med.-Statist di Milano ns 5:94-97, 1859-60.

4440 Bazzoni, C. "Seconde Relazione sulla Sorveglianza alla Prostituzione e sul Nuovo Sifilocomio di Milano Attuato il 1 Gennaio 1861." Atti Accad Fis.-Med.-Statist di Milano ns 6:206-209, 1860-61.

4441 Beam, S. "Nurse Fights VD in Streets." Am Nurse 8(1):3, 13, 16, Jan. '76.

4442 Becerro de Bengoa, M. "Intervencionismo y Abstencionismo, Proxenetismo y Clandestinidad." Bol d Cons Nac de Hig (Montevideo) 1924, xix, 542-580.

4443 Becker, W. "Homosexuality in German Federal Republic." Ther Ggw 110(4):584-601, Apr. '71.

4444 Behrend, F. J. "Notizen uber Bordell- und Hurenwesen Geschlichtlicher, Hygienischer und Sanitats-polizeilicher Hinsicht, besonders in Bezug auf Berlin (aus seinen materialien zu einem kunftigen werke uber syphilis)." Ztscher f d Staatsarznk 42:53-100, 1841.

4445 Behrend, F. J. "Die Prostitution in Berlin und die Gegen Sie und die Syphilis zu Nehmenden Massregeln. Eine Denkschrift, im Auftrage, auf Grund amtlicher Quellen abgefasst und Sr. Excellenz dem Herrn Minister v. Landenberg uberreicht." Ztschr f d Staatsarznk 39(Ergnzngshft.):1-206; 58:385-472, 1849.

4446 Behrend, F. J. "Ueber die in St. Petersburg in Bezug auf Syphilis und Prostitution Getroffenen Maassregeln nach Brieflichen Mittheilungen." Ztschr f d Staatsarznk 60:481-500, 1850.

4447 Bejarano, J. "Critical Examination..." Inform Enferm Ven pp. 12-18, Oct. '46.

4448 Bejarano, J. and S. Gallego Calatayud. "Latent Form of Venereal Lymphogranuloma in Prostitutes." Cron Med (Valencia) 37:721-730, Oct. 15, 1933; also Actas Dermo-sif 26:265-271, Jan. '34.

4449 Beltran, J. R. "Illegal Practice of Medicine in Relation to Regulation of Prostitution; medicolegal study." R Asoc Med Argent 48:1311-1315, Nov. '34.

4450 Benech, J. and A. Spillman. "Difficulties of and Necessity for Detection of Beginning Syphilis in Prostitutes." Bull Soc Franc de Dermat et Syph (Reunion Dermat) 42:48-52, Jan. '35.

4451 Benech, J. (Causes). Prophylax Antiven 1:712-733, Dec. '29.

4452 Benech, J. and A. Chiclet. "Epidemiology and General Pathology of Syphilis in Relation to Prostitution; Attempts at Control." An d Mal Ven 29:881-888, Dec. '34.

4453 Benech, J. "Hygenic Aspects of Regulation." Rev d Hyg 56:442-48, Jun. '34.

4454 Benech, J. and A. Chiclet. "Need for Centralization of Sanitary Surveillance." Ann d Mal Ven 30:6-14, Jan. '35.

4455 Benech, J. "Specimen of Medical and Social Record of Prostitutes Kept by City of Nancy; importance in campaign against venereal diseases." Ann d Mal Ven 24:707-12, Jul. '29.

4456 Benech, J. "Statistics on Syphilis in Prostitutes." Ann d Mal Ven 26:721-727, Oct. '31.

4457 Benjamin, Harry. "Prostitution Re-assessed." Int J Sexol 4:154-160, '51. Prime reason for repression of prostitution (VD) is no longer sound because of anti-biotics. Says "promiscuity is normal form of sex behavior" though monogamous behavior desireable.

4458 Bennett, R. (Problem). Practitioner 172:381-388, Apr. '54.

4459 Beral, V. "Cancer of the Cervix: a sexually transmitted infection?" Lancet 1(865):1037-40, May 25, 1974.

4460 Berault, G. La Maison de Tolerance Consideree au Point de Vue Hygienique et Social. Paris: 1904.

4461 Beretervide, J. J. Glandulas Endocrines y Prostitucion. Buenos Aires: 1934, 254 pp.

4462 Bergamini, M. "The Medico-social Aspects of Prostitution in Italy." Minerva Med 57(57):varia 941+, Jul. 21, 1966.

4463 Bergeret, ____. "La Prostitution et les Maladies Veneriennes dans les Petite Localites." Ann d'Hyg (Paris) 25:342-359, 1866, 2, s.

4464 Bergh, R. "I Anledning af den Forestaaende Reform af Prostitutionsvaesenet." Hosp.-Tid (Copenhagen) 6:81-83, 1863.

4465 Bergmann, H. W. "Problems of Promiscuity." Dermat Wchnschr 121:91-96, 189-92, 277-288, '50.

4466 Beristain, P. "Medidas Tendientes a la Disminucion de la Prostitucion y Regeneracion de las Prostitutas." Seman Med (Buenos Aires) 1925, xxxii, pt.1, 977-980.

4467 Berner, H. "Kontrol Med de Veneriske Sygdomme i Kristiania." Tidsskr f Prakt Med 9:105-108, 1889.

4468 Bernheim, S. "Tuberculose et Prostitution." Cong Franc de Med C. r. Paris 2:528-541, 1902.

4469 Bernstein, B. B. Die Prostitution in Ihrer Beziehung zu den Geschlechtskrankheiten; besprechung alter und neuer Praventivmittel. Munich: 1878.

4470 Bertarelli, E. "La Prostitution e la Malattie Sessuali." Attualita Med (Milan) 4:676-688, '15.

4471 Berthenson, L. "Die Ueberwachung der Prostitution In Russland." Med Reform (Berlin) 14:565-568, 1906.

4472 Bertherand, E. L. "Etudes sur les Mesures Medico Administratives les plus Propres a Prevenir la Propagation des Maladies Veneriennes." J de Med et Pharm de l'Algerie (Alger) 9:148, 184, 1884.

4473 Berthod, P. "Le Peril Venerien; la reglementation actuelle de la prostitution; ruine du systeme." J de Med de Par 11;107-110, 1899, 2, s.

4474 Bertin, ______. (Abolition Movement). Echo Med du Nord 4:340-348, Aug. 25, 1935.

4475 Bestieu, R. (Regulation). Clinique (Paris) 32:291-292, Nov. (B) '37.

4476 Bettley, F. R. "Medical Conduct of Brothel." Brit J Ven Dis 25:56-66, Jun. '49.

4477 Beurey, J., et al. "Syphilis, Epidemiology, Biology, Treatment." Maroc Med 51(549):479-92, Aug.-Sep. '71.

4478 Beveridge, M. M. "Social Factors in Male Gonococcal Infectors." Public Health 78:268-72, Jul. '64.

4479 Bianchi, Antonio. Il Libertinaggio, Examinato al Solo Lume della Regione Naturale, con in Fine, Undescorso di Augusto al Cavalieri Celibatari. Milan: C. Orena, 1818, 388 pp.

4480 Bieberbach, W. D. "Venereal Disease and Prostitution." Boston Med and S J 172:201-208, 1915.

4481 Biedenkap, ___. "Proposition Respecting Regulations of Measures for Prevention of Venereal Diseases." Tidsskr f Prakt Med 8:90, 111, 1888.

4482 Bierhoff, Frederick. "The Control of Prostitution and Venereal Diseases in This Country and Abroad." Am J Urol Jul. '11.

4483 Bierhoff, Frederick. "Further Notes in the Sanitary Control of Prostitution in Some European Cities." NY Med J 96:569-574, 627-633, 688-692, '12.

4484 Bierhoff, Frederick. "Venereal Disease a Sanitary and Social Problem." Conf Char and Correc 1911:344-9.

4485 Bierhoff, Frederick. "Zur Frage der Prostitution und er Venerischen Krankheiten." New Yorker Med Monatschr 24:1-19, 1913-14.

4486 Bijkerk, H. "Incidence of Venereal Diseases in the Netherlands." Brit J Vener Dis 46(3):247-61, Jun. '70.

4487 Bisno, A. L., et al. "Human Immunity to Gonococci: studies of opsonization by sera of prostitutes and nuns." Trans Assoc Am Physicians 87:195-204, '74.

4488 Bisno, A. L., et al. "Human Immunity to Neisseria Gonorrhoeae: acquired serum opsonic antibodies. J Lab Clin Med 86(2):221-9, Aug. '75.

4489 Bizard, L. "Causes and Prevention of Extensive Prostitution." Prophylax Antiven 2:758-761, Dec. '30.

4490 Bizard, L. "Results of Wassermann Reaction in Houses of Prostitution." Bull Soc Franc de Dermat et Syph 35:574-578, Jul. '28.

4491 Bizard, L. "Statistics of Syphilis in Houses of Prostitution in Paris, 1917-1926." Bull Soc Franc de Dermat et Syph 34:106-110, Feb. '27.

4492 Bizard, L. "Syphilis in Prostitutes in Paris." Bull Med (Paris) 45:93-95, Feb. 14, '31.

4493 Bizard, L., and Bralez,___. "Statistiques des Syphilis Contagieuses Observees chez les Prostituees Parisiennes de 1910 a 1921." Ann de Mal Ven (Paris) 17:617, 1922.

4494 Blackwell, E. Essays in Medical Sociology. 2v in 1. Arno Press, 1972.

4495 Blaschko, Alfred. Hygiene der Prostitution und der Venerischen Krankheiten. Jena, 1900.

4496 Blaschko, Alfred. "Das Merkblatt der Deutschen Gesellschaft zur bekampfung der Geschlechtskrankheiten." Berl Klin Wchnschr 41:341-343, 1904.

4497 Blaschko, Alfred. "Prostitution et Maladies Veneriennes en Allemagne." Confer Internat p la Prophyl de la Syph et d Mal Ven (Brussels) 1(2):661, 1899; 2(com pt.2):28, 1900.

4498 Blaschko, Alfred. Syphilis and Prostitution. Berlin: S. Karger, 1893.

4499 Blaschko, A. "Les Systemes de Reglementation Actuellement en Vigueur ont-ils eu une Influence sur la Frequence et la Dissemination de la Syphilis et des Maladies Veneriennes?" (Report) Confer Internat p la Prophyl de la Syph et d Mal Ven (Brussels, 1899).

4500 Blaschko, A. "Zur Prostitutionsfrage." Berlin Klin Wchnschr 29:430-435, 1892.

4501 Block, F. "Aerztliche Aufsicht Uber Unkontrollierte Prostituierte." Ztschr f Bekampf d Geschlechtskr 6:19-23, 1907.

4502 Boeck, W. "Prostitution in Relation to National Health." *Am J Syph and Dermat* 1:130-135, 1870.

4503 Boisen, P. O. "Prostitutionssagen." *Ugesk f Laeger* 1:461-473, 1880, 4, R.

4504 Boisseau and Spinetta. "Need of Antigonococci Prophylaxis in Prostitutes." *Ann d Mal Ven* 34:41-46, Feb. '40.

4505 Boisseau, et al. "Rarity of Neurosyphilis in Prostitutes." *Press Med* 47:1658-1660, Dec. 20-23, 1939.

4506 Borelli, G. B. "La Questione dei Sifilicomi." *Gior d Soc Ital d'Ig* (Milan) 10:409-422, 1888.

4507 Bosch, R. "El Problema de la Prostitucion." *Rev Med Leg Jur Med* 1:183-230, '35.

4508 Bosredon, R. D. L. *Peril Venerien et Prostitution*. Bordeaux: 1906.

4509 Bourdon, J. "Homosexuality." *Brux Med* 49(11):733-8, Nov. '69.

4510 Bourgeois,____. "Rapport sur l'Etat Sanitaire de la Ville au Point de Vue de la Prostitution et de la Frequence des Maladies Veneriennes; (ville de Bruxelles)." *Confer Internat p la Prophyl de la Syph et d Mal Ven* 1(2):873-882, 1899.

4511 Braestrup,____. "Note sur la Prostitution dans la Ville e Copenhague et sur les Mesures Prises en Danemark pour Empecher la Propagation de la Syphilis, d'apres un document manuscrit, communique au Congres General d'Hygiene." *Cong Gen d'Hyg de Brux, Compt.-rend* 1852:416-429.

4512 Branchat, R. "De la Prostitucion en sus Relaciones con la Administracion Publica y la Higiene." *Prensa Med de Granada* 3:401-406, 1881.

4513 Bre, Ruth, "Das Recht auf die Mutterschaft; eine Forderung zur Bekampfung der Prostitution, der Frauen- und Geschlechtskrankheiten." *Monatschr f Soziale Med* (Jena) 1:104-113, 1904.

4514 Breda, A. "La Profilassi delle Malattie Veneree in Italia; studio e proposte." *Gior Ital d Mal Ven* (Milan) 18:224, 265, 1883.

4515 Bremermen, L. W. "Prostitution and Gonorrhea." *Urol and Cutan R* 20:203, 1916.

4516 Breton, E. *Syphilis et Prostitution a Marseille*. Montpellier, 1900.

4517 British Medical Assn. Homosexuality and Prostitution; a memorandum of evidence prepared by a special committee of the Council of the British Medical Assn. London: 1955.

4518 Broadbent, P. A. "'Tis Pity She's a Whore. (John Ford 1586-1639)." Health Visit 45(1):9, Jan. '72.

4519 Brown, W. J. "The Essential Elements of a Syphilis Control Program." Bol of Sanit Panam 70(1):59-65, Jan. '71.

4520 Bruck, F. "Danger of Venereal Infection." Munchen Med Wchnschr 74:2188-2189, Dec. 23, '27.

4521 Buchwala, H. "Course of Syphilis in Prostitutes." Arch f Dermat u Syph 181:385-394, '40.

4522 Budde, V. "Nyere Oplysninger om Prostitutionsvaesenets Ordning i Forskjellige Lande Med Saerligt Hensyn til Dennes Virkninger i Hygiejnisk Retning." Ugesk f Laeger 14:311-322, 1886, 4, R.

4523 Budde, V. "Prostitutionsspørgsmaalet." Ugesk f Laeger 15:81, 105, 1887, 4, R.

4524 Buret, F. Syphilis in the Middle Ages and in Modern Times. Tr. by A. H. Ohmann-Dumesnil. Philadelphia: F. A. Davis, 1895.

4525 "Bureau of Social Hygiene." Outlook 103:287-8, Feb. 8, 1913.

4526 Burke, E. T. "Toll of Secret Disease." Nineteenth Cent 102:675-86, Nov. '27.

4527 Butler, Henry. Is the Pleasure Worth the Penalty?; a common-sense view of the leading vice. Bound with, National Society for the Promotion of Purity, Laws et 1875. Others included. 76 pp.

4528 Butte, L. "Etat Sanitaire, au Point de Vue de la Syphilis, des Filles Soumises dans les Maisons de Tolerance de Paris Depuis 1872 Jusqu'en 1903 Inclus." Ann de Therap Dermat et Syph 3:289-294, 1903; J de Med de Par 15:221, 1903, 2, s. Med Anecdot (Paris) 1903:180, 184; Rev de Med Leg (Paris) 10:173-177, 1903; Rev Prat d'Obst et de Gynec (Paris) 1903:170-174; Ann de Therap Dermat et Syph (Paris) 3:553-559, 1903.

4529 Butte, L. Influence des Expositions Universelles sur l'Etat Sanitaire des Prostituees a Paris. Paris: 1901.

4530 Butte, L. "Modifications Apportees au Systeme Actuel de Reglementation de la Prostitution a Paris; suppression de la reglementation des maisons de rendez-vous et des maisons de tolerance." Ann de Therap Dermat et Syph 4:169-171, 1904.

4531 Butte, L. "De la Prophylaxie de la Syphilis par la Surveillance Medicale des Prostituees; action du dispensaire de salubrite de la ville de Paris pendant les trente derniers annees." Cong Internat de Dermat et de Syph (Paris, 1889) 1890:806-834.

4532 Butte, L. "La Prostitution et l'Assistance Publique (nouveau projet d'Organisation du service sanitaire des prostituees)." Ann de Therap Dermat et Syph 4:289-294, 1904.

4533 Butte, L. "La Prostitution a Paris, comparison entre l'etat sanitaire, au point de vue de la syphilis, des prostituees inscrites et celui des prostituees insoumises a Paris de 1872 a 1904." Ann de la Policlin de Par 15:121-129, 1905.

4534 Butte, L. Prostitution et Syphilis; La surveillance medicale de prostituees a Paris de 1872-1904. Paris: 1905.

4535 Butte, L. "Refutation du Rapport Communique a la Commission Extra-parlementaire du Regime des Moeurs par M. le Prof. Augagneur, maire de Lyon: De la prostitution sur la morbidite venerienne." Ann de Therap Dermat et Syph (Paris) 4:481-498, 1904.

4536 Butte, L. "La Surveillance Medicale des Prostituees a Paris en 1906." Soc Franc de Prophyl San et Mor Bull (Paris) 7:274-279, 1907.

4537 Calderone, F. "Serodiagnostic Reactions for Syphilis Made as Routine in Houses of Prostitution." Gior Ital di Dermat e Sifil 71:171-188, Feb. '30.

4538 Call (y Morros), J. Prostitucion y Profilaxia de la Sifilis. Madrid: 1885.

4539 Callari, I. "La Blenorragia e la Sifilde nelle Prostitute." Rassegna Internaz d Med Mod (Catania) 4:135, 149, 1902-3.

4540 Calloch, "De la Syphilis dans ses Rapports avec la Prostitution Autorisee et clandestine; rapport..." J de la Sect de Med Soc Acad Loire-Inf (Nantes) 33:193-228, 1857.

4541 Calvet Nava, J. "A Puntes Sobre la Prostitution de Barcelona Dificultades en el Diagnostico del Chancro Simple y dei Syfilitico, y Frecuencia Relativa de Uno y Orto." Gae Med Catal (Barcelona) 8:293-300, 1885.

4542 "Campaign Against Venereal Diseases and Prostitution." Prophy Sanit Morale 33:267-70, Dec. '61. In French.

4543 Camano, O. A. L. Dia Med 21:1161, Jun. 13, '49.

4544 Cambas, ___. "La Prostitution en Espagne; prophylaxie de la syphilis." Ann de Dermat et Syph 3:188-213, 1871-2.

4545 Capinski, T. Z. "Critical Evaluation of the Current System of Syphilis Control in Poland." Folia Med Cracov 9(4):521-81, '67.

4546 Cardia, Mario. "Trichomoniase et Prostitution." Acta Gyn et Obs Hispanolusitana IV-4, 7 pp.

4547 Carle, ____. "Discovery of Carriers of Venereal Diseases Among Prostitutes and Necessity of Forcing Them to Submit to Therapy." Ann d Mal Ven 30:1-5, Jan. '35.

4548 Carle, ____. "Effects of Regulation of Prostitution in Prevention of Venereal Disease." Vie Med 8:361-64, Feb. 25, '27.

4549 Caro-Paton, Tomas. La Mujer Caida: Memorias y Reflexiones de un Medico de la Lucha Antivenerea. Madrid: M. Montal, 1956, 230 pp.

4550 Carrera, ____. "Prostituta Epilettica." Arch di Psichiat (etc.) (Torino) 14:266, 1893.

4551 Carrera, J. L. "Deficient Attempts of Vigilance of Prostitution for Prevention of Venereal Diseases." Prensa Med Argent 17:923-930, Nov. 30, '30.

4552 Carter, H. D. Sin and Science. Heck-Catell, 1946, 216 pp.

4553 Carter, W. "On the Medical Control of Prostitution." Liverpool M and S Rep (London) 5:145, 1871.

4554 Cartwright, Frederick F. Disease and History. New York: Thomas Y. Crowell Co., 1972. p.60.

4555 Castaldo, F. E. "Medicosocial Problem." Rev Med Latino-Am 24:364, Jan.; 463, Feb. '39.

4556 Castells, F. "Las Cardiopatias en las Prostitutas." Gac Med Catal (Barcelona) 9:230, 263, 1886.

4557 Castiglioni, Pietro. Sorveglianza sulla Prostituzione e Modi per Impedire la Diffusione della Sifilide. Rome: G. Via, 1872, 202 pp.

4558 Cavaillon, A. "Effect of Closure of Houses of Prostitution on Incidence of Venereal Diseases." Prophylax Antiven 19:540-43, Aug. '47.

4559 Cavaillon, A. "Prostitution and Venereal Diseases From Adolf Hitler's Point of View." Prophylax Antiven 6:81-86, Feb. '34.

4560 Cavaillon, A. "Prostitution and Voluntary or Obligatory Treatment of Venereal Diseases in Abolitionist Countries; comparative results of inquiry asked of International Union

Against Venereal Peril by Commission of White Slavery of League of Nations. Prophylax Antiven (Assemb. Gen.) 6:58-123, Feb. '34.

4561 Cervia, T. and R. Luelmo. "Investigation of Tuberculosis Among Prostitutes." Rev Espan de Tuberc 18:405-411, Jun. '49.

4562 Cervia, T. "Tuberculosis in Prostitutes and Its Mediosocio Problem; experience in Ofra Sanatarium." Rev Espan Tuberc 206:677-86, Nov. '51.

4563 Chanfleury van Ijsselstein, J. L. La Visit des Prostituees au Point de Vue d l'Hygiene Publique. Geneva: Federation Abolitionniste Internationale, n. d., before 1902. Also published in German.

4564 Chapman, ____. "De la Prostitution en Angleterre et des Effets Sanitaires des Actes du Parlement sur les Maladies Contagieuses." Cong Period Internat d Sc Med Compt.-rend (Brussels and Paris, 1875) 4:162-170, 1876; Discussion, 116-126.

4565 Charpy, A. "Des Organes Genitaux Externes chez les Prostituees." Ann de Dermat et Syph (Paris) 3:271-279, 1871-2.

4566 Chaves, B. "La Reglementation de la Prostitution au Bresil." Confer Internat p la Prophy de la Syph et d Mal Ven, 1899. Brussels: 1900, ii, com., 57-69.

4567 Chevallier, P., et al. "Dwarf Chancre of Vulva in Prostitute." Ann d Mal Ven 33:400-401, Jun. '38.

4568 Chiarotti, C. "Gonodeviation Test in Relation to Contagiosity of Gonorrhea." Soc Internaz di Microbiol., Boll d Sez Ital 9:108-112, May '37. Also Gior di Batteriol e Immunol 21:419-430, Sep. '38.

4569 Chicago Bar Assn. War Activity Committee. Brief on the Subject Prostitution--Venereal Disease Control Program. Chicago: Chicago Law Ptg Co., 1944.

4570 Chizh, V. F. "Mental Diseases of Prostitutes." Obozr Psichiat., Nevrol. (etc.) (St. Petersburg) 11:785-801, 1906.

4571 Chu, L. W. and C. H. Huang. "Gonorrhea Among Prostitutes; survey of incidence and attempt at oral sulfadiazine (sulfonamide) prophylaxis. Chinese Med J 66:312-318, Jun. '48.

4572 Civis. "Word About Venereal Disease." English R 23:505-12, Dec. '16.

4573 Clark, C. W. "Medical Examination of Prostitutes." Postgrad Med 12:162-66, Aug. '52.

4574 Clark, M. V. B. "Medico-legal Aspects of the Social Evil." Omaha Clinic 7:309-311, 1894-5.

4575 Clarke, W. "Commercialized Prostitution and Disease Transmission." J Soc Hygiene 23:77-9, Feb. '37.

4576 Clarke, C. W. "On Guard." Today's Health 31:13, Aug. '52.

4577 Clarke, W. Prostitution and Alcohol. Am. Social Hygiene Assn., 1917.

4578 Clec'h, R. La Maison de Prostitution au Point de Vue Sanitaire. Lyon: 1932, 118 pp.

4579 Close, Kathryn. "Sick Men Can't Fight: San Antonio's police commissioner and the health authorities cleaned up the appalling number of new cases of venereal disease in army camps near their city. Survey Graphic 32:80-4+, Mar. '43.

4580 Cobb, W. B. "Women's Court in its Relation to Venereal Diseases." Soc Hygiene 6:83-92, Jan. '20.

4581 Cocks, O. G. Social Evil and Methods of Treatment. Y. M. C. A., 1912.

4582 Colin, L. "Prostitution et Syphilis." Rev San de Bordeaux 1884-5, ii, 161-165.

4583 Commenge, O. Hygiene Sociale. La Prostitution Clandestine a Paris. Paris: 1897 and 1904.

4584 Commenge, O. La Prostitution Devant l'Academie de Medecine de Belgique. Paris: 1888.

4585 Commenge, O. Recherches sur les Maladies Veneriennes a Paris dans leurs Rapports avec la Prostitution Clandestine et la Prostitution Reglementaire de 1878 a 1887. Paris: 1890.

4586 Commenge, O. Syphilis et Prostitution chez les Insoumises Mineures 1878-1887. Paris: 1893.

4587 Committee of Fifteen. Prostitution and Venereal Diseases. Bul. v.1, no.3. Chicago: Jan. '20, 4 pp.

4588 Compston, H. F. B. The Magdalen Hospital: the Story of a Great Charity. S. P. C. K., 1917, 237 pp.

4589 "Compulsory Medication of Prostitutes." (editorial) Westm 106:137; Westm Rev, Am ed (New York) 1876:64-88.

4590 Coni, E. R. "Instrucciones para la Organizacion y Funcionamiento de un Servico Sanitario de la Prostitucion." <u>Rev Med Quir</u> (Buenos Aires) 17:261, 288, 1880-1.

4591 Coni, E. R., et al. "Proyecto de Reglamento para la Prostitucion." <u>Rev Med Quir</u> 17:245-251, 1880-81.

4592 <u>Contagious Diseases Act, 1878</u>; new regulations, etc. London: Knight, 1878.

4593 "The Control of Prostitution." <u>Brit M J</u> 1:630-632, 1870.

4594 "Control of Venereal Diseases and Problem of Prostitution in City of New York; report of subcommittee of Committee on Public Health Relations of New York Academy of Medicine." <u>NY State J Med</u> 36:451-455, Mar. 15, 1936.

4595 Corbillon, A. "Le Probleme Medicale de la Prostitution." <u>Centre de Sante</u> no. 32. Oct./Nov. '59, 6 pp.

4596 Corlieu, A. "Prostitution et Syphilis." <u>Paris Med</u> 11:469, 493, 505, 518, 529, 541, 565, 1886.

4597 Correa da Costa, L. A. and H. Duek. "Incidence of Nicolas-Favre Disease in Prostitutes of Rio de Janeiro." <u>An Cong Brasil Ginec e Obst</u> 3:305-329, '42. Also <u>Hara Med Rio de Janiero</u> 2:9-23, Sep. '44.

4598 Correia, Alberto C. Germanos. <u>Prostitucao e Profliaxia Anti-venerea India Portuguesa</u> (Tipografin Rangel Bastorica India Portuguesa, 1938), p.36.

4599 Costa Carvalho, G. da. (Medical Aspects). <u>Folha Med</u> 23:27-35, Feb. 5, 1942.

4600 Costa Ferraz. "Da Regulamentacao da Prostituicao." <u>Ann Acad de Med do Rio de Jan</u> 1889-90, 6. s., v, 259-278.

4601 Costea, V. "Biological, Social, Economic and Psychological Factors in the Spread of Venereal Diseases." <u>Rev Med Chir Soc Med Nat Iasi</u> 76(2):502-7, Apr.-Jun. '72.

4602 Council of National Defense. Sub-committee for Civilian Cooperation in Combating Venereal Diseases. <u>Do Your Bit to Keep Him Fit</u>. New York: 1917, 14 pp.

4603 Coutagne, Henry. <u>Notes sur la Sodomie</u>. Paris: Librairie A. Drouin, 1880. Basically this deals with heterosexual anal intercourse; and he examined numerous prostitutes (446 all told). Also deals with pederasty. Pamphlet says it is an extract of Lyon Medical, Aug. 29 and Sep. 5, 1880.

4604 Coutts, W. E. and O. Donoso Barthet. "Nasopharyngeal Gram-negative Cocci in Secretion of Cervix Uteri of Prostitutes." <u>Brit J Ven Dis</u> 12:75-78, Apr. '36.

4605 Coutts, W. E., et al. "Presence of Spirochaetae in Oral Cavity in Chronic Cervicitis Among Prostitutes." <u>Dermat Wchnschr</u> 101:1242-1244, Oct. 5, 1935.

4606 Cowell, R. O. "Rehabilitation of Tuberculous Prostitute Through Social Case Work." <u>Am J Orthopsychiat</u> 16:525-535, Jul. '46.

4607 Crawford, J. B. "Pornografia." <u>St Louis M and S J</u> 39:412-416, 1880.

4608 Creighton, L. <u>Social Disease and How to Fight It</u>. Longmans, 1914.

4609 Crocq and Rollet. "Prophylaxie Internationale des Maladies Veneriennes; rapport fait au nom de la Commission nommee par le Congres Medicale International de Paris de 1867." <u>Cong Med de Toutes les Nations</u> (Bologne, 1869) 2:258-294, 1870.

4610 Cross, D. K. <u>Social Hygiene</u>. Cape Town: 1913, 23 pp.

4611 Cruyl, L. "De la Prophylaxie Publique en Matiere de Maladies Veneriennes." <u>Ann Soc de Med e Gand</u> 68:226-239, 1889.

4612 Csatary, L. de. "Mesures Prises en Hongrie contre la Propagation des Maladies Syphilitiques." <u>Gaz Hebd d Sc Med de Montpel</u> 6:19, 1884.

4613 Csillag, J. "The Present Position of the Aetiology of Uleus Venereum;..." <u>Orvosi Hetil</u> (Budapest) 43:288, 302 314, 326, 1899.

4614 Cucca, C. "I Lazzaretti." <u>Morgagni</u> (Naples) 27:13-16, 1885.

4615 Cuillert, J. "Modern Moral and Hygenic Campaign Against Prostitution; obligatory sanitary inspection and prophylaxis of all prostitutes in Lyon." <u>Bull Soc Med de Saint Luc</u> 40:34-61, Feb. '34.

4616 Curran, W. J. "Venereal Disease Detention and Treatment: prostitution and civil rights." <u>Am J Public Health</u> 65(2):180-1, Feb. '75.

4617 Cvejic, S., et al. "Venereal Disease in Vojvodina." <u>Med Pregl</u> 22(5):229-41, '69.

4618 Czobos, K. "Zur Verhutung Venerischer und Sifilitischer Infektionen." <u>Wien Med Presse</u> 23:962, 1882.

4619 d'Agostino, M. "Abolition and Regulation From Point of View of Prophylaxisis of Syphilis." <u>Semana Med</u> 2:1879-1886, Dec. 13, 1934.

4620 Dalla Volta, Amadeo. I Fondamente Biologici della Prostituzione. Rome: Casa ed. Leonardo da Vinci, 1924, 201 pp.

4621 The Dangers of False Prudery. Pearson, 1912, 121 pp.

4622 Daniels, J. "Disease and Punishment." Nation 153:162, Aug. 23, 1941.

4623 Dauden and Mora. "Periodic Examination of Prostitutes in Dermatologie Dispensary for Prophylactic Purposes." Actas Dermo Sif 37:767-780, Mar. '46.

4624 Davis, Katherine B. "The Problem of Prostitution," in Int. Conf. Women Physicians, Proceedings 6:56-62, 1920.

4625 De Amorim, P. J. "Venereal Diseases." Hospital (Rio de Janeiro) 70(6):1739-45, Dec. '66.

4626 Deck, L. Syphilis et Reglementation de la Prostitution en Angleterre et aux Indes; etude de statistique medicale de 1866 a 1896. Paris: 1898.

4627 "Decrees Regulating Sanitary Control in Marseille." Prophylax Antiven 13:324-344, Oct. '41

4628 De Goes e Siqueira, J. Breve Estudio Sobre a Prostituicao e a Syphilis no Brasil. Rio de Janeiro: 1877.

4629 Deguy, ____. "Medical Surveillance of Prostitutes." Prophylax Antiven 3:579-585, Sep. '31.

4630 Delune, H. "Epidemiological Trend of Gonorrhoea in Recent Years." Brit J Vener Dis 47(5):377, Oct. '71.

4631 Derata, O. "Remarks on Gonorrhea of Harlots." Sankwa Fujinkwa Gaku Zasshi (Tokyo) 5:138-146, 1903.

4632 Descamps, M. J. D. La Prostitution a Lille et la Prophylaxie de la Syphilis par la Reglementation de la Prostitution. Lille: 1906.

4633 De Souza, H. C. "Aspects of Prostitution and of Anti-venereal Countries." Brazil Med 54:745-750, Nov. 9, 1940.

4634 Dibot, H. Extinction des Maladies Veneriennes; moyens preservatifs, generaux, particuliers et speciaux, avec un expose de la prostitution. Paris: 1873.

4635 Dickinson, R. L. "Gynecologist Looks at Prostitution Abroad; with reference to electrocautery treatment of gonorrheal cervicitis und urethritis." Am J Obst Gynec 14:590-602, Nov. '27; Tr Am Gynec Soc 52:107-122, '28.

4636 Diday, P. Exposition Critique et Pratique des Nouvelles Doctrines sur la Syphilis; suivie d'une etude sur de nouveaux moyens preservatifs des maladies veneriennes. Paris: 1858.

4637 Diday, P. Le Peril Venerien dans les Familles. Paris: 1881.

4638 Dieckhofer, K. and T. Vogel. "Social and Legal Problems in the So-called Poriomania, With Special Reference to Desertion and AWOL." Schweiz Arch Neurol Neurochir Psychiatr 115(2):337-48, '74.

4639 "Discussion sur le Nouveau Projet de loi Concernant la Prostitution et la Prophylaxie des Maladies Veneriennes." Soc Franc de Prophyl San et Mor Bull 7:148-164, 1907.

4640 "The Disinfection of Formosa." Med Times and Gaz (London) 2:413, 1869.

4641 "Diskussion i det Medicinske Selskab om Prostitutionssporgsmaalet i Almindelighed og Visitationen i Saerdeleshed." Ugesk f Laeger (Copenhagen) 1:313-327, 1880, 4, R.

4642 "Diskussion Uber die Prostitutionsfrage." Wien Med.-Halle 5:8, 1864.

4643 Dispensario de Higiene Social de Lisboa Regras da Profilaxia para Evitar as Doencas Venereas. 1936, 16 pp.

4644 Divella, M. "Abolition of Brothels and Reorganization of Antivenereal Services." Igiene e San Pub 1:243-256, Apr.-Jun. '45.

4645 Divella, G.M. "Results of Serologic Examination of Prostitutes for Syphilis in Bari, 1937." Dermosifilografo 13:198-202, Apr. '38.

4646 "Do the Contagious Diseases Acts Succeed?" Westm 152:608-27; 153:135-58, Dec. 1899 and Feb. 1900.

4647 Dock, Lavinia Hygiene and Morality.Putnam, 1910.

4648 Dock, Lavinia R. Hygiene and Morality: a Manual for Nurses and Others. New York: G. P. Putnam's Sons, 1911, 200 pp.

4649 Doerks, G. "Health Control of Prostitutes and Paragraph 28 of the Law on the Control of Venereal Diseases." Oeff Gesundheitsdienst 22:94-99, Jun. '60. In German.

4650 Dolmage, G. "Remarks on Prostitution, with a view to the adoption of measures for the checking of venereal diseases." Med Circ (London) 24:328, 344, 1864.

4651 Donglier, M. "The Attraction of Prostitution and the Prostitute." Acta Neurol Belg 64:719-24, Jul. '64. In French.

4652 Dooremaal, ___ van. "Het Toezicht Over de Prostitutie." Nederl Tijdschr v Geneesk 16:49-51, 1880, 2, R.

4653 Dooremaal, ___ van. Reglementeering der Prostitutie, Hygienisch Gerechtvaardigd?; openbare brief aan G. van Overbeck de Mijer, door S. R. Hermanides, te Geldermalsen. n. p., n. d.

4654 Doros, G. "Blood Examinations of Prostitutes in Budapest." Orvosi Hetil 71:1310-1313, Nov. 6, '27.

4655 Draper, W. F. "The Detention and Treatment of Infected Women as a Measure of Control of Venereal Diseases in Extra-cantonment Zones." Am J Obstet 80:642-646, '19. Discussion, pp.726-741.

4656 Droin, E. "Le Reclassement des Prostituees." Praxis (Swiss) no.45, Nov. 5, 1959, 8 pp.

4657 Droin E. "The Rehabilitation of Prostitutes." Praxis 48:1023-4, Nov. 5, 1959.

4658 "Sur la Prophylaxie de la Syphillis." Cong Internat de Dermat et de Syph C. r. 1889, Paris, 1890, 843-846.

4659 Drysdale, C. "Prostitution et Maladies Veneriennes en Angleterre." Confer Internat p la Prophyl de la Syph et d Mal Ven (Brussels) 1(2):1-20, 1899.

4660 Drysdale, C. R. Prostitution Medically Considered; with some of its social aspects. A paper read at the Harveian Medical Society of London. With a report of the debate. London: 1866.

4661 Drysdale, George. The Elements of Social Science: or Physical, Sexual and Natural Religion. 3d ed enlarged London: Trulove, 1860.

4662 Ducrey, C. "The Spread of Syphilis as an International Problem." Minerva Derm (Italian) 37:346-54, Oct '42.

4663 Duenas, A., et al. "Herpesvirus Type 2 in a Prostitute Population." Am J Epidemiol 95(5):483-9, May '72.

4664 Dugniolle, ___. "Rapport sur le Service Sanitaire de la Prostitution." J de Med., Chir et Pharmacol (Brussels) 12:27-32, 1851.

4665 Dugteren, ___ van. "La Surveillance Sanitaire Doit-elle Etre Consideree Comme Indispensable la Sante Publique?" Confer Internat p la Prophyl de la Syph et d Mal Ven (Brussels,

1899) 2(com):51-56, 1900.

4666 Dulacska, G. "A Prostitutio Rendezese." Allamorvos (Budapest) 2:121-125, 1877.

4667 Dunham, G. C. (Control). Rev Filipina de Med y Farm 24:489-496, Oct. '33.

4668 Dunlop, et al. "Improved Tracing of Contacts of Heterosexual Men With Gonorrhoea. Relationship of Altered Female to Male Ratios. Br J Vener Dis 47(3):192-5, Jun. '71.

4669 Dunlop, E. M. "Some Moral Problems Posed by Sexually Transmitted Disease." Br J Vener Dis 49(2):203-8, Apr. '73.

4670 Dupouy,____. "La Police des Moeurs, les Maladies Veneriennes a Paris." Medecin (Paris) iv, no.42, 1, 1878.

4671 Dupouy, E. La Prostitution dans l'Antiquite dans ses Rapports avec les Maladies Veneriennes; etude d'hygiene sociale. 3d ed. Paris: 1895.

4672 Duque, M. La Prostitucion; sus causes, sus males; su higiene. Havana: 1914.

4673 Durban, P. "Social Factors and Etiologic Atmosphere of Prostitution." Hyg Ment 40:13-27; 48-54, '51.

4674 During, E. von. Prostitution und Geschlechtskrankheiten. Leipzig; 1905.

4675 During, E. von. "Prostitution et Maladies Veneriennes en Turquie." Confer Internat p la Prophyl de la Syph et d Mal Ven (Brussels) 1(2):93-97, 1899.

4676 Duverne, J. "Results One Year After Closing of Houses of Prostitution in Saint-Etienne." Ann de Dermat et Syph (Bull Soc Franc de Dermat et Syph 1) 7:83-85, Feb. '47.

4677 Dyer, A. S. "Syphilis et Prostitution." Presse Med Belge (Brussels) 34:121-125, 1882.

4678 Dyer, L. "Some Casual Remarks on Prostitution and Venereal Diseases in Their Relation to the Public." Medicus (Frederick) 8:33-37, 1900; Phil Med J 5:354-357, 1900.

4679 East, W. N. "Prostitution." Practitioner 158:335-342, Apr. '47.

4680 Eckeroom, A. "Huru Bor Provinsiallakarnes Embetsstallning Ordnas, sa att den Kan Motsvara Bade Helso-och Sjukvardens Kraft?" (How Ought the Public Position of Provincial Physician to be Regulated So That It May Respond to the Demands of Hygiene and Care of the Sick?) Eira (Goteborg) 1885, ix, 591-601.

4681 Edwards, T. C. "Social Protection--a Workable Plan." J Soc Hygiene 38:373-81, Dec. '52.

4682 Edwards, W. M. "A Study of Progonasyl Using Prostitutes in Nevada's Legal Houses of Prostitution." J Reprod Med 11(2):81, Aug. '73.

4683 Edmundson, W. F. "Antivenereal Control by Means of Prophylactic Application of Penicilin to Much Exposed Group." Bol Ofic San Panam 34:347-50, Apr. '53.

4684 Ehlers, ____. "Prostitution et Maladies Veneriennes en Danemark." Confer Internat p la Prophyl de la Syph et d Mal Ven (Brussels) 1(2):98-124, 1899.

4685 Ekstrom, K. "Patterns of Sexual Behavior in Relation to Venereal Disease." Br J Vener Dis 46(2):93-5, Apr '70.

4686 Ekunina-Fiveiskaya, Mariya K. "Medical Inspection of Prostitutes, Performed in the Free City Dispensary of Moscow." Trudi Syezda Russk Vrach v pam Pirogova 1891, Moscow, 4:179-184, 1892.

4687 The Elements of Social Science; or physical, sexual, and natural religion. An exposition of the true cause and only cure of the three primary social evils: poverty, prostitution, and celibacy. By a doctor of medicine. London: 1884.

4688 Engelsted, S. "Measures Adopted in Denmark to Prevent the Spread of Venereal Disease." Tr Internat M Cong (Philadelphia, 1876) 1877:745-760.

4689 "Estudio de la Prostitution en Barcelona." Rev de Hyg y Pol San (Barcelona) i:193-195, 1890.

4690 Etienne, ___. "Morbidite Venerienne chez les Hommes en Relatio avec l'Activite et l'Efficacite de la Surveillance sur la Prostitution." Confer Internat p la Prophyl de la Syph et d Mal Ven 2(com):48-50, 1900.

4691 Eulenburg, A. "Das Sozial Uebel." Deutsche Med Wchnschr 29:452, 1903.

4692 Ewing, S. "The Medical-legal Supervision of Prostitution." Denver M Times 19:290-299, 1899-1900.

4693 Eyckmans, R. "Law Suppressing Official Regulation." Arch Belges Dermat et Syph 8:415-19, Dec. '52.

4694 Fabre, M. "Organization of Service for Antivenereal Prophylaxis. Rev d Hyg 61:698-704, '40.

4695 Fadrhoncov, A. A. "Study on Gonorrhea. I: Analysis of the Data from the Epidemiologic Aspect." Cesk Dermatol 49(3):176-89, Jun. '74.

4696 Falconer, M. P. "Report of the Committee on Social Hygiene." Conf Char and Correc 1915:241-52.

4697 "Fallen Women as a Constant Pathologic Danger." J Am Med Assn 79:2109, '22.

4698 Fanti, G., and R. Willhelm. "Die Prostitution und die Bekampfung der Geschlechtskrankheiten." Ztschr f Bekampf d Geschlechtskrankh (Leipzig) 18:253-269, 1917-18.

4699 Fauser, A. "Die Handhabung der Sanitatspolizeilichen Prophylaxe der Venerischen Krankheiten in Stuttgart." Med Cor.-Bl d Wurttemb Arztl Ver (Stuttgart) 60:27-31, 1890.

4700 Fedoroff, A. I. "Prostitution in St. Petersburg and Its Supervision by the Medical Police." Vestnik Obsh., Hig., Sudeb i Prakt Med (St. Petersburg) 13(1):36-75, 1892. Trans: Arch f Dermat u Syph 25:395-439, 1893.

4701 Fedoroff, A. I. Sketch of the Supervision of Prostitution by the Medical Police in St. Petersburg. St. Petersburg: 1897.

4702 Fernandes Braganca, J. A. Breves Consideracoes Sobre a Prostituicao Debaixo do Ponto de Vista da Hygiene e da Moral. Lisbon: 1875, 73 pp.

4703 Fessler, A. "Importance of Cervical Control of Wassermann Reaction and of Cervical and Urethral Secretion in Examination of Prostitutes." Mitt Deutsch Gesellsch z Bekampf d Geschlechtskr 26:23-27, Feb.-Mar. '28.

4704 Fessler, A. "Venereal Disease and Prostitution in Reports of Poor Law Commissioners, 1834-1850." Brit J Ven Dis 27:154-157, Sep. '51.

4705 Feulard, H. "Nouveaux Reglements sur la Prostitution et de Prophylaxie des Maladies Veneriennes mis en Vigueur en Italie le ler aout 1888." Gaz Hebd de Med (Paris) 25:833-836, 1888.

4706 Feulard, H. "Syphilis et Prostitution; l'eternel debat pour on contre la reglementation. Gaz Hebd de Med (Paris) 41:37, 1894.

4707 Fiaux, F. L. L'Armee et la Police des Moeurs: Biologie Sexualle du Soldat. 1917, 325 pp.

4708 Fiaux, L. "La Prostitution en France." Progres Med (Paris) 2:392, 423, 1895, 3, s.; 7:241, 257, 310, 1898, 3, s.

4709 Fiaux, L. Sur le Pretendue Sterilite Involontaire des Femmes Ayan Exerce la Prostitution. Paris: 1892.

4710 Finger, ___. "L'Organisation Actuelle de la Surveillance Medicale de la Prostitution est-elle Susceptible d'Ameliorations?" (Report) Confer Internat p la Prophyl de la Syph et d Mal Ven (Brussels, 1899) 1(fasc. 1)(2. quest):1-39, 1899; 2(com pt. 2):9-12, 1900; also, trans. Wien Klin Wchnschr 12:892, 927, 1899.

4711 Flatten. H. "Ueber die Microscopische Untersuchung der Secrete bei der Sanitatpolizeilichen Controle der Prostituierten." Vrtljschr f Gerichtl Med (Berlin) 6(suppl.-heft):91-103, 1893, 3, F.

4712 Fleischer, M. "Reglementierungsfrage der Prostitution." Deutsche Prax (Munich) 14:165, 197, 1905.

4713 Flesch, M. "Prostitution und Frauenkrankheiten." Fortschr d Off Gsndhtspflg (Frankfurt a. M.) 5:221-269, 1896.

4714 Flesch, M. "Social Measures for Regulation of Prostitution and Venereal Diseases." Mitt d Deutsch Gesellsch z Bekampf d Geschlechtskr 25:50, May 1, '27.

4715 Flesch, M. "Ueber die Gesetzliche Berrichtigung der Zwangsheilung der Prostituirten." Ztschr f Bekampf d Geschlechtskrankh (Leipzig) 2:322, 1903-4.

4716 Flexner, Abraham. "Civilization Must Fling Down the Gauntlet." J Soc Hygiene 22:419-20, Dec. '36.

4717 Flexner, Abraham. Next Steps in Dealing with Prostitution. American Social Hygiene Assn.

4718 Fokker, A. P. "De Prostitutie." Nederl Tijdschr v Geneesk (Amsterdam) 21:309-312, 1885.

4719 Fonseca, Aureliano de, et al. "Accao do Dispensario de Higiene Social do Porto na Vigilancia Sanitaria das Prostitutas." O Medico no.369, 1959. 12 pp.

4720 Fonseca, Aureliano de. "As Doenca Venereas e a Prostitucao." O Medico no.181, 1955, 15 pp.

4721 Foote, Edward B. Plain Home Talk. New York: Murray Hill Pub. Co., 1887.

4722 Forssman, D. T. "Om Prostitutionen i Helsingfors och Medlen att Hamma den Veneriska Smittan." Finska Lak Sallsk Handl 16:173-211, 1874.

4723 "Fortune Survey: is legalized prostitution the best way to cure the national evil of venereal disease." Fortune 15:164+, Jan. '37.

4724 "Fortune Survey of Public Opinion Regarding Legalized Prostitution as a Public Health Measure." J Soc Hygiene 22:421, 427-30, Dec. '36.

4725 Fosdick, R. B. "Prostitution and Public Health." Month Bull N Y State Health Dep ns 13:84-86, 1918.

4726 Fouquet, ____. "L'Examen du Sang et le Traitment des Prostituees par le 606 d'apres un Article de M. le Prof. Neisser." Soc Franc de Prophyl San et Mor, Bull (Paris) 12:141-145, 1912.

4727 Fouquet, ___. "La Visite Medicale Prostituees; d'apres un article de M. Douglas McMurtrie de New York." Soc Franc de Prophyl San et Mor, Bull (Paris) 22:1-6, 1917.

4728 Fournier, A. "De l'Abolitionnisme." Bull Med (Paris) 16:717-722, 1902.

4729 Fournier, A. "Projet sur la Prophylaxie Publique de la Syphilis." Bull Acad de Med (Paris) 19:155-160, 1888, 2, s.

4730 Fournier, A. "Prophylaxie Publique de la Syphilis." Bull Acad de Med (Paris) 17:592, 630, 1887, 2, s.; Ann d'Hyg 18:55-108, 1887, 3, s.

4731 Fracastor, _____. Contagion. Tr. by W. C. Wright. New York: G. P. Putnam's Sons, 1930.

4732 Franchi, F. and C. Pesa. "Sex Hygiene in France, Spain, and Portugal; comparative study." Minerva Med 2:1078-1081, Oct. 17, 1953.

4733 Frasey, ____. "A Propos du Projet de Loi sur la Prostitution." Bull Med (Paris) 21:220, 1907.

4734 Freed, L. F. "Summarized Findings of Medicosociologic Investigation Into Problem of Prostitution in Johannesburg." South African Med J 22:52-56, Jan. 24, 1948.

4735 Freier, A. "Die Doppelbewertung der Prostitution." N Generation (Leipzig) 21:129-136, '25.

4736 French, E. (Prostitution) Br J Ven Dis 31:113-116, Jun. '55.

4737 Freuenberg, C. "Sollen die Prostituierten auf Gonorrhoe Untersucht und Behandelt Werden?" Deutsche Med.-Ztg (Berlin) 19:487, 1898.

4738 Frosner, G. G. and P. A. Berg. "Change of the Prevalent Subtype of Hepatitis B Antigen in Acute Hepatitis B Infections." Z Immunitaetsforsch 150(3):259-66, Sep. '75.

4739 Frosner, G. G., et al. "Prevalence of Hepatitis B Antibody in Prostitutes." Am J Epidemiol 102(3):241-50, Sep. '75.

4740 Funes, J. M. and C. L. Aguilar. "Solution of Oxophenarsine Hydrochloride and Alkyl Aryl Sulfate in Prophyaxis of Gonorrhea in Prostitutes." Bol Ofic San Panam 33:121-125, Aug. '52.

4741 Funk, J. C. Vice and Health: Problems; Solutions. Lippincott, 1921, 174 pp. Contents: Prostitution and its causes; Prostitution and its manifestations; Business side of prostitution; Results of prostitution; The government's fight; Medical measures; Law enforcement; Medico-legal measures; Education; Welfare and rehabilitation; Good government.

4742 Fyodoroff, A. I. "Pozorniy Promisel." (Shameful Profession). Vestnik Obsh Hig, Sudeb i Prakt Med (St. Petersburg) 1900(2):1175-1185.

4743 Gallarani, C. "Reglamentacion de la Prostitucion; fundamentos de esta importante medida de hijiene publica; proyecto adaptable a la ciudad del Rosario." Rev Med.-quir (Buenos Aires) 6: 268, 285, 302, 1869-70.

4744 Gallia, C. "Increase in Clandestine Prostitution and Syphilis; statistics." Dermosifilografo 3:606-612, Nov. '28.

4745 Gandevia, B. and F. M. Forster. "Fecundity in Early New South Wales: an evaluation of Australian and Californian experience." Bull NY Acad Med 50(10):1081-86, Nov. '74.

4746 Garcia Belenguer, R. "La Prostitucion ante la Hygiene." Espana Med (Madrid) 1:73, 97, 121, 145, 1884.

4747 Garle, H. E. Social Hygiene To-day. George Allen, 1936 and in London Digest of Laws, p.205-323.

4748 Garnier, G., et al. "Present Status of Antivenereal Prophylaxis of Prostitutes in the Paris Area." Prophyl Sanit Morale 37:12-8, Jan. '65. In French.

4749 Garofalo, J. "La Prostitucion y la Sifilis; consideracion sobre la mision del medico; analisis de la obra; la prostitucion no debe ser reglamentada, sino combatida; preservativos de la sifilis; la campana de Manuecos; belleza de esta obra." Siglo Med (Madrid) 8:72-74, 1861.

4750 Garzon, R., et al. "Promiscuity and Venereal Diseases." Arch Argent Derm 12:143-50, Jun. '62. In Spanish.

4751 Gate, J. and P. Robin. "Effects of Suppression of Law on Prostitution and Closing of Houses of Prostitution on Frequency of Venereal Diseases in Rhone District." Prophylax

Antiven 20:248-251, Mar. '48.

4752 Gate, J. and J. P. Robin. "Use of the Fichier Sanitaire et Social de la Prostitution in the Department of the Rhone from 1947 to 1960." Prophyl Sanit Morale 33:122-12+, May '61. In French.

4753 Gaujoux, E. and P. Vigne. "Syphilis in Prostitutes in Marseille; statistical study." Bull Soc Franc de Dermat et Syph (Reunion Dermat, Strasbourg) 40:1025-1027, Jul. '33.

4754 George, B. J., jr. "Legal, Medical and Psychiatric Considerations in Control of Prostitution." Mich Law R 60:717-60, Apr '62.

4755 Geardy, J., et al. "Prostitution and Venereal Disease in the Liege Region." Arch Belg Med Soc 22:601-11, Nov.-Dec. '64. In French.

4756 Geheime,____. "(Die) Prostitution." Allg Wien Med Ztg 25:49, 1880.

4757 Gelabert y Gaballeria, E. "De la Prostitution en sus Relaciones con la Higiene en el Doble Concepto de la Reglamentacion de la Prophylaxis de la Syphilis." Sentido Catol (Barcelona) 8:689-698, 1886.

4758 Gerland, O. "Die Beschrankung der Dirnen auf das Wohnen in Bestimmten Strassen." Deutsche Vrtljschr f Off Gsndhtspflg 37:525-536, 1905.

4759 Gerrish, F. H. "The Duties of the Medical Profession Concerning Prostitution and Its Allied Vices." Tr Maine Med Assn 6:331-350, 1878.

4760 Gibbons, A. H. Compulsory Medication of Prostitutes by the State. Republished from Westminster Rev, July, 1876, by the New York Committee for the Prevention of Licensed Prostitution. New York: 1876.

4761 Gibon, A.L. "Report of the Committee on the Prevention of Venereal Diseases." Am Pub Health Assn Bost. 1881, 6:402-415.

4762 Giersing, O. M. "De Engelske Love for at Hemme Udbredelsen af Syhlia Blandt Armeons of Flaadens Mandskab, Sanit Deres Virkninger." (English Contagious Diseases Acts). Ugesk f Laeger (Kjöbenh) 27:3 R, 403, 421. 1879.

4763 Giersing, O. M. "Prostitution from a Hygienic Standpoint." Maanedsbl udg af Foren imod Lovbesk f Usaedelighed 3:168-176, 1881-2.

4764 Gihon, A. L. "On the Protection of the Innocent and Helpless Members of the Community from Venereal Diseases and their Consequences." Am Pub Health Ass Bost. 1880, 5:55-65.

4765 Girard, ____. "Antivenereal Campaign in Tovlon." Prophylax Antiven 11:515-540, Aug. '39.

4766 Glascow, M. "Prostitution: an analysis." Med Woman's J 50(1943):35-40.

4767 Godkins, T. R., et al. "Utilization of Stimulated Patients to Teach the 'Routine' Pelvic Examination." J Med Educ 49(12):1174-8, Dec. '74.

4768 Goetz, F. H. G. De Prostitutione Atque de Prophylaxi et Oppressione Syphilidis Morbi. Lipsiae, 1850.

4769 Goodman, H. "Experiences With Repression and Regulation of Prostitution With Emphasis on Medical Aspects." M Times 56:150-157, Jun. '28.

4770 Goodman, H. "Prostitution and Community Syphilis." Am J Pub Health 9:515-520, 1919.

4771 Gottheil, E. and A. Freedman. "Sexual Beliefs and Behavior of Single, Male Medical Students." JAMA 212(8):1327-32, May 25, 1970.

4772 Gottschalk, H. "Statistical Bases for Prophylactic Bismuth Therapy of Syphilis." Dermat Wchnschr 108:1453-1457, Oct. 31, 1936.

4773 Gouin, J., et al. "Inapparent Syphilis Diagnosed by Leukocyte Reaction; later clinical confirmation of diagnosis; significance of case in prostitute." Bull Soc Franc de Dermat et Syph 42:318-320, Feb. '35.

4774 Gould, W. G. "Legal Control of Venereal Disease." Nat Conf Social Work 1946:468-76.

4775 Gould, W. G. "Prostitution, Promiscuity, Venereal Disease." Pub Health Nursing 38:173-177, Apr. '46.

4776 Gounelle, H. "Effect of Closure of Public Houses of Prostitution on Venereal Diseases; study among soldiers." Bull Soc Franc de Dermat et Syph (Reunion Dermat, Strasbourg) 40:911-912, Jul. '33.

4777 Gounelle, H. and P. Girault. "House of Prostitution and Antivenereal Prophylaxis." Arch Med Sociale 2:69-81, Feb. '46.

4778 Graff, ____. "Sind die Physicatsarzte Verpflichtet, die Gesundheit der Lustdirnen in Bordellen zu Uberwachen?" Ztschr f d Staatsarznk (Erlang.) 33:250-255, 1837.

4779 Graham, Sylvester. Lecture to Young Men. Providence: Weeden and Cory, 1834. Reprinted New York: Arno Press, 1974. pp.32-33.

4780 Grandhomme and Grunwald. "Uebersicht Uber die in der Zeit von 1893 bis 1902 bei den Frankfurter Prostituierten Festgestellten Geschlechtskrankheiten." Festschr z i Cong d Deutsch Gesellsch z Bekampf d Geschlechtskrankh (Frankfurt a. M.) 1903:62-75.

4781 Grandier-Morel, Dr. Voyages d'Etude Physiologique Chez les Prostituees des Principaux Pays du Globe. Paris: P. Fort, 1901, 352 pp.

4782 Grant, L. "Essential Preventives." Caledon M J 16:13-17, Jan. '37.

4783 Gratsianoff, ____. "Po Povodu Satyi Desyatova: Vrachi i Prostitusiya." (Apropos of Desyatoff's Essay: Physicians and Prostitution). Ejened Jour "Prakt Med" (St. Petersburg) 5:11-19, 1898.

4784 Gratsianoff, P. "On the Projected New Order of the St Petersburg Committee of Medical Police." Russk Med Vestnik 6:4-14, 1904.

4785 Gratsianoff, P. "Ten Years of Medical Inspection of Prostitution in Minsk." Russk Med Vestnik 5(15):13; (16):14.

4786 Gratsianski, P. "K Vopr. o Reglament. Prostitut." Voyenno-Med J (St. Petersburg) 157(3):305-332, 1886; Protok Russk Sif i Dermat Obsh (St. Petersburg 1885-6) 1(suppl.):1-28, 1887.

4787 Gravagna, _____. "Importance of Treating Prostitutes Having Latent Syphilis." Dermosifilografo 4:76-78, Feb. '29.

4788 Gregorio, E. de and T. Cisneros. "Results of Frei Reaction in Prostitutes in Relation to Their Venereal Infection." Rev Argent Dermatosif 26:544-550, '42.

4789 Greco, N. V. "Abolition of Law 12331 for Prophylaxis of Venereal Diseases; consequences." Semana Med 2:1114-1118, Nov. 25, 1948.

4790 Greer, J. H. The Hidden Plague; diseases propagated by prostitution. Ipswich, 1916, 16 pp.

4791 Griffith, F. "Observations Upon the Protective Value of the Inspection of Public Women as Carried Out in Paris." Med Rec (New York) 65:651, 1904; South Calif Pract (Los Angeles)

19:170-174, 1904.

4792 Gruber, M. von Die Prostitution vom Standpunkte der Sozialhygiene aus Betrachtet. Vienna: 1905, 47 pp. (Forms no.3, Vortr. Sozial wiss. Bildungsverein Wein); Bull Soc Internat de Prophyl (etc.) (Brussels) 1:171-176, 1901.

4793 "Guarding the Olympic Games." J Soc Hygiene 14:290-2, May '28.

4794 Guiard, F. P. "Le Danger Venerien pour la Sante Publique; urgence d'une reglementation nouvelle de la prostitution pour le combattre. J de Med de Paris 11:18-24, 1899, 2, s.

4795 Gumbiner, ____. "Die Ueberwachung der Prostitution vom Sittlichen und Sanitats-polizeilichen Standpunkte Betrachtet." Wchnschr f d Ges Heilk (Berlin) 1850:481, 503, 516.

4796 Gunning, J. W. Een Medisch Votum op Zedelijk Gebied. s'Gravenhage, 1889.

4797 Gunning, J. W. "Ter Kenschetsing van de Prostitutiek Westie." Nederl Tijdschr v Geneesk (Amsterdam) 17:149-153, 1881, 2, R.

4798 Gunsett, A. "Zur Frage der Gonokokkenuntersuchung der Prostituierten." Strassb Med Ztg 2:177-179, 1905.

4799 Guth, G. "Mikroskopische Gonorrhoekontrolle der Prostituierten, Insbesondere in der Praxis der Berliner Sittenpolizei." Ztschr f Bekampf d Geschlectskrankh 14:1-18, 1912-13.

4800 Guth, G. "Syphilisserodiagnostik bei Prostituierten." Ztschr f Bekampf d Geschlehctskrankh 18:221-229, 1917-18.

4801 Guthe, T. and R. R. Willcox. "The International Incidence of Venereal Disease." R Soc Health J 91(3):122-33, May-Jun. '71.

4802 Haack, K. "Comparative Capillaroscopic Examination of Prostitutes and of Patients Visiting Skin and Venereal Disease Clinic." Dermat Ztschr 59:95-103, Aug. '30.

4803 Haberling, Wilhelm. Das Dirnenwessen in den Heeren und Seine Bekampfung. Leipzig: J. A. Barth, 1914, 103 pp.

4804 Hackett, C. J. "On the Origin of Human Treponematoses." Bull WHO 29(1963):7-14.

4805 Hall, A. On the Great Prevelence of Venereal Diseases in Great Britain; showing the necessity of additional sanitary laws to arrest their progress. Glascow: 1847.

4806 Haltrecht, N. Ehe 1:151-154, Nov.1, '26.

4807 Hamilton, Alice. "Prostitutes and Tuberculosis." Survey 37:516-17, Feb. 3, 1917.

4808 Hahnlein, V. "Zur Psychogenese der Dirne." Arch f Menschenk (Dresden) 1:215-219, 1925-26.

4809 Hanauer, W. "Zur Aetiologie und Behandlung der Prostitution." Monatschr f Harnkr u Sex Hyg (Leipzig) 1:70-75, 1904.

4810 _____. "Die Prostitution und die Dienstboten." Monatschr f Harnkr f Sociale Med (Jena) 1:417-425, 1904.

4811 Harding, T. S. "Our Studious Indifference to the Obvious (Prostitution and Control of Venereal Disease)." M Rec 151:20(adv. paging), Jan. 3, '40; 20(adv. paging), Jan. 17, '40; 21(adv. paging), Feb. 7, '40.

4812 Haro, A. S., and O. Kilpo. "Venereal Diseases Among Prostitutes in Helsinki, 1945-57." Acta Dermatovener (Stockholm) 41:309-19, '61.

4813 Hart, G. "Factors Influencing Venereal Infection in a War Environment." Br J Vener Dis 50(1):68-72, Feb. '74.

4814 Hart, G. "Psychological Aspects of Venereal Disease in a War Environment." Soc Sci Med 7(6):455-67, Jun. '73.

4815 Hart, G. "Role of Preventive Methods in the Control of Venereal Disease." Clin Obstet Gynecol 18(1):243-63, Mar. '75.

4816 Hart, G. "Social and Psychological Aspects of Venereal Disease in Papua New Guinea." Br J Vener Dis 50(6):453-8, Dec. '74.

4817 Hart, G. "Social Aspects of Venereal Disease. I: Sociological Determinants of Venereal Disease." Br J Vener Dis 49(6):542-7, Dec. '73.

4818 Hart, G. "Social Aspects of Venereal Disease. II: Relationship of Personality to Other Sociological Determinants of Venereal Disease." Br J Vener Dis 49(6):548-52, Dec. '73.

4819 Haslund, A."Nogle Oplysninger i Anledning af Debatten om Prostituierten og Visitationen." Ugesk f Laeger (Copenhagen) 1:245-249, 1880, 4, R.

4820 Haslund, W. E. "Laegerne og Prostitutionskontrollen." (Physicians and the Control of Prostitution). Ugesk f Laeger (Copenhagen) 8:385-396, 5, R, 1901.

4821 Hassing, M. De Colica Scortorum Disquisito. Havnia, 1848.

4822 Havas, A. "A Prostitutiorol." Kozeg es Torveny Orvos (Budapest) 1896:9-16.

4823 Heidingsfeld, M. L. "The Control of Prostitution and the Prevention of the Spread of Venereal Diseases." JAMA 42:305-309, 1904.

4824 Heite, H. J., and O. M. Maucher. "Circulating Sperm Antibodies in Prostitutes." Munch Med Wchnschr 117(46):1845-8, Nov. 14, '75.

4825 Hellwig, A. "Medical Supervision of Prostitutes According to Law For Prevention of Venereal Diseases." Mitt d Deutsch Gesellsch z Bekampf d Geschlechtskr 26:4, Jan. 1, '28.

4826 Henderson, H. and S. Shaw. "V. D. for Sale." Collier's 718:22-3, Nov. 23, 1946. Also in Lee, A. M. and E. B. Lee, eds., Social Problems in America, pp.503-06. Holt, 1949.

4827 Henigst, W. "Letter: Sexual Transmission of Infections Associated with Hepatitis-B Antigen." Lancet 2(842):1395, Dec. 15, '73.

4828 Henry, M. H. "The Discussion on the Prevention of Syphilis, with Reference to the Regulation of Prostitution, at the Third International Medical Congress, held at Vienna, August, 1873, with additional remarks." Am J Syph and Dermat 5:17-28, 1874.

4829 Hermanides, S. R. "De Concept-wet tot Bestrijding van Syphilitische en Venerische Zickten." Neder Tijdschr v Geneesk 18:321-337, 1882, 2, R.

4830 Hermanides, S. R. "Reglementeering der Prostitutie, Hygienisch Gerechtvaardigd? Openbare brief aan Prof. Dr. G. van Overbeck de Meijer." Nederl Mil Geneesk Arch (etc.) (Utretcht) 7:666-685, 1883.

4831 Hermann, J. "Die Impfug ud die Prostitution vor dem Forum des Internationalen Medizinischen Congresses zu Wien im Jahren 1873." Allg Wien Med Ztg 18:469, 481, 1873.

4832 Hermann, J. "Die Prostitution und das Gesundheitsbuch." Allg Wien Med Ztg 22:22, 31, 1877.

4833 Hermann, J. "Die Prostitution und die Syphilis." Wien Med Wchnschr 12:123, 139, 155, 1862.

4834 Hermann, J. "Directe Vorschlage zur Regelung der Prostitution." Oesterr Ztschr f Prakt Heilk (Vienna) 9:865-869, 1863.

4835 Hervas, A. "La Prostitucion; juicio critico; profilaxis." Siglo Med (Madrid) 42:566, 1895.

4836 Hesbacher, E. N. "Problem of Venereal Disease Control in Extracantonment Area." Ven Dis Inform 24:189-193, Jul. '43.

4837 Hesse, P. G. "Aspects of Venereology in General Medicine." Z Aerztl Fortbild (Jena) 68(11):544-50, Jun. 1, '74.

4838 Higginson, A. "Harmful Action of Regulated Prostitution." Cron Med (Lima) 54:299-302, Sep. '37.

4839 Haustein-Berlin, Hans. Geschlectskrankheiten und Prostitution in Skandinavien. Berlin: 1925, 24 pp.

4840 Hill, J. H. "General Problem of Control," in Silent Enemies; the story of the diseases of war and their control, pp.187-97. Putnam, 1942.

4841 Hippe, J. "Die Bordellfrage vom Standpunkte des Juristen." Ztschr f Bekampf d Geschlechtskr 4:88-110, 1905.

4842 Hissard, R. "Role of House of Prostitution in Syphilitic Morbidity." Prophylax Antiven 19:178-481, Jun. '47.

4843 Hissard, R. "Sanitary Surveillance and Augmentation of Syphilis." Bull Soc Franc de Dermat et Syph (Reuniom Dermat, Strasbourg) 40:992-995, Jul. '33.

4844 Hoeffel, ____. "Si l'on se Place a un Point du Vue Exclusivement Medical, y a-t-il Avantage a Maintenir les Maisons de Tolerance on Vaut-il Mieux les Supprimer?" (Report) Confer Internat p la Prophyl de la Syph et d Mal Ven (Brussels) 1899, i, fasc. i, 3.quest., 1-13.

4845 Hoerig, D. "Development of Venereal Diseases in the Dresden District with Reference to the Social Hygiene Questions, Problems of Prostitution and Domestic Servants, Research on Sources of Infection." Z Aerztl Fortbild 54:100-11, Sep. 1, '60. In German.

4846 Hoffman, K., et al. "Studies on the Epidmiology of Ornithosis of the Population in the Essen Area on the Basis of Antibody Determination With the Complement Fixation Test." Arch Hyg Bakteriol 150(3):330-47, Aug. '66.

4847 Holst, A. "Prostitution et Maladies Veneriennes en Norwege." Confer Internat p la Prophyl de la Syph et d Mal Ven (Brussels) 1(2):125-142.

4848 "Homosexuality and Prostitution: B. M. A. memorandum of evidence for departmental committee." Br Med J (Supp) pp.165-170, Dec. 17, '55.

4849 "Homosexuality, Prostitution and the Law." (Report of the Roman Catholic Advisory Committee on Prostitution and Homosexual Offenses and the Existing Law; with text). *Dublin R* 230(471):57-65, '56.

4850 Hooker, E. B. "Abatement of Prostitution." *New Eng Med Gaz* (Boston) 50:64-71, Feb. '15.

4851 Hooker, E. H. "Case Against Prophylaxis." *Soc Hygiene* 5:163-84, Apr. '19.

4852 Horacek, J. "Control of Venereal Diseases in the South Moravian Region." *Cesk Dermatol* 48(5):332-9, Oct. '73.

4853 Hornemann, E. "Public Hygiene and Prostitution." *Hyg Medd* (Copenhagen) 3:211-244, 1879-80, n. R.

4854 Hossain, A. S. "Sexual Behavior of Male Pakistanis Attending Venereal Disease Clinics in Great Britain." *Soc Sci Med* 5(3):227-41, Jun. '71.

4855 Huart, Louis. *Physiologie de la Grisette... Nouvelle Edition Augmentee d'une Notice sur la Vie de l'Auteur.* Brussels: 1882, 80 pp.

4856 Hubner, H. "Die Errichtung und Aufgaben des Neuen Prostitutuiertenpavillons der Hautklinik des Stadtischen Krankenhauses zu Frankfurt a. M." *Munchen Med Wchnschr* 4:392-394, 1908.

4857 Hudson, E. H. "Treponematosis and African Slavery." *Br J Vener Dis* 40:43-52, Mar. '64.

4858 Hudson, E. H. "Treponematosis and Man's Social Evolution." *Am Anthropologist* 67:885-901, Aug. '65.

4859 Hudson, E. H. "Treponematosis in Perspective." *Bull WHO* 32(1965):735-748 and in *Treponematosis*. New York: Oxford University Press, '46.

4860 Huet, G. D. L. "Vervolg van het Verslag van den Gecommitteerde tot Onderzock Naar de Werking der Reglementation op de Prostitutie Hier te Lande." *Nederl Tijdschr v Geneesk* (Amsterdam) 4(2 Afd.):326-337, 2, R.

4861 Huet, G. D. L. "Opmerkingen Naar Aanleiding van het Rapport der in 1882 Benoemde Comm. der Maatsch. tot Bevord der Geneesk., om na te gaan de gebreken, die aan het tegenvordig toezigt op de Prostitutie, waar dit bestaat, kleven, enz." *Nederl Tijdschr v Geneesk* (Amsterdam) 19:405-409, 1883, 2, R.

4862 Hugel, F. "Ueber die Quastionirung und Losung der Prostitutionsfrage." *Ztschr f Gerichtl Med* (Vienna) 3:477, 488, 499, 509, 1867.

4863 Huguet, F. N. "Sobre la Necesidad de Vijilar y de no Permitirse las Casas Libres de Prostitucion." Gac Med (Lima) 5:259, 1879.

4864 Huhner, M. "An Important Factor in the Spread of the Social Evil." Urol Cutan Rev (St. Louis) 25:201-203, '21.

4865 Hund, John. The Physician and the Social Evil; a study of the development of the medical science under religious influence with special reference to the social evil. Milwaukee: Enterprise, 1911, 44 pp.

4866 Hutton, Ulrich von. Of the Wood Called Guaiacum. Tr. by Thomas Paynel. London: Thomas Bertheleti, 1539. p.l.

4867 Ichok, G. "Problem of Prostitution and Prevention of Venereal Diseases in Argentina." Rev d'Hyg 58:124-132, Feb. '36.

4868 Idsoe, O., and T. Guthe. "The Rise and Fall of the Treponematoses. I: Ecological Aspects and International Trends in Venereal Syphilis." Br J Vener Dis 43(4):227-43, Dec. '67.

4869 International Conference of Women Physicians. Proceedings, 1919. Vol.6: Conservation of Health of Women in Marriage," pp.56-73, 1920. Includes "Problem of Prostitution," by K. B. Davis; Prostitution and Prophyaxis of Venereal Disease in Italy," by Clelia Lollini; "Regulation of Prostitution in Sweden," by Alma Sundquist; with discussion.

4870 "International Milestones in the Control of V. D. and Prostitution." J Soc Hygiene 40:184-5, May '54. Chronological listing, 1899-1954.

4871 Ipavic, ____. "Bericht des Sanitaren Comite's in der Prostitutions-Regelungsfrage." Mitth d Ver d Aerzte in Steiermark 14:47-50, 1878.

4872 Istituo di Medicina Sociale. La Piaga Sociale della Prostiuzione. Rome: 1950, 247 pp. An account of the 2d Congress of the Societe de Medicine Sociale.

4873 Jadassohn, J. "Bericht Uber Eine zum Studium der Prostitution und der Prophylaxe der Venerischen Krankheiten Unternommene Reise." Deutsche Vrtljschr f Off Gsndhtspflg (Brnschwg.) 26:193-245, 1894.

4874 Jadassohn, ____. "L'Organisation Actuelle de la Surveillance Medicale de la Prostitution est-elle Susceptible d'Ameliorations?" (Report) Confer Internat p la Prophyl de la Syph et d Mal Ven (Brussels) 1899,i, fasc. i, 2.quest., 41:1899, Brussels: 1900, ii, com. pt.2, 13.

4875 Jadassohn, ____. "Prostitution et Maladies Veneriennes en Suisse." Confer Internat p la Prophyl d la Syph et d Mal Ven (Brussels, 1899) 2(com. pt.2):50.

4876 Jadassohn, ____. Prostitution und Venerische Krankheiten. 1: Die prostitution und die venerischen krankheiten in der Schweiz. 2: Die internationale konferenz zur verhutung der syphilis und der venerischen krankheiten in Brussel (Sep. 1899). Berichte. Bern: 1900.

4877 Janet, J. "Projet de Reglementation Medicale de la Prostituion." Ann de Therap Dermat et Syph 5:217-224, 1905.

4878 Jaubert, ____. "Serodiagnosis of Gonorrhea in Systematic Control of Prostitutes." Bull Soc Franc Dermat et Syph 59:502-504, Nov.-Dec. '52.

4879 Jauneau, M. A. P. Etude sur la Morbidite Venerienne et les Resultats de la Reglementation Prostitutionnelle a Brest. Bordeaux: 1903.

4880 Jeannel, J. Memoire sur la Prostitution Publique et Parallele Complet de la Prostitution Romaine et de la Prostitution Comtemporaine; suivis d'une etude sur le dispensaire de salubrite de Bordeaux, d'une statistique dans la garnison de Bordeaux et d'un essai de statistique de l'infection venerienne dans les garnisons de l'empire francais. Paris: 1862.

4881 Jeannel, "De la Responsabilite des Prostituees qui ont Transmis des Maladie Veneriennes." Mem et Bull Soc Med Chir d Hop de Bordeaux 2:333-335, 1867.

4882 Jeannel, J. "Sur la Prostitution et sur la Prophylaxie des Maladies Veneriennes en Angleterre." Ann d'Hyg (Paris) 1874:101-130, 2. s.

4883 Jersild, O. Undersogelser Over Cervikalsekretet hos Prostituerede; et bidrag til studiet af den gonorrhoiske endometritis. Copenhagen: 1904.

4884 Jessner, S. "Zur Prostitutionsfrage." Monatsh f Prakt Dermat (Hamburg) 15:553-565, 1892.

4885 Jevremovic, M. P. "On Measures for Preventing Venereal Diseases and the Regulation of Prostitution." Srpski Arh za Celok Lek 13:1-14, 1907.

4886 Jewell, D. L. "Suggestions for Community Action Against Venereal Disease." Soc Hygiene 5:497-519, Oct. '19.

4887 Jimenez, F. G. "Prostitucion; indicaciones sobre su etiologie y su Terapentica." Anfiteatro Anat (Madrid) 4:227, 1876.

4888 Johnson, Bascom. Next Steps. 2d ed. New York: American Social Hygiene Association, 1918.

4889 Johnson, Bascom. "The Prostitution 'Racket': related health problems, and a suggested remedy." J Soc Hygiene 25:209-20, May '39.

4890 Johnson, Bascom. "Prostitution and Quackery in Relation to Syphilis Control." J Soc Hygiene 26:6-11, Jan. '40.

4891 Johnson, Bascom. "When Brothels Close, V. D. Rates Go Down; prostitution in the spread of venereal disease in an army cantonment area. J Soc Hygiene 28:525-35, Dec. '42. Bibliography, tables, chart.

4892 Johnson, D. W., et al. "An Evaluation of Gonorrhea Case Findings in the Chronically Infected Female." Am J Epidemiol 90(5):438-48, Nov. '69.

4893 Johnstone, A. "Prostitution and Public Policy." J Soc Hygiene 23:73-76, Feb. '37.

4894 Jordan, ____. "Geschlechtskrankheiten und Prostitution." Munchen Med Wchnschr 1903:997.

4895 Jose de Goes, ___. "A Prostituicao Publica Diante da Hygiene Social." Rev Med (Rio de Janiero) 4:25, 41, 60, 76, 90, 1877.

4896 Joseph, M. "Die Politische Behandlung der Prostituirten und die Notwendigkeit einer Kranken-Unterstutzung fur Prostituirte." Med Reform (Berlin) 11:17-19, 1903.

4897 Joulia, P. "Frequency of Syphilitic Chancres of Cervix and of Vaginal Walls in Prostitutes." Paris Med 1:213-215, Mar. 7, '36.

4898 Joulia, P., et al. "Hidden Factors of Numerous Contaminations: Frequency of Chancre of Uterine Cervix and Vagina in Prostitutes." Bull Soc Franc de Dermat et Syph (Reunion Dermat, Strasbourg) 40:1023-1025, Jul. '33.

4899 Joulia, P. "Need for Early Detection of Primary Syphilis, Especially of Cervix and Vagina; dangers of contamination by prostitutes." Prophylax Antiven 7:600-617, Oct. '35.

4900 Joyeux, B. "Statistical and Clinical Studies of Venereal Diseases in Prostitutes of Hanoi, 1930-39." Bull Soc Med de l'Indochine.

4901 Kato, K. and A. Ogava. "Relation Between Change to Positive Tuberculin Reaction and Roentgenologie Signs of Tuberculosis in Prostitutes." Kekkaku (Abstr. Sect.) 18:9-10, Mar. 24, '40.

4902 Kato, K., et al. "Tuberculin Reactions in Prostitutes." Kekkaku (Abstr. Sect.) 18:9, Mar. 24, '40.

4903 Kaverin, V. "General Prophylaxis in Syphilis." Med Besieda (Veronej) 1:219-226, 1887.

4904 Keighley, E. "Carcinoma of the Cervix Among Prostitutes in a Women's Prison." Br J Vener Dis 44(3):254-5, Sep '68.

4905 Kellogg, J. H. Plain Facts for Old and Young. Burlington, Iowa: 1882. Reprinted Buffalo, New York: Heritage Press, 1974, pp.400-401.

4906 Kelly, H. A. "The Best Way to Treat the Social Evil." Med News (New York) 86:1157-1163, 1905.

4907 Kelly, H. A. "What's the Right Attitude of the Medical Profession Toward the Social Evil?" JAMA 44:679-681, 1905.

4908 Kemp, Tage. Prostitution: An Investigation of Its Causes, Especially with Regard to Hereditary Factors. Copenhagen: Levin and Munksgaard, 1936, 253 pp. Diagrams.

4909 Kennedy, Robert F. The Enemy Within. New York: Popular Library, 1960.

4910 Kerney, J. E. "How Health Officer Can Cooperate in Repression of Prostitution." J Soc Hygiene 19:523-527, Dec. '33.

4911 Kholevinskaya, M. M. "Report of the Examination of the Prostitutes at the Samokat Inspection Point of the Fair of Nizhni Novgorod for 1893." Vrach (St. Petersburg) 15:487-491, 1894; 16:438, 471, 1895.

4912 Kilduffe, R. A. "A Note Upon the Incidence of Positive Wassermann Reactions in Prostitutes." Atlantic Med J (Harrisburg) 28:224, 1924-25.

4913 Kim, J. D., et al. "Syphilis Among the Prostitutes and a New 'Test Plan' for the Serologic Diagnosis of Syphilis." J Korea Med Assn 6:1143-52, Nov. 20, 1963.

4914 Kinberg, O. "On the So-Called Vagrancy; a medico-sociological study." J Crim Law 24:552-70, Sep '33.

4915 King, A. "The First Harrison Lecture, 1974. The life and times of Colonel Harrison." Br J Vener Dis 50(6):391-403, Dec. '74.

4916 Kinoshita, K. "Statistics on Venereal Diseases in Prostitutes." Hifubyog kin Hiniokibyog Zasshi (Tokyo) 5:404-411, 1905.

4917 Kinsie, P. M. "Prostitution--then and now." *J Soc Hygiene* 39:241-8, Jun. '53.

4918 Kneeland, G. J. *Commercialized Prostitution and the Liquor Traffic*. American Social Hygiene Assn., 1916.

4919 Koch, Richard A., and Ray Lyman Wilbur. "Promiscuity as a Factor in the Spread of Venereal Disease." An offprint from the *Journal of Social Hygiene*, 1944.

4920 Kohn, S. R., et al. "Primary Gonococcal Stomatitis." *JAMA* 219(1):86, Jan. '72.

4921 Kokoschka, E. M., et al. "Examination Results in Prostitutes Infected With Venereal Diseases." *Z Haut Geschlechtskr* 47(9):423-32, May 1, '72.

4922 Kolankowski, J. "Town and Country in the Spreading of Venereal Diseases." *Przegl Dermatol* 54(6):651-3, Nov.-Dec. '67.

4923 Kolodny, R. C., et al. "Sperm-agglutinating Antibodies and Infertility." *Obstet Gynecol* 38(4):576-82, Oct '71.

4924 Konopik, J. "The Problem of Venereal Diseases in the Capital Prague." *Cesk Dermatol* 43(1):46-7, Feb. '68.

4925 Kopp,____. "Die Verbreitung der Venerischen Erkrankungen und Speciell der Syphilis durch die Prostitution." *Verhandl d Gesellsch f Deutsch Naturf u Aerzte (Leipzig, 1893) 65(2)313-320, 1894.*

4926 Kopytowski, M. "Ueber die Haufigkeit des Vorkommens von Gonoccen und Anderen Bacterien im Secrete des Cervix Uteri bei Schienbar Gesunden Prostituirten." *Arch f Dermat u Syph* 32:345-348, 1895.

4927 Kopytowski, W. "Looking for Gonococci in the Purulent Discharges of the Sexual Organs in Public Women." *Kron Lek* (Warsaw) 19:257-263, 1898.

4928 Kosack,____. "Ueber die Gegen Verbreitung der Syphilis zu Ergreifenden Sanitats Polizeilichen Massregeln." *Friedreich's Bl f Gerichtl Med* (Nurnburg) 29:45, 89, 1878.

4929 Kozlovski, G. "Syphilis in Moroco in the Region of Fez." *Maroc Med* 50(541):723-8, Dec. '70.

4930 Kraus, B. "Sociale Medizin; die Regelung der Prostitution." *Allg Wien Med Ztg* 20:169, 480, 1875; 21:23, 41, 51, 58, 69, 77, 1876.

4931 Krauss, F. S. "Beischlafausubung als Kulthandlung." *Anthropophyteia* (Leipzig) 3:20-33, 1906.

4932 Krautwig, P. "Geschlechtskrankheiten und Prostitution." Centralbl f Allg Gsndhtspflg (Bonn) 25:211-229, 1906.

4933 Kromayer, ____. "Communication Relative a la Premiere Question (discussion): Les systemes de reglementation actuellement en vigueur ont-ils en une influence sur la frequence et la dissemination de la syphilis et des maladies veneriennes?" Confer Internat p la Prophyl de la Syph et d Mal Ven (Brussels) 1(app.):23-27, 1899; 2(com. pt. 2):62, 1900.

4934 Kromayer, ____. "Communication Relative a la Deuxieme Question." (discussion): La organisation actuelle de la surveillance medicale de la prostitution est-elle susceptible d'amelioration? Confer Internat p la Prophyl de la Syph et d Mal Ven (Brussels, 1899) 1899(1.app.):49; 2(com. pt.2):66-68, 1900.

4935 Krowczynski, Z. "The Relation of the Physician to the Investigation of Prostitution." Przegl Lek (Krakow) 18:137, 149, 163, 175, 1879.

4936 Kuhn, J. Die Prostitution im Neunzehnten Jahrhundert vom Sanitatpolizeilichen Standpunkt aus Betrachtet; oder die prophylaxis der Syphilis. Leipzig: 1871.

4937 Kuhn, J. Die Prostitution im Neunzehnten Jahrhundert und die Verfassers nen Bearbeitet von Dr. Eduard Reich. Leipzig: 1888.

4938 Kullberg, A. F. On Prostitution and the Most Efficient Means to Check Venereal Diseases; with special reference to Stockholm. Lund, 1874.

4939 Kullberg, A. F. "On Prostitution and the Most Efficient Means to Suppress Venereal Diseases." Svens Lak.-Sallsk n Handl (Stockholm) 5(1):33-126, 1873, 2, s.

4940 Kuznetsoff, M. "Istoriko-statisticheskii Ocherk Prostitutsii i Razvitija Sifilisa v Moskvie." Arch Sudebnoi Med (St. Petersburg) 6(4):84-201, 1870.

4941 Kvicera, J. "Anonymous Sources of Venereal Diseases." Cesk Derm 39:383-9, Dec. '64.

4942 Kvicera, J. "On the Prevention of Venereal Diseases in a City." Cesk Dermatol 42(6):404-10, Dec. '67.

4943 Lacassagne, J. and H. Pigeaud. "Abortion, Pregnancy and Maternal Function in Prostitutes." Ann d Mal Ven 25:251-263, Apr. '30.

4944 Lacassagne, J. and F. Lebeuf. "Rare Incidence of Nicholas-Favre's Disease Among Prostitutes; results of Frei reaction." Marseille-Med 1:432-444, April 15-25, '38.

4945 Lacassagne, J. and F. Lebeuf. "Frequency and Date of Development of Syphilis in Prostitutes." Ann d Mal Ven 31:774-777, Oct. '36.

4946 Lacassagne, J. and F. Lebeuf. "Results of Bismuth in Prevention of Syphilis in Prostitutes." Bull Soc Franc de Dermat et Syph (Reunion Dermat., Strasbourg) 43:1189-1191, Jun. '36.

4947 Laird, S. M. "Prostitution and Venereal Disease in Manchester." Brit J Vener Dis 32:181-183, Sep. '56.

4948 Lallemand, Claude-Francois. On Involuntary Seminal Discharges. Tr. by William Wood. Philadelphia: A. Waldie, 1839.

4949 Lamb, A. M. "New Methods of Contact Tracing in Infectious Venereal Diseases." Br J Vener Dis 42(4):276-9, Dec. '66.

4950 Lambinet, J. "La Reglementation de la Prostitution a Liege et la Lutte Contre les Maladies Veneriennes." Soc Franc de Prophyl San et Mor, Bull (Paris) 24:84-90, '24.

4951 Lancucki, J., et al. "Attempt at the Evaluation of the Influence of Environment on the Incidence of Syphilis in Soldiers of Obligatory Service." Przegl Dematol (Suppl) pp.93-9, '69.

4952 Lande, L. Hygiene Publique; les affections veneriennes et leur prophylaxie generale a Bordeaux. Rapport presente a la Societe e Medecine et de Chirurgie de Bordeaux, le 22 Novebre, 1872. Paris: 1873.

4953 Lane, J. R. "On the Prevention of Contagious Venereal Disease." Brit and For M.-Chir Rev (London) 43:196-208, 1869.

4954 Lardier, ____. Les Veneriens des Champs et la Prostitution a la Campagne. Paris: 1882.

4955 Lasegne, C. "De la Fecondite dans ses Rapports avec la Prostitution." Arch Gen de Med (Paris) 2:513-524.

4956 Lassar, O. Die Gesundheitsschadliche Tragweite der Prostitution; eine Social-medicinische Betrachtung. Berlin: 1892.

4957 Lassar, O. "Prostitution un Geschlechtskrankheiten; eine socialmedcinische Betrachtung." Hyg Rundschan (Berlin) 1:1009-1017, 1891.

4958 Lassen, H. A. "Prostitutionssporgsmaalet." Ugesk f Laeger (Copenhagen) 28:67-71, 1879.

4959 Lassen, J. "The Vital Question of the Protection System." Maanedsbl udg af Foren Imod Lovbesk f Usaedelighed (Copenhagen) 2:34-44, 1880-81.

4960 Lasserre, Jean. Le Maisons de Tolerance et la Santepublique. Paris: an extract of La Prophylaxie Antivenerienne, no. 12, 1945. 11 pp.

4961 Latour, A. "Lettre Adressee a M. le Dr. Ricord a Propos de la Prostitution Clandestine." Union Med (Paris) 7:641-643, 1869, 3, s.

4962 Laugier, P., et al. **"Syphilis** in Geneva During the Past Two Years: Epidemiology, Serology and Treatment." Praxis 60(49): 1628-35, Dec. 7, 1971.

4963 Laurent, A. "La Prostitution, la Frequence des Maladies Veneriennes a Rouen et des Moyens de Faire Diminuer Cette Frequence." Normandie Med (Rouen) 7:31-52, 1892.

4964 Laurent, E. "Qu'est ce que la Prostitution?" Independ Med (Paris) 4:183, 1898.

4965 Lecour, ___. "De la Prostitution et des Mesures de Police dont elle est l'Objet a Paris, au point de vue de l'infection syphilitique." Arch Gen de Med (Paris) 2:711-736, 1867.

4966 Le Fort, L. "De la Prostitution dans ses Rapports avec la Propagation des Maladies Veneriennes," in, Oeuvres, 1:743-785. Paris: 1895. First published Paris: 1888.

4967 Leggi, ____. "(Delle) sulla Prostituzione." Atti Cong Gen d Ass Med Ital (Torino) 7:164-166, 1876.

4968 Leloir, H. "A Propos du Danger que Font Courir a la Sante Publique les Filles Publiques Insoumises." Ann de Dermat et Syph (Paris) 9:464, 1888 2, s.

4969 Lentino, W. "Is Prostitution Still a Significant Health Problem?" Med Aspects Hum Sexuality 2:39-46, Oct. '68.

4970 Lentino, Walter. "Medical Evaluation of a System of Legalized Prostitution." AMAJ 158:20-3, May 7, 1955. Leghorn, Italy.

4971 Leonard, P. "Chancres of the Vaginal Walls and Uterine Cervix in Prostitutes as Hidden Factors in Numerous Contaminations." Bull Soc Franc Derm Syph 4:571-2, Aug.-Oct., '59. In French.

4972 Leonard, P. "Relative Frequency of Pregnacies in Prostitutes for the Past 35 Years in Bordeaux." Bull Soc Franc Derm Syph 4:572-73, Aug.-Oct., '59. In French.

4973 Leonhard, S. Die Prostitution; ihre hygienische, sanitare, sittenpolizeiliche und gesetzliche Behampfung. Munich and Leipzig: 1912.

4974 Le Pileur, L. "En se placant a un point de vue exclusivement medical y a-t il interet ou non a maintenir les maisons de tolerance? J de Mal Cutan et Syph (Paris) 12:137, 193, 1900.

4975 Le Pileur, L. "Expose d'un Projet de reglementation sanitaire de la Prostitution." Soc Franc de Prophyl San et Mor Bull (Paris) 7:216-233, 1907.

4976 Le Pileur, L. De l'Hospitalisation des Prostituees Veneriennes. Paris: 1889.

4977 Le Pileur, L. Prophylaxie de la Syphilis; reglementation de la prostitution a Paris. Clermont (Oise), 1887.

4978 Le Pileur, L. "A Propos du Projet de Loi de M. Berenger, Senateur, Visant le recolage sur la Voie Publique." Rev de Med Leg 2:125, 157, 194, 1895.

4979 Le Pileur, L. "Si l'on se Place a un Point de Vue Exclusivement Medical, y a-t-il Avantage a Maintenir les Maisons de Tolerance ou Vaut-il Mieux les Supprimer?" (Report) Confer Internat p la Prophyl de la Syph et d Mal Ven 1(1)(3. quest):43-84, 3 ch.

4980 Lepinay, E. "Attempted Bismuth Prophylaxis of Syphilis in Prostitutes of Restricted Areas." Rev Franc de Dermat et de Venereol 12:171-174, Mar. '36. In French.

4981 Lepinay, E. "Bismuth in Prevention of Syphilis Among Prostitutes of Closed District." Prophylax Antiven 8:230-233, Apr. '36.

4982 Lepinay, E. "La Prostitution au Maroc et la Lutte Contre ses Consequences Veneriennes." Brux Med 6:1221-1236, '25-'26.

4983 Lepinay, E. "Voluntary and Obligatory Treatment of Venereal Diseases in Prostitutes; comparative results according to observations at Casablanca." Prophylax Antiven (Assemb. Gen.) 6:142-145, Feb. '34.

4984 Leppmann, A. "Ueber die zur Verhinderung der Verbreitung der Syphilis Erforderlichen Sanitats-polizeilichen Vorschriften." Vrtljschr f Dermat (Vienna) 10:289, 531, 1883.

4985 Lesser, F. "Die Disziplinierung der Prostitution, ein neues System zur Bekampfung der Geschlechtskrankheiten." Berlin Klin Wchnschr 57:53, 85, 1920.

4986 Lesser, F. "Problem of Prostitution in Prevention of Venereal Disease." Med Welt 2:657, Apr. 28, '28.; 697, May 5, '28.

4987 Leveque, P. Prophylaxie es Maladies Veneriennes et Police des Moeurs; theories abolitionistes. I: Historique. II: Questions Jurisdiques. Lyon: 1905.

4988 Levi, I. "Desirability of Establishing Obligatory 'Prophylaxis Record Book' for Supervised Prostitutes." Dermosifilografo 9:177-179, Mar. '34.

4989 Levy,___. "Hauptbestimmungen des Neuen Danischen Gesetzes zur Bekampfung der Offentlichen Unsittlichkeit und Venerischen Ansteckung." Soziale Med u Hyg 2:143, '07.

4990 Lewin, P. A. "On Prostitution and the Most Efficient Means to Check Venereal Diseases, with special reference to Stockholm." Svens Lak.-Sallsk n Handl 5(2):1-165, 1873-4, 2, s.

4991 Lewis, D. "Clinical Lecture on Obstetrics and Gynaecology; the relationship of syphilis to society; the prophylaxis of venereal diseases; the restriction and regulation of prostiution." Chicago Clin R 4:347-367, 1894-5.

4992 Lewis, D. "The Prophylaxis and Management of Prostitution." St Paul Med J 8:591-600, 1906; Penn Med J 10:24-30, 1906-07.

4993 Lieberman, A. "A Case of Veniferous Venery." J Indiana Med Assn 56:51-5, Jan. '63.

4994 Lignieres, D. de. Prostitution et Contagion Venerienne; un pas vers l'extinction de la syphilis. Paris: 1900.

4995 Lillo, G. de. "Existence of Spermatic Antibodies in Blood of Prostitutes Due to Seminal Resorption by Vagina: experimental study." Rinasc Med 14:519-520, Aug. 15, 1937.

4996 Lion, A. "Ueber Findel- und Waisenhauser im Zusammenhange mit der frage Uber die Prostitution." Monatsbl f Med Statist u Off Gsndhtspflg (Berlin) 1862:61, 69, 77.

4997 Lister, J. "The Open University and Medical Education--Political Pressures--Sex on the State?" New Eng J Med 290(17):952-4, Apr. 25, 1974.

4998 Lizano, A. A. "Venereal Disease in Female Vagrants." J Phillipine M A 27:171-174, Mar. '51.

4999 Lochte,___. "Mikroskopische Gonokokkenbefunde bei Alten und Bei Gefangenen Prostituierten." Monatsh f Prakt Dermat (Hamburg) 33:335-340, 1901.

5000 Lollini, Clelia. "Prostitution and Prophylaxis of Venereal Disease in Italy," in Int. Conf. Women Physicians, Proceedings, pp.62-66. New York: 1920.

5001 Long, W. Baynard, et al, eds. Handbook on Social Hygiene Philadelphia: Lea and Febiger, 1938.

5002 Loughena, A. "Sulla Prostituzione." Gazz d Osp (Milan) 7:601, 699, 617, 1886.

5003 "Lov om Foranstaltninger til at Moderbejde den Veneriske Smittens Udbredelse af 10. April 1874." (Law for prevention of diffusion of venereal diseases). Maanedsbl Udg af Foren Imod Lovbesk f Usaedelighed 1:91-96, 1879-80.

5004 Lowndes, F. W. Lock Hospitals and Lock Wards. London: 1882, 31 pp.

5005 Lucas, A. "Les Medecins des Moeurs Sont-ils Legalement Autorises a Exercer leurs Fonctions?" Gaz d Hop (Paris) 77:1273-1275, 1904.

5006 Lucena, C. E. "Professional Dancers as a Factor in Venereal Propagation; result of systematic medical examination." Rev Med de Rosario 28:981-987, Sep. '38.

5007 Luger, A. "Prevention of Venereal Diseases." Z Haut Geschlechtskr 47(9):399-414, May 1, '72.

5008 Luger, A. "Problems of **Gonorrhea** in Austria." Postgrad Med J 48:Suppl 1:24-35, Jan. '72.

5009 Luger, A. F. "Problems Concerning Gonorrhea in Austria." Br J Vener Dis 47(5):378, Oct. '71.

5010 Luisi, P. "Prostitution and Venereal Diseases in Different Countries." Bol d Cons Nac d Hig 25:410-443, Jun. '31.

5011 Luisinus, Aloysius. Aprohdiasiacus Sive de lue Venerea. Lugduni Batavorum, 1728.

5012 Lunedei, A. "Palatal Purpura in Prostitutes; case due to oral coitus." Valsalva 11:125-144, Mar. '35.

5013 Lutand, A. "La Prostitution en Angleterre." Ann d'Hygiene (Paris) 15:414, 514, 1886, 3, s.

5014 Lutaud, A. "La Prostitution Patentee." J de Med de Par 15:229, 1903, 2, s.

5015 Lutaud, J. "Des Mesures Repressives et Sanitaires Dirigees Contre la Prostitution en Angleterre." Gaz Hebd d Med (Paris) 21:313-323, 1874.

5016 Lydston, G. F. "Social Evil and Its Relations to Social and Sex Hygiene." Privately printed Tomlinson-Humes, 1912.

5017 Lyman, H. M. "State Protection for Syphilo-phobists." Med Rec (New York) 16:122, 1879.

5018 M., F. V. "Prostitution (hygiene publique)." Dict d Sc Med (Paris) 45:480-491, 1820.

5019 Maestre, D. "Medidas que Deben Aeonsejarse a las Autoridades para Evitar la Propagacion de la Sifilis." Bol de Hig (San Fernando) 2:410, 430 1 tab, 508, 1883-5; 3:67, 82, 1886-7.

5020 Maestre, M. G. "Prostitucion: proyecto de reglemento de higiene especial." Monitor de la Salud (Barcelona) 5:38-44, 1884.

5021 Maglin, A. "Sex Role Differences in Heroin Addiction." Social Casework 55(3):160-167, '74.

5022 Malecot, A. "Les Veneriens et le Droit Commun (note relative a la prophylaxie de la syphilis et a la reglementation de la prostitution)." Bull et Mem Soc de Med Prat de Par 1888:200-212; Pratique Med 2:109, 222, 1888; J de Med de Paris 14:409-432, 1888.

5023 Malzberg, B. "Venereal Disease Among Prostitutes." Soc Hygiene 5:539-44, Oct. '19.

5024 Manasein, M. P. "Report of the Commission of the II. Division of the Russian Society for the Preservation of the Public Health on the Medical Inspection of Prostitution in Connection With the General Problem of the Struggle with it." Russk Med Vestnik (St. Petersburg) 6:334, 401, 1904.

5025 Mantegazza, Paul. Die Hygiene der Liebe. O. J. Jena, c1885.

5026 Mantegazza, P. "La Prostituzione," in Gli Amori d. Nomini, 2:175-225. Milan: 1886; also, trans.: L'Amour dans l'Humanite, pp.342-383. Paris: 1886.

5027 Manunza, P. "Question of Spermatotoxic Power of Blood Due to Abundant Absorption of Semen as a Cause of Sterility of Prostitutes." Arch di Anthropol Crim 56:591-613, Sep.-Oct. '36.

5028 Manunza, P. and A. Spanedda. "Question of Spermatotoxic Power of Human Blood due to Seminal Resorption by Vagina Studied in Relation to Possible Etiology of Sterility in Prostitutes; negative results of complement deviation reaction." Arch Ist Biochem Ital 8:495-508, Dec. '36.

5029 Marcondes, R. S. and S. W. Edmonds. "Health Knowledge of Prostitutes in Saigon, Vietnam. A study of health attitudes and habits relating to venereal diseases taken from a group of prostitutes." Rev Saude Publica 1(1):18-23, Jun. '67.

5030 Marcozzi, Aldo. Ipersessualita e Prostiuzione. Rome: Instituto G. Mendel, 1960, 7 pp.

5031 Marcus, J. "Zur Socialen Struktur und Psychologie Aller Geheimen Prostitution." Ztschr f Sexualwissensch (Bonn) 1922-23, pp.217-223.

5032 Marcuse,____. "Zur Ambulatorischen Behandlung der Prostitutuierten." Ztschr f Bekampf d Geschlechtskrankh 5:1-8, 1906.

5033 Margossian,____. "Des Mesures Administratives a Prendre dans le but d'Empecher la Propagation des Maladies Veneriennes a Smyrne." Gaz Med d'Orient (Constantinople) 16:184-6, 1872-3.

5034 Markiewicz, J. "Results of Initial Venereological and Epidemiological Analysis of 2,651 Females Detained by Police in Cracow for Violation of Public Order in the Years 1963-1972." Przegl Dermatol 61(4):469-75, Jul.-Aug. '74.

5035 Marselli, E. "La Prostitucion." Rev de Criminol Psiquiat (Buenos Aires) 8:705-722, '21.

5036 Martinez La Rosa, P. "Abolitionism in Anti-venereal Campaign." Cron Med (Lima) 61:337-341, Nov. '44.

5037 El-Massy, C. H. Etiologie et Prophylaxie de la Prostitution Envisagees dans leur Evolution Actuelle. Paris: 1936, 150 pp.

5038 Masters, F. W. and Greaves, D. C. "The Quasimodo Complex." Br J Plast Surg 20(2):204-10, Apr. '67.

5039 Matsuda, T. "Medical Basis of the Theory of Abolition of the 'Red Light Districts'." Jap J Nurs Art 8:122-32, Aug. '69.

5040 Matthys, R. "Resume du Rapport Fait a la Societe Belge de Dermatologie et de Syphiligraphie sur la Reglementation de la Prostitution." Soc Franc de Prophyl san et Mor Bulletin (Paris) 24:79-83, '24.

5041 Mauriac, C. "De la Contagion des Maladies Veneriennes dans la Ville de Paris Depuis la Fin de 1875 Jusqu'au Commencement de 1881." Ann d'Hyg (Paris) 8:133-162, 1882, 3, s.

5042 Mazzeo, M. "Regulation and Abolition of Prostitution in Relation to Prevention of Syphilis." Morgagni 69:841-863, May 29, '27.

5043 McGaughey, J. B. "The Importance of the Adoption of Measures for the Prevention of Venereal Diseases." Tr Minnesoda M Soc 1878:175-178.

5044 McGinnes, G. F. "Prostitution Abatement in a Venereal Disease Program." J Soc Hygiene 27:355-72, Oct. '41.

5045 "Measures for Prevention of Venereal Diseases." Rep San Com Engal 1864-5 (Calcutta) 1:19, 1866.

5046 Meheus, A., et al. "Prevalence of Gonorrhea in Prostitutes in a Central African Town." Br J Vener Dis 50(1):50-2, Feb. '74.

5047 Meheus, A., et al. "Serological Evidence for Syphilis in Different Population Groups in Rwanda." Trop Geogr Med 27(2):165-8, Jun. '75.

5048 Meissner, P. "Abolitionismus und Hygiene." Monatschr f Harnkr u Sex Hyg 2:42-49, 1905.

5049 Melody, G. F. "Chronic Pelvic Congestion in Prostitutes." Med Aspects Hum Sexuality, pp.103-104, Nov. 1969.

5050 Menczer, J., et al. "Antibodies to Herpes Simplex Virus in Jewish Women With Cervical Cancer and in Healthy Jewish Women of Israel." J Natl Cancer Inst 55(1):3-6, Jul. '75.

5051 Menno Huizinga, J. "Wettelijke Bestrijding der Syphilis." Niederl Tijdschr v Geneesk (Amsterdam) 17:93-98, 1881, 2, R.

5052 "Mesures Adoptes et Realisees en Belgique Contre la Propsgation des Affections Veneriennes." Gaz Med de Par 1:1-4, 1846, 3, s.

5053 Michaelis, C. "Zur Prostitutionsfrage." Cor.-Bl d Arztl u Pharm Kreis-Ver im Konigr Sachs (Leipzig) 12:68, 1872.

5054 Miche, W. "Ueber den Einfluss der Kasernirung der Prostituierten auf die Ausbreitung der Syphilis." Arch d Dermat u Syph (Vienna and Leipzig) 31:359, 32:91, 1895.

5055 Mieczynska-Wojcik, Z. and K. Szwarc. "Migration of Prostitutes and the Effect of This Phenomenon on Delayed Diagnosis of Early Syphilis." Przegl Dermatol 87-91, 1973.

5056 Miehe, Wilhelm. Ueber Einfluss der Kasernirungder Prostituirten auf die Ausbreitung der Syphilis. No cover, no publisher, no date, 85 pp. Gives statistics to 1890.

5057 Militchevitch, ____. "Prostitution et Maladies Veneriennes en Serbie." Confer Internat p la Prophy de la Syph et d Mal Ven (Brussels) 1(2):21-43, 1899.

5058 Miller, ____. "Die Prostitution." Ztschr f Med.-Beamte (Berlin) 20:405-422, 1907.

5059 Miller, E. P. The Treatise on the Cause of Exhausted Vitality; or Abuses of the Sexual Function. New York: John A. Gray and Green, 1867, p.77.

5060 Miner, M. E. Social Hygiene. National Conf. of Charites and Correction, 1916.

5061 Mireur, H. La Syphilis et la Prostitution dans leurs Rapports avec l'Hygiene, la Morale et la Loi. Paris: 1875 and 1888.

5062 Moeller, ____. "La Reglementation de la Prostitution Devant la Science et Devant les Faits." J de Med de Paris 2:673, 709, 1890, 2, s.; J de Mal Cutan et Syph (Paris) 2:297-315, 1890-91.

5063 Moghissi, K. S. and H. C. Mack. "Epidemiology of Cervical Cancer: study of a prison population." Am J Obstet Gynecol 100(5):607-14, Mar. 1, '68.

5064 Mol, Albert. The Profession. Universal Pub. and Dist. Corp., 1970.

5065 Moller, M. "The Microscopic Examination of the Secretions in the Inspection of Prostitutes." Hygiea (Stockholm) 59(2):321-331, 1905.

5066 Moller, Magnus. "Der Standige Kundenkreis der Prostitution." Zeitschrift fur Bekampfung der Geschlechtskrankheinten VIII. Leipzig: 1909.

5067 Monge, A. "Al Ilmo. Sr. D. Angel Pulido, director general de sanidad; higiene de la prostitucion." Rev Espan de Sif y Dermat (Madrid) 3:241-253, 1901.

5068 Monrier, ____. "Which are the Diseases Against Which the Contagion Act of 1874 is Directed, and how far does the same extend to obligatory visitation?" Maanedsbl Udg af Foren Imod Lovbesk f Usaedelighed (Copenhagen) 2:138-150, 1880-81.

5069 Montano, W. M. "Allies of Prostitution." Cron Med (Lima) 60:275-285, Oct. '43.

5070 Montesano, V. "La Prostituzione e la sua Regolamentazione in un Libro Recente." Rassegna di Studi Sess (Rome) 1921, i:26-28.

5071 Montesano, V. "A Proposito di Reglomentazione ed Abolizianismo." Rassegna di Studi Sess (Rome) 1921, i, 254-257.

5072 Moral, A. M. del "La Prostitucion; una pagina para su estudio higienico-social." Higiene (Havana) 1(39):2-4, 1891-2.

5073 Morhardt, P. E. Les Maladies Veneriennes et la Reglementation de la Prostitution au Point de Vue de l'Hygiene Sociale. Paris: 1906.

5074 Mori, A. (Statistik uber Uleus molle bei den Prostituierten, Res. pt. 2, 3) Hifubyog kin Hiniokibog Zasshi (Tokyo) 3:40-62, 1903.

5075 Morin, A. "Louis Fiaux; obituary, life and work, especially in campaign against prostitution; partial bibliography." Prophylax Antiven 9:131-155, Mar. '37.

5076 Morton, R. S. "Venereal Diseases in Bangladesh." Br J Vener Dis 50(1):64-7, Feb. '74.

5077 Motta, E. "Policia Sanitaria; a prostituicao em general." J Soc d Sc Med de Lisb 34:167, 193, 225, 1870, 2 s.; 35:38, 225, 1871.

5078 Mourier, __. "Prostitutionssporgsmaalet." Ugesk f Laeger 28:21, 113, 1879.

5079 Muller, ____. "Zur Bordell-frage." Med Ztg Berl 20:63, 1851.

5080 Muller, M. "Die Bedentung der Mikroskopischen Sekretuntersuchung fur die Kontrolle der Prostituierten und die Prophylaxie der Gonorrhoe." Strassb Med Ztg 2:143-149, 1905.

5081 Muller, M. "Nochmals die Bedeutung der Mikrokopischen Sekretuntersuchung fur die Kontrolle der Prostituierten und die Prophylaxie der Gonorrhoe: replik an Dr. Gunsett." Strassb Med Ztg 2:206, 1905.

5082 Mullo, ____. "Informe Sobre el Proyecto de Reglementacion de las Casas de Tolerancia, leido en la Asociacion Medica Bonaerense." Rev Med.-quir (Buenos Aires) 6:365-369, 1869-70.

5083 "Muster-Reglement Uber die Prostitution." Wien Med Bl 3:1077, 1101, 1880.

5084 Necessarian, A. The Contagious Diseases Acts and the Royal Commission. Manchester: Alexander Ireland, 1871. Other pamphlets.

5085 "Nederlandsche Maatschappijtot Bevordering der Geneeskunst Amendementen der Afdeelingen op het Voorstel van de Comissie tot Bestrijding der Syphilis."Ned Tijdschr v Geneesk Amst. 1882, 2,R. 17:433-436.

5086 Nedoma, K., and J. Sipova. "Gynecological and Health Profile of Prostitutes." Cesk Gynecol 38(6):425-7, Jul. '73.

5087 Nedoma, K., and J. Sipova. "Gynecological and Health Profile of Prostitutes." Isis 64(222):425-7, Jun. '73.

5088 Nedoma, K., and J. Sipova. "Gynecological and Health Profile of prostitutes." J Natl Med Assoc 65(4):425-7, Jul. '73.

5089 Neisser, A. "Dans quel sens peut-on reformer la reglementation de la prostitution?" (Report) Soc Franc de Prophyl San et Mor Bull (Paris) 5:276, 331, 1905; 6:245, 1906.

5090 Neisser, A. "Is It Really Impossible to Make Prostitution Harmless as Far as Infection is Concerned?" Am J Urology and Sexology 12:289-99, Jul. '16.

5091 Neisser, A. "Ueber die Mangel der zur zeit ublichen Prostituiertenuntersuchung." Deutsche Med Wchrschr 16:834-837, 1890.

5092 Neisser, A. "Ueber die Verbreitung der Venerischen Krankheiten Unter den Prostituirten." Wien Med Wchnschr 40:885, 1890.

5093 Nelson, N. A. "'Prostitution' and Genitoinfectious Disease Control." Canad J Pub Health 34:251-260, Jun. '43.

5094 Nelson, N. A. "The Repression of Prostitution for Venereal Disease Control." Charts. Baltimore Health N 20:101-8, Jan. '43. Same, with title: "Medical Treatment and Law Enforcement Are Not Enough." Charts. J Soc Hygiene 28:89-96, Feb. '43.

5095 Ness, E. "National Campaign for Venereal Disease Control in Wartime; social protection in cooperative program." J Soc Hygiene 30:186-189, Apr. '44.

5096 Ness, E. "Social Protection in the Cooperative Program of the National Campaign for Venereal Disease Control in Washington." J Soc Hygiene 30:186-9, Apr. '44.

5097 Ness, E. "Social Protection in Venereal Disease Control." J Soc Hygiene 30:226-31, Apr. '44.

5098 Ness, E. "Venereal Disease Control in Defense." Ann Am Med Acad 220:89-93, Mar. '42. Bibliography.

5099 Neumann, L. "Prophylaxie de la Syphilis et Surveillance de la Prostitution." Cong Internat de Dermat et de Syph C. r. 1889 (Paris) 1890:847-855.

5100 Neumann, L. "Die Prophylaxis der Syphilis; ein Beitrag zur Losung der Prostitutionsfrage." Klin Zeit.-u Streitfragen (Vienna) 3:141-170, 1885(?).

5101 "New York Academy of Medicine on Plain Words About Venereal Disease." Am J Pub Health 32:113, Jan. '42.

5102 Newman, A. "VD in London; battle of Picadilly Circus among our army's worst." Newsweek 21:60+, Jun. 14, 1943.

5103 Nicolau, S. "Individual Prophylaxis of Venereal Diseases, With Special Consideration of Various Methods Applied to Prostitutes." Rev San Mil (Bucarest) 35:712-725, Jul. '36.

5104 Niehans, P. Statistische Untersuchungen zum Problem der Prostitution und der Geschlechtskrankheiten vom Standpunkt der Sozialen und Forensischen Medizin. Zurich: 1914.

5105 Nielsen, R. "Sensitivity of Gonococci to Antibiotics in Strains Isolated From 'Prostitutes' in Copenhagen." Br J Vener Dis 6(2):153-5, Apr. '70.

5106 Niemineva, Kalin. "A Study of Factors Influencing Fertility of Prostitutes." Intl J Sexology 6:77-83, '52. Aso Acta Genetica Statistica Medica II.

5107 Nikolski,___ "Precautions Against Syphilis in the Ekaterinburg Community." Vrach Vaidom (St. Petersburg) 7:3420-3424, 1882.

5108 Nissen, Henry W. "Social Behavior in Primates" in, Comparative Psychology New York: Prentice Hall, 1951. pp.423-57.

5109 "Noch Einmal die 'Regelung der Prostitution'." Wien Med Wchnscr 19:131-133.

5110 "Noch ein Wort fur ein Prostituionsgesetz." Wien Med Wchnscr 13:555, 571, 1863.

5111 Norcross, G. E. "The Regulation of Prostitution." Mass M J 25:335-340, 1905.

5112 "Note and Comment." Soc Hygiene 3:28-98 Apr. '17.

5113 Notzel, K. "Oeffentliche Hauser in Russland; auf Grund neuen Materials." Ztchr f Bekampf d Geschlectskrankh 5:41, 81, 1906.

5114 Novotny, F. "Sex Education in the School and Its Possible Effect on the Incidence of Gonorrhea." Cesk Dermatol 49(3):206-9, Jun. '74.

5115 Obadia, Leon. La Prostitution, Role Sociol-legal du Medecin. Univ. of Montpellier, 1947, 130 pp.

5116 Oboznenko, P. E. Prostitution of St. Petersburg Under Supervision, after data of the committee of medical police and the Kalinkin Hospital. St. Petersburg: 1896.

5117 Oller, L. Z. and T. Wood. "Factors Influencing the Incidence of Gonorrhea and Non-Gonoccal Urethritis in Men in an Industrial City." Br J Ven Dis 46(2):96-102, Apr. '70.

5118 Omizzolo, F. B. "Pulmonary Tuberculosis in Prostitutes in Italy; statistics, contagion and social aspects." Minerva Med 1:585-589, Jun. 23, '36.

5119 Omori, I., et al. "Report on the Venereal Diseases of the Clandestine Prostitutes an Sendai." Chingai lji Shinpo (Tokyo) 1891(278):14-21.

5120 Onchukova, Mme. M. S. "Conditions of Prostitutes in Odessa." Trudi Odessk otd Russk Obsh Okhran Narod Zdrav (St. Petersburg) 4:49-57, 1904.

5121 "On Dolorosa Street, Free Clinic in San Antonio, Texas." Time 38:54, Sep. 15, 1941.

5122 "Opinion of the Committee Based on Reports (Dictamne sobre los temas de la seccion VII: prostitucion)." Arch Mex Ven.-Sif y Dermat 3:39-58, Mar.-Apr. '44.

5123 "L'Organization Actuelle de la Surveillance Medicale de la Prostitution Est-elle Susceptible d'Amelioration?" Available from Geneva: Federation Abolitionniste Internationale, n. d., 12 pp.

5124 Osoba, A. O. "Epidemiology of Urethritis in Ibadan." Br J Vener Dis 48(2):116-20, Apr. '72.

5125 Ostrander, Katharin. "Social Service and the Venereal Carrier." Pub Health (Mich.) n s 7:15-21, Jan. '19.

5126 Ottolenghi, S. "Prostituzione e Criminalita." Rassegne di Studi Sess (Rome) 1921, i, 312.

5127 van Overbeck de Meijer, ___. "Het Geneeskundig Toezicht op de Prostitutie." Nederl Tijdschr v Geneesk (Amsterdam) 20:125-137, 1884, 2. R; 23:470, 645, 1887, 2. R.

5128 van Overbeck de Meijer, ___. "Het Geneeskundig Toezicht op de Prostitutie, op nien verdedigh." Nederl Tijdschr v Geneesk 19:821-845, 1883, 2, R.

5129 van Overbeck de Meijer, ___. "Maatregelen, van Overheidswege te Nemen tot Betengeling vag de Uitbreidling van Venerische Ziekten." Nederl Tijdschr v Geneesk 18:601-605, 1882, 2, R.

5130 van Overbeck de Meijer, ___. "Een Nieuw Tijdperk in den Strijd Tegen het Geneeskundig Toezicht op de Prostitutie." Nederl Tijdschr v Geneesk (Amsterdam) 22:397-401, 1886, 2, R.

5131 Ozenne, E. "Prostitution et Maladies Veneriennes en France." Confer Internat p la Prophyl de la Syph et d Mal Ven (Brussels, 1899) 1(2):143-203.

5132 Ozoux. (in Reunion) Ann d Mal Ven 29:808-825, Nov. '34.

5133 **Packalen, T. "Gonorrhea: Its Specificity and Its** Behavior in Prostitutes." Acta Soc Med Fenn Duodeum Ser. A, fasc.1, pt.2. 17:1-250. '34.

5134 Pais, L. "Repeated Serologic Tests for Syphilis of Prostitutes." Dermosifilografo 14:236-242, Apr. '39.

5135 Papaevangelou, G. "Hepatitis-associated Antigen in VD Clinic Patients." Br J Med 3(872):172, Jul. 21, '73.

5136 Papaevangelou, G., et al. "Hepatitis B Antigen in Prostitutes." Br J Vener Dis 50(3):228-31, Jun. '74.

5137 Papaevangelou, G., et al. "Prevalence of Hepatitus B Antigen and Antibody in Prostitutes." Br Med J 2(913):256-8, May 4, '74.

5138 Pappenheim, L. "Medicinische Ueberwachung der Prostitution." Monatschr...d. San.-Pol (Berlin) 2:35-43, 1860.

5139 Pappenheim, L. "Prostitutions-Polizei." Beitr...d. San.-Pol (Berlin) 1862(4):78-105.

5140 Pappritz, Anna. Eine Kundgebung des Abolitionismus." Monatschr f Harnkr u Sex Hyg 3:490-495, 1906.

5141 "Parecer da Commissao de Hygiene Sobre hum Plano de Reforma Sanitaria das Meretrizes,..." J Soc d Sc Med de Lisbon 4:328-333, 1836.

5142 Parent-Duchatelet, A. J. B. La Syphilis et les Autres Maladies Veneriennes Chez les Prostituees de Paris. Paris: Pierrefort, 1900.

5143 Parent-Duchatelet. "Physiologische und Pathologische Verhaltnisse der Offentlichen Dirnen Nach...von Bluff." J f Geburtsh Leip. 1837, 7:666-674.

5144 Parran, Thomas. Shadow on the Land. (Syphilis). New York: American Social Hygiene Assn., 1937.

5145 Patze, A. Ueber Bordelle und die Sittenverderbuiss Unserer Zeit; Eine medicinalpolizeiliche abhandlung fur staats- und polizeibeamte, sittenlehrer, sittenrichter, aerzte sowie fur jeden, den die aufrechthaltung der allgemeinen sittlichkeit interessirt. Leipzig: 1845.

5146 Pauli, H. "Geschlechtskrankheiten und Prostitution." Hyg Volksbl (Berlin) 4:211, 223, 1903.

5147 Payenneville. "Nouvelle Organisation de la Lutte Antivenerienne Chez les Prostituees a Rouen." Rev Pra d'Hyg Municip (Paris) 1921, 16:6-14.

5148 Peetermans, N. "Quelques Considerations sur les Moyens a Employer pour Arreter les Progres de la Maladie Venerienne, en Response a Cette Question: Quelles sout les mesures de police medicale les plus propres a arreter la propagation de la maladie syphilitique?" Ann Soc d Sc Med et Nat de Brux 1836:10-15.

5149 Pelman, C. Ueber die Stellung des Staates zur Prostitution." Centralbl f Allg Gsndhtspflg (Bonn) 4:181-199, 1885.

5150 Pemberton, J., et al. "Socio-medical Characteristics of Patients Attending a VD Clinic and the Circumstances of Infection." Br J Vener Dis 48(5):391-6, Oct. '72.

5151 Pequignot, H. "Modern Problems of Antivenereal Campaign; closing of houses of prostitution." Semaine d Ho Paris (Suppl) 22:204-205, Sep. 21, '46.

5152 Pellegrin,____. "Antivenereal Campaign in the Maritime Alps During the Year 1962." Prophyl Sanit Morale 35:161-6, Jun. '63. In French.

5153 Pellegrin,____. "Apropos of the Suppression of the Health and Social Card-Index of Prostitution." Prophyl Sanit Morale 33:12-33, Jan. '61. In French.

5154 Pellegrin, J., et al. "Remarks on Recent Syphilis Among Prostitutes." Prophyl Sanit Morale 36:17-9, Jan. '64. In French.

5155 Pennink,____. "Wetelijke Regeling van het Toezight op de Prostitutie is Staatspligt." Versi v de Vereen t Verbet d Volksgzndht (Ultrecht) 5:90-95, 1870.

5156 Pepin, P. La Prostitution Cause de l'Accroissement Continu de la Syphilis dans la Region Parisienne. Paris: 1929, 82 pp.

5157 Percy, J. F. "Prostitution: its cause and the relation of the medical profession to its abolishment." Tri-state Med J (Keokuk) 1:61-73, 1893-4.

5158 Perdrup, A. "Effect of the Development of Social Hygiene on the Occurence of Gonorrhea." Arch Klin Exp Dermatol 227(1):640-4, '66.

5159 Perin, L., et al. "Occurence of Trichomonas Vaginalis in Prostitutes; possible role of etiology of urethritis in general." Bull Soc Franc Dermat et Syph 58:364-367, Jul.-Oct. '51.

5160 Perin, L., et al. "Penicillin Therapy in Syphilis of Prostitutes." Bull Soc Franc Dermat et Syph 59:258-62, May-Jun. '54.

5161 Perin, L., et al. "Systematic Frei Reaction in Prostitutes." Ann de Dermat et Syph 6:23-26, Jan. '46.

5162 Perin, L., et al. "Venereal Morbidity of Prostitutes of Parisian Region: conclusions to be drawn." Semaine Hop Paris 26:4351-4354, Nov. 14, '50.

5163 Persenaire,____. "Eenige Opmerkingen Betreffende het Onderzoek van Postituees." Tijdschr v Inland Geneesk (Batavia) 8:17-23, 1900.

5164 Petersen, O. "Prostitution et Maladie Veneriennes en Russe." Confer Internat p la Prophyl de la Syph et d Mal Ven (Brussels) 1(2):261-305, 1899.

5165 Petithan,___. "De la Prostitution." Ann Soc Med.-Chir de Liege 26:122-129, 1887.

5166 Petrini de Galatz,_____. "Prostitution et Maladies Veneriennes en Roumanie." Confer Internat p la Prophyl de la Syph et d Mal Ven 1(2):44-76, 1899.

5167 Pfeiffer. "Das Wohnungselend der Grossen Stadte und Seine Beziehungen zur Prostitution und den Geschlectskrankheiten." Ztschr f Bekampf d Geschlechtskrankh 1:135-144, 1903.

5168 "Physician Discusses the False Security Provided by Licensed Prostitution." J Soc Hygiene 23:209-12, Apr. '37. France.

5169 Pibarot, J. A Propos du Controle de la Prostitution; une novelle phase; le sanitarisme. Lyon: St-Etienne, 1948, 103 pp.

5170 Picek, S. "Corporeal and Sexual Constitution of Prostitutes of Lower Social Classes; importance of intersexualism in their sexology." Cesk Dermat 16:301-308, '36. Abstract in J Obst and Gynaec Brit Emp 45:89-91, Feb. '38.

5171 Pierson, H. Een Onderzoek Naar de Prostitutie Kwestie. 'sGravenhage, 1879.

5172 Pierson, H. Openbare Brief aan A. Aletrino Naar Aanleiding van Diens Brochure: "Over Eenige Oorzaken der Prostitutie". Amsterdam, 1902.

5173 Pierson, H. Prostitutie van de Wetenschap; Antwoord aan A. P. Fokker, hoogleeraar in de hygiene, op diens brochure: "De prostitutiekwestie." s'Gravenhage, 1879.

5174 Pierson, H. Die Prostitutionsfrage vom Standpunkte der Medizinischen Wissenschaft, des Rechtes und der Moral. Mulheim a. d. Ruhr: 1885.

5175 Pietra Santa, P de. "Reorganisation du Service Sanitaire Relatif a la Prostitution." J d'Hyg (Paris) 15:349-355, 1890.

5176 Pignier, F. "Ignorance and Predjudice in the Matter of Prostitution." Prophyl Sanit Morale 34:19-30, Jan. '62. In French.

5177 Pinard, M. "Question of Regulating of Prostitution in Prevention of Venereal Diseases." Bull Gen de Therap 188:51057, '37.

5178 Pinard, M. "Transmission of Venereal Diseases by Prostitutes; danger of regulation of prostitution." Prophylax Antiven 10:367-373, Jul. '38. Comment by Perin 10:583-595, Oct. '38. Comment by Robert 10:596-599, Oct. '38.

5179 Pini, C. Dati Statistici dall' anno 1869 al 1887 sulle Visite Mediche nelle Malattie Venereo-sifilitiche in Relazione alla Questione Igienica. Firenze. 1887.

5180 Pini, G. "Sorveglianza sulla Prostituzione." Gior d Soc Ital d'Ig (Milan) 5:525-543, 1883.

5181 Pinkus, F. "Beitrage zur Kenntnis der Berliner Prostitution. Die Syphilis der Prostituierten." Arch f Dermat u Syph (Vienna and Leipzig) 113:805-814, 1912.

5182 Pinkus, F. "Prevelence of Syphilitic Infections Among Prostitutes in Berlin; statistics." Med Klin 24:1077-1078, Jul. 13, '28.

5183 Pinkus, F. "Venereal Diseases in Prostitutes." Med Klin 23:1888-1889, Dec. 9, '27.

5184 Pippingskold, J. "Des Mesures Hygieniques a l'Egard de la Prostitution en Finlande; communication faite aussi Congres period. internat. d. sciences medicales a Berlin, 1890." Finska Lak Sallsk Handl 33:1-19, 1891.

5185 Pippingskold, J. "La Surveillance de la Prostitution au Pointe de Vue Prophylactie de la Syphilis." Fisnska Lak.-sallsk Handl 30:57-66, 1888.

5186 Pippingskold, J. "View and Questions on Hygienic Treatment of Prostitution." Finska Lak Sallsk Handl 32:419-434, 1890.

5187 Platts, W. M. "Venereal Disease in New Zealand." Br J Vener Dis 45(1):61-6, Mar. '69.

5188 Poenaru-Caplescu, C. "Sifilisul si Prostitutia." Spitalul (Bucarest) 23:348-356, 1903.

5189 Poenaru-Caplescu, C. "Sifilisul si Prostitutuinea in Romania." Presa Med Rom 8:4-6, 1902; Bull Med (Bucarest) 5:4, 1902.

5190 Poggio, R. H. "La Prostitucion y la Sifilis." Gac Med (Madrid) 9:265, 273, 281, 289, 1853.

5191 Pokrovskaya, M. I. "Prostitutsiya i Alkoholizm." J Russk Obsh Okhran Narod Zdrav (St. Petersburg) 15:216-223, 1905.

5192 Polenz, J. M. "New Therapy?" Am J Psychiatry 127(6):844, Dec. '70.

5193 Pontoppidan, E. "Kontrollen Med Prostitutionen og de Veneriske Syndommes Udbredelse." (...and propagation of venereal diseases). Hosp.-Tid (Copenhagen) 10:517-527, 1892, 3, R.

5194 Pontoppidan, E. "The Hygienic Measures Against Prostitution." Ugesk f Laeger (Copenhagen) 5:1129-1134, 1898, 5, R.

5195 Pontoppidan, E. "La Raison de Bon Sens." Bull Soc Internat de Prophyl... (Brussels) 1:140-155, 1901.

5196 Pontoppidan, E. "De l'Unite Administrative de la Visite et du Traitement Hospitalier des Prostituees." Confer Internat p la Prophyl de la Syph et d Mal Ven 1(app):45-48, 1899.

5197 Pontoppidan, E. "What can be done, apart from the control of prostitution, to combat the spread of venereal disease?" Ugesk f Laeger 7:289-301, 1900, 5, R.

5198 Pontoppidan, E. "Physicians and the Control of Prostitution." Ugesk f Laeger (Copenhagen) 8:241, 268, 1901, 5, R.

5199 Posada, J. L. "Health Conditions of Prostitution in a Semirural District." Actas Dermo-Sif 30:581-588, May '39.

5200 Pospelow, __. "De la Surveillance de la Prostitution a Moscou." Cong Internat de Dermat et de Syph C. r. Paris, 1890, 835-843.

5201 Pospieloff, A. "Sanitary Supervision of Prostitution in Paris and Brussels." Veqstnik Obsh Hig Sudeb i Prakt Med (in Russian) St. Petersb. 8:2;105-138, 1890

5202 Potuzil, F. "The Legal Remedy for Prostitution." Cesk Zdrav 14(11):613-5, Nov '66.

5203 Powers, A. H. "Prostitution and Venereal Diseases." N Eng M Gaz (Boston) 40:559-561, 1905.

5204 "The Practical Working of the Laws Against Syphilis in Paris." Med Times and Gaz (London) 1:44, 1870.

5205 Prakken, J. R. "Hygienists and Moralists in the Fight Against Venereal Disease in the 19th Century." Med Tijdschr Geneeskd 117(28):1042-9, Jul. 14, '73.

5206 Pressl,___. "Syphilis und Prostitution." Oesterr San Beamte (Vienna) 1:112, 133, 1888.

5207 "Projet de loi Concernant la Prostitution et la Prophylaxie des Maladies Veneriennes." Soc Fran de Prophyl San et Mor Bull Par., 7:34-44, 1907.

5208 "Prophylaxie Publique de Syphilis." Pratique Med (Paris) 1:205-277.

5209 "Sur la Prophylaxie de la Syphilis." (discussion) Bull Acad de Med (Paris) 18:155, 187, 1888.

5210 "Die Prophylaxis der Syphilismit Bezeihung auf die Regelung der Prostitution." Wien Med Presse 14:865-872, 1873.

5211 "A Proposito di una lettera del Prof. Celso Pellizzari sulla Prostituzione e Profilassi Pubblica della sifilide; soliloquio di un vecchio medico." Osservatore (Torino) 39:582-592, 1888.

5212 "Prostitution." Compt.-rend Soc Med de Chambery 1854:52-56.

5213 "Prostitution." (editorial) Med Times and Gaz (London) 16:90, 1858.

5214 "Prostitution et Syphilis." Press Med Belg Brus. 1882.

5215 "Prostitution: a health or law enforcement problem." J Soc Hygiene 10:363-5, Jun. '24.

5216 "Prostitution: its medical aspects." Lancet (London) 1:173, 198, 1858.

5217 "Prostitution and National Health." Westm 92:179.

5218 "De la Prostitution (in Lyons)." Compt Rend Cons d'Hyg Pub du Rhone 1891:417-428.

5219 "Prostitution is an Axis Partner." Am J Pub Health and Nation's Health 32:85, Jan. '42.

5220 "Prostitutionssporgsmaalet." Ugesk f Laeger 17:686-691, 1888, 4 R.

5221 "La Prostituzione data alla sorvrglianza dei municipai." Gior Ital d Mal Ven (Milan) 17:355-360, 1876.

5222 Prowe, ___. "Gonorrhoe und Prostitution." Berl Klin Wchrschr 38:1142-1144, 1901.

5223 "Public Health's Progress to Prevent Young Women and Girls From Involvement in Prostitution and Promiscuity." Survey 79:152, May '43.

5224 Puschmann, T. "Zur Prostitutionfrage." Wien Klin Wchnschr 7:387-389,1894.

5225 Pusey, William Allen. The History of Epidemiology of Syphilis. Springfield, Ill.: Charles C. Thomas, 1933, p.5. See also Jeanselme, E., Histoire de la Syphilis. Paris: G. Doin, 1931.

5226 Quantin, Emile. "Prostitucion y Sifilis." (Transl.) Rev Espan de Sif y Dermat (Madrid) 2:250-256, 1900.

5227 Quantin, Emile. Prostitution et Syphilis. Paris: F. Savy, 1863, 70 pp.

5228 "Quelles sont les mesures de police medicale les plus propres a arreter la propagation de la maladie syphilitique?" Ann Soc d Sc Med et Nat de Brux 1836:15-18.

5229 "Quelles sont les mesures de prophylaxie publique a prendre, sous forme de dispositions legales, contre les maladies veneriennes notamment en ce qui concerne les points suivants relativement a la prostitution; 1: La prostitution des mineures; 2: L'action des pouvoirs publics, soit dans l'internat de la moralite et de la tranquillite publiques, soit au point de vue sanitaire; 3: Les proxenetes et les souteneurs." Confer Internat p la Prophyl de la Syph et d Mal Ven (Brussels, 1902) 2:54-276, 1903.

5230 "Question of State Interference to Provide for the Disinfection of Prostitutes." Rep Med Off Privy Council, 1868 (London) 11:10-20, 1869.

5231 Queyrat, L. "Hygenic Aspects of Regulation." Rev d'Hyg 49:481-498, Jul. '27.

5232 Quinche, ___. "Ueber die Prostitution und deren Beausichtigung." Med Ztg (Berlin) 20:165, 169, 1851.

5233 Rabut, R. "Is the Suppression of the Medical Card Index on Prostitution Responsible for the Resurgence of Syphilis?" Prophyl Sanit Morale 33:199-203, Oct. '61. In French.

5234 Raddi, A. "L'igiene in rapporto alla quistione sociale." Gior di Med Pubb (Naples) 24:353-370, 1893.

5235 Ramanos, R. "Venereal Disease and Prostitution on Northern Boundary." Dia Med 21:934, May 16, 1949.

5236 Ramazzotti, P. "Parte dei Servizi Governativi in Milano per la Profilassi Generale delle Malattie Veneree (dispensario celtico; vigilanza sanitaria alle meretrici)." Gior d r Soc Ital, d'Ig (Milan) 29:1-38, 1907.

5237 Ramirez, J. J. "La Reglamentacion de la Prostitucion como Elemento Profilactico de la Syphilis." Actas y Mem d IX Cong Internac de Hig y Demog (Madrid, 1898) 2:211-216, 1900.

5238 "Rapporto della Commissione Incaracata daala Reale Accademia Medico-Chirurgica d'investigare Quale Siano i Provvedimenti piu atti a Minorare la Diffusione delle Malattie Veneree." Goir d r Accad Med-Chir di Torino 2s. 3:347-361, 1848.

5239 Rappaport, M. F. "After Ten Years; helping prostitutes help themselves." J Soc Hygiene 39:209-15, May '53.

5240 Rapport der Heeren Prof. van Overbeck de Meijer, Prof. A. P. Fokker en Dr. Menno Huizinga, aan de Nederlandsche Maatschappij tot Bevordering der Geneeskunst (...toSt betengeling van syphilitische en venerische ziekten). s'Gravenhage, 1882. Abstract in Nederl Tijdschr v Geneesk (Amsterdam) 18:161-168, 1882, 2, R.

5241 Ratcliff, J. D. "War Against Syphillis; America's first quarantine hospital for diseased women." Collier's 111:14-15+, Apr. 10, 1943.

5242 Rause, F. de "Note Statistique sur la Fecondite des Prostituees." Bull Soc d'Anthrop de Par 12:214-216, 1877, 2, s.

5243 Rawls, W. E. "The Association of Herpesvirus Type 2 and Carcinoma of the Uterine Cervix." Am J Epidemiology 89(5):547-54, May '69.

5244 Reclam, C. C. "Die Ueberwachung der Prostitution." Deutsche Vrtljschr f Off Gsndhtspflg (Brnschwg.) 1:379-395, 1869.

5245 "The Registration of Infectious Disease." San Rec (London) 1879, x, 51.

5246 Regnault, F. "Syphilis et Prostitution." Presse Med (Paris) 14:601, 1906.

5247 "The Regulation of Prostitution as a Sanitary Measure." Med Rec (New York) 1879, xvi, 205.

5248 "The Relations of Medical Officers of Health." Med Eng (Liverpool) 2:149-151, 1876.

5249 "Relazione delta Commissione incaricata dello studio del quesito: Sorveglianza delle prostituzione e provvedimenti sanitarii relativi." Gior Veneto Med Venezia, 13:308-326, 1870.

5250 Relu, L. La Syphilis et la Reglementation de la Prostitution. Montpellier, 1911, 35 pp.

5251 Renault, P. "Prostitution in Relation to the Spread of Syphilis; importance of medical surveillance in prevention." Rev de Med (Paris) 50:729-738, Dec. '33.

5252 "Report on an Inquiry by Public Health Offices on the Occurence of Venereal Diseases." Z Haut Geschlechtskr 46(24):857-60, Dec. 15, 1971.

5253 "De la Responsibilite du Medicin Charge d la Visite Sanitaire des Prostituees." J de Med de Par 19:152, 1907, 2, s.; Rev de Med Leg 15:117-119, 1907.

5254 Reuss, L. "Influence de la Prostitution Habituelle sur la Sante des prostituees; frequence des maladies communes et generales chez les prostituees." Ann d'Hyg (Paris) 19:289-303, 1888, 3, s.

5255 Reuss, L. La Prostitution au QPoint de Vue de l'Hygiene et de l'Administration. Paris: 1889.

5256 Rev Med Franc d Extreme-Orient 17:131-141, Feb. '39. (article).

5257 Rey, A. "Du Bulletin Sanitaire des Filles Publiques." Alger Med 1881, 9:179-183.183.

5258 Rey, A. and L. Julien. "Prostitution et Maladies Veneriennes en Algerie." Confer Internat p la Prophyl de la Syph et d Mal Ven (Brussels) 1899, i, fasc.2, pp.726-732.

5259 Reynolds, C. R. "Prostitution as a Source of Infection With Venereal Diseases in the Armed Forces." Am J Pub Health 30:1276-82, Nov. '40.

5260 Reynolds, J. B. "Recent Progress in Social Hygiene in Europe." Soc Hygiene 1:165-82, Mar. '15.

5261 Ries, K. "Zur Prostitutionsfrage." Med Cor Bl d Wurttemb Arztl Ver (Stuttgart) 71:445, 457, 469, 1901; Aerztl Rundschan (Munich) 11:337, 437, 1901.

5262 Rietema, F. A. "Die Prostitutionsfrage." Monatsch f Prakt Dermat (Hamburg) 12:329, 376, 425, 1891.

5263 Rittmann, ____. "Die Prostitution vom Standpunkte der Phisiologie, Anthropologie und Pathologie." Allg Wien Med Ztg 17:107, 115, 123, 132, 140, 149, 156, 165, 175, 204, 216, 259, 274, 290, 326, 342, 356, 394, 411, 428, 1872.

5264 Robinson, O. D. E., and J. G. Wilson. "Tuberculosis Among Prostitutes; report of investigation made in connection with a study of the disease in Cincinnati." Am J Public Health 6:1164-72, Nov. '16. Tables. Report of this investigation is published as Public Health Bulletin no.73 by the U. S. Public Health Service. The investigation was made at the joint request of the Board of Health and Anti-Tuberculosis League of Cincinnati, extending from Mar. '14, to Apr. '15.

5265 Robinson, W. J. "How to Deal With the Problem of Prostitution." Am J Urol 9:381-390, 1913.

5266 Rodet, A. "Des Mesures d'Hygiene Publique qui Doivent etre Conseillees a l'autorite pour empecher la propagation du virus syphilitique." Union Med (Paris) 10:162, 199, 306, 355, 1861, 2. s.

5267 Rodiet, A. "La Prostitution Surveillee a Paris Depuis a Guerre." Ann d Med Leg (Paris) 4:486-488, 1924.

5268 Rodrigues Alves, Luis. O Servico do Estasdo. Sao Paulo: 1952.

5269 Rohe, G. H. "The Prevention of Syphilis." Balt Phys and Surg 5:33, 1876.

5270 Rona, ___. "Prostitution et Maladies Veneriennes en Hongrie." Confer Internat p la Prophyl de la Syph et d Mal Ven (Brussels, 1899) 1(2):207; 2(com pt.2):0, 1900.

5271 Rosenstein, Julius. Our Nation's Health Endangered by Poisonous Infection Through the Social Malady. San Francisco: Town Talk Press, 1913, 56 pp.

5272 Rosenstirn, J. "Should the Sanitary Control of Prostitution be Abandoned?" Med Record (New York) 85:1066-1071, '14.

5273 Rosenthal, T. and G. Kerchner. "Venereal Disease in Prostitutes." Am J Syph, Gonor and Ven Dis 32:256-264, May '48.

5274 Rosso, G., and G. Bottino. "Current Pathogenetic Aspects of Carcinoma of the Uterine Cervix." Minerva Ginecol 27(4):304-10, Apr. '75.

5275 Rozanoff, P. "Prostitution, Venereal Diseases, and their Treatment in Manchuria." Russk Vrach (St. Petersburg) 1:503, 1902.

5276 Ruggles, E. W. "The Physician's Relation to the Social Evil." N Y Med J (etc.) 85:159-161, 1907.

5277 Russia. Ministry of the Interior. Medical Department. Special Commission. "Rules of the Commission to Examine into the Matter of Establishing a Committee of Medical Police in Moscow, in Connection With the Project of a General Organization of Supervision of Prostitution in the Empire." Vestnik Obsh Hig, Sudeb i Prakt Med (St. Petersburg) 1901:41-58.

5278 Saavedra, A. M. (article). Medicina 16:117-121, Sep. 25, 1936 (suppl). Mexico.

5279 Saavedra, A. M. "Problem in Mexico." 20:173 (suppl), Nov. 10, '40; 20:181 (suppl), Nov. 25, '40; 20:187 (suppl), Dec. 10, '40.

5280 Sainte-Croix, A. de, et al. "Closing of Houses of Prostitution in Strasbourg has Caused Diminution in Venereal Diseases, particularly Syphilis." Prophylax Antiven 2:267-294, May '30.

5281 Salomonsen, L. W. "Prostitutionssporgsmaalet." Ugesk f Laeger (Copenhagen) 1:165-179, 1880, 4, R.

5282 Samson, J. W. "Sexual-hygienische Bedeutung der Prostituierten-Tuberkulose." Arch f Frauenh u Eugenetik (Berlin) 9:52-56, '23.

5283 Samson, J. W. "Tuberkulose und Prostitution." Berl Klin Wchnsche 1921, lviii, 1078-1081.

5284 Sandman, F. "Studier Ofver Gonnorre hos Prostituerade." Hygiea (Stockholm) 6:1029-1055, 1906, 2, f.

5285 Sandouville,____ de. Des Mesures Administratives a Prendre dans le but d'Empecher la Propagation des Maladies Veneriennes. Avec des notes de M. Trebuchet. Paris: 1849.

5286 Sandwith,____. "Prostitution et Maladies Veneriennes en Egypte." Confer Internat p la Prophyl de la Syph et d Mal Ven 1(2):713-725, 1899.

5287 "Sane Program." La State Bd Health Q Bull 8:167, S '17. Program adopted and agreed to by the delegates at a conference on suppression of venereal diseases held in San Francisco, Jul. 31, 1917, is given.

5288 "Sanitary Supervision of Prostitutes." Brit and For M.-Chir Rev (London) 45:87-110, 1870.

5289 Sanjuan, M. "De la Prostitution Clandestinaen su Relacion con las Enfermedades Venereas." Rev Soc Espan de Hig (Madrid) 2:193-193, 1884.

5290 Santoliquido, Rocco. Le Malattie Veneree. Available in 1946 from Geneva: Federation Abolitionniste Internationale, 23 pp.

5291 Sarason, D. "Vorschlag Einer Neuen Organisation des Prostitutionswesens." Ztschr f Bekampf d Geschlechtskrankh 16:217-232, 1915-1916.

5292 Scareuzio and Soffiantini. "Craniometria della Prostituzione." Arch di Psichiat (etc.) (Torino) 7:29, 1886.

5293 Scheiber, A. Un Fleau Social: Le probleme medico-policier de la prostitution. Paris: Librairie de Medicis, 1946, 317 pp.

5294 Schemitz, R. "Tuberculosis, Important Cause of Misery and Prostitution." Gazz Internaz Med.-chir 34:163, Mar. 15, '29.

5295 Schlasberg, H. J. "Zur Frage von der Heilbarkeit der Gonorrhoe bei Prostituierten." DermQat Ztschr (Berlin) 20:953-967, 1913.

5296 Schlenzka, A. "Bekampfung der Gesclechtskrankheiten und Prostitution." Ztschr f Bekampf d Geschlechtskrankh (Leipzig) 17:227-236, 1916-17.

5297 Schmid, F. "Die prostitution und die venerischen Krankheiten in der Schweiz." San Demog Wchnbull d Schweiz (Bern) 1900:217, 231, 252, 266, 286, 300, 347, 360, 380, 412. Also, transl: Confer Internat p la Prophyl de la Syph et d Mal Ven (Brussels, 1899) 1(2):226, 1899; 2(com.)(2):48, 1900.

5298 Schneider, F. "Voorstel ter Wering van Prostitutie en Syphilis." Geneesk Courant Tiel 43(32-33), 1889.

5299 Schneider, Karl. Studien Uber Personlichtkeit und Schicksal Eingeschriebener Prostituierter. Berlin: J. Springer, 1921, 229 pp.

5300 Schofield, C. B., et al. "Blood Ethonal Concentration in Patients Attending Special Clinics in Glascow." Br J Vener Dis 51(5):340-4, Oct. '75.

5301 Schrank, J. "Die Prostitution in Paris und deren Regelung." Allg Wein Med Ztg 35:591, 605, 1890.

5302 Schrank, J. "Reformen bei der arztlichen Untersuchung der unter Controle stehenden Prostituirten." Compt.-rend Cong Internat de Med (Moscow 1897) 7:415-419, 1900.

5303 Schrank, J. "Ueber die neueren Gesichtspunkte bei der arztlichen Untersuchung der unter Controle stehenden Prostituirten." Oesterr San.-Wes (Vienna) 6:710-718, 1894.

5304 Schrank, J. "Ueber die Wichtigkeit und die Ausfuhrung der Mikroskopisch-bacteriologischen Untersuchung der Urogenitalsekrete der Unter Controle Stchenden Prostituirten." Allg Wien Med Ztg 36:309, 321, 1891.

5305 Schrank, J. "Vorschlage zur Eindammung der Schadlichen Folgen der Prostitution." Allg Wien Med Ztg 48:375, 1903.

5306 Schwann, A. "Die Unzulanglichkeit der Heutigen Prostituirtenuntersuchung und -behandlung im Allgemainen wie Speziell in Koln, nebst Vorschlagen zu ihrer Verbesserung." Munchen med Wchnschr 1903:1405.

5307 Schweizer,_____. "Ein Beitrag zur Bordellfrage in Rechtlicher Beleuchtung." Monatschr f Harnkr u Sex Hyg (Leipzig) 1:133-139, 1904.

5308 Sciarra, O. "On the Merlin Law--prevention of syphilis: reporting by name of cases of contagious syphilis--official procedure for the crime of contagion." Arch Ital Sci Med Trop Parassitol 46(11):441-4, Nov.-Dec. '65.

5309 Sebek, V. "Current Course of Female Gonorrhea." Cesk Gynekol 37(1):47-8, Feb. '72.

5310 Selhorst, S. B. "Prostitution et Maladies Veneriennes dans les Pays-Bas." Confer Internat p la Prophyl de la Syph et d Mal Ven (Brussels) 1(2):77-92, 1899.

5311 Seligman, E. R. A. "The Sanitary Supervision of Prostitution." Social Dis (N. Y.) 2(1):5-17, 1911.

5312 Sellier, O. M. L'Evolution de la Prophylaxie Antivenerienne chez les Prostituees. Paris: 1943, 74 pp.

5313 Serebryakoff, V. M. "Venereal Diseases Among Tramping Prostitutes of Moscow." Protok Mosk Ven i Dermat Obsh 7:25-31, 1897-8.

5314 Sernaque, F. "Prostitution and Venereal Diseases." Cron Med (Lima) 56:286-288, Oct. '39.

5315 Serra Bartra, M. "La Prostitucion y la Sifilis." Bol Med (Lerida) 6:1025, 1041, 1057, 1907.

5316 Servier,___. "A Propos de la reglementation de l'exercice de la Prostitution des Droits des Populations sur la Femme Prostituee." Ann de Dermat et Syph 2:121-126, 1869-70.

5317 Shtremberg, Kh. F. "Mixed Bed and Dispensary Treatment of the Prostitutes of Yuryeff from Syphilis." Russk J Kozhn i Ven Boliezn (Kharkov) 4:547, 649, 1902; 5:120, 290, 470, 1903.

5318 Shtremberg, Kh. F. "Results of Bacteriological Examinations in Inspection of the Conditions of the Health of the Prostitutes of Yuryev." Russk J Koahn i Ven Boliezn (Kharkov) 2:612, 760, 958, 1901.

5319 Siboulet, A., and L. Egger. "Medico-epidemiologic Problems Posed by Masculine Gonococcal Urethritis (apropos of 10,000 cases)." Bull Inst Natl Sante Rech Med 21(4):737-80, Jul.-Aug. '66.

5320 Sica, M. "Important Problem of Sanitary Organization; hygenic vigilance in communities." Igiene e San Pub 1:236-242, Apr.-Jun. '45.

5321 Sichel, M. "Der Geisterzustand der Prostituierten." Zsch f d Ges Neur u Psychiat 14:445-483, '13.

5322 Sighele, S. and Niceforo, A. "La Mala Vita dans les Grandes Villes." (Transl.) Arch d'Anthrop Crim (Lyon and Paris) 14:663-676, 1899.

5323 Sigmund,___ von. "Ein Gesetz fur die Regelung der Prophylaxis der Syphilis mit Beziehung auf die Regulung der Prostitution." Wien Med Presse 14:697-701, 1873.

5324 Silva, L. "Question of Relations to Anomalies of Teeth." Arch Policia e Ident 1:293-310, '37.

5325 Silva Cardeira, L. da. "Hygiene Publica da Prostitucao." Escholiaste Med (Lisbon) 17:229-232, 1866.

5326 Simon, C., and J. Bralez. "So-called Primary Adenopathy With Presence of Treponema But Without Inoculation Chancre: case of prostitute after ill-founded accusation of contamination; new problem for health dispensaries." Bull Soc Franc de Dermat et Syph 44:111-118, Jan. '37; also Bull Med Paris 51:120-122, Feb. 20, '37.

5327 Singer, A. "Cervical Dysplasia in Young Women." Proc R Soc Med 68(4):236, Apr. '75.

5328 Sirlin, L. (article). Cron Med (Lima) 60:353-356, Dec. '43.

5329 Sirlin, L. "Prostitucion y Enfered des Venereas." Semana Med (Buenos Aires) 1921, xxviii, 556-560.

5330 Smith, H. "Medicosocial Study of Syphilis." Union Med du Canada 74:165-174, Feb. '45.

5331 Snow, W. F. "Relations of Police and Health Officials to the Problems of Prostitution and the Venereal Diseases." J Soc Hygiene 18:340-4, Jun. '32.

5332 Sobrado, L. de. "Es o no Indispensible Tolerar la Prostitucion? En todo caso, como debe vigilarse?" Gac Med (Madrid) 3:116-118, 1847.

5333 "The Social Evil." (editorial) Medicine (Detroit) 12:614, 673, 1906.

5334 "The Social Evil Bill." Weekly M Rev (St. Louis) 23:155, 1891.

5335 Social Health (New Delhi). July 1962-, v.1-, Quarterly.

5336 "Social Hygiene; the problem of prostitution." Conf Char and Correc 1914:197-256.

5337 "Social Hygiene; report of the committee," in Nat. Conf. of Charities and Corrections, Proceedings, 1914, pp.197-205.

5338 "The Social Plagues: syphilis and prostitution." Prophyl Sanit Morale 36:150-51, Jun. '64. In French.

5339 "Social Protection in Peacetime." J Soc Hygiene 32:90-98, Feb. '46.

5340 Solari, Enrique Felix. "Improved Regulation Necessary for Prevention of Venereal Diseases in Buenos Aires." Semana Med 2:1531-1536, Dec. 1, '27.

5341 Soltz-Szots, J., and H. Kokoscka, H. "Treatment of Gonorrhea With Penicillin, Cephloridine, and Doxycycline." Br J Vener Dis 49(2):177-80, Apr. '73.

5342 Somoza, P. "Es Posible Reprimer Eficazmente la Prostitucion? De que medios podran balerse los gobiernos para atenuar sus inconvenientes?"Siglo Med (Madrid) 26:434, 497, 562, 658, 690, 754, 1879.

5343 Sonnenberg, E. "Regulation of Prostitution." Medyeyna (Warsaw) 33:195, 216, 233, 1905.

5344 Sormani, J. "De la Prophylaxis de las Enfermedades Venereas y Especialmente de la Syphilis." Rev Med.-quir (Buenos Aires) 20:95, 148, 160, 179, 1883-4. Also, trans., (abstract) Canada Lancet 16:97-100, 1883-4.

5345 Sousa, C. P. de, and F. N. Brando. "Epidemiological Aspects of Lymphogranuloma Venereum: a study of a group of prostitutes." Br J Vener Dis 37:179-82, Jun. '61.

5346 Souza, J. F. de. "Memoria sobre as medidas a adoptar contra a prostituicao no paiz." Ann Brazil de Med (Rio de Jan.) 38:317, 343, 372, 1876-7.

5347 Souza Costa, ____. "Da Prostituicao Como Causa d Desenvolvimento e Propagacao da Syphilis; necessidade de um Regimen Sanitario para a Prostituicao no Rio de Janiero." Uniao Med (Rio de Janiero) 1:19-26, 1881.

5348 Spault, L. "Sexual Behavior and Affective Disorders." Dis Nerv Syst 36:644-7, Dec. '75.

5349 Sperk, Eduard L. Oeuvres Completes--Syphilis, Prostitution, Etudes Medicales Diverses. 2v. Paris: O. Doin, 1896.

5350 Sperk, Eduard L. "On the measures to prevent the spreading of syphilis and prostitution." Arch Sudebnoi Med (St. Petersburg) 5(pt.3, no.3):67-84, 1869.

5351 Sperk, Eduard L. "Scientific contributions to the propositions in the report of the city committee on general health, concerning medico-police reforms in regulating prostitution and controlling syphilis." Voyenno-med J (St. Petersburg) 158(3):151-182, 1887.

5352 Sperk, Eduard L. "Theories of statistics of disease and death resulting from prostitution and syphilis." Vestnik Sudeb Med... (St. Petersburg) 1(3):1-21; 2:1-36, 1885. Also, transl.: Vrtljschr f Dermat (Vienna) 13:411-435, 1886.

5353 Spillman, A. "Discovery and Therapy of Carriers of Virulent Spirochaeta Pallida Among Supervised Prostitutes." Ann d Mal Ven 29:732-736, Oct. '34.

5354 Spillman, L., and A. Spillman. "Good Results of Epidemiologic Method in Antisyphilitic Prophylaxis and in Combat Against Clandestine Prostitution." Ann d Mal Ven 30:330-336, May '35.

5355 Spillman, A. "Researches on Origin of New Cases of Syphilis; hospitaliztion of contagious persons ; role of prostitution in contamination; statistics from Fournier Dispensary in 1934." Prophlax Antiven 7:429-439, Jul. '35.

5356 Spillman, L., and Zuber. "Syphilis et Prostitution a Nancy." Rev Med d l'est (Nancy) 45:639-648, 1913.

5357 Spillmann, P. "Internationale Enquete uber die Beziehungen Zwischen Prostitution und Tuberkulose." Tuberculosis (Leipzig) 5:32-35, 1906.

5358 Spillmann, P. "Tuberculose et Prostitution." Cong Internat de la Tuberc (Paris, 1905) 2:576-579, 1906.

5359 Spindler, A. "Relation Between Frequency of Chancroid and Frequency of Prostitution." Arch f Dermat u Syph 154:292-299, '28.

5360 Spool, A. R. "Remarks on the Question of Prostitution." Duodecim (Helsinki) 21:209-212, 1905.

5361 Stamm, H. T. Die Verhutung der Geschlectlichen Ansteckung. Zurich: Schmidt, 1886.

5362 Staveren, W. B. van. De Bezwaren Gehandhaafd; Critiek op de "Bedenkingen" der Heeren T. Broes van Dordt, arts M. Polak en arts C. F. Th. von Ziegenweidt in zake de reglementeering der prostitutie. Leiden: 1901.

5363 Stern, C. "Die Reform der Arztlichen Aufsicht uber Prostituierte." Ztschr f Bekampf d Geschlechtskr (Leipzig) 6:113-127, 1907.

5364 Stites, F. M. "The Protection of the Innocent from Venereal Disease Infection and Prostitution." Kentucky Med J 59(2):16-21, 1907.

5365 Stoffer, S. S. "A Gynecologic Study of Drug Addicts." Am J Obstet Gynecol 101(6):779-83, Jul. 15, '68.

5366 Stokes, J. H. "In Control of Venereal Diseases." Arch Mex Ven Sif y Dermat 2:5-11, '43.

5367 Stokes, H. "Prostitution in Venereal Disease Control." Pa Health pp.6-7+, Jan. '43.

5368 Stokes, J. H. "A Statement on Prostitution in Venereal Disease Control." Ven Dis Information 23:195-8, May '42.

5369 Stokes, J. H. "Statement on Prostitution in Venereal Disease Control." Rev de Med y Cir (Barranquilla) (num 7) 14:39-51, Jul. '47.

5370 Stone, A. K. "Prostitution; the relation of the experience of Europe to the solution of the problem in Boston." Boston M and S J 1895, 133:29-32. Discussion, 42-45.

5371 Stoukowenkoff, ____. La Reglementation Jugee Theriquement au Point de Vue la Syphiligraphie Moderne. Geneva: Federation Abolitionniste Internationale, 1889.

5372 Strauss, H., and I. Grunstein. "Sulfathiazole (Sulfonamide) therapy of 500 Prostitutes; control of venereal disease in wartime." JAMA 121:1187-1190, Apr. 10, 1943.

5373 Stravino, A. La Iperemia Abituale e la Flogosi nei Genatali delle Meretrici. Naples: 1885.

5374 Strielnikoff, E. "Syphilis and the Protective Measures in St. Petersburg." Arch Sudebnoi Med (St. Petersburg) 7(3):23-33, 1871.

5375 Strohl, E. "Zur Prostitutions-Frage." Vrtljschr f Gerichtl Med (Berlin) 24:101-124, 1876, n, F.

5376 Strohmberg, C. Die Prostitution Ein Beitrag zur Offentlichen Sexualhygiene und sur Staadtlichen Prophylaxe der Geschlechtskrankheiten; eine socialmedicinische studie. Stuttgart: Enke, 1899, 218 pp. (Abstr): Confer Internat p la Prophyl de la Syph et d Mal Ven (Brussels) 1(app):159-166, 1899.

5377 Strohmberg, C. "Yuryev Dispensary for Prostitutes. (Inspection Point)" Russk J Kozhn i Ven Boliezen Kharkov, 2:636-639, 1901.

5378 Strohmberg, C. "Die Abnahme der Gonorrhoe bei den Dorpater Prostituirten seit dem Jarhe 1898." St Petersb Med Wehnschr 30:69-72, 1905.

5379 Stroppiana, L., et al. "Medico-social Problems of Prostitution and Its Regulation from the Beginning to Modern Times." Att Accad Stor Arte Sanit 30:141-153, Sep.-Oct. '64. In Italian.

5380 Struve, ___. "Geschlechtskrankheiten und Prostitution." Deutsche Med Wchnschr (Leipzig and Berlin) 46:463-465, 1920.

5381 Stuart, J. "La Prostitution et sa Reglementation; les actes sur les maladies contagieuses en Angleterre et leur influence reelle au point de vue sanitaire." Tribune Med (Paris) 30:268-273, 1898, 2, s.

5382 "Studies on Orgasm." Br Med J 1(801):644, Mar. 11, '72.

5383 "Study of 280 Patients in Venereal Disease Isolation Hospitals of Puerto Rico, February, 1944; report on study of prostitution conducted by Bureau of Medical Social Services of Puerto Rico Department of Health." J Soc Hygiene 30:269-287, May '44.

5384 Stumpf, R. Het Liefdeleven der Romeinen; naar de klassieke bronnen bewerkt en nit medisch oogpunt beschouwd. Amsterdam: n. d.

5385 Sturgis, F. R. "Prostitution; its suppression and control." Medicine (Detroit) 7:470-479, 1901.

5386 Sudhoff, Karl. "The Earliest Printed Literature on Syphilis," in Sigerist, Henry, ed., Monumenta Medica, v.3. Florence: R. Lier and Co., 1925. Facsimile reproductions.

5387 Sudhoff, Karl. Der Ursprung der Syphilis. Leipzig: F. C. W. Vogel, 1913.

5388 "Suite de la Discussion sur le Nouveau Projet de Loi Concernant la Prostitution et la Prophylaxie des Maladies Veneriennes." Soc Franc de Prophyl San et Mor Bull (Paris) 7:148, 172, 1907.

5389 "The Supervision of Prostitutes and the Control of Venereal Diseases." Med News (New York) 70:637, 1897.

5390 "Suppression of Prostitution For the Public Health." Cal State Bd Health Monthly Bul 13:57-8, Aug. '17.

5391 "Surveillance de la Prostitution et Prophylaxie de la Syphilis." (Discussion) Semaine Med (Paris) 9:359, 1889; Rev San de la Province (Bordeaux)6:121, 1889.

5392 Suyematsu, J. "Venereal Diseases of Prostitutes." Kokka Igaku Kwai Zasshi (Tokyo) 1895:215, 260, 296.

5393 "Syphilis et Prostitution." Cong Period Internat d Sc Med Compt-rend 1873. Bruss. and Par., 44-63, 1876.

5394 "Syphilis und Prostitutionsverhaltnisse im Konigreiche Italien." Wien Med Press 14:808-810, 1873.

5395 Tamponi, M. "Syphilitic Contagion From Prostitute Free From Specific Manifestation and With Negative Serological Reactions." Dermosifilografo 9:504-512, Sep. '34.

5396 Tate, J. H. "The Board of Health and Prostitution." Cincin M Rep 2:97-101, 1869.

5397 Taylor, C. B. "On the Impossibility of Detecting Syphilis in the Persons of Women, who are, nevertheless, the most frequent sources of contagion, and the consequent folly and danger of all regulations which ordain the forcible introspection of women for that purpose." Med Enq (Liverpool) 3:153-156, 1877.

5398 Teodoresco, S. "Suggestion for Prophylaxis of Venereal Disease by Suppression of Prostitution." Bull Acad de Med de Roumanie 4:515-520, '39.

5399 Terada, ___. "Statistics of Venereal Diseases in Prostitutes at the Susaki Hospital in Tokyo." Hifubyog kiu Hiniokibyog Zasshi (Tokyo) 3:303-307, 1903.

5400 "Territorial Quarantine." Ariz Med 30(2):108-9, Feb. '73.

5401 Teutsch, R. "Essai de Prophylaxie des Maladies Veneriennes; comment il fant organiser les lupnars." Med Anecdot (Paris) 1902:37-46.

5402 Thomson, W. "Some Results of the Contagious Diseases Acts." Med Press and Cir Lond. 1879, 27:341-344.

5403 Texier, L., et al. "Current Epidemiological and Clinical Problems of Recent Syphilis." J Med Bordeaux 140:1404-9, Sep. '63. In French.

5404 Thiry. "Hygiene Sociale; de la Prostitution." Bull Acad Roy de Med de Bel 20:648-772, Brus. 1886.

5405 Tisne, C. "Prophylaxie de la Syphilis." Ann Med Chir Fran et Etrang Par. 1887, 3:249-264.

5406 Tissot, S. A. D. Dissertatio de Febribus Biliosis---Tentamen de Morbis ex Maustupratione. Lausanne: Marci-Mic Bousequet, 1758.

5407 Tjaden,___. "Geschlechtskrankheiten und Prostitution." Klin Wchn-Berl 2:312-315, 1923.

5408 Tommasoli,_____. "Prostitution et Maladies Veneriennes en Italie." Confer Internat p la Prophyl de la Syph et d Mal Ven (Brussels) 1899, i, fasc.2, 517; 650: 1900, ii, com. pt.2, 42; J de Med de Paris 12:336, 348, 358, 413, 423, 437, 448, 1900, 2, s.; Rev de Med Leg (Paris) 7:229, 278, 311, 1900.

5409 Tomowitz,___. "Ein Beitrag zur Prostitutionsfrage, nach Erfahrungen im Garnisons Spitale No. 2 in Wien." Allg Mil.-arztl Ztg (Vienna) 9:495-497, 1868.

5410 Tooker, H. V. "Venereal Disease, Far From Beaten." Harper 189:545-53, Nov. '44.

5411 Touraine, A., and Solente. "Focus of Syphilis in House of Prostitution; discovery of four chancres of uterine cervix and one of tonsil among inmates." Bull Soc Franc de Dermat et Syph 43:118-123, Jan. '36.

5412 Touraine, A. "Prostitution and Venereal Disease." Presse Med 61:355-57, Mar. 11, '53.

5413 Touraine, A. "Reflections of Doctor A. Touraine on Prostitution, Proxenetism, Homosexuality and the Prevention of Venereal Diseases." Prophyl Sanit Morale 33:112-21, May '61. In French.

5414 Touraine, A., and P. Renault. "Venereal Diseases in Free and Supervised Prostitution." Bull Soc Franc de Dermat et Syph 40:1329-1332, Jul. '33.

5415 Tovar de Lemos, A. A Fecundidade nas Prostitutas. Lisbon: 1946.

5416 Tovar de Lemos, A. Inquerito Acereca da Prostituicao e Doencas Veneras em Portugal, 1950. Lisbon: 1953, 146 pp. A detailed study on prostitution and venereal disease in Portugal in 1950, comparing the results with a similar study made by the author in 1940.

5417 Tovar de Lemos, A. O Servic o de Inspeccao de Toleradas, no ano de 1947. Lisbon: 1948, 56 pp.

5418 Tracy, J. L. "The Attitude of the Medical Profession Towards Prostitution." Cincin Med J 4:196-198, 1889.

5419 Travagli, F. "Prostituzione e Sifilede." Rass Stud Sess 6:157-160, '20.

5420 Treiger, R., et al. "Incidence Sof Frei Reaction in Prostitution of Capital of Sao Paulo." Hospital, Rio de Janeiro 39:239-243, Feb. '51.

5421 Trizar, J. M., et al. "Inform de la Comesion Especial Nombrada para el Estudio de las Conclusiones del Trabajo del Dr. Emilio J. Bansinasi, Sabre Prostitucion." Rassegna di Studi Sess (Rome), 1921, i, 312.

5422 Turanov, N. M. "Progressive Ideas in the Control of Social Diseases in the Pre-October Period." Vestn Dermatol Venerol 43(8):3-9, Aug. '69.

5423 Turanov, N. M., et al. "State of Venereal Disease Morbidity Abroad." Vestn Dermatol Venerol 47(7):60-6, Jul. '73.

5424 Tylvest, B. "Seasonal Variation in Incidence of Crab Lice Among Loose Women in Copenhagen." Acta Dermat Venerol 31:676-78, '51.

5425 Ude, J. "Der Kerpunkt des Prostitutions Problems." Arzt als Crzieher (Munich) 1921, xvii, 53-55.

5426 "Ueberwachung der Prostitution." Gen.-Ber u d Off Gsndhtsw im Rgrngsbz Konigsb (1883-85) 1887:81.

5427 "Ullersperger, J. B. "Die Prostitution." Ztschr f Gerichtl Med (Vienna) 2:60, 72, 115, 1866.

5428 United States. Public Health Service. Case Against the Red Light District. (V. D. no. 54). 8 pp.

5429 United States. Public Health Service. Open Forum on the Open House. 1921.

5430 United States. Public Health Service. What Representative Citizens Think About Prostitution. (V. D. no. 66). 1921, 8 pp.

5431 "V. D. Among the Amateurs." Time 41:46, Mar. 29, 1943.

5432 Valdes-Morel, A. "Prostitution et Maladies Veneriennes au Chili." Confer Internat p la Prophyl de la Syph et d Mal Ven (Brussels) 1(2):733-762, 1899.

5433 Valdettaro, A. "In Favor of Regulation." Cron Med (Lima) 53:128-132, Mar. '36.

5434 Valtan, O. "Larynx in Prostitutes." Morgagni 71:765-767, Apr. 14, '29.

5435 Van Buskirk, E. F. "Social Hygiene." Natl. Conference of Social Work. Proceedings 1924:261-5.

5436 Van Goudoever, L. C. "Een veel Besproken Onderwerp." Ned TijdschQr v Geneesk Amst. 1880, 16:181-192.

5437 Vasconcelos, T. de. "Prostitution." J Med (Portugal) 51:565, Jul. 13, '63.

5438 Vass, H. "The Prostitute and Venereal Disease." World R pp.50-51, Feb. '44.

5439 Vaucel, M., et al. "Frei and Ito-Reenstierna Reactions in Prostitutes of Hanoi." Bull Soc Med Chir de l'Indochine 14:1261-1265, Nov. '36.

5440 Venegas, O. "Precautions to be Taken Against Venereal Disease by Men and Women in Houses of Prostitution." Primer Cong de Med y Cir Nav y Mil de Chile, p.400, 1929.

5441 Vernes, A. "Improving Conditions." Arch Inst Prophylac 8:153-158, '36.

5442 "Venereal Diseases. Extract from the Annual Report of the Chief Medical Officer of the Department of Health and Social Security for the Year 1968." Br J Vener Dis 46(1):76-83, Feb. '70.

5443 Venot, J. "Hygiene. Rapprochments Statistiques entre les deux prostitutions (inscrite et clandestine) au point de vue de la syphilis." J de Med de Bordeaux 2:159-174, 1857, 2, s.

5444 Verchere, F. "Filles Soumises et Insoumises." (Abstr.) Med Mod (Paris) 9:462, 1898.

5445 Verchere, F. "Prostitution et Syphilis." J de Med de Par 10:223, 244, 255, 266, 1898, 2, s. Also (abstr.) Rev Prat d'Obst et de Gynec (Paris) 14:122-131, 1898.

5446 Verchere, F. "Quelle Part Revient a la Prostitution dans la Propagation de la Syphillis et des Maladies Veneriennes?" Confer Internat p la Prophyl de la Syph et d Mal Ven 1(1, C):1-31.

5447 Vibert, ___. "Premier Rapport sur la Prostitution dans ses Rapports avec la Police Medicale, avec la transmission et la prophylaxie des affections syphilitiques." Bull Soc de Med Pub, 1883 (Paris) 6:330-358, 1884; discussion, 434-440.

5448 Vibert, ___. "Reglementation de la Prostitution." Rev d'Hyg (Paris) 5:912-940, 1883; discussion, 6:62-68.

5449 "Vice Rings Flourishing, says Parran." Christian Cent 59:204-5, Feb. 18, '42.

5450 Vicente, C. de. "Hygiene de la Prostitution." Confer Internat p la Prophyl de la Syph et d Mal Ven (Brussels, 1899) 2(com):17-26, 1900.

5451 Vidoni, G. "Il Fattore Costituzionale nella Prostituzione." Note e Riv di Psichiat (Pesaro), 1920, 3, s., viii, 257-287.

5452 Vigne, P., and J. Bonnet. "Results of Study of Frei Reaction with Human Antigen in Prostitutes; 11 cases." Bull Soc Franc de Dermat et Syph (Reunion Dermat., Nancy) 43:228-233, Feb. '36.

5453 Vignes, F. Considerations Medicales et Bio-anthropologiques sur un Groupe de Prostituees Mineures. Paris: 1936, 125 pp.

5454 Villela, E. "Aspects of Antivenereal Campaign." Arch Mex Ven Sif y Dermat 2:17-25, '43.

5455 Villela, E. "Why Repression of Prostitution is Necessary in Control of Venereal Diseases." Inform Enferm Ven pp.3-11, Oct. '46.

5456 Villette, Armand. Du Trottoir a Saint-Lazare. Paris: H. Parville, 1925.

5457 Vinay, C. "La Suppression du Service des Moeurs." Lyon Med 103:1032-1036, 1904.

5458 Vineta Bellaserra, J. "La Sifilis en las Prostitutes." Gaz San de Barcel 14:47-59, 1902.

5459 Virgitti, M. H. and B. Joyeux. "Venereal Danger in Suburban Zone of Hanoi; need of control." Bull Soc Med Chir de l'Indochine 15:73-108, Jan. '37.

5460 Voina, A. "Prostitution and Venereal Diseases in Rumania." Cron Med.-quir de la Habana 56:363, Aug. '30.

5461 Von Peterson, O., and C. Von Sturmer. Die Verbreitung der Syphilis, der Venerischen Krankheiten und der Prostitution in Russland. Berlin: S. Karger, 1899, 170 pp.

5462 Von Sacher-Masoch, L. Die Messalinen Wiens; Geschihcten aus der Guten Gesellschaft. Berlin: n. d.

5463 Vorberg, G. "Freiheit oder Gesunheitliche Ueberwachung der Gewerbsunzucht." Aerztl Rundschau (Munich) 17:133, 146, 160, 173, 1907.

5464 "Vote sur les Conclusions Relatives a la Prostitution." Bull Acad Roy de Med de Belg (Brussels) 1:638-705, 1887, 4, s.

5465 Vvedenski, A. A. "On the Diseases Among Prostitutes upon the Vizhegorod; from the data of the Women's Hospital." Vestnik Obsh Hig., Sudeb i Prakt Med (St. Petersburg) 26(2):170-190, 1895.

5466 Vvedenski, A. A. "Syphilis Among the Prostitutes of Licensed Houses of St. Petersburg (after a one-day census)." Vestnik Obsh Hig, Sudeb i Prakt Med 31(2):71-80, 1896.

5467 W., I. "Die Prostitution und die Nothwendigkeit Ihrer Gesetzlichen Regelung." Wien Med Wchnschr 7:699, 715, 771, 819, 1857; 8:11, 107, 187, 308, 451, 595, 659, 1858.

5468 Wailes, M. A. "Social Aspect of Venereal Diseases; contact tracing and prostitute." Br J Ven Dis 21:15-17, Mar. '45.

5469 Wallis, C. "Problem of Prostitution and Campaign Against Venereal Disease." Arch Mex Ven y Dermat 5:177-189, Jul.-Aug. '46.

5470 Wanatabe, F. "Examination for Diplococcus Gonorrhoeae in Licensed Prostitutes in Taihoku City." Taiwan Igakkai Zasshi 36:2644, Dec. '37.

5471 "War on Venereal Ills; U. S. Public Health Service plans all-out attack." Science N L 42:300, Sep. 7, 1942.

5472 Ward, A. P., et al. "The Incidence of Substances in the Sera of Fertile and Infertile Women Agglutinating Seminal Plasma-Coated Particles." J Reprod Fertil 35(1):97-103, Oct. '73.

5473 Washington, J. E. "A Social Evil Act Needed." Nashville Med J M and S 20:175-183, 1877.

5474 Waugh, M. A. "Studies on the Recent Epidemiology of Early Syphilis in West London." Br J Vener Dis 48(6):534-41, Dec. '72.

5475 Waugh, M. A. "Venereal Diseases in Sixteenth-century England." Med Hist 17(2):192-9, Apr. '73.

5476 Webster, B. "Venereal Disease Control in the United States of America." Br J Ven Dis 46(5):406-11, Oct. '70.

5477 Wegner, A. "Die Grundgedanken Eines Neuen Deutschen Strafgesetzbuchs und die Bekampfung der Prostitution." Dermat Wchnschr (Leipzig and Hamburg) 81:1741-1747, '25.

5478 Weidmann, A. "Current Problems of Venereal Diseases in Women." Munch Med Wchnschr 108(38):1837-43, Sep. 23, '66.

5479 Weissenbacher, E. R., et al. "Investigations on the Incidence of Mycoplasma in the Female Urogenital Tract." Geburtshilfe Frauenheilkd 33(10):763-9, Oct. '73.

5480 Welander, E. "Prostitution et Maladies Veneriennes en Suede." Confer Internat p la Prophyl de la Syph et de Mal Ven (Brussels) 1(2):455-516, bis 1 ch., 1899.

5481 Wenger, P. "Keeping Young Girls From Going Astray." Ztschr f Kinderschutz 20:175, Nov. '28.

5482 Werner, S. "Ueber die Sterblichkeit und die Hautigkeit der Heretitaren Syphilis bei den Kindern der Prostituirten." Monatsh f Prakt Dermat (Hamburg) 24:183, 244, 1897.

5483 Wernich, ____. "Der Gegenwartige Stand der Prostitutionsfrage." Tagebl d Versamml Deutsch Naturf u Aerzte (Cologne, 1888) 61:283, 1889.

5484 "The Westminster Review on the 'Compulsory medication of prostitutes by the state'." Med Eng (Liverpool) 2:125-127, 1876.

5485 Whitwell, J. R. Syphilis in Earlier Days. London: H. K. Lewis and Co., 1940. pp.8-12.

5486 Wigfield, A. S. "Changes Over a Quarter of a Century in the Medico-Social Aspects of Venereal Disease on Tyneside." Br J Vener Dis 49(2):157-62, Apr. '73.

5487 Wilcox, R. R. "Prostitution and Venereal Disease; proportion of venereal disease acquired from prostitutes in Asia; a comparison with France, the United Kingdom, and the United States of America. Br J Vener Dis 38:7-42, Mar. '62.

5488 Willcox, R. R. Progress in Venerology. London: William Heinemann, 1953.

5489 Williams, D. H. "The Suppression of Commercialized Prostitution in the City of Vancouver." J Soc Hygiene. 27:355-72, Oct. '41.

5490 Willson, R. N. "The Relation of the Medical Profession to the Social Evil." JAMA 47:29-32, 1906.

5491 Wilson, H. M. The Medical Control of Prostitution. Geneva: International Abolitionist Federation, 1914.

5492 Wilson, J. M. "Sex in Retrospect." J Am Geriatr Soc 21(9):409-13, Sep. '73.

5493 Wilson, R. N. "The Eradication of Social Diseases in Large Cities." Tr Internat Cong Hyg and Demog (Washington, 1912) 4:115-126, '13.

5494 Willig, D. "Public Health in Soviet Russia, with particular reference to prostitution." M Life 44:197-225, May '37.

5495 Wines, F. H. "Minority Report of the Committee on Prevention of Venereal Diseases." Boston: Am. Public Health Assn., Report 8:334-336, 1883.

5496 Wolbarst, A. L. "Evidence that the Suppression of Public Prostitution is a Factor in the Dissemination of the Venereal Diseases." Am Med (Burlington, Vt.) ns 30:275-287, 1924.

5497 Wolff,____. "Si l'on se Place a un Point du Vue Exclusivement Medical, y a-t-il avantage a maimtenir les maisons de tolerance ou vaut il mieux les supprimer?" (Report) Confer Internat p la Prophyl de la Syph et d Mal Ven (Brussels) 1(1)(3.quest):15-42, 1.ch., 1899.

5498 Wolff,____. "Zur Kasernierungsfrage." Ztschr f Bekampfung d Geschlechtskr (Leipzig) 4:73-76, 1905.

5499 Wolffsheiim, F. S. "Ueber Bordelle." Med Argos (Leipzig) 5:318-329, 1843.

5500 Wood, C. A. "The Question of Prostitution and Its Relations to the Public Health." Canad M Rec (Montreal) 9:49-60, 1880-81; 14:289-300, 1885-6.

5501 Worthington, G. E. "Prostitution: what a city should know about itself." Am City 30:63-6, Jan. '24.

5502 Woolston, Howard Brown. Prostitution in the U. S. New York: Century Co., 1921, 360 pp.

5503 Wren, B. G. "Gonorrhea Among Prostitutes." Med J Aust 1(17):847-9, Apr. 29, '67.

5504 Yabe, T. "Necessite d'une Surveillance Sanitaire sur la Prostitution dans les Ports." Sei-i-Kwai Med J (Tokyo) 18:6-12, 1899. and Confer Internat p la Prophyl de la Syph et de Mal Ven (Brussels) 1899, i, app., 51: 1899, Brussels, 1900, ii, com., 201-209.

5505 Yarros, R. S. "Prostitute as a Health and Social Problem," in Nat. Conference of Social Work, Proceedings, 1919. 1920, pp.220-4.

5506 Yeltzina, Zinaida Ya. (Sanitary Inspection of the Prostitutes of the Samokat Point of the Nizhegorod fair for the Last Five Years). Protok Russk Sif i Dermat Obsh 1892-3 (St. Petersburg) 8:190-204, 1894.

5507 Zablotniak, R. "Antivenereal Activity of the Polish Eugenics Society in Warsaw (1916-39). History of Medical Societies." Przegl Dermotol 57(6):785-91, Nov.-Dec. '70.

5508 Zablotniak, R. "Social Antivenereal Activity of the Polish Eugenic Society in Warsaw (1916-1939). A contribution to the history of medical societies." Pol Med J 10(4):1024-30, '71.

5509 Zarubin, V. I. "Prostitusiya, Venericheskiya, Boliezni i Nizhegorodskaya Yarmarka." (Prostitution, Venereal Diseases, amd the Fair of Nizhni-Novgorod). Meditsina (St. Petersburg) 8:387-390, 1896.

5510 Zahn, M. A., and J. C. Ball. "Patterns and Causes of Drug Addiction Among Puerto Rican Females." Addict Dis 1(2):203-13, '74.

5511 Zeledon, Joaquin. "Proyecciones de la Etapa Antibiotica Sobre la Prostitucion en Centro America." Revista Medica de Costa Rica, pp.4-11, Oct. 1957-58. A special number of the Revista dedicated to Zeledon who founded the review and was interested in the battle against venereal disease.

5512 Zepler, G. "Ueber die Notwendigkeit Einer Kranken-Unterstutzung fur Prostituirte und Einege Andere Maassnahmen zur Bekampfung der Geschlechtskrankheiten." Krankenpflege (Berlin) 2:512-552, 1902-03.

5513 Zinsser, W. H. "Fighting Venereal Diseases--a public trust." Soc Hygiene 4:497-524, Oct. '18.

Not all publications are cited but a sampling are, primarily ones we were able to consult.

5514 Der Abolitionist. Organ fur di Bestrebungen der Internationalen Foderation zur Bekampfung der Staatlich Reglementierten Prostitution. Monthly. Started in 1902 in Dresden.

5515 American Federation for Sex Hygiene and the American Vigilance Assn. were consolidated December, 1913 and the name adopted is the American Social Hygiene Assn., incorporated. The purpose of the Association is to acquire and diffuse knowledge of the established principles and practices which promote social health, to advocate the highest standards of morality, to suppress commercialized vice, etc. Quarterly magazine and monthly bulletin, proceedings, book reviews, and special literature published.

5516 Association for Moral and Social Hygiene. Prostitution. London: by the Assn., 1960, 4 pp.

5517 Association for Moral and Social Hygiene. Held several national conferences, for example: The Second All-India Conference on Moral and Social Hygiene. Calcutta: 1951, 116 pp. Some discussion on prostitution.

5518 American Social Hygiene Association. Formed in 1913. Many publications including: State and Federal Laws, 1916.

5519 American Social Hygiene Association. State Laws Concerning White Slave Traffic. 1916. table.

5520 Britischer, Continentaler, and Allgemeiner Bund. Beschusse des Genfer Congresses. Neuenburg: Bureau des Bulletin Continental, 1877, 20 pp.

5521 British Vigilance Association and the National Committee for the Suppression of Traffic in Persons. Formed in 1885. Issued annual reports. 68th Annual Report Since the Foundation of the National Vigilance Association in 1885. London.

5522 British Vigilance Association and the National Committee for the Suppression of Traffic in Persons. 72nd Annual Report. London: 1959.

5523 Brussels. De l'Organisation de la Traite des Blanches a Bruxelles. Brussels; 1881, 32 pp.

5524 Brussels. Die Organisation der Weissen Sclaverei in Brussel. Berlin: 1882, 32 pp.

5525 Bulletin Abolitionniste. Originally called Le Bulletin Continental. This is the publication of the Federation Abolitionniste Internationale. Originally founded in 1875, it was later combined with Journal du Bien Public. It went through several series, latest starting in 1949.

5526 Bulletin de la Societe de Moralite Publique de Belgique. Issued trimestrially. Was being published in Brussels, 1902.

5527 Committee of Fifteen. Issued annual reports such as Seventeenth Annual Report; for the year ended December 31, 1925. Chicago.

5528 Committee of Fourteen. Issued annual reports. Annual Report for 1926. New York: 1927, 54 pp.

5529 Commonwealth Club of California. Red Light Abatement Law. (Transactions, v.9, no.8). 1914, 35 pp.

5530 Constitution of the National Assn. for the Promotion of Social Purity. (1870?). A series of pamphlets bound under this name are in the British Museum.

5531 "Convention on Traffic in Persons Adopted by Assembly." United Nations Bulletin 8:56-9, Jan. 1, 1950.

5532 Coote, W. A. A Vision and its Fulfillment; history of the origin of the work of the Vigilance Assn. for the Suppression of the White Slave Traffic. National Vigilance Assn., 1910, 189 pp.

5533 Crowdy, R. E. "Opium Traffic and the Work of the Social Section of the League of Nations," in Geneva Institute of International Relations, Problems of Peace, 2d series. 1st-7th series 1927-33, pp. 195-211.

5534 Crowdy-Thornhill, Rachel. International Bureau for the Suppression of Traffic in Persons; history and program of the work. London, 1952. 8 pp.

5535 Dokumente der Frauenqqq_. Vienna: bimonthly. Was being published in 1902.

5536 Dyer, Alfred. Six Years Labour and Sorrow; the fourth report of the London Committee for Suppressing the Traffic in British Girls for the Purposes of Continental Prostitution. London: Dyer Bros., 1885, p.2.

5537 Echanges. No. 43 Toussaint, 1949, Paris, 40 pp. A review devoted to battling female slavery, but considerable material on prostitution.

5538 Falconer, M. P. "Report of the Committee on Social Hygiene." National Conference of Charities and Correction. Proceedings 1915:241-52.

5539 Fallot, T. La Femme Esclave. Geneva: Federation Abolitionniste Internationale, n. d., before 1902.

5540 Federation Abolitionniste Internationale Contre la Reglementation de la Prostitution. Aspects Actuels de la Prostitution. Congres de Bruxelles. Sep. 6-9, 1947. Paris: 1947, 88 pp.

5541 Federation Abolitionniste Internationale. Bulletin Abolitionniste. Geneva: 1939-.

5542 Federation Abolitionniste Internationale. Proceedings of the various Congresses: 1877, 1883, 1889, 1904, 1908, 1913, 1927. Separate volumes.

5543 Federation Abolitionniste Internationale. L'Integrite Intersexuelle des Peuples et les Gouvernements, XXXII, 811 pp. n. d.

5544 Federation Abolitionniste Internationale. Un Noveau Regime des Moeurs, 512 pp., n. d.

5545 Federation Abolitionniste Internationale. La Lutte Contre la Regelementation de la Prostitution. 27 pp., before 1942.

5546 Federation Abolitionniste Internationale. Qu'est-ce que la Federation Abolitionniste, 8 pp., before 1942.

5547 Federation Abolitionniste Internationale. Situation Abolitionniste Mondiale. 6 pp., 1944.

5548 Federation Abolitionniste Internationale. Responses Donnees par Deux Souverains Pontifes...a un appel en faveur de la FAI. Geneva: 1955, 16 pp.

5549 Femmes Esclaves. Supplement au no. 193 de Sillage (Paris). 1955(?).

5550 Guardian Society, London. Report of the Provisional Committee of the...for the preservation of public morals by providing temporary asylum for prostitutes (etc.). London: 1816.

5551 Het Maandblad. The Hague: published monthly in 1902.

5552 House of Mercy; a reformatory for fallen women and girls, New York City. Annual Reports of the managers. New York: 1874-5.

5553 International Abolitionist Federation. London: F. C. Bank, 1877, 98 pp.

5554 International Bureau for the Suppression of Traffic in Persons. Annual Report, 1955. London: 8 pp.

5555 International Bureau for the Suppression of Traffic in Persons. Traffic in Persons. (Annual Report, 1959). London: 8 pp.

5556 International Bureau for the Suppression of Traffic in Women and Children. Traffic in Women and Children: Past Achievements, Present Task. London: 1949.

5557 International Congress for Suppression of the Traffic in Women and Children. Report of the Proceedings, 1924.

5558 International Congress for the Suppression of the Traffic in Women and Children. "Report of the Proceedings, June, 1927." Journal of Social Hygiene 13:417-20, Oct. 1927.

5559 International Congress of the World's Purity Federation. Meeting, Louisville, Ky., Nov. 8-14, 1917. International headquarters, La Crosse, Wis.

5560 International Congress on Social Morality. Prostitution. Geneva: Federation Abolitionniste Internationale, 1935.

5561 International Federation for the Abolition of State Regulation of Vice. Congres International; compte rendu officiel des travaux du congres.

5562 Jewish Assn. for the Protection of Girls and Women. Official Report; on suppression of traffic in girls and women. 1910, 267 pp.

5563 Jorissen, Luise. Die Lage der Prostitution in Deutschland. Koln-Klettenberg, 1957. Prepared for the 20th Congress of the FAI.

5564 Der Korresponden fur das Rettungswek an den Gefallenen und fur die Arbeit zur Hebung der Sittlichket. Mulheim a. d. Ruhr: was being published in 1902.

5565 Korrespondenzblatt zur Bekampfung der Offentlichen Sittenlosigket. Berlin: was being published in 1902.

5566 League of Nations. Secretariat. Advisory Committee on Social Questions. Enquiry into Measures of Rehabilitation of Prostitutes. Part I: Prostitutes--their early lives.; Part II: Methods of Rehabilitation of Adult Prostitutes.; Parts III and IV: Conclusions and Recommendations. Geneva: 1938-39, 157 pp. C 218 M 12 1938 IV, C 83 M 43 1939 IV.

5567 League of Nations. Advisory Committee on Social Questions. Enquiry into Measures of Rehabilitation of Prostitutes. Social Services and Venereal Disease. Geneva: 1938. C 6 M 5 1938 IV.

5568 League of Nations. Advisory Committee on Social Questions. Prevention of Prostitution; a study of measures adopted or under consideration particularly with regard to minors. Geneva: 1943, 182 pp. C 26 M 26 1943 IV, IV Social 1943 IV 2.

5569 League of Nations. Advisory Committee on Social Questions. Report on the Work of the Committee in 1937. 1st Session, Geneva C 235 M 169 137 IV; 2d Session, Geneva, 1938 C 147 M 88 1938 IV; 3d Session, Geneva, 1939 C 214 M 142 1939 IV.

5570 League of Nations. Advisory Committe on Social Questions. Summary of Annual Reports 1922-39.

5571 League of Nations. Advisory Commission for Protection of Women and Girls. Jewish Association for the Protection of Girls and Women. Geneva: 1938, 8 pp. CTFE265.

5572 League of Nations. Advisory Commission for the Protection and Welfare of Children and Young People. Report for 1927: Traffic in Women and Children, cont.. Neuchatel: 1928. CTFE 371.

5573 League of Nations. Advisory Commission for the Protection of Children and Young People. Digest of the Comments by Private Organizations on the Report of the League of Nations Commission of Enquiry into Traffic in Women and Children in the East. Geneva: 1934, 20 pp. CTFE 613. Geneva, 1924, C 217 M 71 1924 IV; 4th Sess: Geneva, 1925, C 382 M 126 1925 IV; 5th Sess: Geneva, 1926, C 233 M 84 1926 IV; 6th Sess: Geneva, 1927, C 338 M 113 1927 IV; 7th Sess: Geneva, 1928, C 184 M 59 1928 IV; 8th Sess: Geneva, 1929, C 294 M 97 1929 IV.

5574 League of Nations. Advisory Commission for the Protection and Welfare of Children and Young People. Traffic in Women and Children Committee. Report. 1st Sess: Lausanne, 1922, A 9(1)1922 IV C 438(1)1922 IV. 2d Sess: Geneva, 1923, C 184 M 73 1924 IV. 3d Sess: Geneva, 1924, C 184 M 73 1924 IV. 4th Sess: Geneva, 1925, A 22 1925 IV (C 293(1) 1923). 5th Sess: Geneva, 1926, C 240 M 89 1926 IV. 6th Sess: Geneva, 1927, A 25 1927 IV. 7th Sess: Geneva, 1928, C 154 1928 IV. 8th Sess: Geneva, 1929, C 170 1929 IV. 9th Sess: Geneva, 1930, C 216 M 104 1930 IV. 10th Sess: Geneva, 1931, C 267 M 122 1931 IV. 11th Sess: Geneva, 1932, C 390 M 220 1932 IV. Later Reports issued in Report of Advisory commission.

5575 League of Nations. Commission of Enquiry into Traffic in Women and Children in the East. Report to the Council. Geneva: 1933, 556 pp. C 849 M 393 1932 IV. Also, Summary of the Report to the Council. Geneva: 1934, 41 pp. CTFE

606.

5576 League of Nations. Committee on Traffic in Women and Children. Abolition of Licensed Houses. Geneva: 1934. C 221 M 88 1934 IV, IV Social 1934 IV 7.

5577 League of Nations. Committee on Traffic in Women and Children. Concise Study of the Laws and Penalties Relating to Souteneurs. Geneva: 1931, 30 pp. C 441 M 188 1931 IV. Some 50 countries listed which never had or abolished such houses including Japan and France. Municipalities too.

5578 League of Nations. Advisory Commission for the Protection and Welfare of Children and Young People. Traffic in Women and Children Committee. Abstract of the Reports from Governments on the System of Licensed Houses as Related to Traffic in Women and Children. Geneva: 1927. CTEE 336. IV Social 1927 I V 14.

5579 League of Nations. Advisory Commission for the Protection of Children and Young People. Traffic in Women and Children Committee. Licensed Houses--Abstract; additional information received from governments of countries where the system of licensed houses has been abolished. Geneva: 1929, 91 pp. CTFE 336.

5580 League of Nations. Traffic in Women and Children Committee. Amendments to the Conventions of 1910 and 1921: Elimination of the Age Limit. Report of the Secretary. Geneva: 1932, 8 pp. C 503 M 244 1932 IV.

5581 League of Nations. Traffic in Women and Children Committee. Central Authorities. Geneva: 1932, 20 pp. C 504 M 245 1932 IV.

5582 League of Nations. Traffic in Women and Children Committee. Conference of Central Authorities in Eastern Countries, Bandoeng, Java. Geneva: 1937. C 228 M 164 1937 IV.

5583 League of Nations. Traffic in Women and Children Committee. Conference of Central Authorities in Eastern Countries, Minutes, Bandoeng, Java, Feb. 2-13, 1937. Geneva: 1937. C 476 M 318 1937 IV.

5584 League of Nations. Traffic in Women and Children: the Work of the Bandoeng Conference. Geneva: 1938. C 516 M 357 1937 IV, IV Social 1937 IV 11.

5585 League of Nations at Bandoeng (Java), in Feb. 1937; notes on the conference of Central Authories in Far Eastern Countries. Assn. for Moral and Social Hygiene in India, n. d., 19 pp.

5586 League of Nations. Diplomatic Conference Concerning Suppression of Traffic in Women of Full Age. Report. Geneva: 1933, 29 pp. C 590 M 276 1933 IV.

5587 League of Nations. Diplomatic Conference Concerning Suppression of Traffic in Women of Full Age. Records. Geneva: 1933. C 649 M 310 1933 IV.

5588 League of Nations. Draft Protocol for the Suppression of Traffic in Women of Full Age. Geneva: 1933. A 24 1933 IV IV Social 1933 IV 3.

5589 League of Nations. Traffic in Women and Children Committee. Position of Women of Russian Origin in the Far East. Geneva: 1935, 16 pp. A 12 1935 IV.

5590 League of Nations. Traffic in Women and Children Committee. I: Rapporteuer's Report Adopted by the Council on June 5, 1928. II: Report of the Council of the Traffic in Women and Children Committee. Geneva: 1928, 11 pp. A 9 1928 IV.

5591 League of Nations. Report of the Special Body of Experts On Traffic in Women and Children. Geneva: 1927. 2 v. C 52 M 52 1927 IV and C 52(2)M 52(1) 1927 IV.

5592 League of Nations. Traffic in Women and Children Committee. Report, 1927. Assn. Catholique Internationale des Oeuvres de Protection de la Jeune Fille. Geneva: 1928. CTE 375.

5593 League of Nations. Traffic in Women and Children Committee. Resolutions Adopted by the Assembly, the Council and the Traffic in Women and Children Committee, 1920-29. Geneva: 1929 CTFE 359(1)IV Social 1929 IV 10.

5594 League of Nations. Traffic in Women and Children Committee. Study of Laws and Regulations with a View to Protecting Public Order and Health in Countries Where the System of Licensed Houses Has Been Abolished. Geneva: 1930, 93 pp. C 380 M 164 1930 IV.

5595 League of Nations. Committee on Traffic in Women and Children. Suppression of the Exploitation of Prostitution of Others. Geneva: 1938 IV,. A 13 1938 IV Social 1938 IV 10. Addendum; further government answers received. A 13 1938 IV Addendum.

5596 League of Nations. Traffic in Women and Children Committee. Report of the Fifth Committee to the Assembly. Geneva: 1923, A 75 1923 IV; 1926, A 75 1926 IV; 1927, A 73 1927 IV; 1929, A 60 1929 IV; 1930, A 76 1930 IV.

5597 League of Nations. Services Sociaux et Maladies Veneriennes. Geneva: n. d., 73 pp.

5598 League of Nations. L'Action Preventive Contre la Prostitution. Geneva: 1943, 201 pp.

5599 League of Nations. Full summary of the Report of the Special Body of Experts on Traffic in Women and Children. 12 pp.

5600 League of Nations. International Conference on Traffic in Women and Children: General Report On the Work of the Conference. Geneva: 1921, 33 pp. C 227 M 166.

5601 "League of Nations and Traffic in Women." Educational Review 74:11-12, Jun. 1927.

5602 Ligue Francaise Pour le Relevement de la Moralite Publique. Une Institution qui Deshonore Notre Pays: la Reglementation. Geneva: Federation Abolitionniste Internationale, 1936.

5603 London. Central Vigilance Committee. Manual on the English Law on the Repression on Immorality. London: 1883, 19 pp.

5604 London. Committee For Obtaining the Repeal of the C. D. Acts. Seven Reasons for Repeal. London: 1883, 11 pp.

5605 London. Committee for the Suppression of Traffic in English Girls. Report. London: 1881, etc.

5606 London. International Bureau for the Suppression of the White Slave Traffic. Prospectus. 1910, 7 pp.

5607 London. National Vigilance Association. Annual Report of the Executive Committee. London: 1888, etc.

5608 Longo, G. "Problem and the League of Nations." Igiene e San 2:241-24‹, Jan.-Jun. '46.

5609 Luisi, Dra. P. Una Verguenza Social: La Regementacion de la Prostitucion. Geneva: Federation Abolitionniste Internationale, n. d., 44 pp.

5610 Maanedsblad; organe de la Danish section of the Federation. Copenhagen: monthly. Was being published in 1902.

5611 Madras Vigilance Assn. Various tracts written in the 1930's against prostitution.

5612 Magdalen Hospital, London. An account of the rise, progress, and the present state of the Magdalen Charity; with the rules and list of subscribers. London: 1761.

5613 The Mascot. New Orleans: weekly. Published in the eighteen-eighties and 'nineties. It gave news of the underworld of New Orleans and to the houses of prostitution there.

5614 Meuron, A. de. La Federation et le Christianisme. Geneva: Federation Abolitionniste Internationale, before 1942, 29 pp.

5615 Miner, C. E., Adams, K. J., Palmer, A. W. "Three Views of a Year's Work; the Committee of Fifteen." J Soc Hygiene 14:139-47, Mar. '28.

5616 National Society for the Promotion of Social Purity. Laws and Operations of the Society. 1875, 67 pp.

5617 Neues Frauenleben. Vienna: monthly. Was being published in 1902.

5618 New York Society for the Suppression of Vice. Annual Reports. 1912-1917 by the Society.

5619 Nyurin, N. D. "Analysis of League of Nations Report on Prostitution." Sovet Urach, Zhur. 43:565-572, May 30, 1939.

5620 Orgaan van der Nederlandschen Vrouenwenbond. Gravenhage: was being published in 1902.

5621 Parker, Daniel. Les Trafiquants de Femmes. 5th ed. Geneva: Federation Abolitionniste Internationale, 1942, 16 pp.

5622 Parker, Daniel. Triomphe due Mensonge et de la Corruption. Geneva: Federation Abolitionniste Internationale, 1940, 31 pp.

5623 The Participants in Prostitution; reports of the FAI Congress in Athens, Sep. 9-12, 1963. Geneva: Federation Abolitionniste Internationale, 1963.

5624 The Philanthropist. New York: quarterly "for the promotion of social purity." Was being published in 1902.

5625 Pieczynska, E. La Federation et l'Hygiene. Geneva: Federation Abolitionniste Internationale, 30 pp. n. d.

5626 Powell, Aaron Macy, ed. The National Purity Congress, Its Papers, Addresses, Portraits: An Illustrated Record of Papers and Addresses of the First National Purity Congress, held under the auspices of the American Purity Alliance in Baltimore, Oct. 14, 15, amd 16, 1895. New York: American Purity Alliance, 1896, 453 pp.

5627 La Principio de la Movada por Casta Vivo. Geneva: Federation Abolitionniste Internationale, 29 pp. n. d.

5628 La Relevement Social; organ of Ligne Francaise de la Moralite Public. 2 rue Balay, St-Etienne: was being published in 1902.

5629 Sainte-Croix, Avril de, Mme Ghenia. League of Nations. Traffic in Women and Children. Report on the International Women's Associations. Geneva: 1925. CTFE 234.

5630 Sainte-Croix, Avril de, Mme Ghenia. Report on the International Women's Associations, 7th Session. Geneva: League of Nations, 1928. CTFE 370.

5631 Scheiber, A. Un Fleau Sociale. Geneva: Federation Abolitionniste Internationale, 1947, 317 pp.

5632 Searchlight. Lost Souls. A. H. Stockwell, 1925, 64 pp.

5633 Sedlighets-Vaennen; organ of the Swedish section of the Federation. Blasiholmstorg: quarterly. Was being published in 1902.

5634 The Shield; official organ of the British Committee of the Federation for the Abolition of State Regulation of Vice. London: New series vol.1 no.1--vol.15 no.155. May 1897-Jan. 1916. Third series Apr. 1916- .

5635 Social Health. New Dehli: quarterly. Vol.1- . Jul. '62- .

5636 Society for the Suppression of Vice. Abolition of the Red-Light Districts in Baltimore. 1915.

5637 Solano Rodriguez, Susana Matilde H. de Perez Trevino, and Carlos A. Bambaren, under the rubric of Comite Abolicionista Peruano. Lima: 1958, 32 pp. Pamphlet dealing with prostitution.

5638 Tidsskrift for Arbeidet til Fremme af Sedelighed. Kristiania, 1902.

5639 Union Internationale Contre le Peril Venerrien. Assemblee General (Liege, 1939) and the texts and debates. Prophylaxie Antivenerienne. Paris: Jan. '46.

5640 United Nations. Etude sur la Traite des Etres Humanis et la Prostitution, 1959. 60 pp.

5641 United Nations. Economic and Social Council. Traffic in Women and Children. Summary of Annual Reports for 1946-47 (etc.); prepared by the Secretriat. Lake Success, 1948-.

5642 United Nations. International Convention for the Suppression of the Traffic in Women and Children. Opened for signature at Geneva from Sep. 30, 1921 to Mar. 31, 1922. Amended by the protocol signed at Lake Success, New York, Nov. 12, 1947. 1948, 9 pp.

5643 United Nations. _International Convention for the Suppression of the Traffic in Women of Full Age_. Signed at Geneva Oct. 11, 1933. Amended by the protocol signed at Lake Success, New York, Nov. 12, 1947. Lake Success, 1948, 8 pp.

5644 United Nations. Secretariat. _Study on Traffic in Persons and Prostitution: Suppression of the Traffic in Persons and the Exploitation of the Prostitution of Others_. New York: Dept. of Economic and Social Affairs, 1959, 57 pp.

5645 World Peace Foundation. International Conference. _Records on Traffic in Women and Children_. 1922.

5646 "Abnormality of Vice." _Charities and the Commons_ 20:87-8, Apr. 18, 1908.

5647 Abraham, Karl. _Selected Papers_. Tr. by Douglas Bryan and Alix Strachey. London: The Hogarth Press, 1942.

5648 Ball, J. D. and G. H. Thomas. "A Sociological, Neurological, Serological and Psychiatric Study of a Group of Prostitutes." _Am J Insanity_ 74(1918):647-666.

5649 Barag, G. "Zum Psychanalyze der Prostitution." _Imago_ 23:330-362, '37.

5650 Borelli, Siegfried. _Die Prostitution als Psychologisches Problem_. Berlin: Springer, 1957, 271 pp.

5651 Bowman, Karl M. _Sexual Deviation Research_. Printed by Assembly of the State of California as requested by the Judiciary Subcommittee on Sex Research, Mar. '52. Primarily on homosexuality.

5652 Bredmose, G. V. "Psychiatric Examinations in Copenhagen, Especially With Reference to Mental Hygenic Precautionary Measures." _Nord Med Tidskr_ 16:1456-1458, Sep. 17, '38.

5653 Bullard, W. N. "State Care of High-Grade Imbecile Girls." _Conf Char and Corr_ 1910:229-303.

5654 "Causes of Sex-delinquency in Girls." _J Soc Hygiene_ 13:109-14, Feb. '27.

5655 Chambers, C. D., et al. "Narcotic Addiction in Females: a race comparison." _Int J Addict_ 5(2):257-78, Jun. '70.

5656 Chideckel, Maurice. _Female Sex Perversion_; the sexually aberrated woman as she is. New York: Eugenics Pub. Co., 1935, 331 pp.

5657 Clarke, W. "Prostituion and Alcohol." _J Soc Hygiene_ 3(1917):75-90.

5658 Clarke, W. "Prostiution and Mental Deficiency." _Soc Hygiene_ 1:364-87, Jun. '15.

5659 Clouzet, Maryse (Choisy). _Psychoanalysis of the Prostitute_. New York: Philosophical Library, 1961, 138 pp. French study of the essential motives of the prostitute, psychology of pimp and customer.

5660 Cluss, Adolf. _Die Alkoholfrage vom Physiolgischen, Sozialen und Wirtschaftlichen Standpunkt_. Berlin: 1906. Some discussion of prostitution and alcoholism.

5661 Cole, William Graham. Sex in Christianity and Psychoanalysis. New York: Oxford Univ. Press, 1955.

5662 Enge, J. "Legal Aspects of Confining Prostitutes on Grounds of Mental Incapacity." Ztschr f Psych Hyg 14:78-86, '42 and Alleg Ztschr f Psychiat 120, Hft. 1-2, '42.

5663 Erkens, J. "La predisposizione individuale e le influenze ambientale sulla prostituzione," in Arch di Antrop Crim Psichiat e Med Leg 54:8-15, 1934. Individual predisposition and environmental influence. Corroboration of Lombroso's theory.

5664 Ferenczi, Sandor. Contributions to Psychoanalysis. Boston: Richard C. Badger, 1916.

5665 Friedlander, Kate. Psychoanalytic Approach to Juvenile Delinquency. New York: International Universities Press, 1949. Deviants have not developed into fully socialized adults.

5666 Friedman, Irit and Ilana Peer. "Drug Addiction Among Pimps and Prostitutes." Int J Addictions, 1967. Israel.

5667 Freud, Anna, et al. The Psycho-analytic Study of the Child. New York: International Universities Press, 1949, 493 pp. Vol. 3 and 4.

5668 Freudenberger, H. J. "A Patient in Need of Mothering." Psychoanal R 60(1):7-14, 1973.

5669 Giel, R. "Freud and the Devil in Ethiopian Psychiatry." Psychiatr Neurol Neurochir 71(2):177-83, Mar.-Apr. '68.

5670 Gilder, S. S. "Tattoed Ladies." Canad Med Assn J 98(25):1203, '68.

5671 Glover, Edward. The Psychopathology of Prostitution. 2d ed London: Institute for the Study and Treatment of Delinquency, 1957, 20 pp. Also in Glover, The Abolition of Tolerated Prostitution. London: ISTD no. 2, 1945 and in Glover, The Roots of Crime. New York: International Universities Press, 1960, pp.244-67.

5672 Goitein, L. "The Potential Prostitute." J Crim Psychopathology 3:359-367, '42.

5673 Gokhale, B. B. "The Visiting Client (a pilot study on the client of the prostitute)." Ind J Psychiat 4(1):39-45, Jan. '62.

5674 Greenwald, Harold. "The Call Girl: a social and psychoanalytic study." Psychoanalysis 6:20-44, '58.

5675 Greenwald, Harold. The Call Girl; a social and psychoanalytic study. Ballantine Books, 1958, 245 pp., bibliography.

5676 Greenwald, Harold. The Elegant Prostitute; a social and psychoanalytic study. New York: Walker, 1970, 305 pp.

5677 Grzywo-Dabrowska, M. Psychologja Prostytutek. Lodz: 1925, 37 pp.

5678 Gurvitch, B. R. "The Psychopathic Effect of Exogenius Factors Upon the Personality." Zh Nevro Patol i Psikhiat 1:97-103, '31. Personality of prostitute divided into three character stages.

5679 Hollender, M. H. "Prostitution, the Body and Human Relatedness." Int J Psychoanal 42:404-13, Jul.-Oct. '61.

5680 Horney, Karen. Our Inner Conflicts. New York: W. W. Norton and Co., 1945.

5681 Jonsson, G. "Psychiatric Examination of Female Prostitutes." Acta Psychiat et Neurol 13:463-476, '38.

5682 Kenyon, F. E. "Homosexuality in the Female." Br J Psychiatry spec no. 9:185-200, '75.

5683 Kneeland, G. J. "Commercialized Prostitution and the Liquor Traffic." Soc Hygiene 2:69-90, Jan. '16.

5684 Krevelen, D. A. van, "Analysis of a Prostitute." Acta Paedopsychiatr (Basel) 33(4):109-17, Apr.-May '66.

5685 Lafora, G. R. "Relation to Mental Deficiency and Psychopathy." Med Ibera 1:717-720, Jun. 2, '34.

5686 Legrun, A. "Handwriting of 'Easy' Girls." Prax Kinderpsychol Kinder Psychiatr 17(1):29-31. Cont., Jan. '68.

5687 Lion, Ernest G. et al. An Experiment in the Psychiatric Treatment of Promiscuous Girls. San Francisco: City and Dept. of Public Health, 1945.

5688 Lubart, J. M. "Field Study of the Problems of Adaption of Mackenzie Delta Eskimos to Social and Economic Change." Psychiatry 32(4):447-58, Nov. '69.

5689 Maerov, A. S. "Prostitution: a Survey and Review of 20 Cases." Psychiatric Q 39(4):674-701, Oct. '65.

5690 Malzberg, B. "Mental Defect and Prostitution." Eugenics R 12:100-4, Jul. '20.

5691 Martimor, E. "'Shameful Relationships': their role in determining various crimes." Ann Med Psychol (Paris) 2(3):343-50, Oct. '68.

5692 Moraglia, G. B. Die Onanie Beim Normalen Weike und bei den Prostituierten. Paris: Scient. London Press, 1906.

5693 Muller-Eckhard, Hans. "Ein Assimilitiertes Judas-Schicksal und die Versperrte Zuflucht in die Psychose." Psyche Heidel 6:34-48, '52. Case history of a prostitute.

5694 Nedoma, K. and I. Sipova. "Heterosexual Relations of Women With Prostitution Behavior." Cesk Psychiatr 68(1):23-6, Feb. '72.

5695 Pabian, J. "Psychiatric Analysis of Some Causes of Prostitution." Przegl Lek 31(12):1000-4, '74.

5696 Parry, A. "Tatooing Among Prostitutes and Perverts." Psychoanalitic Q 3:476-482, Jul. '34.

5697 Perez Morales, F. "Aspects of the Analysis of a Prostitute." Rev Psicoanal 17:66-81, Jan.-Mar. '60. Spanish.

5698 Picek, S. "Somatic and Sexual Constitution of Prostitutes; rare case of nymphomania." Casop Lek Cesk 86:820-824, Jul 11, '47.

5699 "Psychiatric Studies of Delinquent Women." Soc Hygiene 6:604-8, Oct. '20.

5700 Putnam, S. "Psychopathology of Prostitution," in Schmalhausen, S. D. and V. F. Calverton, eds., Women Coming of Age, pp.310-39. Liveright, 1931.

5701 Rado, Sandor. Psychoanalysis of Behavior. New York: Grune and Stratton, 1956.

5702 Reich, Wilhelm. The Sexual Revolution. Tr. by Theodore P. Wolfe. 4th ed New York: The Noonday Press, 1962. Wrote on this at great length.

5703 Ringel, E. "The So-called Warbrides--10 Years Later. A Follow-up Examination of Critically Treated Young Female Psychopaths." Wien Med Wschr 113:30-5, Jan. 5, 1963.

5704 Rosenthal, O. Alkoholismus und Prostitution. Berlin: 1905.

5705 Scott, P. D. "Battered Wives." Br J Psychiatry 125:433-41, Nov. '74.

5706 Scott, Peter D. and Denis Pan. "Psychiatric Aspects of the Wolfenden Report." Brit J Delinqu 9:20-43, '58.

5707 Schachter, M. "Prostitution as a 'Gratuitous Act': a contribution to the psychopathology of rebellious..." Archivos de Criminologia, Neuropsiquiatria y Disciplinas Conexas (1961):294-304.

5708 Schneider, C. Studien uber Personlichkeit und Schicksal Eingeschriebner Prostituierter. Berlin: 1921, 229 pp. (Abhandlungen aus dem Gesamtgebiete der Kriminalpsychologie, Heft 4).

5709 Schulze, E. "Intoxication Psychoses in Prostitutes Following Abuse of Preludin." Oeff Gesundheitsdienst 23:287-291, Jul. '61. In German.

5710 Schulze, R. "On the Problem of Prostitution and of Frequent Changes in Sexual Partners in its Current Signifigance." Z Aerztl Fortbid 54:1017-26, Sep. '60. In German.

5711 Siedow, Helmut. "Untersuchungen mit dem Farbpyramidentest an Psychopathischen Personenlichkeiten." Z Diagnost Psychol 6:18-38, '58. Studies with the Coln Pyramid Test on psychopathic personalities.

5712 Sigusch, V. "The Antipathetic Gradient vis a vis Sexual Deviant Groups." Nervenarzt 39(3):114-23, Mar. '68.

5713 Sipova, I. and K. Nedoma. "Family Setting and Childhood in Socially and Sexually Deprived Women." Cesk Psychiatr 68(3):150-3, Jun. '72.

5714 Staak, M. "Psychopathological and Medicosocial Aspects of Homicide in Sexual Relations between Strangers on Chance Acquaintances." Med Leg Domm Corpor (Paris) 4(3):258-61, Jul.-Sep. '71.

5715 Staak, M. "Situations of Homocide in Heterosexual and Homosexual Transient Partnerships." Z Rechtsmed 71(1):39-46, '72.

5716 Standard Statistics of Prostitution, Gonorrhea and Syphilis. New York: American Social Hygiene Assn., 1919.

5717 Sullivan, Harry Stack. Conceptions of Modern Psychiatry. New York: W. Norton, 1940.

5718 Thompson, G. N. "Psychiatric Aspects of Control." Am J Psychiat 101:677-681, Mar. '45.

5719 Treadway, W. L. et al. Psychiatric Studies of Delinquents. U. S. Public Health, 1920.

5720 Vella, G. and A. Petizio. "Contribute all Conoscenza del Compartamento della Prostituta." Quaderni di Criminologia Clinica 2/3(1960):317-344.

5721 Wengraf, F. "Fragment of Analysis of a Prostitute." *J Crim Psychopath* 5:247-253, Oct. '43.

5722 Wolfenden, J. "Evolution of British Attitudes Towards Homosexuality." *Am J Psychiatry* 125(6):792-7, Dec. '68.

5723 Agonston, T. "Some Psychological Aspects of Prostitution: the Pseudo-personality." Int J Psycho-Anal 26:62-67, '45. "Addendum" 27:59, '46 with 10 item bibliography.

5724 Aichorn, August. "Some Remarks on the Psychic Structure and Social Care of a Certain Type of Juvenile Delinquents," in The Psychoanalytic Study of the Child, vol.3-4. New York: International Universities Press, Inc., 1949, pp.439-448.

5725 Aigrisse, G. "Aspects Psychologiques de la Prostitution." Le Service Social, no. 2, '55. 11 pp.

5726 Anthony, K. "Psychology of Delinquency." New Rep 31:130-3, Jun. 28, 1922.

5727 Arago, Jacques Etienne Victor. Femme Entretenue. Physiologie du Protecteur. Brussels: 1882, 66 pp.

5728 Ardilla, Alfredo. Psicologia y Probemas Sociales en Columbia. Tunja: Universidad Pedalogica y Technologia de Columbia, 1971, 155 pp.

5729 Bauer, B. A. Women and Love. 2v. in 1. Liveright, 1971.

5730 Berg, Charles. Fear, Punishment, Anxiety and the Wolfenden Report. London: George Allen and Unwin, Ltd., 1959. Not very useful.

5731 Bernocchi, F. "Risultati di un Esperienza di Recupero della Prostituta." Igeiene Mentale 7(1963):105-178.

5732 Biro, B. "Studies of Prostitutes." Arch f Kriminol 98:213-215, May-Jun. '36.

5733 Blake, Roger. The Promiscuous Wife. Cleveland: K. D. S., Inc., 1966.

5734 Borelli, Siegfried and Willy Starck. Die Prostitution als Psychologischen Problem. Berlin: Springer-Verlag, 1957. Standard treatment.

5735 Carle. "Reasons for Becoming a Prostitute." Paris Med (annexe) 1:i-iii, Mar. 7, 1936.

5736 "The Clients of Prostitutes." Brit J Med 5215:1794-5, Dec. 17, 1960.

5737 Comfort, Alex. Sexual Behavior in Society. New York: The Viking Press, 1950.

5738 Constant. Les Compagnes de la Nuit. Paris: 1954, 254 pp. Similar to the movie by the same name. Deals with the lives of the prostitutes.

5739 Cross, Harold H. Unite. *The Lust Market*. London: Torchstream Books, 1959, 261 pp.

5740 Curran, F. J. and M. Levine. "A Body Image Study of Prostitutes. *J Crim Psychopath* 4:93-116, '42. Use of Schnieder's Body Image Questionnaire.

5741 Davis, Katherine B. *Factors in the Sex Life of Twenty-Two Hundred Women*. New York: Harpers, 1929.

5742 Dongier, M. and Suzanne Dongier. "L'Attract de la Prostituee." *Acta Neurologica et Psychiatrica Belgica* 64(7):719-724, '64. The attraction towards prostitution and of the prostitute.

5743 Durban, P. "Psychology of Prostitutes." *Ann Med Psychol* (Paris) 124(2):169-92, Feb. '66.

5744 Durban, P. *La Psychologie des Prostitutees*. Paris: Maloine, 1969, 238 pp.

5745 Ellis, Albert and Edward Sagarin. *Nymphomania*; a study of the oversexed woman. New York: Gilbert, 1964, 255 pp.

5746 Ellis, Albert. "Why Married Men Visit Prostitutes." *Sexology* 25:344-347, '59.

5747 Ellis, Havelock. *Studies in the Psychology of Sex*. New York: Random House, 1936. Vol.2 pt.3, "Sex in Relation to Society."

5748 Ford, Clellan S. and Frank A. Black. *Patterns of Sexual Behavior*. New York: Harper and Bros., 1951, pp.98-99, 127-128. See also Henriques, *op cit*, I, 371-425.

5749 Fournier, Christine. *Ces Filles Perdues*. Paris: 1964, 176 pp. Includes some interviews with prostitutes.

5750 Glover, E. *The Psycho-pathology of Prostitution*. London: Institute for the Scientific Treatment of Delinquency, 1945, 16 pp.

5751 Goitein, P. L. "The Potential Prostitute: the role of anorexia in the defence against prostitution desires." *J Crim Psychopath* 3:359-367, '42.

5752 Greenwald, Harold. *The Call Girl*; a social and psychoanalytic study. New York: Ballantine Books, 1958. A revised edition published under the title *The Elegant Prostitute*. New York: Walker and Co., 1970. One of the better psychiatric studies.

5753 Hall, Susan and Bob Adelman. *Gentleman of Leisure*; a year in the life of a pimp. New York: Times Mirror, New American Library, 1972, 189 pp.

5754 Hall, W. S. "Intoxicants and the Social Evil." Miss R 42:335-6, May '19.

5755 Hammer, W. Ueber Prostitution und Homosexualitat, Zugleich ein Beitrag zur Lehre von den Enthaltsamkeitsstorungen. Leipzig: Verl. d. Monat. f. Harnkr., 1905.

5756 Hertoft, P. "Investigation Into the Sexual Behavior of Young Men." Dan Med Bull (Suppl) 1:1-96, Mar. '69.

5757 Hoffman, R. "Why Men Pay For Love; interviews." Cosmop 139:124-7, Jun. '55.

5758 House, Samuel. Is Our Civilization Over-sexed? Freud Has Lifted a Great Incubus of Shame From Man. Girard, Kan.: Haldeman-Julius Pub., 1929, 32 pp.

5759 Hollender, M. H. "Prostitution, the Body, and Human Relatedness." Int J Psycho-Anal. 42(4-5):404-413, '61.

5760 Hyman, E. C. "Holding the Promiscuous Girl Accountable For Her Behavior." Nat Probation Assn. Yrbk 1948:190-201.

5761 Kemp, T. Physical and Psychological Causes of Prostitution and the Means of Combating Them. League of Nations Advisory Committee on Social Questions, pt.4. C 26 1943.

5762 Kronhausen, Phyllis and Eberhard. Sex Histories of American College Men. New York: Ballantine Books, 1960.

5763 Jacobs, Jerry. Deviance: Field Studies and Self-disclosures. Palo Alto, Calif.: National Press, 1974, 190 pp. Readings on deviant behavior and way handled by courts, bureaucratic agencies.

5764 Karpman, B. Case Studies in Psycho-Pathology of Crime. Washington: Medical Science Press, 1944, 738 pp. Vol. II, cases 6-9. Case 7 deals with the Mann Act.

5765 Karpf, Maurice J. "The Effects of Prostitution on Marital Sex Adjustment." Int J Sexol 6:149-154, '53.

5766 Karpman, B. "Emotional Background of White Slavery: Toward the Psychogenesis of So-Called Psychopathic Behavior." J Crim Law 39:1-18, May/Jun. '48.

5767 Kempny, L. "Contribution to the Psychological Study of Prostitution." Kwart Psychol 11:26-40, '39. Czech.

5768 Kohberg, L. "Sittliche Abwegigheit Frau und Ihre Sozialen Folgen." (Moral Deviation of Women and Its Social Consequences). Schweiz Med Wschr 70(1):82-86, 96-102, '40. Report of Zurich social agency.

5769 League of Nations. Advisory Committee on Social Questions. Prostitutes: Their Early Lives. Geneva: League of Nations, 1938, 139 pp.

5770 LeBaron, Joseph. Sex Life of the American Prostitute. North Hollywood, Calif.: Brandon House, 1962, 159 pp.

5771 Mamoru, Iga. "Cultural Factors in Suicide of Japanese Youth With Focus on Personality." Sociology and Social Research 46(1), Oct. '61.

5772 Mancini, Jean-Gabriel. Prostitutes and Their Parasites. London: Elek Books, 1963, 109 pp. Tr. into English by M. D. G. Thomas.

5773 **Manuel, P.** Prostitution and Volkserziehung. Coln: Kratz, 47 pp.

5774 **Merimee, Prosper.** The Prostitute and Her Lover. Girard, Kan.: Little Blue Books, 64 pp.

5775 Mertz, P. A. "Mental Deficiency in Prostitutes." J Am Med Assn 72:1597-1599, May 31, 1919.

5776 Morharat, ____. "Sexualite et Prostitution." Rev Anthrop 23:352-357, 1913.

5777 Mortensson, G. and E. Vestergaard. "Efterundersogelse af 300 Unge Prostituerede Kvinder." Nordisk Tidsskrift for Kriminalvidenskab 55(1965):246-258.

5778 Muller, C. "Die Psyche der Prostituierter." Verh d Gesell Dtschr Naturforsch u Aerzte 80:375-377, '09.

5779 Nedoma, K. and Sipova, I. "Heterosexual Relations of Prostitutes." Ceskoslovenska Psychiatrie 68(1):23-26, Feb. '72.

5780 Nedoma, K. and Sipova, I. "Sexual Behavior and Reactivity in Prostitutes." Ceskoslovenska Psychiatrie 68(4):214-217, Aug. '72.

5781 Nissen, Henry W. "Social Behavior in Primates," in Stone, Calvin P., Comparative Psychology, pp.423-57. New York: Prentice Hall, 1951. See also Wiskler, Wolfgang, The Sexual Code: The Social Behavior of Animals and Men, pp. 217-18. Garden City: Doubleday and Co., 1972.

5782 Origlia, Dino. Indagine Psicologica sulla Personalita della Prostituta. Rome: 1950, 123 pp.

5783 Petiziol, Adolfo. La Prostituta: Profilo Psicologi Storico Sociale. Rome: Edizioni Nazionali, 1962, 251 pp.

5784 Podolsky, E. "What Drives the Prostitute?" GP 21:122-3, Feb. '60.

5785 Preble, Z. E. "She Was Lonesome; How an Age-old Problem is Being Answered." Sunset 43:28-30, Sep. '19.

5786 "Psychology and Prostitution." Time 71:64-6, Mar. 3, 1958.

5787 Putnam, Samuel. "The Psychopathology of Prostitution," in Schmalhausen, Samuel and V. F. Calverton, eds., Woman's Coming of Age, A Symposium. New York: Horace Liverwright, Inc., 1931.

5788 Rabut, R. "Intellectual Level of Prostitutes; results of mental tests." Paris Med 1:207-210, Mar. 3, '34.

5789 Rabut, R. "Previous History of Prostitute; a statistical survey." Prophylax Antiven 8:365-383, Jul. '36.

5790 Rappaport, Mazie F. "After 10 Years: helping prostitutes to help themselves." J Soc Hygiene 39(1953).

5791 Rappaport, Mazie F. "The Psychology of the Female Offender." NPPA J 3(1), Jan. '57.

5792 Reik, Theodore. Psychology of Sex Relations. New York: Farrar and Rinehart, Inc., 1945.

5793 Rizzo, C. and G. Argenta. "Contribution to the Psychological Study of Prostitution With the Rorschach Method." Riv Neurol (Nap) 29:545-62, Sep.-Oct., '59. Italian.

5794 Roheim, G. "Dreams of a Somali Prostitute." J Crim Psychopath 2: 162-170, '40.

5795 Rubin, Theodore Issac. In the Life. New York: Macmillan, 1961, 166 pp.

5796 Saxon, S. Sex is a Private Affair. Doubleday, 1966.

5797 Schachter, M. and S. Cotte. "Prostitution Feminine et Test de Rorschach." Arch Int Neurol 67:123-138, '48. Comparison of Rorschach findings for 100 prostitutes and 30 normal female subjects.

5798 Sipova, I. and K. Nedoma. "Personality of Socially and Sexually Depraved Women." Cas Lek Cesk 109(26):609-13, Jun. '70.

5799 Sirlin, L. "Psychology of the 'Gigolo' and of Exploiting of Women." Med Rev Mex 41:207-09, May 10, 1961. Spanish.

5800 Stein, Martha L. Lovers, Friends, Slaves: Nine Male Sexual Types: Their Psycho-Sexual Transactions With Call Girls. New York: Berkley Pub. Co. and P. T. Putnam's Sons, 1974. Outstanding study.

5801 Talvas, Abbe A. La Psychologie des Prostitutees. Lectures given on prostitution at the Institute Catholique de Paris, mimeographed, 46 pp. Available from the Institute in 1953.

5802 Tenenbaum, Joseph. The Riddle of Woman: a Study in the Social Psychology of Sex. New York: Lee Furman, 1930.

5803 Unwin, J. D. Sexual Regulations and Human Behavior. London: Williams and Norgate, 1933. pp. ix-x, 85, 87, 108. Also Unwin, Sex and Culture. London: Oxford Univ. Press, 1934, Passim.

5804 Verbeke, Nelly. "Une Therapeutique Psychologique." Revue Abolitionniste Nov./Dec. '60. Reprinted as a pamphlet at Geneva by FAI, 1961.

5805 Weitz, R. H. and H. L. Rachim. "Mental Ability and Educational Attainment of 500 Venereally Infected Females; Psychologic Study of Sexual Promiscuity and Venereal Disease." J Soc Hygiene 31:300-342, May '45.

5806 Weitz, R. D. "Occupational Adjustment Characteristics of a Group of Sexually Promiscuous and Venereally Infected Females." J App Psychol 30:248-54, Jun. '46. Bibliography.

5807 Wells, John Warren. Tricks of the Trade: A Hooker's Handbook. New York: Signet, NAL, 1975.

5808 Wile, Ira S., ed. The Sex Life of the Unmarried Adult. Vanguard Press, 1934.

5809 Winick, C. "Prostitutes' Clients' Perception of the Prostitutes and of Themselves." Int J Social Psychiatry 8(1962):289-297.

5810 Zara, E., et al. "Psycho-Sociological Considerations on Adolescent Prostitution." Osp Psichiatr 33(1):41-116, Jan.-Jun., '65.

5811 Acton, William. Prostitution Considered in its Moral, Social and Sanitary Aspects in London and Other Large Cities With Proposals for the Mitigation and Prevention of its Attendant Evils. London: J. Churchill, 1857.

5812 Addams, J. "Challenge to the Contemporary Church." Survey 28:195-8, May 4, '12.

5813 ____. "New Conscience and an Ancient Evil." McClure 38:3-13, 232-40, 338-44, 471-8, 592-8, Nov. '11-Mar. '12.

5814 Aiyer, Sir P. S. Sivaswamy. Evolution of Hindu Moral Ideas. Calcutta: Calcutta Univ. Press, 1935.

5815 "Ancient Evil." Outlook. 101:103-5, May 18, '12.

5816 "Ancient Evil and its Modern Cure." Catholic Charities Review 2:137-41, 167-71, May-Jun. '18.

5817 Andrew, E. and Bushnell, K. Heathen Slaves and Christian Rulers. Woman's Correspondence Bible Class, Oakland, Cal.

5818 Asmussen, J. P. "Bemerkungen zur Sakralen Prostitution im Alten Testament." Stud Th 11(2):167-92, '57.

5819 Assn. for Moral and Social Hygiene. Defence Regulation 33. Rev ed London: Mar. '46, 8 pp.

5820 Astour, M. C. "Tamar the Hierodule: an Essay in the Method of Vestigal Motifs (Gen. 38)." J Bib Lit 85:185-96, Jun. '66.

5821 Barrell, Leah. The White Slave. Oakland: Messiah's Advocate, 1914, 49 pp.

5822 Bailey, Derrick Sherwin. Sexual Relation in Christian Thought. New York: Harper and Bros., '59.

5823 Bailey, J. A. "Initiation and the Primal Woman in Gilgamesh and Genesis 2-3." J Bib Lit 89:137-50, Jun. '70.

5824 Batista da Costa Valente, Nautilde. Servico de Recuperacao Moral e Social de Mulher Prostituida. Sao Paulo: 1952. 2d ed. Discussion of the activities of the service for moral and social recuperation of prostitutes.

5825 Benjamin, Harry. Prostitution and Morality. New York: Julian, 1964, 495 pp.

5826 Berne, L. Un Grave Probleme de Moeurs Publiques; la repression de la debauche au regard de l'opinion Catholique. Geneva: Federation Abolitionniste Internationale, 1942, 44 pp.

5827 Bethell, L. "Guardian of the Gate." Sunset 33:349-53, Aug. '14.

5828 Betts, F. W. History of the Moral Survey Committee of Syracuse. American Social Hygiene Assn.

5829 "Billy Sunday's Advocacy of Vice Districts." Survey 35:447-8, Jan. 15, '16.

5830 Blackmore, John. The London by Midnight Mission. London: Robson and Avery, 1860, 324 pp.

5831 Bouhdiba. Islam et Sexualite. Univ. Rene Descarte, 1972.

5832 Brachwitz, R. "Morals in Old Berlin; historical-cultural study." Arch f Gesch d Med 35:339-347, '43.

5833 Brazao, Arnaldo. O Encerramento das Casa de Tolerancia Como Medida de Defensa Moral da Familia. Lisbon: 1944, 12 pp. Argues that the closing of tolerated houses is an essential defence of family morality.

5834 Brinckman, A. Note on Rescue Work. London: 1894, 10 pp.

5835 Brown, W. F. "Church and Prostitution." Dublin Review 170:111-20, Jan. '22.

5836 Buschan, G. "Ueber Tempelprostitution." Zsch P Sex-wiss u Sex-pol 18: 452-458, '32. Temple prostitution traced through several ancient cultures (Babylonia, Greece).

5837 Bussey, Charles de (Charles Marchal). Les Courtisanes Deveneues Saintes. Paris: 1859.

5838 Carr, A. "The Moralists Permit Prostitution." Homiletic and Pastoral Review 67:520-21, Mar. '67.

5839 A Catholic Bishop of Ireland. Un Voix Catholique. Geneva: Federation Abolitionniste Internationale, n. d. (before 1902).

5840 Chapin, Edwin Hubbell. A Discourse on Shameful Life. New York: Thatcher and Hutchinson, 1859, 25 pp. Sermon: Go and sin no more.

5841 Chesser, Eusatace. Live and Let Live. New York: Philosophical Library, 1958. The moral of the Wolfenden Report.

5842 "Church and the Magdalen." Lit Digest 44:992, May 11, '12.

5843 "Church Crusade on the Barbary Coast." Survey 37:694-5, Mar. 17, '17.

5844 Church of England. Moral Welfare Council. Sexual Offenders and Social Punishment. Comp. and ed. by D. S. Bailey. Westminster, Eng.: Church Information Board, 1956, 120 pp.

5845 Church of England. Moral Welfare Council. The Street Offenses Bill: a Case for its Amendment. 1959, 15 pp.

5846 Coffee, R. I. "Pittsburgh Clergy and the Social Evil." Survey 29: 815-6, Mar. 8, '13.

5847 Cole, J. M. "Moral Welfare Work in the Church of England." Int R Missions 37:146-62, Apr. '48.

5848 Cole, William Graham. Sex in Christianity and Psychoanalysis. New York: Oxford Univ. Press, 1955, pp. 199-236.

5849 Collard-Huard, Mme G. and H. Martin. "Attitude of Catholic Physician in Present Campaign Against Regulated Prostitution." Bull Soc Med de Saint Luc 39:265-53, Sep.-Oct. '33.

5850 Comfort, A. "Matter of Science and Ethics; Reflection of B. M. A. Committee's Report on Homosexuality and Prostitution." Lancet 1:147-49, Jan. 21, '56.

5851 Craisson, D. De Rebun Venereis ad Usum Confessariorum. Paris: 1870.

5852 Davis, Kingley. Factors in the Sex Life of 2,200 Women. London: Harper and Bros., 1929.

5853 Deichert, Erlangen A. Die Moralstatistik in Ihrer Bedeutung fur Eine Socialethik. 3d ed 1882, pp.289-346.

5854 Duncan, F. "Road from Jerusalem to Jericho." Good Housekeeping 56:362-7, Mar. '13.

5855 Editions de l'Amicale du Nid. Les Richesses de Celles que l'on Croyait Perdues. Clichy, 1964, 120 pp.

5856 Edmondson, J. The Moral Forces Which Defeat the Regulation of Vice. London: 1882, 12 pp.

5857 Epstein, Louis M. Sex Laws and Customs in Judaism. New York: Ktav Publishing House, 1948, p.155.

5858 F., M. Prostitution. The Moral Bearings of the Problem. Catholic Social Guild, 1917, 239 pp.

5859 Federated Churches of Cleveland. Vice Conditions in Cleveland, Year Ending April 30, 1916. Federated Churches of Cleveland, 1916.

5860 Fey, H. E. "Miss Royden and War Prostitution." Christian Century 54:186-7, Feb. 10, '37.

5861 Flower, B. O. "Prostitution Within the Marriage Bond." Arena 13:59-73, Jun. 1895.

5862 ______. "Wellsprings and Feeders of Immorality." Arena 11:56-70, Dec. 1894; 11:167-75, Jan. 1895; 11:399-412, Feb. 1895; 12:337-52, May 1895.

5863 Frankignoul, Louis. Proces Moral de la Prostitution et de sa Reglementation. Geneva: Fed. Abolit. Inter., 1952, 16 pp.

5864 Garcia D. Figar, Antonio. La Mujer Caida y Su Redencion. Madrid: 1952, 125 pp. A study of the causes and moral implications of prostitution.

5865 Garrison, W. "La Question Agraire Dans Ses Rapports Avec la Prostitution." Rev de Morale Soc I:348-353, 1899.

5866 Goitein, L. "The Potential Prostitute." Journal of Criminal Psychopathology 3:359-367, 1942.

5867 Goldberg, B. C. The Sacred Fire: the Story of Sex in Religion. New York: University Books, 1958.

5868 Gotto, S. "Changing Moral Standard." Nineteenth Century 84:717- 30, Oct. 1918.

5869 Greenwald, Harold. "The Call Girl: A Social and Psychoanalytic Study." Psychoanalysis 6:20-44, 1958.

5869A Gregory, M. The Crowning Crime of Christendom. London: 1896, 31 pp.

5870 Hardt, R. Is Die Kaernierung der Dirnen ein Auswig im Kampf gegen die Prostitution?. Stuttgart: 1954. A two page pamphlet published by the Evangelic Church in Germany as part of a conference held in Hamburg in 1954.

5871 Herter, H. "Die Soziologie der Antiken Prostitution im Licte des Heinischen und Christlichen Schrifttums." Jahrbuch fur Antike und Christentum 3:70-111, 1960.

5872 Holtz, E. "Ein Beitrag zur Doppelten Moral. (A Contribution to the Double Standard of Morals.)" Frau 44: H.5, 1937.

5873 Hopkins, J. E. The Present Moral Crisis. London: 1886, 24 pp.

5874 Kardiner, Abram. Sex and Morality. Indianapolis: Bobbs-Merrill and Co., 1954.

5875 Kennedy, Charles. The Necessary Evil. New York: Harper and Bros. Pub., 1913.

5876 Kohberg, L. "Social Results of Immorality of Women." Schwez Med Wchschr 70:82, Jan. 24, 1940; Feb. 3, 1940.

5877 Kubushiro, O. "Anti-prostitution." Jap Chr Q 21:328-9, Oct. '55.

5878 Kuykendall, J. W. "Martyr to the Seventh Commandment: John R. McDowall." J Pres H 50:288-305, Winter '72.

5879 Laburu, P. Jose A. de, S. J. Es Licito Moral ye Socialmente, Oficializar la Prostitucion. Buenos Aires: 1949, 22 pp.

5880 Laurence, Henry W. The Not Quite Puritans. Boston: Little Brown and Co., 1928.

5881 Laveleye, E. de. Regulated Vice in Relation to Morality. London: 1884, 17 pp.

5882 Lehman, F. M. and Clarkson, N. K. White Slave Hell. Christian Witness, n. d.

5883 Levy, Reuben. The Social Structure of Islam. Cambridge: University Press, 1957.

5884 "Look at Sin." Newsweek 39:86, Feb. 25, 1952.

5885 Louttit, H. I. "Build-up for International Tragedy." Jap Chr Q 21:160-5, Apr. '55.

5886 MacMunn, Sir George. The Religions and Hidden Cults of India. Q London: Sampson Low, Marston and Co., 1932.

5887 Marchal, Jean. Comment Defendre la Moralite Publique. Paris: Editions Sociales Francaises, 1962, 119 pp.

5888 Mardaan, A. Deva-Dasi. New York: The Macaulay Co., 1952.

5889 Masaki, H. "Opinion of the Anti-prostitution Bill, an Interview." Jap Chr Q 21:330-2, Oct. 1955.

5890 Mason, M. H. "Public Morality; Some Constructive Suggestions." Nineteenth Century 82:185-94, Jul. 1917.

5891 Moal, L. Ce Que les Parents Doivent Savoir et Dire de la Prostitution. Paris: Centre Catholique d'Education Familiale de l'Institut Catholique de Paris, 1959.

5892 Modern Heathenism Caused by Christian Faithlessness. London: 1884, 14 pp.

5893 Morgan, Kenneth W., ed. The Religion of the Hindus. New York: Ronald Press, 1953.

5894 Muninger, D. "Gateway to Hope," tr. by O. Pfenninger. Jap Chris Q 28:192-6, Jun. 1162.

5895 Murray, E. and Villiers, L. de. Geknakte Lelies. (On the Work of the Magdalenahuis, Claremont). Stellenbosch, 1941, 32 pp.

5896 "Outrage Public aux Moeurs et Prostitution." Extract of the Report of the Legislative Commission of Neuchatel in Revue de Morale Progessive nos. 16-17, Geneva: 1892.

5897 Paddock, Z. "Prostitution." Meth Q 19:455.

5898 Pardoe, Geoffrey. Traffic in Souls. London: A. Halle, 1959, 113 pp.

5899 Patai, Raphael. Sex and Family in the Bible. New York: Doubleday, 1959.

5900 Patil, B. R. "The Devadasis." Indian Jour of Soc Work 35(4):377-389, Jan. 1975.

5901 Penzer, N. M. "Sacred Prostitution," in Poison Damsels and Other Essays. London: 1952.

5902 Preuss, Julius. "Prostitution und Sexuelle Perversitaten Nach Bible und Talmud" Monatshefte fur Prakt. Dermatologie 43 (1906).

5903 "Progress in Moral Housecleaning." Scientific Temperance J 27:133-4 , S '18.

5904 Prosser, Rev. William A. The Scarlet Woman and Her Accusers. Pittsburgh: United Peoples Church, 1915, 122 pp. unbound.

5905 "Prostitution, the Christan Harem." Westm 122:105.

5906 "Psychology and Prostitution." Time 71:64-6, Mar. 3, 1958.

5907 Report of the Moral Survey Committee on the Social Evil. Syracuse, New York: 1913.

5908 Reynolds, J. B. "Revolution in Morals." Nat Munic R 12:586-91, Oct. '23.

5909 Rocco, P. U. "Current Aspects of Prostitution. The Moral Aspects." Minerva Med 57(57):varia 940+, Jul. 21, '66.

5910 Roche, John P. and Gordon, Milton M. "Can Morality Be Legislated?" New York Times Magazine, May 22, 1955.

5910A Rogeat, M. Moeurs et Prostitution. 1935, 354 pp.

5911 Rosebury, Theodor. Microbes and Morals. New York: Viking Press, 1971.

5912 Rousseau, Jean Jacques. The Confessions. New York: Modern Library, n. d., Bk VII, p.325.

5913 Royal, Dorothy. "Seven Questions on Morals Answered by Bernard Shaw." World R, May '44, pp.3-5.

5914 Rubin, Theodore Isaac. In the Life; a composite case history. New York: Ballantine Books, 1961.

5915 Russell, Bertrand. Marriage and Morals. London: George Allen and Unwin, 1929.

5916 Schricker, H. F. "Ramparts We Watch." J of Soc Hygiene 38:241-9, Jun. '52.

5917 Schults, Raymond L. Crusader in Babylon: W. T. Stead and the Pall Mall Gazette. Lincoln, Neb.: University of Nebraska Press, 1972.

5918 Scremin, Luigi. Considerazioni Morali sulla Toleranza del Meretricio. Roma: 1935.

5919 Scremin, L. La Prostitution e la Morale Moeur. Milan. 1945, 99 pp.

5920 "Seek New Prostitution Code." Christ Cent 81:1516, Dec. 9, 1964.

5921 "Should Teen-age Boys Be Exposed to This?" Christ Cent 63:709, Jun. 5, 1946.

5922 "Sins of the Holy Land: a View of Today." Survey 32:169-70, May 9, 1914.

5923 Snaith, N. H. "Cult of Molech." Vet Test 16:123-4, Jan. '66.

5924 "Social Evils." Can Munic J 14:362, Nov. 1918.

5925 Southard, M. M. White Slave Traffic, versus the American Home. Pentecostal Pub., 1914.

5926 The State and Sexual Morality. Geneva: Fed. Abolit. Inter., 77 pp.

5927 Stead, William T. If Christ Came to Chicago. Chicago: Laird and Lee, 1894.

5928 ________. Satan's Invisible World Displayed. New York: R. F. Fenno, 1897.

5929 Talbot, Lady Edmund. Rescue Work. London, 1901, 16 pp.

5930 Tod, I. M. S. The Necessity of Stronger Representation of the Religious Feeling Against the State Regulation of Vice. London: 1884, 16 pp.

5931 Tyrrell, F. G. and Neil, H. The Shame of the Human Race: the White Slave Traffic. Bible House, 1909.

5932 "Vice Fought by the Golden Rule." Lit Digest 46:234, Feb. 1, 1913.

5933 "Vice Rings Flourishing Says Parran." Christ Cent 59:204-5, Feb. 18, 1942.

5934 Vorwahl, H. "Zur Ethischen Problematik der Prostitution." Neue Generation 27:108-113, 1931.

5935 Wake, Charles Staniland. "Sacred Prostitution." Anthropologia 1:156-164, 1873/75. Privately Printed in 1929, 114 pp.

5936 Wardlaw, Ralph. Lectures on Female Prostitution. Glascow: James Macelhose, 1842. Series of lectures by a minister dealing with prostitution, but some information, particularly on the Lock and Magdalen Hospitals.

5937 Warren, G. C. "Under Restraint by Devine and Civil Law." N Church R 26:237-49, Apr. 1919.

5938 Wembridge, E. R. "Morals Among the Immoral." Am Mercury 9:467-71, Dec. 1926.

5939 Westermarck, Edward. The Origin and Development of the Moral Ideas. London: Macmillan, 1906, 2v.

5940 Willard, V. "Go and Sin No More." Sunset 38:11-12, Mar. 1917.

5941 Willis, W. N. Anti-Christ in Egypt. Anglo-Eastern Pub. Co., 1915, 168 pp.

5942 Wolfenden, Sir John. Live and Let Live; the moral of the Wolfenden Report. New York: Philosophical Library, Inc., 1958.

5943 "Women and Morality." English R 14:624-36, Jun. '13.

5944 "Abolition of Licensed or Tolerated Houses of Prostitution: Report of the Committee on Traffic in Women and Children." J Soc Hygiene 22:422-5 Dec. '36.

5945 Addams, Jane. A New Conscience and an Ancient Evil. New York: Macmillan, 1913, 219 pp. Also in Spectator 108:873-4, Jun. 1, 1912.

5946 Addams, Jane. "Sheltered Woman and the Magdalen." Ladies Home J 30:25, Nov. '13.

5947 Addition, H. S. "Work Among Delinquent Women and Girls." Annals of the American Academy of Political and Social Science 79:152-60, Sep. '18.

5948 "Advertising Campaign Against Segregated Vice." Am City 9:3-4, Jul. '13.

5949 Aitekar A. S. The Position of Women in Hindu Civilization. Banaras: Motilala Banaras; Dass, 1956, pp.5-6.

5950 Allen, A. W. "How to Save Girls Who Have Fallen." Survey 24:684-96, Aug. 6, 1910.

5951 Almada Santini, Enrique. La Prostitution en Sus Relaciones con la Criminalidad. Mexico: 1957, 61 pp.

5952 American Social Hygiene Assn. Why Let It Burn. By the Assn., 1928.

5953 Andermann, Joachim. Prostituion Oder Geschlechtsfreiheit. Friedewald-Dresden: Verlag Aurora, 1917, 77 pp. unbound.

5954 Anderson, Nelson, ed. Studies of the Family. Gottingen: Vanderhoeck and Ruprecht, 1958.

5955 "Anti-vice Program of a Woman's Club." Survey 33:81, Oct. 24, '14.

5956 Asbury, Herbert. The Gangs of New York. Garden City Pub. Co., 1928 and Blue Ribbon Books, Inc., 1939.

5957 Austin, M. "One Love." Harp W 58:9-11, Feb. 21, 1914.

5958 Ayscough, Florence. Chinese Women: Yesterday and Today. Boston: Houghton and Mifflin, 1937.

5959 Baer, M. "Der Internationale Madchenhandel," in Grossstadt-Dokumente, Bd. 37, 1908, 96 pp.

5960 Banerjee, G. R. "Prostitution Requires Prohibition." Ind J Soc Work 19(1):11-17, '58.

5961 Barclay, Kathryn and Gallemore, Johnny L. "The Family of the Prostitute." Corrective Psychiatry and Journal of Social Therapy. 18(4):10-16, '72.

5962 Barclay, S. Bondage: the Slave Traffic in Women Today. New York: Funk and Wagnalls, 1968.

5963 Barnes, Harry Elmer. Society in Transition. New York: Prentice Hall, 1952. Ch. 17 on "Prostituion as a Social Evil."

5964 Barton, Roy F. The Half-way Sun: Life Among the Headhunters of the Phillipines. New York: Brewer and Warren, 1930, p. 52.

5965 Bauer, Bernard Adam. Women and Love. 2v. New York: Dingwell-Rock, 1934. Originally published in Vienna as Wie Bist du Weib? by Rikola, 1923.

5966 Beard, M. R. Women's Work in Municipalities. 1915, p. 97-130. Ch. on "Social Evil."

5967 Bebel, A. La Socialisme et la Prostitution. Geneva: Federation Abolitionniste Internationale, n. d., before 1902.

5968 Bebel, August. Woman Under Socialism. Tr. from the 33d German ed by Daniel de Leon. New York: N. Y. Labor News, 1904, p.5.

5969 Becker, Walter. "Die Bekaempfung der Prostitution im Entwurf Eines Neuen Strafgesetzbuches." Z Evang Ethik 1959, p. 304-389.

5970 Bell, M., ed. "Social Corrections for Delinquency," in Yearbook of the National Probation Assn. 39:328, 1946.

5971 Benjamin, Harry and Albert Ellis. "An Objective Examination of Prostitution." Int J Sexol 8(2):100-105, Nov. '54.

5972 Benjamin, Harry and R. E. L. Masters. The Prostitute in Society. Mayflower, 1966.

5973 Benjamin, Harry and R. E. L. Masters. Prostitution and Morality: A Definitive Report on the Prostitute in Contemporary Society and an Analysis of the Causes and Effects of the Suppression of Prostitution. Intro. by Walter C. Alvarez. New York: Julian, 1964, 495 pp.

5974 Besterman, Theodore. Men Against Women; A Study of Sexual Relations. London: Methuen, 1924, p.l.

5975 Biot, Rene "The Play in Prostitution." An address given at the 17th Congress of the International Abolitionist Federation, Sep. 1947. Reprinted from The Shield. London: n.d.

Assn. for Moral and Social Hygiene, 1948.

5976 Blackwell, Elizabeth. Essays in Medical Sociology. London: Ernest Bell, 1902. Generally an essay on sexuality but feels prostitution is debasing. In many ways she is ahead of her time.

5977 Bloch, Iwan. The Sexual Life of Our Time. Rev 6th ed New York: Allied Books Co., n. d.

5978 Block, Herbert A., ed. Crime in America: Controversial Issues in Twentieth Century Criminology. New York: Philosophical Library, 1961, 355 pp.

5979 Blom-Cooper, Louis. "Prostitution: A Socio-legal Comment on the Case of Dr. Ward." Brit J Socio 15(1):65-71, Mar. '64.

5980 Bonger, W. A. Criminality and Economic Conditions. 1916; pp.321-56.

5981 "Boy Who Likes Girls." Time 60:18, Aug. 25, 1952.

5982 Bosio, B. "Question of Prostitution as Inherent Quality of a Certain Race, Nationality, or Religion." Semana Med 1:302-306, Jan. 24, 1935.

5983 Bowler, A. C. "Social Factors Promoting Prostitution." J Soc Hygiene 17:477-81, Nov. '31.

5984 Breckinridge, Mrs. D. "New Hope," in National Conference of Charities and Correction, Proceedings, 1914, p.217-22.

5985 British Social Biology Council. Women of the Streets; a sociological study of the common prostitute. Ed. by C. H. Rolph. London: Secker and Warburg, 1955, 248 pp.

5986 Brown, Julia S. "A Comparative Study of Deviation from Sexual Mores." Am Socio R Apr. 17, 1952, pp.135-46.

5987 Browning, Norma Lee. City Girl in the Country. Chicago: Henry Regnery, 1955. Includes stories from Chicago Tribune on prostitution.

5988 Bryan, J. H. "Apprenticeships in Prostitution." Social Problems 12(1965):287-296.

5989 Bryan, J. H. "Occupational Ideologies of Call Girls." Social Problems 13(1966):441-449.

5990 Bullough, Vern L. The History of Prostitution. New Hyde Park, New York: University Books, 1964, 304 pp.

5991 Bullough, Vern L. "Problems and Methods for Research in Prostitution and the Behavioral Sciences." J of the Hist of the Behav Sci 1(3):244-251, Jul. '65.

5992 Bullough, Vern L. "Streetwalking, Theory and Practice." *Sat R* 4 8:52-4, Sep. 4, 1965.

5993 Bullough, Vern L. *The Subordinate Sex*. Urbana: Univ. of Illinois Press, 1973.

5994 Burgess, W. *World's Social Evil*. Saul Bros., 1914.

5995 Burks, John and Jerry Hopkins. *Groupies and Other Girls*. New York: Bantam Books, 1970.

5996 Burnham, J. M. "First Stone." *Forum* 51:365-72, Mar. '14.

5997 Butlers, J. E. "Lovers of the Lost." *Contemp* 13:16.

5998 Cain, H. P. "Blitzing the Brothels." *J Soc Hygiene* 29:594-600, Dec. '43.

5999 "Call Girls on Tape." *Time* 73:78, Jan. 26, 1957.

6000 "Call Wives: Long Island Housewives." *Newsweek* 63:18, Feb. 17, 1964.

6001 "Campaign Against Vice." *Outlook* 66:874-6, Dec. 8, 1900.

6002 Caprio, Frank S. *Unfaithful* (Former title: Marital Infidelity). Greenwich, Conn.: Fawcett Pub. Inc., 1956, 239 pp.

6003 Carstens, C. C. "Rural Community and Prostitution," in (National) Conference of Charities and Correction. *Proceedings* 1915:267-72. Also in *J Soc Hygiene* 1:529-44, Sep. '15.

6004 Cartel Romand d'Hygiene Sociale. *Jeune File Moderne, Femme de Demain*. Lausanne: Cartel Romand d'Hygiene Sociale, 1945, 20 pp.

6005 Carver, J. L. "Slavery's Last Stronghold." *U. N. World* 2:24-7, Jun. '48.

6006 "Case Against Prostitution." *J Soc Hygiene* 25:240-1, May '39.

6007 "Causes and Remedies of Prostitution." *Liv Age* 21:385.

6008 "Changed Problem and the Committee of 14." *Survey* 28:412-3, Jun. 8, 1912.

6009 Chaterloin, Lis. *En 1963 aun Existe la Trata Blancas*. Barcelona: Rodegar, 1963, 143 pp.

6010 Chesser, Eustace, et al. *The Sexual, Marital and Family Relationships of the English Woman*. London: Hutchinson, 1956.

6011 Chesser, Eustace. Women. London: Jarrolds, 1958.

6012 Christensen, Harold T. "Cultural Relativism and Premarital Sex Norms," Am Socio R 25:31-39, Feb. '60.

6013 Christensen, Harold T. and Carpenter, Geo. R. "Value-Behavior Discrepancies Regarding Premarital Coitus in Three Western Cultures." Am Socio R 27:66-74, Feb. '62.

6014 Christy, Richard. The Money Lovers. Van Nuys, Calif.: Triumph News, Inc., 1968, 188 pp.

6015 Clarke, Walter. "From the Green Notebook." J Soc Hygiene 11:321-33, Jun. '25.

6016 Clarke, Walter. Prostitution and Mental Deficiency. American Social Hygiene Assn., 1915. Reprinted from Social Hygiene 1(3), Jun. '15.

6017 Clinard, Marshall B. Sociology of Deviant Behavior. New York: Rinehart and Co., 1957.

6018 "Code Message." Newsweek 22:39, Jun. 12, 1943.

6019 Cohen, Y. A. "Sociology of Commercialized Prostitution in Okinawa." Social Forces 37:160-8, Dec. '58. Bibliography.

6020 Colbron, Grace I. "Divertibility of Public Regarding Prostitution." Public 17:174-5, Feb. 20, '14.

6021 Colcord, J. C. "Fighting Prostitution." Survey 68:214-15, Aug. '42.

6022 Cole, William E. and Charles H. Miller. Social Problems: A Sociological Interpretation. New York: David McKay, 1965, 519 pp. Pt.3, Ch.12 on "Prostitution and Homosexuality."

6023 Cook, F. J. "Corrupt Society." Nation 196:478, Jun. 1, 1963.

6024 Cooper, C. R. Designs in Scarlet. Little, 1939, 372 pp.

6025 Cormack, Margaret. The Hindu Woman. New York: Teachers College Columbia, 1953. Primarily modern.

6026 Coutsoumaris, Aristotle. La Femme Victime de la Traite des Blanches. Athens: 1963, 48 pp.

6027 Crane, F. "Lure." Forum 51:115-8, Jan. '14.

6028 Creighton, L. The Social Disease and How to Fight It. Longmans, 1914, 87 pp.

6029 Cressey, Paul. Taxi Dance Hall. Chicago: Univ. of Chicago Press, 1932.

6030 Croog, Sydney H. "Aspects of the Cultural Background of Premarital Pregnancies in Denmark." Social Forces 30(1951-52):215-19.

6031 Crook, Evelyn B. "Cultural Marginality in Sexual Delinquency." Am J Soc 39:493-500, Jan. '34.

6032 "Danger Signal." Outlook 94:426-7, Feb. 26, '10.

6033 Davis, Kingsley. Factors in the Sex Life of 2,200 Women. London: Harper and Bros., 1929.

6034 Davis, K. B., et al. "Memorandum on the Relationship Between Low Wages and the Vice Problem," in New York (state). Factory Investigating Com. Fourth Report, 1915, v.1, p. 389-417.

6035 Davis, Kingsley. "Prostitution," in Merton, Robert K. and Robert A. Nisbet, Contemporary Social Problems; New York: Harcourt Brace and World, 1961, pp.262-288.

6036 Davis, Kingsley. "The Sociology of Prostitution." Am Soc R 2:744-55, Oct. '37. One of the most cited sociological articles.

6037 Davis, Kingsley. "Notes on the Sociology of Prostitution," in Lee, A. M., ed., Social Problems in America: a Source Book. Holt, 1949, p.508-11.

6038 Davis, Kingsley. "A Study of Prostitutes," in Kneeland, G. J., Commercialized Prostitution in New York City. New York: Century, 1913, p.163-288.

6039 Deardorff, N. R. "Measurement of Progress in the Repression of Prostitution." J Soc Hygiene 18:301-14, Jun. '32.

6040 De Leeuw, Hendrik. Sinful Cities of the World. New York: Citadel Press, 1934.

6041 De Leeuw, Hendrik. Woman, The Dominant Sex. London: Arco Pub., 1957.

6042 "Despair of Our Efforts to End Vice." Lit Digest 48:494-5, Mar. 7 , 1914.

6043 Deutsch, A. "No Glamour," in Lee, A. M. and Lee, E. B., Social Problems in America: A Source Book. Holt, 1949, p. 507.

6044 Devine, Thomas. "Weapons for the Cities' War on Prostitution: Techniques for Social Protection and Venereal Disease Control Developed Sucessfully During the War." _Am City_ p.85-6, Jan. '46.

6045 Diehe, B. and D'Amico, T. "From Caves to Cafes." _Am Mercury_ 77:85-90, Sep. '53.

6046 Dingwall, Eric John. _The American Woman_. New York: Rinehart and Co., 1957. Paperback reprint by Signet, 1958.

6047 Dixon, K. _Address to Men on Prostitution_. Singapore: 1919, 8 pp.

6048 Dorr, R. C. "Breaking the Great Taboo," in _What Eight Million Women Want_, p.183-225.

6049 _Downward Paths_; an inquiry into the causes which contribute to the making of a prostitute. London: G. Bell, 1916, 200 pp. Several anonymous writers.

6050 Droin, E. _Social Restoration of Prostitutes and Their Exploiters_. Geneva: FAI, 1953, 16 pp.

6051 Durand, Andre. _Operation Trottoir_. Paris: Monde Ouvrier, 1954, 66 pp. An enquiry into prostitution.

6052 Durban, P. "Facteurs Sociaux et Atmosphere Aetiologique de la Prostitution." _L'Hygiene Mentale_ (Supplement de l'Encephale) 40(1951):13-27, 48-54.

6053 Edholm, M. G. C. "Traffic in White Girls." _Calif M_ 2:825.

6054 Edwards, T. C. "Social Protection--A Workable Plan." _J Soc Hygiene_ 38:373-81, Dec. '52.

6055 Ehrmann, W. W. "Male and Female Reports on Pre-Marital Coitus." _Soc Problems_ 1:155-158, '54.

6056 Ehrman, Winston. _Premarital Dating Behavior_. New York: Henry Holt, 1959.

6057 Elliott, A. W. _Cause of the Social Evil and the Remedy_. Southern Rescue Mission, 1913.

6058 Elliott, A. W. _Cause of the Social Evil_. 3d ed Macon, Ga.: A. W. Elliott, 1919.

6059 Elliott, Mabel and Francis E. Merrill. _Social Disorganization_, Ch VIII, "The Prostitute." 2d ed Harper and Bros., 1950. 4th ed 1961.

6060 Ellis, Albert. "Female Sexual Response and Marital Relations." _Sexual Problems_ 1:152-154.

6061 Ellis, Albert. "Why Married Men Visit Prostitutes." _Sexology_ 25(1959):344-347.

6062 Ellis, H. "Last of Prostitution." _Soc Hygiene_ 4:496, Oct. '18.

6063 Ellis, H. "Mrs. Puritan and the Prodigal." _Forum_ 50:577-87, Nov. '13.

6064 Ellis, J. "Welfare and Community Action." _J Soc Hygiene_ 31:261-266, May '45.

6065 Eltzroth, Majorie. "Vocational Counseling for Ghetto Women with Prostitution and Domestic Service Backgrounds." _Vocational Guidance Q_ 22(1):32-38, '73.

6066 Engels, Frederick. _The Origin of the Family, Private Property and the States_. 4th ed reprinted New York: Internationale Pub., 1942, p.49.

6067 Erkens, J. "Individual Predisposition and Environmental Influence." _Arch di Antropol Crim_ 54:8-15, Jan.-Apr., '34.

6068 Everett, R. H. "Failure of Segregation as a Protector of Innocent Womanhood." _Soc Hygiene_ 5:521-31, Oct. '19.

6069 Fairchild, J. E. _Women, Society and Sex_. New York: Premier Books, 1962.

6070 Fairfield, L. "Notes on Prostitution." _Brit J Delinq_ 9(3):164-173, Jan. '59.

6071 Falconer, M. P. "Part of the Reformatory Institution in the Elimination of Prostitution." _Soc Hygiene_ 5:1-9, Jan. '19.

6072 Falconer, M. P. "Reformatory Treatment of Women," in National Conference of Charities and Corrections. _Proceedings, 1914_, pp. 253-6.

6073 Falconer, M. P. "Report of the Committee on Social Hygiene of the National Conference on Charities and Corrections." _Soc Hygiene_ 1:514-28, Sep. '15.

6074 Faris, R. E. L. and H. W. Dunham. _Mental Disorder in Urban Areas_. Chicago: Univ. of Chicago Press, 1939.

6075 Faris, Robert E. R. _Social Disorganization_. 2d ed New York: Ronald Press, 1955.

6076 Faulkner, T. A. _A Lure of the Dance_. Los Angeles: by the author, 1916.

6077 Filhol, Paul. _Le Monde des Particulieres, etc_. Paris: 1959, 262 pp.

6078 "'Les Filles' Ces Mal-aimees." Moissons Nouvelles, special no. 19, Clichy, 1956, 58 pp.

6079 "Les 'Filles' Ces Sans-Famille." Moissons Nouvelles, Numero Special, Clichy, 1957, 90 pp.

6080 "Filles san Joie." Newsweek 85:42 Jun. 23, '75. Strike.

6081 Fink, A. E. "Public Welfare Agencies in the Social Protection Program." Nat Conf Social Work 1944:285-93.

6082 Fischer, E. "Zum Reformationsfest." Deutsche Rundschau 173:1-17, Oct. '17.

6083 Fitzhugh, G. "The Universal Trade; Excerpt from 'Cannibals all!'," in Lynn, K. S., ed., The American Society. Braziller, 1963, pp.91-96.

6084 Flexner, Abraham. "Next Steps in Dealing With Prostitution." Soc Hygiene 1:529-38, Sep. '15 and in National Conference of Charites and Corrections, Proceedings, 1915, p.253-60.

6085 Flexner, Abraham. Prostitution in Europe. New York: Bureau of Social Hygiene. Publications, 1914, 455 pp. Reprinted by Rittenhouse, 1965.

6086 Flower, B. O. "Prostitution Within the Marriage Bond." Arena 13:59.

6087 Ford, Corey. "Fighting the Debauchery of Our Boys and Girls." Vanity Fair 34:48-49, 74, Jul. '30.

6088 French, A. T. "Need for Industrial Homes for Women." Soc Hygiene 5:11-13, Jan. '19.

6089 Frere, C. F. "In Protection of Women." Spectator 108:833-4, May 25, 1912.

6090 Frothingham, O. B. "Causes and Remedies of Prostitution." Nation 4:153, 220.

6091 Funk, J. C. "Social Hygiene Program and the Citizen." J Soc Hygiene 18:65-70, Feb. '32.

6092 Gagnon, J. H. "Sex Research and Social Change." Arch Sex Behavior 4(2):111-41, Mar. '75.

6093 Gaillard, Jean-Jacques. Retour a la Vie. Lausanne: 1956, 16 pp. Return to normal life of the "victims" of prostitution.

6094 Gemaehling, P. Bilan d'une Reforme. Geneva: FAI, 1950, 16 pp.

6095 Gemaehling, Paul and Daniel Parker. Les Maisons Publiques: Danger Public. Paris: Ligue Francaise pour le Relevement la Moralite Publique, 1945, 77 pp.

6096 Gibbens, T. C. and M. Silberman. "The Clients of Prostitutes." Brit J of Venereal Disease 36:113-7, Jun. '60.

6097 Gibbens, T. C. N. "Men and Prostitutes." New Society 43(2):6-7, Jul. 25, 1963.

6098 Gilman, Charlotte. "The Oldest Profession in the World." The Forerunner 4:65, Mar. '13.

6099 Glenn, M. W. "Social Causes of Prostitution," in National Conference of Charities and Correction, Proceedings, 1914, p.229-36.

6100 Glueck, S. and E. T. Glueck. Five Hundred Delinquent Women. New York: Knopf, 1934.

6101 Goldman, Emma. Mother Earth 8(1913):211.

6102 Goldman, Emma. and A. Shulman. The Traffic in Women and Other Essays on Feminism. New York: Times Change Press, 1971, 63 pp.

6103 Goode, William J. "Illegitimacy, Anomie and Cultural Penetration." Am Soc R 26(1961):910-925.

6104 Goodnow, E. Market for Souls. New York: Kennerley, 1910.

6105 Gordon, Gary. Sins of Our Cities. Derby, Conn.: Monarch Books, 1962.

6106 Gosling, J. and D. Warner. Shame of a City. Allen, 1960.

6107 Grant, E. E. "Scum From the Melting Pot." Am J Soc 36:641-51, May '25.

6108 Gray, D. "Turning Out. A Study of Teenage Prostitution." Urban Life and Culture 1:401-405, '72.

6109 Greenwald, Harold. The Call Girl: A Social and Psychoanalytic Study. New York: Ballantine Books, 1958, 245 pp.

6110 Greenwald, Harold. A Study of Deviant Sexual-occupational Choice by Twenty New York Women. Ann Arbor: University Microfilms, 1956, no.19, 242.

6111 Greer, J. H. Social Evil: Its Cause, Effect and Cure. Chicago: by the author, 1910 and by Regan Pub., 1921. 64 pp.

6112 Greer, J. H. Prostitution. Raymer's, n. d.

6113 Groetzinger, Leona Prall. The City's Perils. Chicago(?): 1910(?), 220 pp.

6114 Groothuyse, Johan Wilhelm. Die Arbeidsstructuur van de Prostitutes. Deventer: Van Loghum Slaterus, 1910, 217 pp.

6115 Groves, Ernest R. The American Woman. New York: Greenberg, 1937.

6116 Guyot, Yves. Etudes de Physiologie Sociale: La Prostitution. Paris: Charpentier et Cie, 1882, 580 pp.

6117 Hall, G. M. Prostitution: A Survey and a Challenge. Williams, 1933, 1966 pp.

6118 Hall, Gladys Mary. Prostitution in the Modern World: A Survey and a Challenge. New York: Emerson, 1936, 200 pp.

6119 Hall, J. Graham. "The Prostitute and the Law." Brit J Delinq 9(3):174-181, Jan. '59.

6120 Hall, Susan. Ladies of the Night. New York: Trident Press, 1973, 249 pp.

6121 Hall, Williams, J. E. "The Wolfenden Report: An Appraisal." Pol Q 29(2):132-143, Apr./Jun. '58.

6122 Hardwick, K. B. "A Warning Against Neoregulation." Reprinted from The Shield, Sep. '46. London: 7 pp.

6123 Harland, R. O. Vice Bondage of a Great City. Young People's Civic League, 1912 and Int. Purity Assn.

6124 Harris, Sara. "Key Club--Sin Club." True Confessions 71:6-7, 15, 16, 71, Sep. '63.

6125 Havel, J. E. La Condition de la Femme. Paris: Librairie Armand Colen, 1961, 221 pp.

6126 Healy, W. "Social Evil." Nat Munic R 1:84-6, Jan. '12.

6127 Heath, L. J. "Sampling Public Opinion." Soc Hygiene 8:327-41, Jul. '22,

6128 Henriques, Fernando. Love in Action. New York: E. P. Dutton and Co., 1960.

6129 Henriques, Fernando. "Modern Sexuality," Prostitution and Society (Vol.3). London: MacGibbon and Kee, 1968, 349 pp.

6130 Henriques, Fernando. Prostitution and Society, A Survey. London: MacGibbon and Kee, 1962-, 3v. and New York: Citadel Press, 1963.

6131 Henshel, A. M. "Swinging: A Study of Decision Making in Marriage." Am J Soc 78:885-891, 1973.

6132 Hijmans, A. Vrouw en Man in die Prostitutie; een Sociologisch-psychologische Studie. 's-Gravenhage, Van Keulen, 1956, 183 pp.

6133 Hirsch, P. Verbrechen und Prostitution als Soziale Krankheitserscheinungen. Berlin: Burchh. Vorwarts, 1907, 184 pp.

6134 Hirschfeld, Magnus. Men and Women: The World Journey of a Sexologist. Tr. by O. P. Green. New York: G. P. Putnam's Sons, 1935.

6135 Hirschi, Travis. "The Professional Prostitute." Berkeley J of Sexology 7(1):33-50, Spr. '62.

6136 Hoenig, J., et al. "Social and Economic Aspects of Transsexualism." Brit J Psychiatry 117(537):163-72, Aug. '70.

6137 Holloway, J. W., Jr. "Social Workers and Prostitution." J Soc Hygiene 10:193-202, Apr. '24.

6138 Holt, W. L. Social Evil. Cosmopolis Press, 1922. Also, Critic and Guide Co., n. d.; and New York: The Altrurians, 1909, 26 pp. unbound.

6139 Hooker, Elbert L. "The Urban Tourist Camp." Stud in Soc 1(1).

6140 Horowitz, Irving Louis, ed. Power, Politics and People; the collected essays of C. Wright Mills. New York: Oxford Univ Press, 1963, 657 pp.

6141 Horton, Paul B. and Gerald R. Leslie. The Sociology of Social Problems. New York: Appleton Century Crofts, 1960.

6142 "How to Create Good Will." Time 69:91, Mar. 4, 1957.

6143 "How to Deal With Prostitution." Westm 93:477.

6144 Howard, M. "Clients of the Prostitutes and the Ponces." Spectator 202:108, Jan. 23, 1959. Gt. Britain.

6145 Hubert, H. La Reclassment des Prostituees par la Tutelle Sociale. Brussels: 1948. Presented to obtain diploma of "Assistante Sociale."

6146 Hulstaert, Gustave. "Le Marriage des Nkundo," in Institute Royal Colonia Belge, Memoires I(1839):44, 64-69.

6147 Iga, Mamoru. "Sociocultural Factors in Japanese Prostitution and the 'Prostitution Prevention Law'." J of Sex Research 4:127-46, May, '68.

6148 "Increasing Prostitution Challenges Community Action." Minn Munic 30:433-5, Nov. '45.

6149 Inghe, Gunnar. "Social Psykologiska Synpunkter pa Losdrivare och Prostituerade," in, Sweden. Inrikesdepartementet. Utredning Med Forslag om Losdrivarlagens Upphavande, etc. Bilaga 2, '49. (Statens Offentliga Utredninger, 1949:4).

6150 "International Convention for the Suppression of the Traffic in Women of Full Age." J Social Hygiene 9:537-8, Dec. '33.

6151 International Federation for the Abolition of State Regulation of Vice. Congress, Rome, 1950. La Prostitution; les problemes qu'elle pose aujourd'hui. Geneva: Secretariat de la FAI, 1951, 95 pp.

6152 "Is Commercialized Prostitution Returning: an analysis of a series of 2,372 studies made by the American Social Hygiene Assn, Jan. 1, 1940--Mar. 31, 1946 in 1,170 communities." J Soc Hygiene 32:255-6, May '46. Charts.

6153 Istituto di Medicina Sociale. La Piaga Sociale della Prostituzione. Rome: 1950. Pt 1: Atti del II Convegno della Societa di Medicina Sociale sull'Argumento--Relazioni Dei Proff. Cesare Coruzzi e Italo Levi-Luxardo, communicazioni dei proff. F. Franchi, [et al] e resoconto; Pt. 2: Indigine Psicologica del Dr. Dino Origlia sulla Personalita della Prostituta.

6154 Jackson, Nelson C. "Social Protection Among Negroes." Reprint from J Soc Hygiene, 1945.

6155 Jackman, Norman R., Richard O'Toole and Gibert Geis. "The Self-image of the Prostitute." Sociol Q 4(2):150-161, Spr. '63.

6156 Jagand-Pages, Gabriel (pseud. Taxil, Leo). La Prostitution Contemporaine. Paris: Lib Populaire, 1884, 508 pp.

6157 James, Lionel. "On the Game." New Society 555(24):426-429, May 24, 1973.

6158 "Jane Addams' Call to a New Crusade." Cur Lit 51:656-8, Dec. '11.

6159 Jarrett, Kay. Sex is a Private Affair. Garden City: Doubleday, 1966, 234 pp. Chicago.

6160 Jersild, Jen. Boy Prostitution. Tr. from the Danish by Oscar Bojesen. Copenhagen: GEC Gad, 1956, 101 pp.

6161 Joesten, Joachim. Vice, Inc. New York: 1954, 159 pp. A study of prostitution around the world but especially in Canada and U. S.

6162 Johnson, Bascom. "Are We Holding Our Own Against Prostitution?" J Soc Hygiene 33:57-64, Feb. '47.

6163 Johnson, Bascom. "Attitudes of Governments Toward Foreign Prostitutes." J Soc Hygiene 14:129-38, Mar. '28.

6164 Johnson, Bascom. "Civic Housecleaning." J Soc Hygiene 14:464-7 1, Nov. '28.

6165 Johnson, Bascom. "Current View of Prostitution and Sex Delinquency." J Soc Hygiene 22:389-402, Dec. '36.

6166 Johnson, Bascom. "Facing an Old Problem; How American Communities Are Dealing With Commercialized Prostitution." J Soc Hygiene 21:24-31, Jan. '35.

6167 Johnson, Bascom. "International Traffic in Women and Children." Police J pp.4-5, Mar.-Apr., '29.

6168 Johnson, Bascom. "Next Steps." Soc Hygiene 4:9-23, Jan. 4:9-23, Jan. '18.

6169 Johnson, Bascom. "Social Hygiene and National Defense From the Viewpoint of the Voluntary Agency and the Community." J Soc Hygiene 26:420-5, Dec. '40.

6170 Johnson, Bascom. "We Need Not Tolerate Prostitution: Facts and Fallacies Concerning the Prostitution Problem and Its Effects on Community and Industrial Life; Milestones in the March Against Commercialized Prostitution." J Soc Hygiene 27:421-32, Dec. '41.

6171 Johnstone, A. "Postwar Progress Against Prostitution." J Soc Hygiene 33:49-52, Feb. '47.

6172 J Soc Hygiene. (Special Issue). "Measurement of Progress in the Repression of Prostitution," by N. R. Deardorff; "The Relation of Prostitution to Economic Conditions," by Virginia Murray; "Social Hygiene and Unemployment; from the Medical Point of View," by C. G. Heyd; "Relations of Police and Health Officials to the Problems of Prostitution and the Venereal Diseases," by W. F. Snow. 18:301-44, Jun. '32.

6173 J Soc Hygiene. (Special Wartime Issue--Prostitution, Social Protection and the Police). Oct. '42. "New Offensive Along Police Front," by Eliot Ness; "Recommendations For Improving Procedures in Dealing With Prostitution Cases in New York City," "Local Control of Prostitution in Wartime," by E. T. Weatherly; "Planning for 'The Kind of Help They Need'," "A Study of Protective Measures in the City of Boston," and "Police and Health Department Functions in Repressing

Prostitution and Controlling Venereal Diseases," by W. F. Snow; "No Certification For Prostitutes," "Commercialized Prostitution and Disease Transmission in New York City," by Walter Clarke.

6174 *J Soc Hygiene* for Apr. '49 is devoted to "A progress report in the case of the people vs. the prostitution 'racket'."

6175 Kagan, Herman. *Prostitution and Sexual Promiscuity Among Adolescent Female Offenders*. Dissertation, University of Arizona, 1969, 167 pp.

6176 Kamarovsky, Mirra. "Cultural contradictions and sex roles." *Am J Soc* 52:184-90, Nov. '46.

6177 Karpf, Maurice J. "The Effects of Prostitution on Marital Adjustment." *Int J Sexology* 6(3):149-154, '53.

6178 Keane, W. *The Subject People Don't Like to Talk About*. New York: American Social Health Assn., 1958.

6179 Kemp, T. *Prostitution: An Investigation of Its Causes, Especially With Regard to Hereditary Factors*. Copenhagen: Levin and Munksgaard, 1936.

6180 Khalaf, Samir. "Correlates of Prostituion: A Comparative View of Some Popular Errors and Misconceptions." *Sociol Int* 5(1):110-122, '67.

6181 Khalaf, Samir. *Prostitution in a Changing Society*; a sociological survey of legal prostitution in Beirut. Beirut: Khayats Booksellers and Publishers, 1965.

6182 Kirkendall, Lester A. *Premarital Intercourse and Interpersonal Relationships*. Ner York: Julian Press, 1961. Bibliography of titles.

6183 Kirkpatrick, Clifford and E. Kanin. "Male Sex Aggression on a University Campus." *Am Socio R* 22:52-58, Feb. '57.

6184 Klare, Hugh. "Society and the Prostitute." *Socialist Commentary* 19:81-3, Mar. '55. British law and administration.

6185 Kneeland, G. J. *Commercialized Prostitution in New York City* New York: Century, 1913.

6186 Krich, A. M. *Women*. New York: Dell Pub., 1953.

6187 Krishnaswamy, S. "A Study of the Responses of Sex-delinquents, Prostitutes, and Non-delinquent Girls." *Int J Sexology* 8(1954):97-99.

6188 Kumar, Pramond. "Prostitution: A Socio-psychological Analysis." Ind J Soc W 21(4):425-430, May '61.

6189 "Ladies of the Night." Nation 188:466, May 23, 1959.

6190 Landis, Paul H. Social Problems. Philadelphia: J. B. Lipponcott, 1959. Ch. 16 on prostitution.

6191 Langstaff, Josephine. Adam's Rib. London: George Allen and Unwin, 1954. A popular look at women.

6192 Lanoux, Armand. "Physiologie du Demi-Monde en 1900," in Les Oeuv res-libres ns no. 179, pp. 131-162. Paris.

6193 Lapham, Lewis. "The Streets of Dreams and Death." USA 1(1):69-71.

6194 LeBlond, Albert and Arthur Lucas. Du Tatouage Chez les Prostituees. Paris: Soc. d'Editions, 1899, 96 pp.

6195 League of Nations. Advisory Committee on Social Questions. Enquiry Into Measures of Rehabilitation of Prostitutes. New York: Columbia Univ. Press, 1938. 4 pts in 3v. Pt. 1: Prostitutes--Their Early Lives; Pt. 2: Social Services and Venereal Disease; Pt. 3: Methods of Rehabilitation of Adult Prostitutes; Pt. 4: Conclusions and Recommendations. Also published by Int. Documents Service, 1938, 140 pp.

6196 League of Nations. Advisory Committee on Social Questions. Prevention of Prostitution: A Study of Measures Adopted or Under Consideration, Particularly With Regard to Minors. Int. Documents Service, 1943, 182 pp. and by Columbia Univ. Press, 1943.

6197 League of Nations. Suppression of the Exploitation of the Prostitution of Others. Int. Documents Service, 1938, 8 pp.

6198 Lemert, Edwin M. Social Pathology. New York: McGraw-Hill, 1951.

6199 Lewis, Lionel S. and D. Brissett. "Sex as Work: Study of a Voctional Counseling." Social Problems 15:8-17.

6200 Little, Kenneth. "Some Urban Patterns of Marriage and Domesticity in West Africa." Sociol R 7(1):65-97, '59.

6201 "Lucrative Feudalism." Time 64:20, Jun. 26, 1954.

6202 Lukas, E. J. "Digging at the Roots of Prostitution." Probation 22:97-100+, Apr. '44.

6203 Luzzatto Fegiz, Pierpaolo. Il Volto Sconosciuto dell'Italia: Diec i Ann di Sondazzi DOXA. Milan: A. Giuffre, 1958, 1353 pp.

6204 Lytle, H. M. _Tragedies of the White Slave_. New York: Padell Book and Magazine Co., 190 pp.

6205 The Maharani of Baroda and S. M. Mitra. _The Position of Women in Indian Life_. New York: Longmans Green and Co., 1911.

6206 Manners, Dorine. _Sin Street_. New York: Pyramid Books, 1957, 157 pp.

6207 Marchant, J. _The Master Problem_. Stanley Paul, 1917, 371 pp. and Moffat, 1917.

6208 Marlowe, Kenneth. "An Intimate Look at Today's Prostitute." _Sexology_, May '66, pp.652-655.

6209 Martineau, L. _La Prostitution Clandestine_. Paris: 1885.

6210 Masry, Youssef el. _Daughters of Sin_. New York: McFadden Bartell Corp., 1964(?).

6211 Maurer, D. "Prostitutes and Criminal Argots." _Am J Socio_ 44(1939):546-550.

6212 Mayer, J. "Passing the Red Light District--Vice Investigations and the Results." _Soc Hygiene_ 4:197-209.

6213 McClure, "Tammanyizing of a Civilization." _McClure_ 34:117-28, Nov. '09.

6214 McCord, C. P. "One Hundred Female Offenders: A Study of the Mentality of Prostitutes and Wayward Girls; With Discussion," in, New York (state). Bd. of Charities. _Report, 1915_, v.1, p.1146-75, 1916.

6215 McPartland, John. _Sex in Our Changing World_. New York: Rinehart and Co., 1947.

6216 Merlin, Lina. _Chiusura della Case di Tolleranza_. Rome: 1949, 62 pp.

6217 Merrill, Francis E. _Social Problems in the Home Front_. Harper and Bros., 1946. Ch. 6 on War and Prostitution.

6218 Michelson, M. "Vice and the Woman's Vote." _Sunset_ 30:344-8, Apr. '13.

6219 "Milestones in the March Against Commercialized Prostitution, 1886-1942." _J Soc Hygiene_ 27:428-32, Dec. '41.

6220 "Milestones in the March Against Prostitution: 1942-46." _J Soc Hygiene_ 33:65-72, Feb. '47.

6221 "Milestones in the March Against Commercialized Prostitution: 1946-1949." J Soc Hygiene 35:167-9, Apr. '49.

6222 Miller, James. Prostitution Considered to Its Cause and Cure. Edinburgh: Sutherland and Knox, 1859, 38 pp. pamphlet. Causes: seduction, force of habit, poverty, poor housing, vanity, intemperance, ignorance, irreligion, looseness of morality, slackness of civil rule. Opposed to regulation.

6223 Milner, Christina Andrea. Black Pimps and Their Prostitutes; social organization and value system of a ghetto occupational substructure. Dissertation, 1971, Univ. of Calif., Berkeley, 327 pp.

6224 Milner, Christina and Richard. Black Players. Boston: Litle Brown and Co., 1972. Pimps.

6225 Milner, M. E. "Report of Committee on Social Hygiene." Soc Hygiene 1:81-92, Dec. '14.

6226 Miner, Maude Emma. Slavery of Prostitution: A Plea For Emancipation. New York: Macmillan, 1916, 308 pp.

6227 Minnis, Mhyra S. "Prostitution and Social Class; As Viewed in Recent Popular Literature." Proc Southwest Soc Assn 13:1-6, 1963.

6228 "Miseries of Prostitution." Colburn 1:239.

6229 Mitchison, L. "Hall of a Thousand Mirrors." New Statesman 54:688+, Nov. 23, 1957.

6230 Morley, J. "On a Social Evil; Contemporary Opinions." (reprint). Fortnightly 181(175):109-13, Feb. '54.

6231 Mortimer, Lee. Women Confidential. New York: Julian Messner, 1960.

6232 Moss, Rose A. "A Valid Focus for Case Work Service in a Rapid Treatment Center," in Wessel, R., A Case Work Approach to Sex Delinquents, 1947, pp.35-37. Philadelphia: Pennsylvania School of Social Work, 1947.

6233 "Mrs. Warren's Profession." Nation 143:6, Jun. 4, 1936.

6234 "Municipalities and Vice." Municipal Affairs 5:376-87, Jun., '01.

6235 Murtagh, J. M. and S. C. Harris. Cast the First Stone. McGraw, 1957 and 1963; W. H. Allen, 1958. Prostitution in New York City. Reviewed by Powell, H. in Sat R 40:15, Apr. 27, 1957.

6236 Murtaugh, J. M. and Beatrice S. Burstein. "Problems and Treatment of Prostitution." Correction (New York) 23:3-8+, Jan. '58.

6237 Musgrave, V. "Women Outside the Law." 20th Cent 164:178-84, Aug. '58.

6238 "Need For Prostitution by a Husband." 20th Cent 172:126-8, Spr. '64.

6239 Neilans, A. "International Movement Against Regulated Prostitution: Its Progress and Significance." Int R Mission 22:81-93, Jan. '33.

6240 Neilans, Alison. "The International Traffic in Women." For Affairs (Eng.) 8:309-10, May '27.

6241 Neville-Rolfe, S. K. Poverty and Prostitution. British Social Hygiene Council, 1934, 35 pp.

6242 "New Methods of Grappling With the Social Evil." Cur Opinion 54:308-10, Apr. '13.

6243 "New Weapon Against Vice." Survey 28:630-1, Aug. 10, '12.

6244 New York (city). Bureau of Social Hygiene. Commercialized Prostitution, Nov. 1, 1916; a Comparison Between 1912, 1915, and 1916.

6245 New York. Committee of Fifteen. The Social Evil. Report prepared in 1902, ed. by Edwin R. Seligman. New York: G. P. Putnam's Sons, 1912.

6246 Nystrom, A. K. Om Aktenskapet, Pauperism och Prostitutionen. Stockholm: 1885, 107 pp.

6247 O'Callaghan, Sean. The Slave Trade Today. New York: Crown Pub., 1961.

6248 "On the Local Front; Dealing With Problems of Prostitution." Nat Munic R 32:26-8, Jan. '43.

6249 "Open Letter to Any Community in Search of Freedom From Commercialized Prostitution." J Soc Hygiene 22:412-14, Dec. '36.

6250 Opinions de Quelques Hommes en Vue. (i. e. MM. Bebel, Ador, and Others, on state-regulated prostitution). Geneva: 1896, 4 pp.

6251 Oestereich, Heinrich. Gegenwartsaspekte der Prostitution. Koln-Klettenberg, 1956, 6 pp. Prostitution outside of the traditional forms of houses, and streetwalkers.

6252 Oestereich, Henrich. Neue Formen--Neue Abwehrmittel der Offentlichen Unzucht. Colonga: 1958, 30 pp. Discussion of various forms of prostitution.

6253 O'Sulivan, F. D. In the Orchard of Forbidden Fruit. Chicago: National Publicity Bureau, 1915.

6254 Ouida. "Love vs. Avarice; the Causes Which Make for Social Evil." Lippicott's 83:712-7, Jun. '09.

6255 Owen, Frank. "Fighting the Traffic in Women." World Tomorrow 11 :79-80, Feb. '28.

6256 Paddon, M. E. "Study of Fifty Feeble-minded Prostitutes." J Delinquency 3:1-11, Jan. '18. Tables.

6257 Parker, V. H. "Segregated District." Woman Lit ns 10:26, Sep. '25.

6258 Parker, Daniel. Les Trafiquants de Femmes. 6th ed rev and corr Paris: 1945, 24 pp. Earlier editions in 1939 and 1942.

6259 Parsons, Talcott. "Age and Sex in the Social Structure of the United States." Am Sociol R 7(1942):604-16.

6260 Pasqualuri, F. "Les Peripateticiennes." (The Streetwalkers). Med World (London) 98:226-28, Mar. '63.

6261 Phelan, R. V. "Woman Labour and Moral Strength." Westm 179:215-8, Feb. '13.

6262 Philippon, Odette. L'Esclavge de la Femme dans le Monde Contemporain; ou, La Prostitution Sans Masque. Lettre de Sin Eminence le Cardinal Feltin. Paris: P. Teque, 1954, 232 pp. Many editions.

6263 Phillipon, Odette. La Esclavitud de la Mujer Moderna. Tr. by Antonio Alvarez de Linera. Madrid-Buenos Aires: Ed. Studium, 1956, 253 pp.

6264 Phillipon, Odette. Problemes Sociaux: la Prostitution, l'Alcoolisme, le Logement. Paris: A. Fayard, 1954, 222 pp.

6265 Phillipon, Odette. La Prostitutzione Senza Maschera. Edizione Paoline, 1955, 271 pp.

6266 Phillipon, Odette. La Traite des Etres Humanis. Paris: 1958, 120 pp. This is another in a series of her books on prostitution, this one directed to young women.

6267 Pierce, C. C. "Prostitution: a community problem." Am City 27:217-18, Sep. '22.

6268 Pigneur-Jacques, Madeleine. Le Reclassement Social des Prostituees Adultes. Brussels: 1953-54, 143 pp. Universite Libre de Bruxelles. Written to obtain a diploma as licenciate in criminal science.

6269 "Pimping Game." Time 97:54-5, Jun. 11, 1971.

6270 Pinney, J. B. "How Fares the Battle Against Prostitution?" Soc Serv R 16:224-46, Jun. '42.

6271 Pittman, David J. "The Male House of Prostitution." Trans-Action 8(516):21-27, Mar./Apr. '71.

6272 Playfair, Giles. "How Denmark Reforms Prostitutes." New Society 4(111):18-19, Nov. '64.

6273 Poli, Oddone C. "Gli Aspetti Sociale della Prostituzione i Tavola Rotonda Nella Sala del Grechetto a Milano." Annali Social 3:63-68, '66.

6274 Pomeroy, Wardell B. "Some Aspects of Prostitution." J Sex Res 1(3):177-187, Dec. '65.

6275 "Popular Gullibility and the White Slavery Hysteria." Cur Opinion 56:129, Feb. '14.

6276 Preble, Z. E. "She Was Lonesome; How an Age-old Problem is Being Answered." Sunset 43:28-30, Sep. '19.

6277 "Private Lives, Public Scandal." Economist 247:11-12, May 26, '73.

6278 "Problem of Two Professions." Time 57:81, Jun. 18, 1951.

6279 "Problems of Prostitution Are Often Rooted in Local Situations." Nat Munic R 32:26-8, Jan. '43.

6280 "Programs Against Prostitution." J Soc Hygiene 11:46-7, Jan. '25.

6281 "Prostitutes' Progress." Newsweek 21:28+, May 3, 1943.

6282 "Prostitutes: the New Breed." Newsweek 78:78, Jun. 12, 1971.

6283 "Prostitution in Tenements." Char 6:206-7, Mar. 2, 1901.

6284 "Protection of the Home." Independent 52:2647, Nov. 1, 1900.

6285 Protestations des Dames Contre les Doleances des Femmes Publique. An answer to the Doleance pamphlet.

6286 Quiroga, M. I. "The Current Status of Prostitution." Sem Med (Buenos Aires) 121:1781-86, Nov. 12, 1962. In Spanish.

6287 Quisenberry, W. E. "Eight Years After the Houses Closed." J Soc Hygiene 39(1953):312-332.

6288 Rabut, R. "Home at Ivry for Social Readaption of Former Prostitutes; Plan and Management." Prophylax Antiven 9:116-119, Feb. '37.

6289 Rabut, R. "Home for Rehabilitation of Prostitute at Ivry; results of the First Year's Work." Prophylax Antiven 10:138-139, Apr. '38.

6290 Rabut, R. "Question of Method of Rehabilitation of Prostitutes." Ann d'Hyg 17:193-196, May '39.

6291 Rabut, R. "Rehabilitation of Prostitutes." Prophylax Antiven 9:56-59, Jan. '37.

6292 Rabut, R. "Relation between Syphillis, Prostitution and Unemployment." Bull Med Paris 48:266-69, Apr. 28, 1934.

6293 Ramahandran, P. "Research Reports and Notes on the Problems of Beggars and Prostitutes." Ind J Soc Work 24(1):35-39, Apr. '68.

6294 Rappaport, M. F. "Casework in Social Protection; the Protective Service of the Baltimore Department of Public Welfare; With Discussion by H. G. Corrigan." Nat Conf Social Work 1946:452-67.

6295 Rappaport, Mazie F. "The Possibility of Help for the Prostitute Through Functional Case Work in an Authoritative Setting," in Wessel, R., A Case Work Approach to Sex Delinquents, 1947, pp.9-34. Philadelphia: Pennsylvania School of Social Work, 1947.

6296 Rappaport, Mazie F. "A Social Agency Helps the Prostitute on Probation," in Nat. Probation Assn., Social Correctives for Delinquency Yearbook, 1945. 1946, pp.124-35.

6297 Raven, Simon. "Boys Will Be Boys: the Male Prostitute in London," in Ruitenbeck, Hendrik M., ed., The Problem of Homosexuality in Modern Society, pp.279-290. New York: Dutton, 1963.

6298 "Reaction Against Sex Talk." Survey 31:682-3, Feb. 28, 1914.

6299 Reckless, W. C. "The Distribution of Commercialized Vice in the City: a Sociological Analysis," in Am. Sociological Soc., The City: Proceedings, 1925, pp.164-76, Jun. '26.

6300 Reckless, W. C. "Indices of Commercialized Vice Areas." J App Socio 10:249-57, Jan. '26.

6301 Reckless, W. C. "A Sociologist Looks at Prostitution." Federal Probation 7(1943):12-16.

6302 Reckless, W. C. Vice in Chicago. Univ. of Chicago Press, 1933, 314 pp.

6303 Reade, A. A. The Tragedy of the Streets. Manchester: 1912, 134 pp.

6304 Rees, Seth Cook. Miracles in the Slums. Chicago: S. C. Rees, 1905.

6305 Reinemann, J. O. "Extra-Marital Relations With Fellow Employee in War Industry as a Factor in Disruption of Family Life." Am Socio R 10:399-404, '45.

6306 Reiss, Ira L. "Premarital Sexual Permissiveness Among Negroes and Whites." Am Socio R 29:688-698, Oct. '64.

6307 Reiss, Ira L. Premarital Sexual Standards in America. Glencoe, Ill.: The Free Press, 1960.

6308 Reiss, Ira L. "The Treatment of Pre-Marital Coitus in 'Marriage and Family' Texts." Soc Problems 4:334-338.

6309 Reitman, B. L. The Second Oldest Profession; a study of the prostitute's "business manager." Constable, 1936, 270 pp.

6310 Reynolds, J. B. "Landlord's Encounter With the Underworld." Nat Munic R 8:298-305, Jun. '19.

6311 Ricard, A. M. "New Conception of Rehabilitation of Prostitutes; results of 2 years' experience." Rev Med-Sociale et de Protec de l'Enf 7:59-63, Jan.-Feb. '39.

6312 Richardson, J. "Ten-dollar Understanding; Brothel Behavior of the College Boy." Esquire 62:101+, Sep. '64.

6313 Riis, Jacob. How the Other Half Lives. Reprinted New York: Saganaw Press, 1957.

6314 Rolph, C. H., ed. Women of the Streets; a sociological study of the common prostitute. Secker, 1955, 248 pp.

6315 Robbins, L. C. and R. L. Kile. "'It's Joint Responsibility...'; Typical Community Prostitution Problems, as Discussed by City Manager's Conference." J Soc Hygiene 29:607-611, Dec. '43.

6316 Robinson, Victor, ed. Morals in Wartime. New York: Publishers Foundation, 1943.

6317 Robinson, W. J. The Oldest Profession in the World. New York: Eugenics Pub., 1929, 100 pp. Structure of society prevents abolition. Reviewed in Am J Soc 36:316-17, Sep.

'30.

6318 Roby, Pamela A. "Politics and Prostitution: a Case Study of the Revision, Enforcement and Administration of the New York State Penal Laws on Prostitution." Criminology 9(4):425-477, Feb. '72.

6319 Roby, Pamela A. Revision, Enforcement and Judicial Administration of New York State Penal Laws on Prostitution. Paper presented at the 1971 annual meeting of the Georgia Sociological and Anthropological Assn., Oct. 29-30, 1971, University Club, Athens, Ga.

6320 Roe, C. G. "Newer Methods of Attacking Commercialized Vice." Conf Char and Corr 1912:303-4.

6321 Rolph, C. H. (for and behalf of the British Social Biology Council). Women of the Street; a sociological study of the common prostitute. London: Secker and Warburg, 1955, 248 pp. Also listed under British Social Biology Council.

6322 Roosevelt, T. "Achievement for Humanity." Outlook 103:116, Jan. 18, 1913.

6323 Rosenblum, K. E. "Female Deviance and the Female Sex Role: a Preliminary Investigation." Br J Sociol 26(2):169-85, Jun. '75.

6324 Ross, H. Laurence. "The 'Hustler' in Chicago." J Stud Res 1(1):13-19, Fall '59.

6325 Ross, I. "Sex in the Boom Towns." Am Mercury 55:606-13, Nov. '42.

6326 Royden, A. M., ed., Downward Paths. Macmillan, 1916.

6327 Ruygers, H. "Maatschappelijk Werk in de Werel van de Prostitutie." Tijdschrift Voor Maatschappelijk Werk May '60, pp.143-150.

6328 Saffro, L. "Prostituzione Femminile Contemporania." Rev Psicol Soc 27:271-302, '60.

6329 "Satellites; Oldest Profession." Time 69:34, May 20, 1957.

6330 Scarlet, Iain. The Professional: prostitutes and their clients. London: Sidgwick and Jackson, 1972, 200 pp.

6331 Schmalhausen, Samuel D., ed. and V. F. Calverton. Woman's Coming of Age. New York: Horace Liveright, 1931.

6332 Schmitz, Carl A. "Gesellschaftsordnung und Wandel in Einer Bergbauernkultur in Nordost-Neuguinea." Kol Ztsch Soziol Soz-Psychol 9(2):258-281, '57.

6333 Schneider, Camillo Karl. *Die Prostituierte und die Gesellschaft*. Leipzig: 1908.

6334 Schroeder, T. "Prostitution as a Social Problem." *Arena* 41:196-201, Feb., '09.

6335 Schur, Edwin M. *Crimes Without Victims*. Englewood Cliffs, N. J.: Prentice Hall, 1965.

6336 Selby, B. "Are Prostitutes Really Necessary?" *20th Cent* 165:440, Apr. '59. Reply by R. B. Thompson 165:440, Apr. '59.

6337 Seligman, E. R. A., ed. *Social Evil*. Putnam, 1912.

6338 "Sex O'Clock in America." *Cur Opinion* 55:113-4, Aug. '13.

6339 *Sexual Crime Today*; a symposium held at the Institute of Criminal Law and Criminology. The Hague: University of Leiden, 1960.

6340 Sharma, K. K., P. S. Dubey, and R. S. Bhatia. "Prostitution." *Ind Sociol* 4(3):33-39, Mar. '61.

6341 Sheehy, Gail. *Hustling: prostitution in our wide open society*. New York: Delacorte Press, 1973.

6342 Sholham, S. and Giora Rahavg. "Social Stigma and Prostitution." *Annales Internationales de Criminologie* 6(1967):470-513 and *Brit J Crim* 8:402-12, Oct. '68.

6343 Sholam, S. and Giora Rahav. *Social Stigma and Prostitution*. Ramat-Gan, 1967. A study of North African Jews living in Israel.

6344 "Should Teen-Age Boys be Exposed to This?" *Christ Cent* 63:709, Jun. 5, '46.

6345 Simmat, William E. *Prostitution und Offentlichkeit*; sociologische detrachtungen zur Affare Nitribitt. Schmiden bei Stuttgart, 1959(?). 169 pp.

6346 Smith, Thomas Robert. *The Woman Question*. New York, Boni and Liveright, Inc., 1919, 229 pp.

6347 Smithurst, B. A. and J. L. Armstrong. "Social Background of 171 Women Attending a Female Venereal Disease Clinic in Brisbane." *Med J Aust* 1(11):339-43, Mar. 15, '75.

6348 *The Social Evil*. Bristol: 1883, 20 pp.

6349 "Social Evil." *Outlook* 101:245-8, Jun. 1, '12.

6350 "Social Evil, the Immediate Remedies." Outlook 103:298-9, Feb. 8, '13.

6351 Spencer, A. G. "Social Nemesis and Social Salvation." Forum 50:432-44, Oct. '13.

6352 "Social Vice." Ind 68:109-10, Jan. 13, '10.

6353 "Solid Foundation For Vice Control." Intercol Statesmen 16:95-6, Mar. '19.

6354 Solivetti, L. M. "Some Social Function in Deviant Behavior. Critical Examination of Literature." Quad Criminol Clin 15(4):453-76, Oct.-Dec. '73.

6355 Soto, J. L. "Prostitution and Public Aid." Pasteur 1:91-98, May '45.

6356 Spaulding, E. R. "Mental and Physical Factors in Prostitution," in Nat. Conf. of Charities and Correction. Proceedings, 1914, p.222-9.

6357 Stachouwer, J. D. F. Criminaliteit, Prostitutie en Zelfmootd bij Immigranten in Amsterdam. Utrecht: Nijmegan, 1950, 145 pp.

6358 Stanke, Alain. Un Mois Chez Les Damnes. Montreal: 1957(?), 111 pp. Report on prostitution.

6359 Stearn, Jess. Sisters of the Night. New York: Julian Messner, 1956.

6360 Stein, Martha. Lovers, Friends, Slaves; the nine male sexual types; their psycho-sexual transactions with call girls. New York: Berkley Pub. Corp., 1974, 347 pp.

6361 Stolberg, B. "Social Evil." Sociol R 13:97-103, Apr. '21.

6362 "Streetwalker," in Josephson, Eric and Mary Josephson, Man Alone; Alienation in Modern Society. New York: Dell, 1962.

6363 Svalastoga, Kaare. "The Family in Scandinavia." Marr Fam Living 16:374-80, Nov. '54.

6364 Taft, Donald Reid. Criminology; an attempt at a synthetic interpretation with a cultural emphasis. New York: Macmillan, 1942, p.281.

6365 Taylor, L. From Under the Lid. Published by the author, 1913.

6366 Thornton, R. Y. "Organized Crime in the Field of Prostitution." J Crim Law Crim 46(6):775-779, Mar./Apr. '56.

6367 Turner, G. K. "Traders in Women: First Report of Rockefeller's Bureau for the Study of the Social Evil." Harp W 57:11, Jun. 21, 1913.

6368 "Traffic in Women and Children: Enquiry Concerning System of Licensed Houses in So Far As It Concerns the Traffic." League of Nations Off J 7:1193-200, Sep. '26.

6369 "Traffic in Women and Girls." Spectator 138:472, Mar. 19, '27.

6370 Trout, I. B. World Scourge. 2d ed Lanark, Ill.: by the author, 1915.

6371 "Twelve O'Clock Sharp." Commonweal 10:660-1, Oct. 30, 1929.

6372 Ullerstam, L. "Sexual Latitude: For and Against," in Sexual Latitude: For and Against, pp.202-13. Hart, 1971.

6373 United States. Public Health Service. What Representative Citizens Think About Prostitution. Supt. of Docs., 1921.

6374 Verbeke, Nelly. Detresse des Filles de Joie. Brussels: Editions Universitaires, 1953, 172 pp.

6375 Vincent, C. E. "Ego Involvement in Sexual Relations: Implications For Research on Illegitimacy." AJS 65:287-95, '59.

6376 Vincent, C. E. "Unmarried Fathers and the Mores: 'Sexual Exploiter' as an Ex Post Factor Label." ASR 25:40-46, '60.

6377 Vivien, Robert-Andre. Solution au Probleme de la Prostitution. Paris: 1960, 152 pp. Deals with the ongoing issues in prostitution.

6378 Wagener, Herm. Der Madchenhandel...Zweite Unveranderte Auflage. Berlin: 1911, 113 pp.

6379 Walker, E. C. Marriage and Prostitution. Published by the author, n. d.

6380 Walker, E. C. Vice; Its Friends and Foes. Published by the author, n. d.

6381 Walker, Kenneth and Peter Fletcher. Sex and Society. Harmondsworth, Eng.: Penguin Books, 1955.

6382 "The War Against Prostitution Must Go On." J Soc Hygiene 31:500-07, Nov. '46. Chart.

6383 Washburn, J. Underworld Sewer. Washburn Pub., 1909.

6384 Weinberg, S. Kirson. Social Problems in Our Time. Englewood Cliffs: Prentice Hall, 1960, 600 pp. Ch. 11 on prostitution.

6385 Wessel, Rosa, ed. Case Work Approach to Sex Delinquents. Pennsylvania School of Social Work, 1947.

6386 Wetering de Rooij, J van. "The 'Girls' and the Police Chief." Tijdsch Ziekenverpl 24(8):369-71, Apr. 13, 1971.

6387 Whitin, F. H. "Warfare on Prostitution: the Next Step." Nat Conf of Social Work, Proceedings 1924:209-12.

6388 "White Slave Law and Blackmail." Lit Digest 54:178, Jan. 27, 1917. Manor Law.

6389 "White Slaves and Immigration." Outlook 93:881-3, Dec. 25, '09.

6390 "White Slaves and the Social Evil." Chaut 57:331-3, Feb. '10.

6391 Whittaker, P. The American Way of Sex. Putnam, 1974.

6392 Willis, W. N. The Crime of Silence About the Hidden Plague. Anglo-Eastern Pub. Co., 1915, 188 pp.

6393 Willis, W. N. Western Men With Eastern Morals. Stanley Paul, 1913, 264 pp.

6394 Willis, W. N. White Slaves in a Picadilly Flat. Anglo-Eastern Pub. Co., 1915, 151 pp.

6395 Willis, W. N. The White Slaves of London. Stanley Paul, 1912, 183 pp.

6396 Willis, W. N. Why Girls Go Wrong; how the white slave gangs **work.** 1913, 214 pp.

6397 Wilson, Helen. On Some Causes of Prostitution, With Special References to Economic Conditions. Geneva: FAI, 15 pp. and Assn. for Moral and Social Hygiene, 1916, 14 pp.

6398 Winick, Charles. "Prostitutes' Clients' Perception of the Prostitutes and of Themselves." Int J Soc Psychia 8(4):289-297, Aut. '62.

6399 Winick, Charles and Paul M. Kinzie. Prostitution in the United States. Chicago: Quadrangle Books, 1971. One of the better studies.

6400 Winn, Denise. Prostitutes. London: Hutchinson, 1974, 144 pp.

6401 Winslow, Robert W. and Virginia Winslow. *Deviant Reality: Alternate World Views*. Boston: Allyn and Bacon, 1974, 335 pp.

6402 Winslow, D. J. "The Occupational Superstitions of Negro Prostitutes in Upstate New York City." *NY Folklore Q* 24(1968):294-301.

6403 Withers, P. *Give Us Men!*; a symposium on the Social Evil from a woman's point of view. Cassell, 1914, 119 pp.

6404 Wolbarst, A. L. "Physician's Attitude Toward Prostitution and Juvenile Delinquency." *Urol and Cutan R* 48:220-223, May '44. Abstract in *M Rec* 157:677-678, Nov. '44.

6405 Wolbarst, A. L. "Prostitution and Its Problems." *M Woman's J* 51:22-24, Jan. '44. (Comment on Glasow's article).

6406 Wong Lun Hing, F. J. H. *Prostitutie*. Utrecht: 1962, 168 pp. A social pathological point of view.

6407 Woods, R. A. "Banners of a New Army." *Survey* 29:813-4, Mar. 8, 1913.

6408 Woolton, B. "Sex and Society: a Sociologist's View." *20th Cent* 163:5-15, Jan. '58.

6409 "World Situation With Regard to Prostitution." *J Soc Hygiene* 35:170-6, Apr. '49.

6410 Worthington, G. E. "Prostitution: What a City Should Know About Itself." *Am City* 30:63-6, Jan. '24.

6411 *Women of the Streets*. Ed. by C. H. Rolph. London: Secker and Warburg, 1955. Outstanding. Also listed under Rolfe.

6412 Young, Wayland. "Prostitution," in Gagnon, J. H. and W. Simon, ed., *Sexual Deviance*, p.105-133.

6413 Young, Wayland. "Sitting on a Fortune: The Prostitute in London." *Encounter* 12:19-31, May '59.

6414 Zarrilli, Canio Louis. "A Critical Analysis of the Royal Commission Report on Homosexuality and Prostitution," in Bloch, Herbert, ed., *Crime in America*; controversial issues in twentieth century criminology. New York: Philosophical Library, 1961.

6415 Zimmerman, Jean Turner. *America's Black Traffic in White Girls*. Chicago: 1912, 90 pp.

6416 Zorbaugh, Harvey W. *The Gold Coast and the Slum*. Chicago: Univ. of Chicago Press, 1929.

6423 American Bar Association. Committee on Courts and Wartime Social Protection. *Venereal Disease, Prostitution and War*; a sound legislative program for the control of venereal disease and the repression of prostituion founded upon experience, etc. Washington: 1943.

6424 American Social Hygiene Association. *Vice Repression as a War Policy*. American Social Hygiene Association, 1917.

6425 "Army Cracks Down on Vice That Still Preys on Soldiers." *Newsweek* 20:27-8+, Aug. 31, 1942.

6426 Baker, N. D. "Must Suppress Vice Resorts Near Army Camps: Secretary Baker Warns Mayors of Nearby Towns and County Sheriffs, or Troops May Be Removed." *Official Bulletin* 1:1-2, Aug. 16, 1917.

6427 Benjamin, H. "Sex Problem in the Armed Forces (morals versus morale in wartime)." *Urol and Cutan R* 48:231-244, May '44.

6428 Broughton, Phillip S. *Prostitution and the War*. Geneva: Federation Abolitionniste Internationale, 1942, 31 pp. and New York Public Affairs Committee, 1942.

6429 Buchanan, J. G. "War Legislation Against Alcoholic Liquor and Prostitution." *J Crim Law* 9:520-9, Feb. '19.

6430 Chicago Bar Association. War Activities Committee. *Brief on the Subject: Prostitution-Venereal Disease Control Program*. Chicago.Law Printing Co., Mar. '44, 58 pp. Prepared for the Division of Social Protection, Community War Services, U. S. Federal Security Agency.

6431 Clarke, W. "Social Hygiene in War." *Rocky Mountain Medical J* 40:591-595, '43.

6432 ____. *Vice Repression as a War Policy*. American Social Hygiene Assn., 1917, pub. no. 121.

6433 Close, K. "In May Act Areas." *Survey* 79:67-70, Mar. '43.

6434 ____. "Sick Men Can't Fight; San Antonio's Venereal Disease Control Program." *Survey Graphic* 32:80-4, Mar. '43.

6435 Corbet, W. J. "Immorality of the English Army Abroad." *Westm* 157:237-54, Mar. '02.

6436 Daniels, J. "Soldier's Saturday Nights." *Nation* 152:586, May 17, 1941.

6437 Deveral, R. L. G. "Wild GI's: Our Black Eye in Japan." *America* 90:597-8, Mar. 6, 1954.

6438 "Disneyland East; Brothel Quarter Built Exclusively For American Soldiers." *Time* 87:29-30, May 6, 1966.

6439 Durel, P. "Sanitary Surveillance in Time of War." *Presse Med* 48:59-61, Jan. 16, 1940.

6440 Exner, M. J. *Prostitution in its Relation to the Army on the Mexican Border.* American Social Hygiene Association, 1917. Tables. Also in Gulick, L. H., *Morals and Morale,* p.99-117, 1919.

6441 Falconer, M. P. "Segregation of Delinquent Women and Girls as a War Problem." *Annals of the American Academy of Political and Social Science* 79:160-6, Sep. '18.

6442 Fey, H. E. "Miss Royden and War Prostitution." *Christ Cent* 54:186-7, Feb. 10, 1937.

6443 Fiaux, L. *L'Armee et la Police de Moeurs;* biologie morale du soldat. Geneva: Fed. Abolit. Inter., n. d., 325 pp.

6444 Fosdick, R. B. "Prostitution and the War." *Social Hygiene Bul* 5:1-2, May '18.

6445 Freund, John. "U. S. Starts Clean-up of Camp Followers." *New York Daily News* May 11, 1942.

6446 Hall, E. R. "Syphilis Problem in Relation to Present Emergency." *J Tennessee Med Assn* 35:297-303, Aug. '42.

6447 Hartmann, G. *Girls They Left Behind.* Munksgaard, 1946.

6448 Hironimous, H. "Survey of 100 May Act Violators," *Federal Probation* 7:31-34, '43.

6449 "Intelligence Office as a Feeder for Vice." *Char* 12:255-6, Mar. 5, 1904.

6450 Johnson, Bascom. "Venereal Morbidity in United States Army in El Paso, Texas-Juarez, Chihuahua Area: Importance of Prostitution." *Inform enferm ven* pp.3-16, Jan. '44.

6451 ______. "Vice Problem and Defense." *Survey* 77:140-3, May '41.

6452 Kinsie, P. M. "The Prostitution Racket Today: Summary Report of Field Studies of Prostitution Conditions in 176 Communities Since the Declaration of the Limited Emergency." *J Soc Hyg* 27:327-34, Oct. '41.

6453 "Letter from General Pershing; Licensed Houses of Prostitution Closed To British Expeditionary Force." *Soc Hygiene* 5:124, Jan. 1919.

6454 "Musings in Historical Paths and By-paths (Venereal Diseases in Panama During World War)," Urol and Cutan R 47:58-67, Jan. '43.

6455 Musser, J. H. "Venereal Disease Problems in Mobilization." Texas State J Med 38:214-216, Jul. '42.

6456 "Navy Provides Social Protection For Servicemen in Japan." J Social Hygiene 32:82-9, Feb. '46.

6457 Ness, E. et al. "Federal Wartime Protection Program, Symposium." Natl Probation Assn. Yrbk 1943:52-85.

6458 Ness, E. "Social Hygiene in Wartime; Prostitution Social Protection and Police; New Offensive Along Police Front." J Social Hygiene 28:365-371, Oct. '42.

6459 Newman, A. "Freedom? Brothel Girls Thank Mae For Nothing." Newsweek 28:53, Oct. 21, 1946.

6460 Parker, R. H. "Sex and the Soldier," Coronet 32:103-6, Jun. '52.

6461 Price, A. B. and Weber, F. J. "Control of the Venereal Diseases in Civilian Areas Adjacent to Concentrations of Armed Forces." Am J Pub Health 31:912-16, Sep. '41.

6462 "Prostitutes Blamed; Suppression Near Army Camps Held Essential to the Control of Venereal Disease." Science 42:278, Oct. 31, 1942.

6463 "Prostitution is an Axis Partner." Am J Pub Health 32:85, Jan. '42.

6464 "Prostitution, Major Wartime Threat." Am City 57:71, Feb. '42.

6465 Quintero, E. "Infections Wasting Manpower Can Be Prevented by Isolation, Treatment and Control of Habitual Prostitutes and Readjustment of New Ones." Bol Asoc Med de Puerto Rico 35:319-323, Aug. '43.

6466 Ranshofen-Wertheimer, Egan. "Prostitution and War." Health and Empire 15:6-12, Jun. '40.

6467 Rippin, J. D. "Social Hygiene and the War." Soc Hygiene 5:125-36, Jan. '19.

6468 Robinson, Victor, ed. Morals in Wartime; general survey from ancient times; morals in the first world war; morals in the second world war. Pub. Found., 1943, 205 pp. tables.

6469 Rosenthal, T. "Problems in Epidemiology of Venereal Disease in Wartime." Am J Syph Gonor and Ven Dis 27:581-589, Sep. '43.

6470 Ross, I. "Sex in the Army." Am Mercury 53:661-9, Dec. '41.

6471 Roy, S. L. War and Immorality. Kitab-Mehal, 1944.

6472 Russell, B. "Sick Men Can't Fight; Reply with Rejoinder." Survey Graphic 32:243, Jun. '43.

6473 "Sailors and Sex; Prostitution Flourishes in Japan; Navy Policy Comes Under Attack," Newsweek 26:82+ Nov. 12, 1945.

6474 Shall Prostitution Follow Our Army. Oregon Social Hygiene Society, Apr. '17, 4 pp.

6475 Snow, W. F.; LaGuardia, F. H.; Kinsie, P. M.; Gould, G.; Johnson, B.; Clements, A. S.; McGinnes, G. F.; Pucker, H. "Social Hygiene and National Defense: the Attack on Commercialized Prostitution. Symposium." J Social Hygiene 27:317-63, Oct. '41.

6476 "Social Evil in the American Army." Cur Opinion 54:273-4, Apr. '13.

6477 "Social Hygiene in Wartime; Social Protection Program in Action; Health Services and Legislation." J Social Hygiene 29:306-319, May '43. Various authors.

6478 "Social Hygiene in Wartime; Prostitution, Social Protection and the Police. Symposium," J Social Hygiene 28:365-429. Oct. 1942.

6479 "Social Hygiene in Wartime; Prostitution, Social Protection and Police; Study of Protective Measures in the City of Boston," J Social Hygiene 28:403-418, Oct. 1942.

6480 "Suppression of Prostitution in Army Camps," Am J Pub Health 32:113-14, Jan. 1942.

6481 Taft, C. P. "Second Front Against Prostitution; Techniques For Repressing Unorganized Prostitution, as Recommended by the Special Committee on Enforcement of the National Advisory Police Committee," J Social Hygiene 29:43-5

6482 _____. "Social and Legal Problems in Wartime Venereal Disease Control Program," Ven Dis Inform 24:155-159, Jun. 1943.

6483 Tempest, V. Our Army in India. White Slave Abolition Publications, 1913, 7 pp.

6484 U. S. Army. Medical Dept. Preventive Medicine in World War II. vol. V: "Communicable Diseases." Washington: Office of the Surgeon General, 1960.

6485 U. S. House. Com. on Military Affairs. Act to Prohibit Prostitution Within Reasonable Distance of Military and Naval Establishments: Hearings, March 11-18, 1941 on HR 2475. Washington D. C: Sup. of Docs. 1941, 70 pp.

6486 U. S. House. Com. on Military Affairs. Extention of the Act to Prohibit Prostitution in and Around Military and Naval Establishments Hearings, May 1, 1945, on HR 2992. Washington D. C.: 1945, 30 pp.

6487 U. S. War Dept. Commission on Training Camp Activities. Documents Regarding Alcoholic Liquors and Prostitution in the Neighborhood of Military Camps and Naval Stations. 1918.

6488 U. S. War Dept. Commission on Training Camp Activities. Next Steps: a Program of Activities Against Prostitution and Venereal Disease For Communities That Have Closed Their 'Red Light' Districts. Bascom Johnson, 1918, 23 pp. Reprinted from Social Hygiene, Jan. 1918.

6489 U. S. War Dept. Commission on Training Camp Activities. Standard Forms of Law For the Repression of Prostitution, the Control of Venereal Diseases, the Establishment and Management of Reformatories For Women and Girls, and Suggestions For a Law Relating to Feeble-Minded Persons. 1919.

6490 U. S. Office of Community War Services. Division of Social Protection. Challenge to Community Action. Washington D. C.: 1945.

6491 U. S. Office of Community War Services. Division of Social Protection. "How to Curb Prostitution in Hotels." 1944, 5 pp. Reprinted from the Southern Hotel J Feb. '43. Federal Security Administration, 75 pp.

6492 Velthuijsen, G. "War and Prostitution in Holland." Soc Hygiene 2:617-21, Oct. '16.

6493 "War Program and Prostitution; Municipal, State, and National Legislation to Eliminate Syphilis and Gonorrhea." Am City 57:109+, Sep. '42.

6494 Wickware, F. S. "National Defense vs. Venereal Disease Fights to Protest its New Soldiers." Life 11:128-30+, Oct. 13, 1941.

INDEX OF AUTHORS